Every month I draw a minor character for the official
Dragon Ball website. There's an almost infinite number of
characters to choose from, so I always have fun with it.
The art on this page is usually some kind of self-portrait,
but sometimes we use one of those minor-character
drawings instead.

—Toyotarou, 2021

Toyotarou

To... ...nga adaptation for the *Dragon Ball Z*
... *Ball Z: Resurrection F*. He is also the
... *Dragon Ball Heroes: Victory Mission*,
... *mp* in Japan in November 2012.

Toriyama

... ...for his playful, innovative storytelling and
... ...ous, distinctive art style, Akira Toriyama burst onto the manga
scene in 1980 with the wildly popular *Dr. Slump*. His hit series *Dragon Ball*
(published in the U.S. as *Dragon Ball* and *Dragon Ball Z*) ran from 1984
to 1995 in Shueisha's *Weekly Shonen Jump* magazine. He is also known
for his design work on video games such as *Dragon Quest*, *Chrono Trigger*,
Tobal No. 1 and *Blue Dragon*. His recent manga works include *COWA!*, *Kajika*,
Sand Land, *Neko Majin*, *Jaco the Galactic Patrolman* and a children's book,
Toccio the Angel. He lives with his family in Japan.

DRAGON BALL SUPER 17

SHONEN JUMP Edition

STORY BY **Akira Toriyama**
ART BY **Toyotarou**

TRANSLATION **Caleb Cook**
LETTERING **Brandon Bovia**
DESIGN **Kam Li**
EDITOR **Rae First**

Printed in the U.S.A.

Published by VIZ Media, LLC
P.O. Box 77010
San Francisco, CA 94107

10 9 8 7 6 5 4 3 2 1
First printing, December 2022

VIZ MEDIA
viz.com

SHONEN JUMP

ratings.viz.com RATED T TEEN

PARENTAL ADVISORY
DRAGON BALL SUPER is rated T for Teen and is recommended for ages 13 and up. This volume contains realistic and fantasy violence.

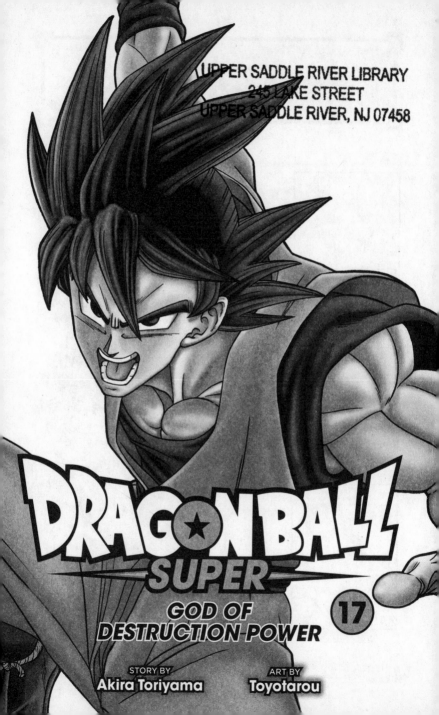

DRAGON BALL
SUPER
GOD OF DESTRUCTION POWER

17

STORY BY
Akira Toriyama

ART BY
Toyotarou

CAST OF CHARACTERS

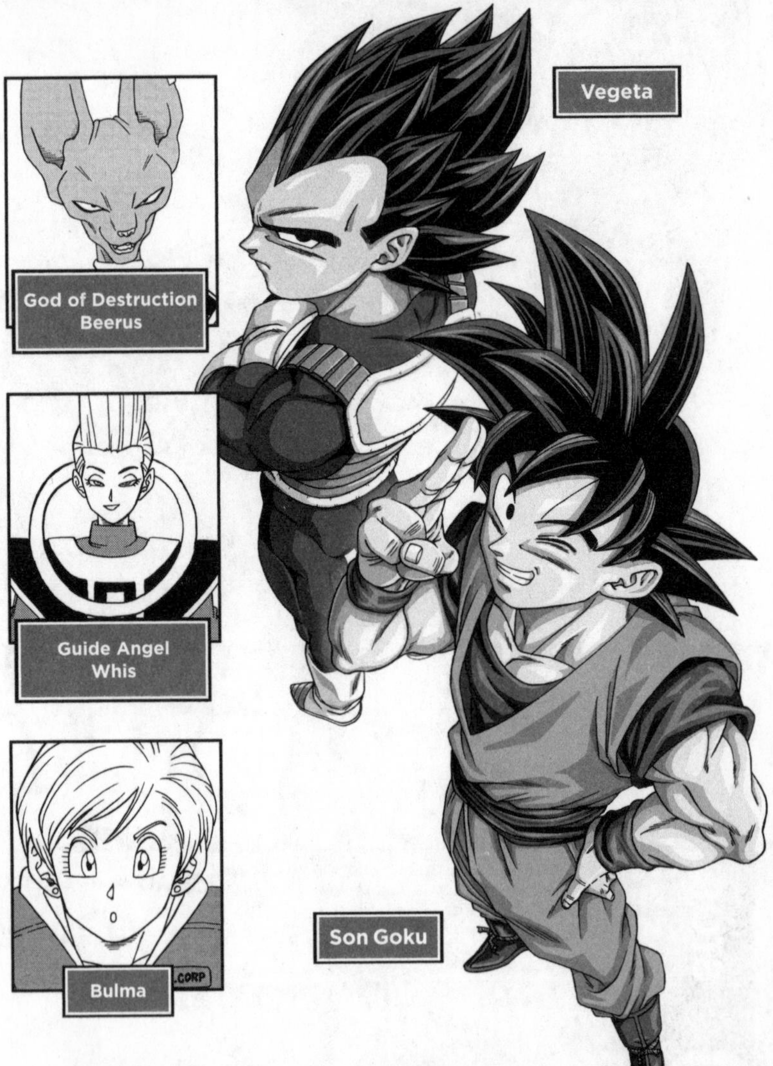
Vegeta
God of Destruction Beerus
Guide Angel Whis
Son Goku
Bulma
C.CORP

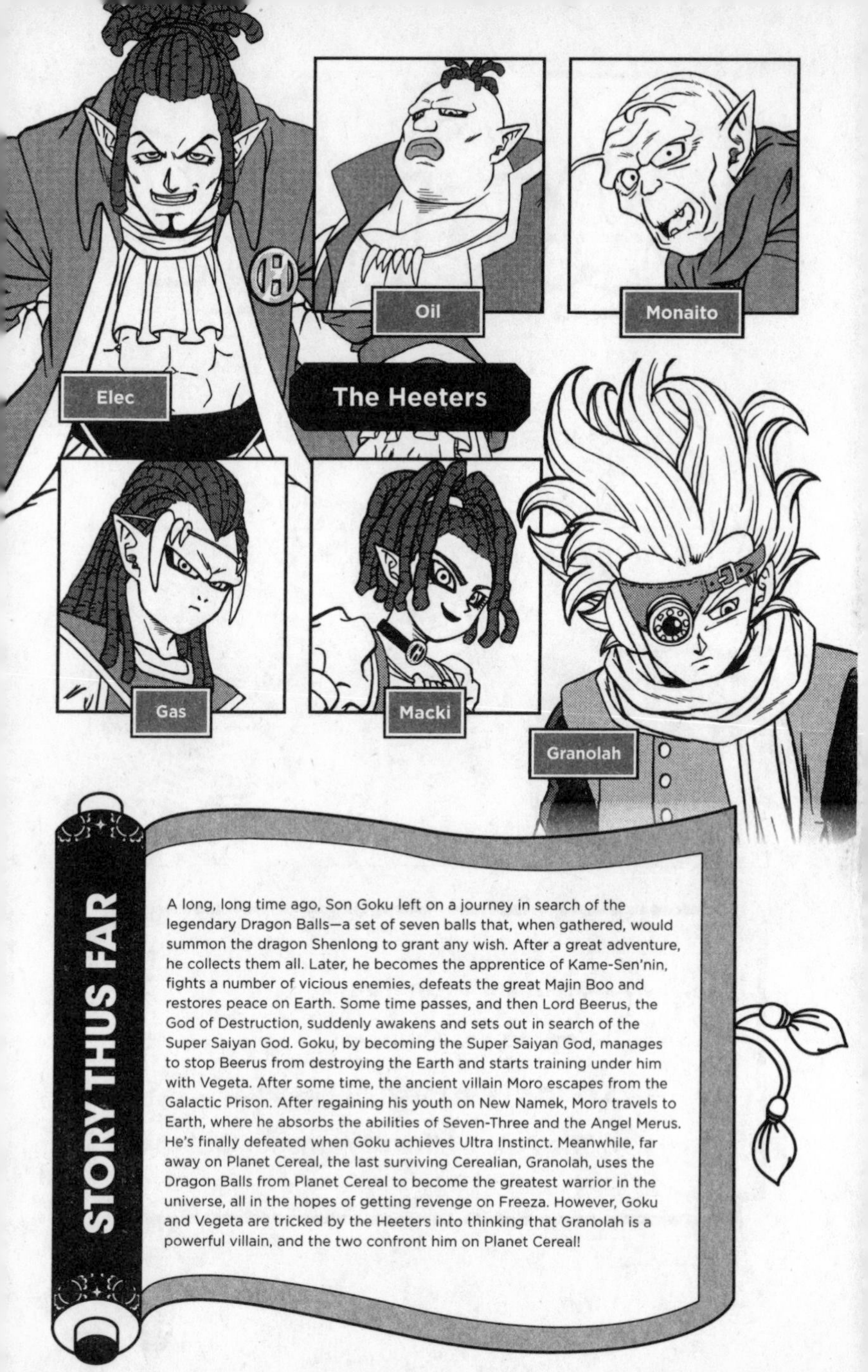
Monaito
Oil
The Heeters
Elec
Granolah
Macki
Gas

STORY THUS FAR

A long, long time ago, Son Goku left on a journey in search of the legendary Dragon Balls—a set of seven balls that, when gathered, would summon the dragon Shenlong to grant any wish. After a great adventure, he collects them all. Later, he becomes the apprentice of Kame-Sen'nin, fights a number of vicious enemies, defeats the great Majin Boo and restores peace on Earth. Some time passes, and then Lord Beerus, the God of Destruction, suddenly awakens and sets out in search of the Super Saiyan God. Goku, by becoming the Super Saiyan God, manages to stop Beerus from destroying the Earth and starts training under him with Vegeta. After some time, the ancient villain Moro escapes from the Galactic Prison. After regaining his youth on New Namek, Moro travels to Earth, where he absorbs the abilities of Seven-Three and the Angel Merus. He's finally defeated when Goku achieves Ultra Instinct. Meanwhile, far away on Planet Cereal, the last surviving Cerealian, Granolah, uses the Dragon Balls from Planet Cereal to become the greatest warrior in the universe, all in the hopes of getting revenge on Freeza. However, Goku and Vegeta are tricked by the Heeters into thinking that Granolah is a powerful villain, and the two confront him on Planet Cereal!

17

DRAGON BALL SUPER

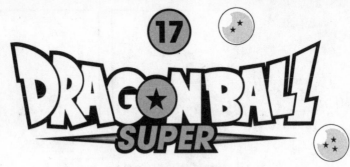

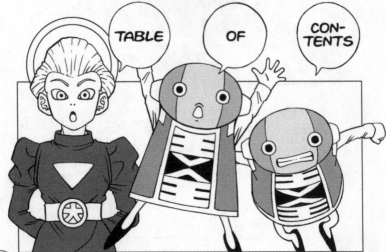

TABLE
OF
CON-
TENTS

DRAGON BALL SUPER

CHAPTER 73: GOKU VS. GRANOLAH

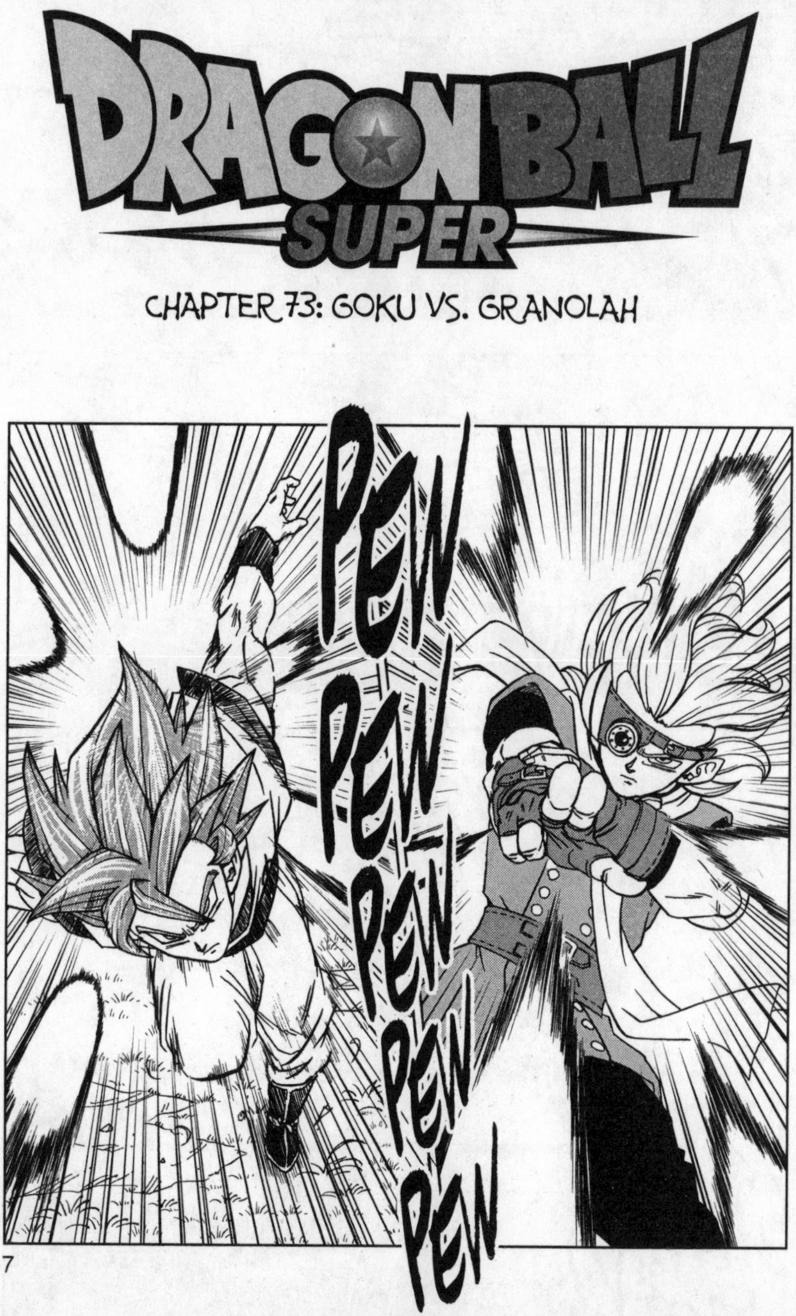
PEW PEW PEW PEW PEW PEW

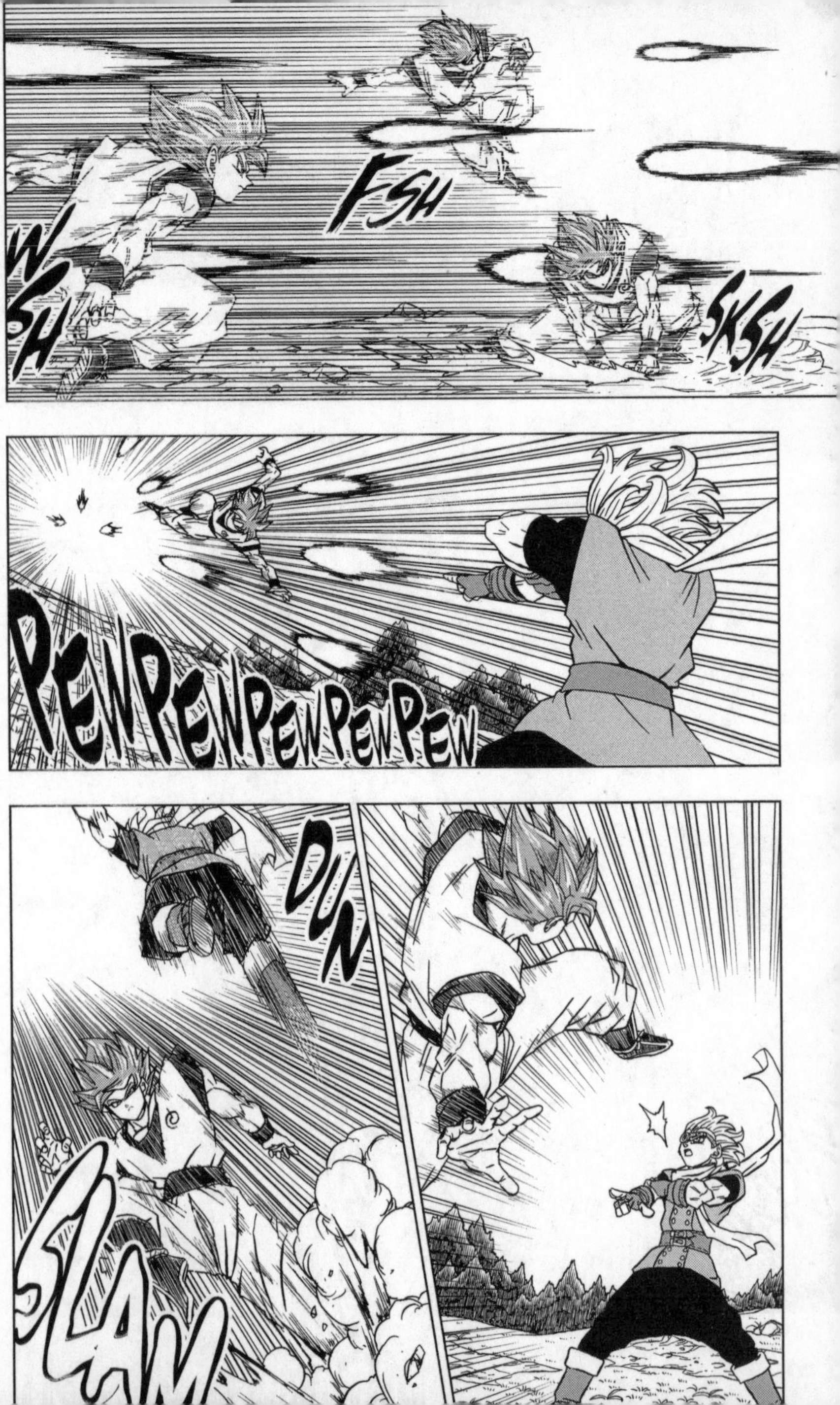
SKSH
FSH
WSH
PEWPEWPEWPEWPEWPEW
DUN
SLAM

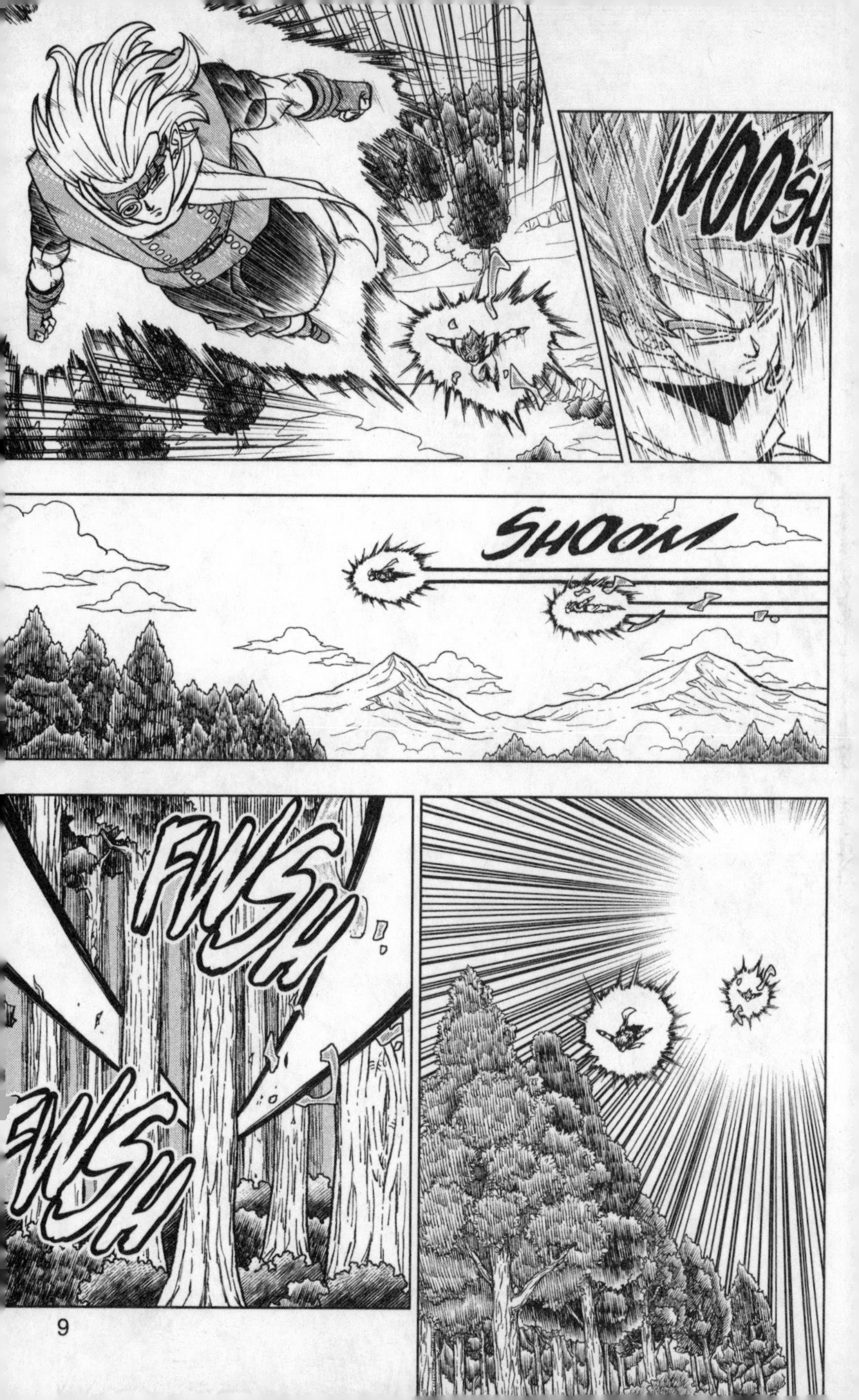
WOOSH
SHOOM
FWSH
FWSH

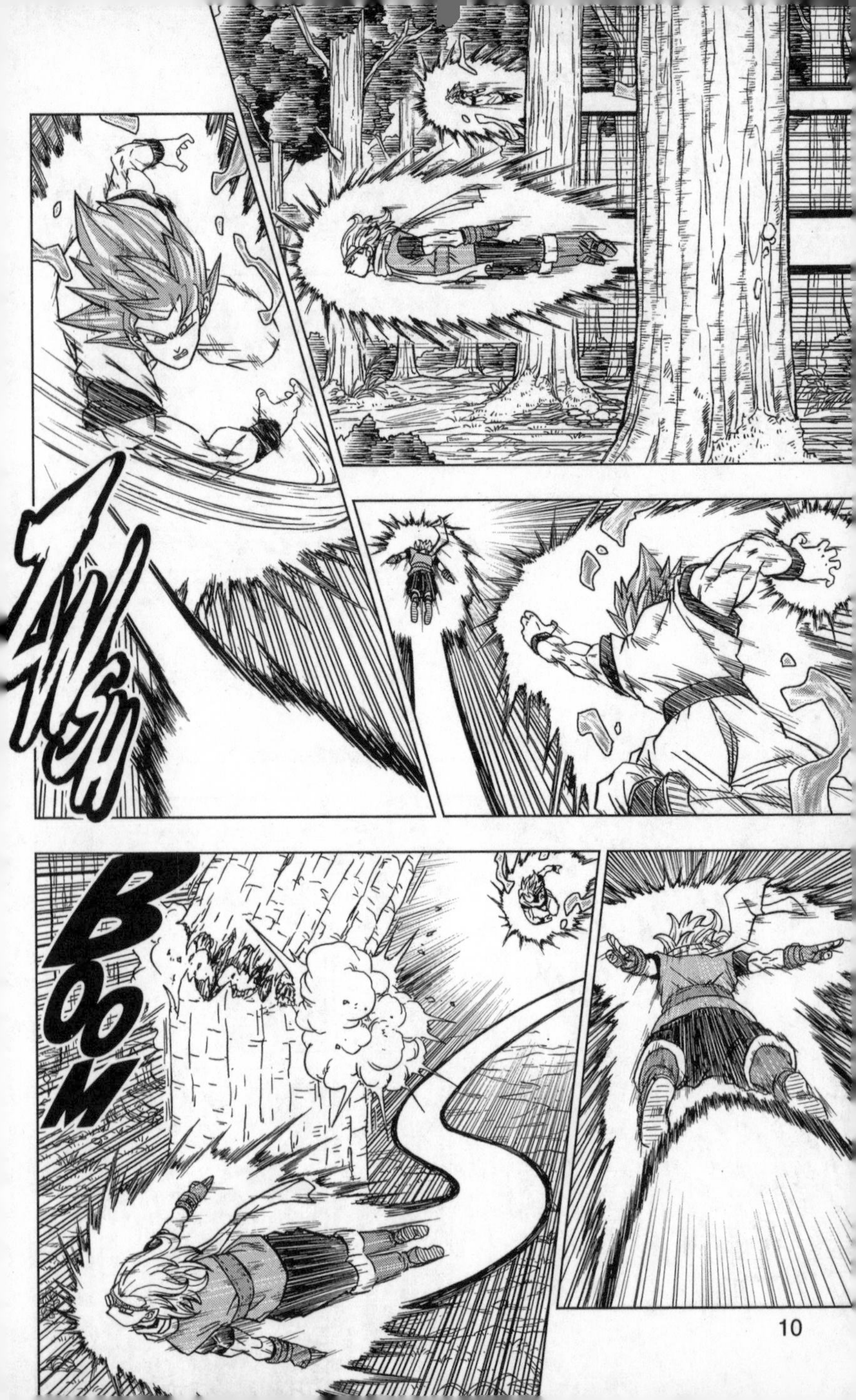
ZWUSH
BOOM

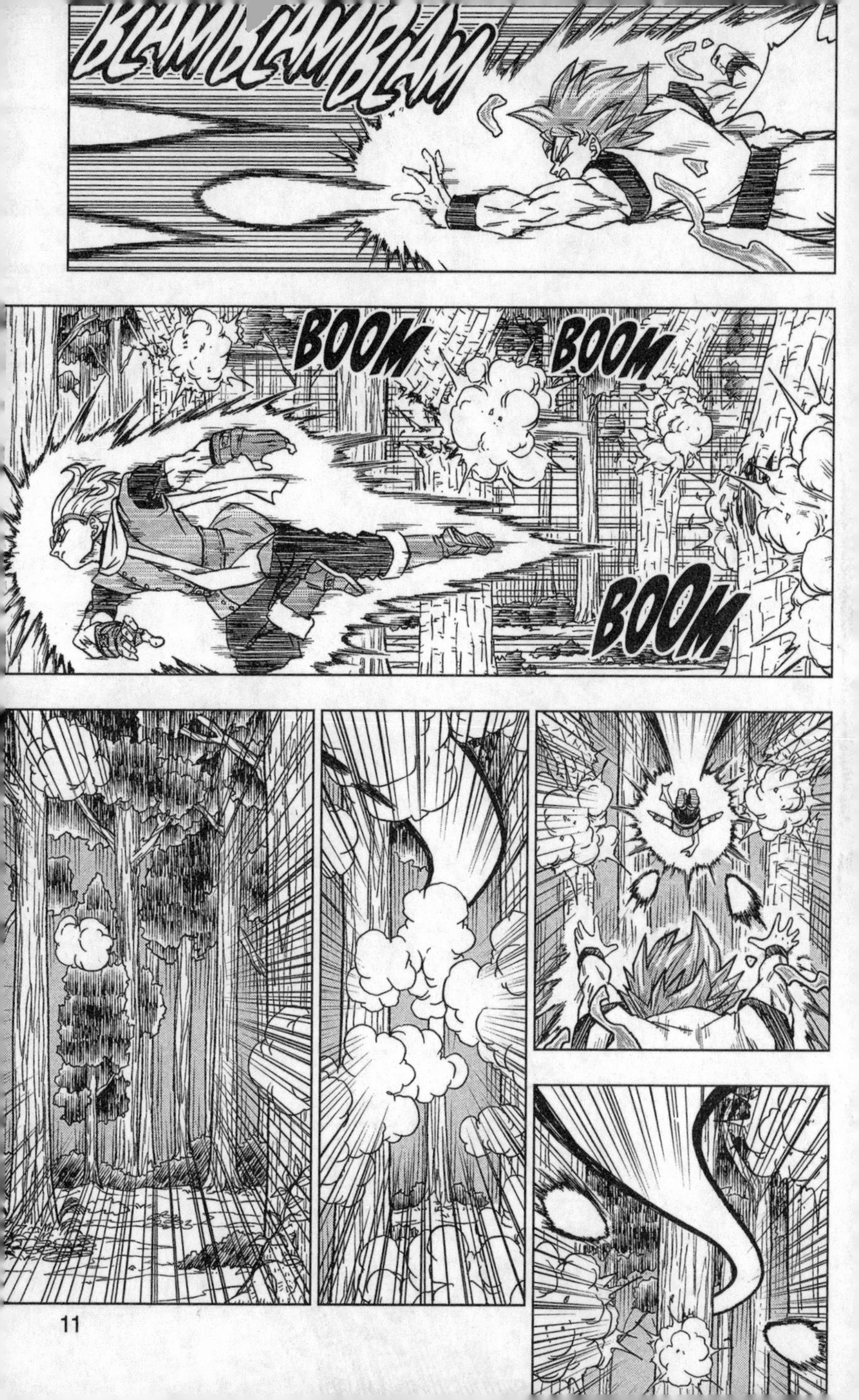
BLAM BLAM BLAM
BOOM
BOOM
BOOM

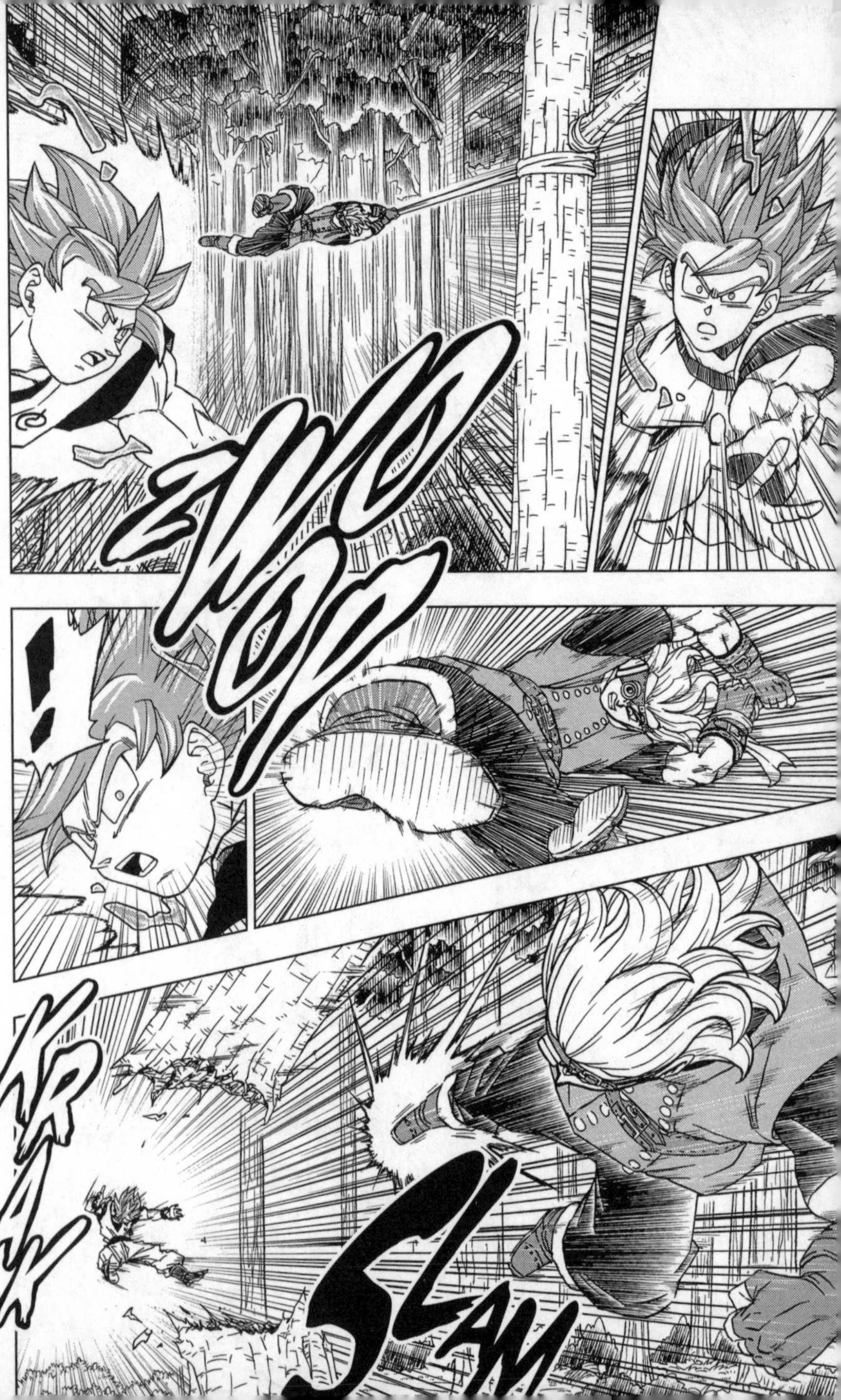
!
SLAM

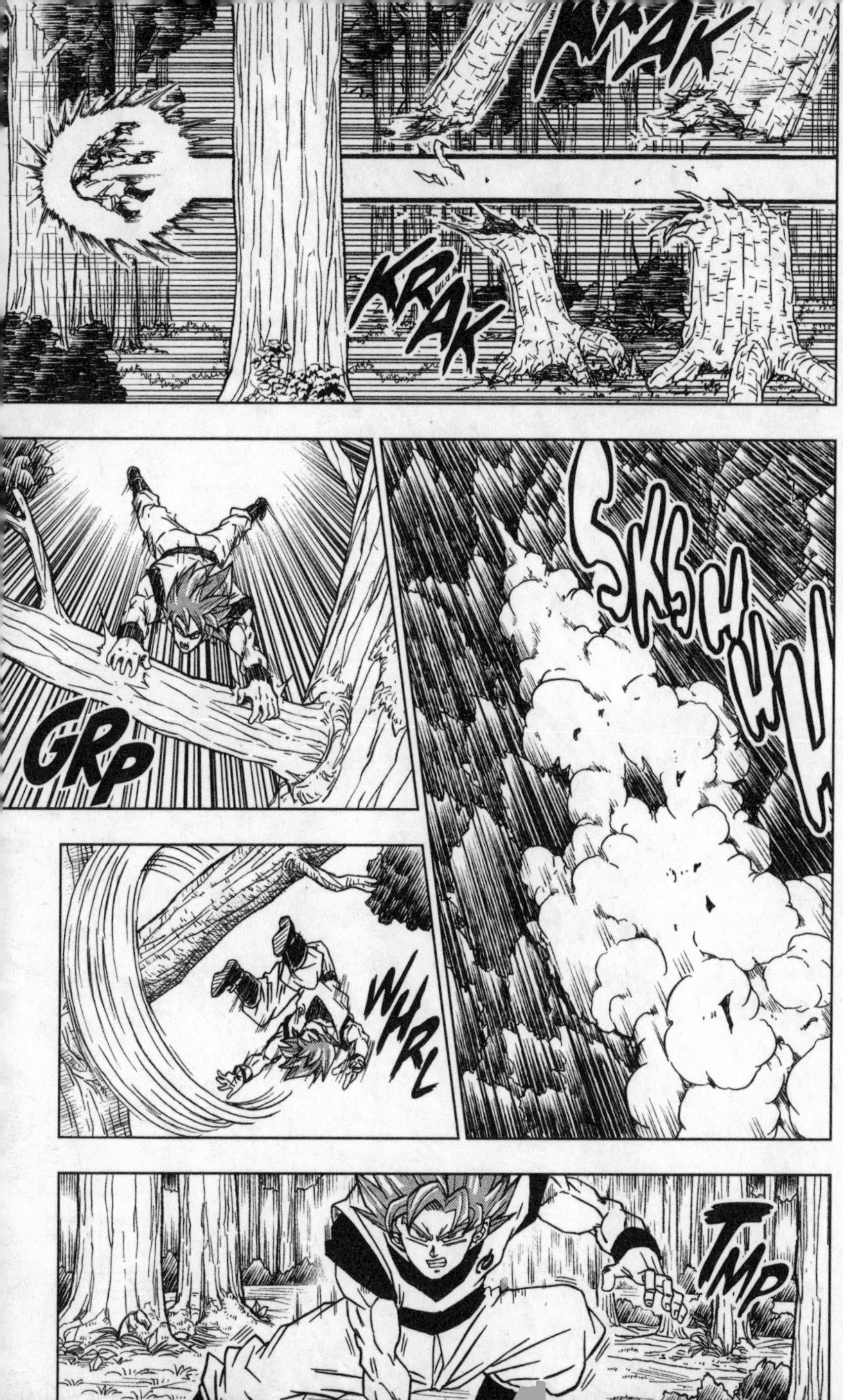

KRAK
KRAK
GRP
WHRL
TMP

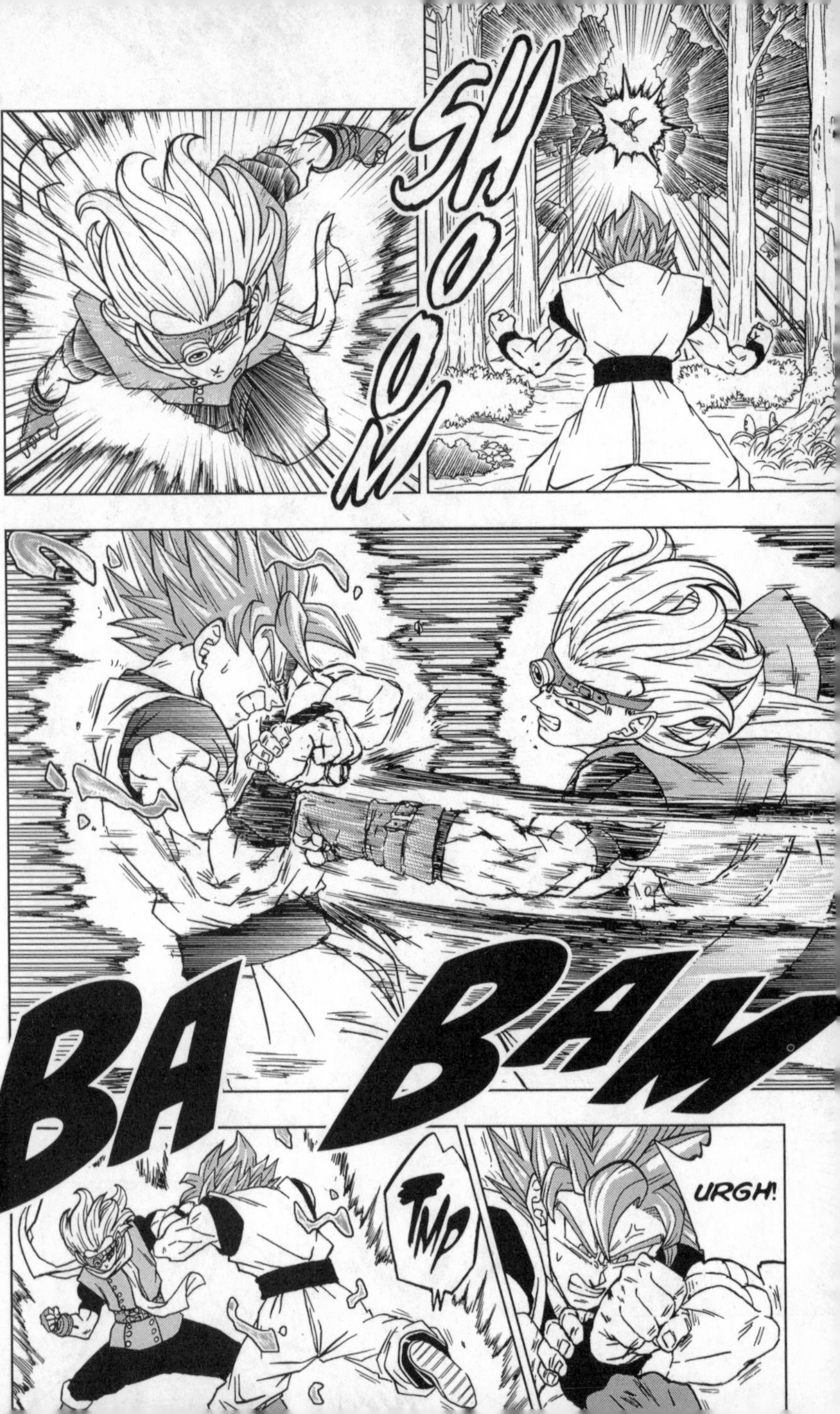
SHOOOM
BA BAM
URGH!
TMP

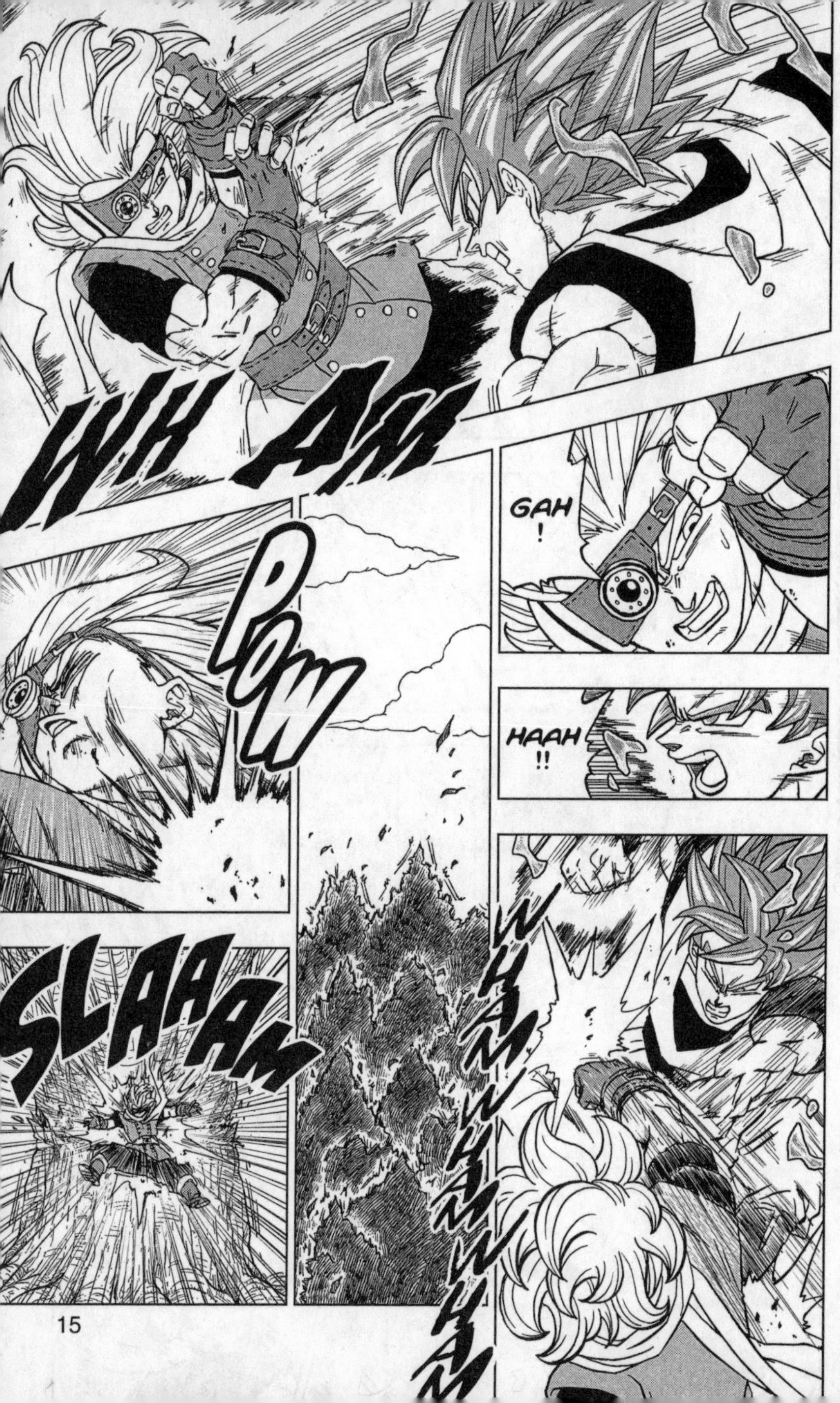

WHAM
GAH!
HAAH!!
POW
WHAMMMMMMMM
SLAAAM

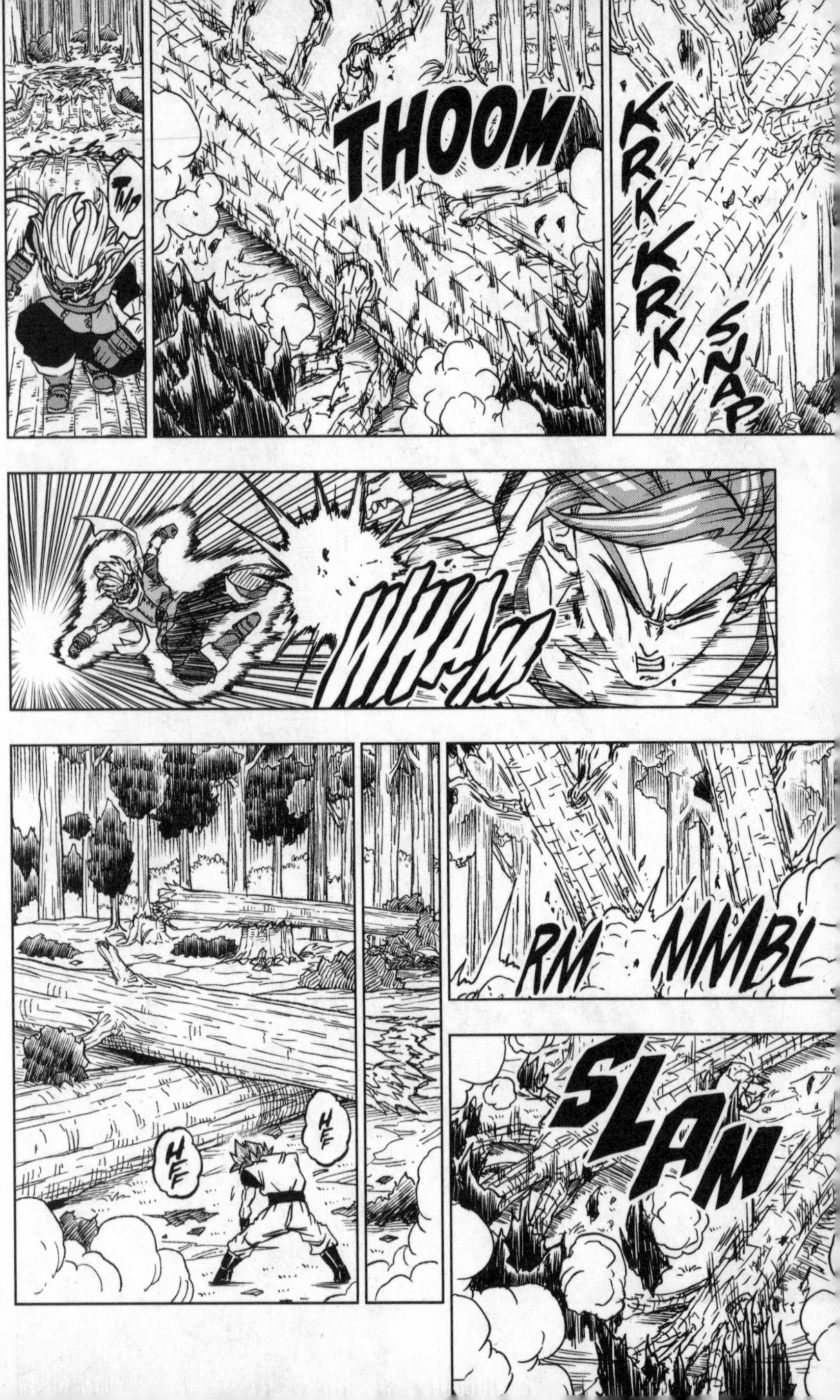
KRK KRK
SNAP
THOOM
TMP
WHAM
RM MMBL
SLAM
HEF
HEF

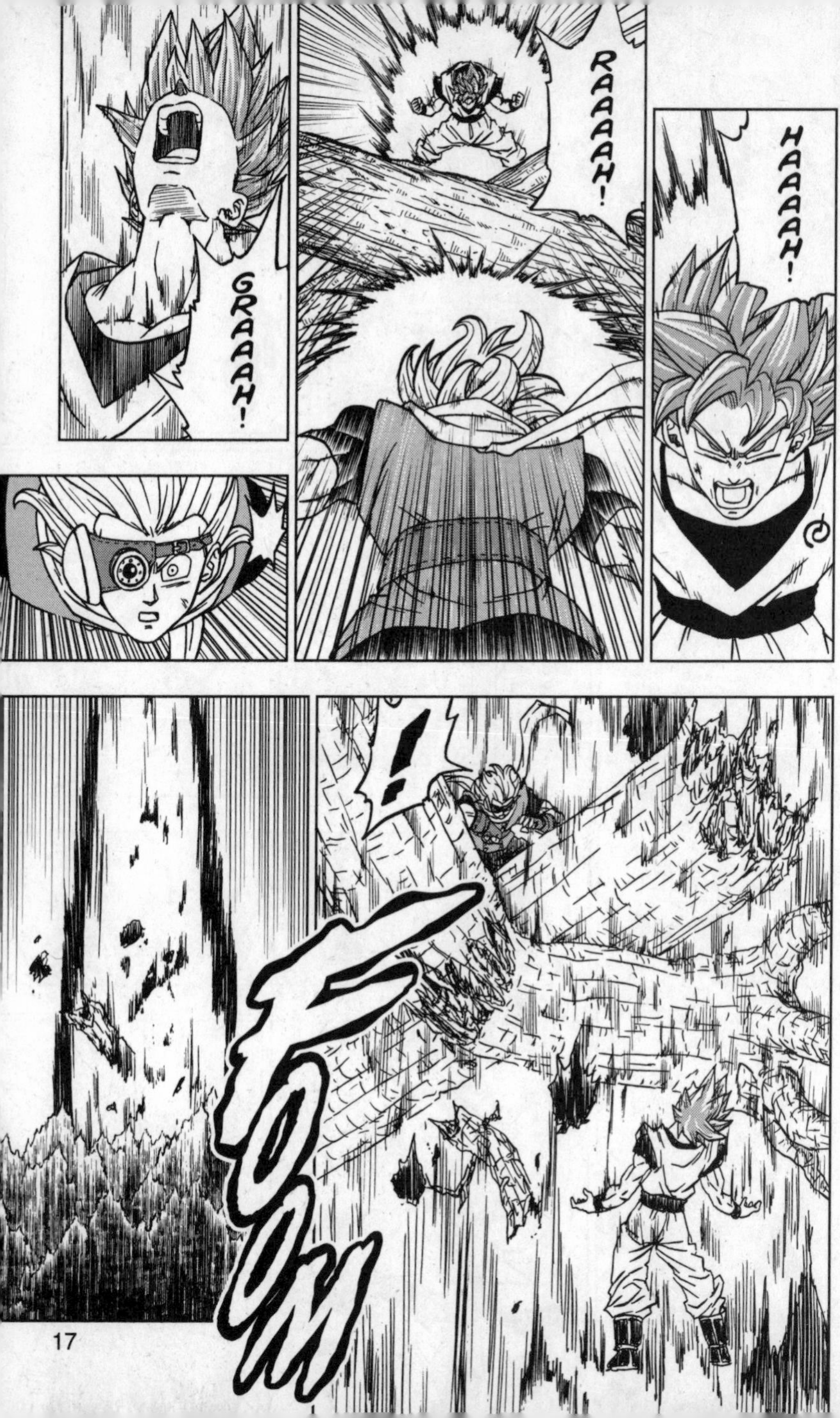
HAAAAAH!
RAAAAAH!
GRAAAAH!
!
VOOOM

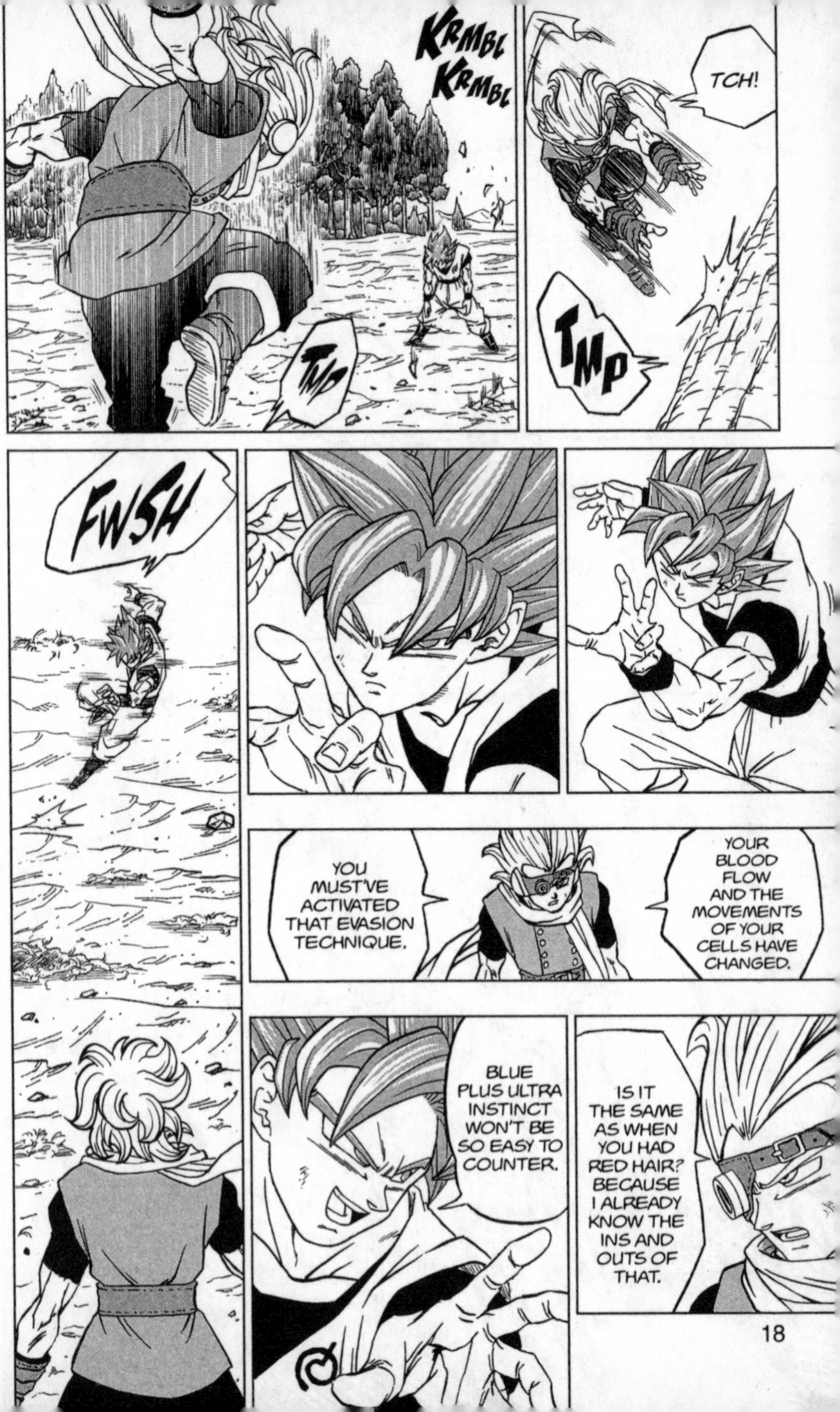
TCH!
TMP
KRMBL KRMBL
TMP
YOUR BLOOD FLOW AND THE MOVEMENTS OF YOUR CELLS HAVE CHANGED.
YOU MUST'VE ACTIVATED THAT EVASION TECHNIQUE.
FWSH
IS IT THE SAME AS WHEN YOU HAD RED HAIR? BECAUSE I ALREADY KNOW THE INS AND OUTS OF THAT.
BLUE PLUS ULTRA INSTINCT WON'T BE SO EASY TO COUNTER.

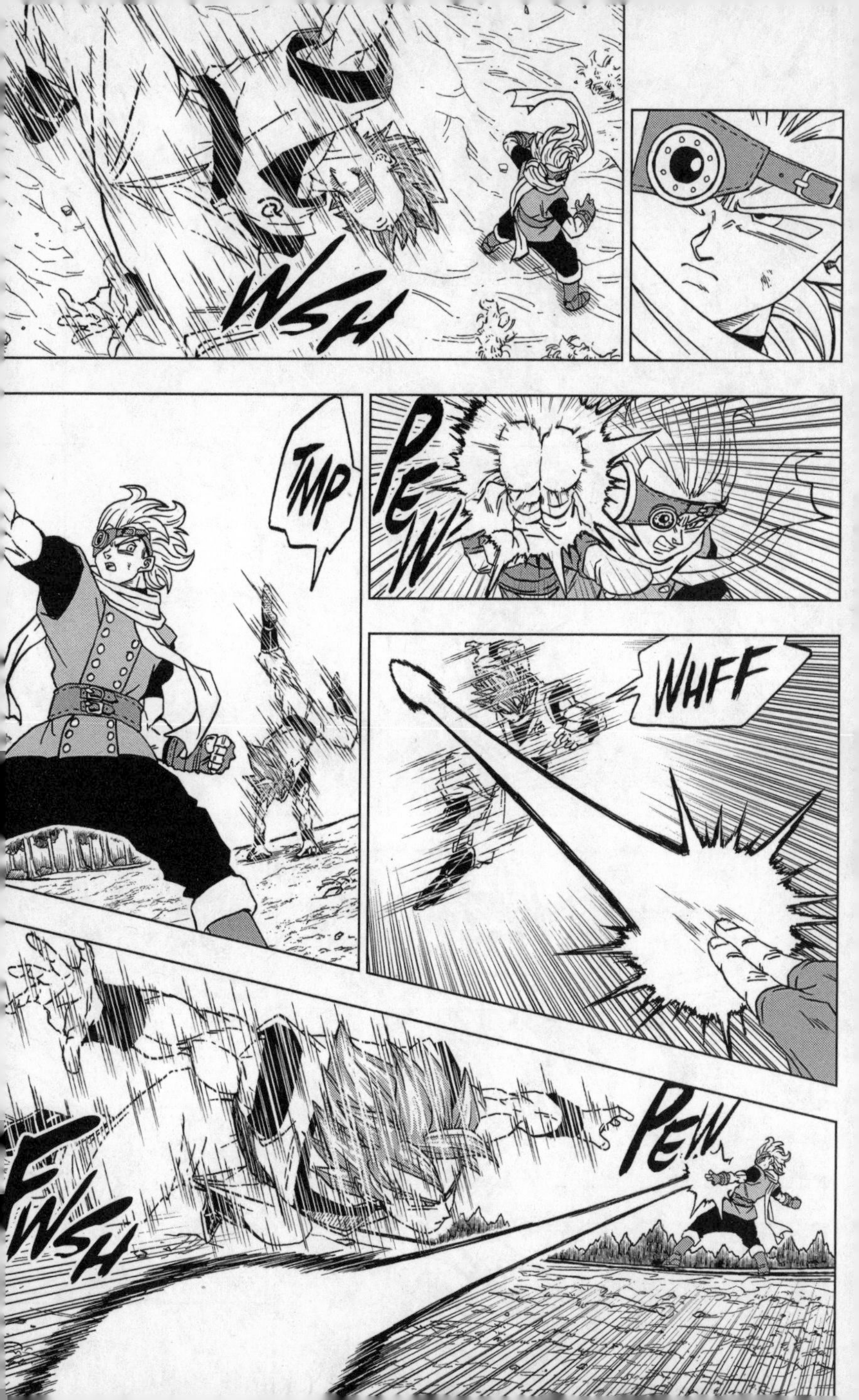
WSH
PEW
WHFF
TMP
PEW
FWSH

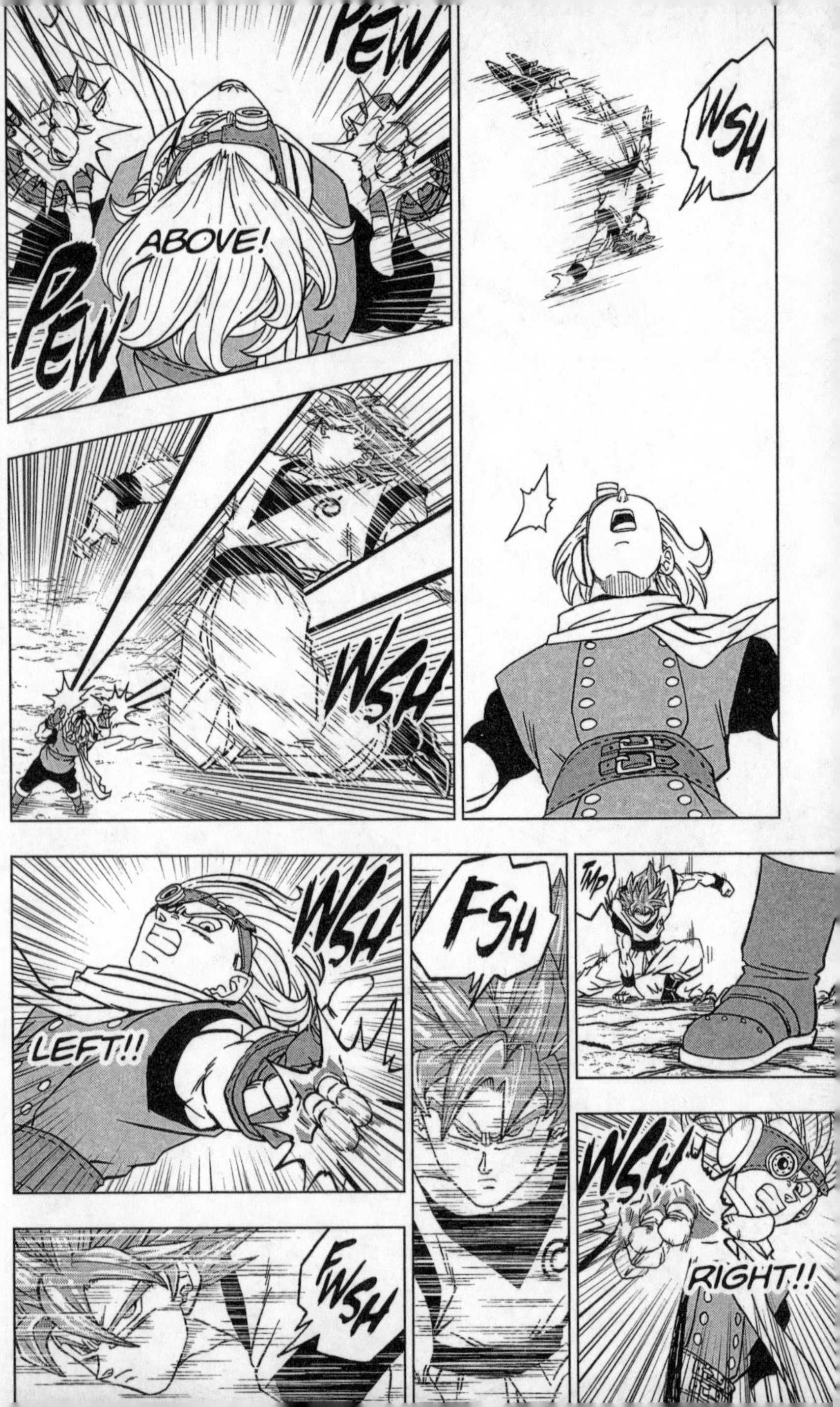
WSH
PEW
ABOVE!
PEW
WSH
TMP
WSH
RIGHT!!
FSH
WSH
LEFT!!
FWSH

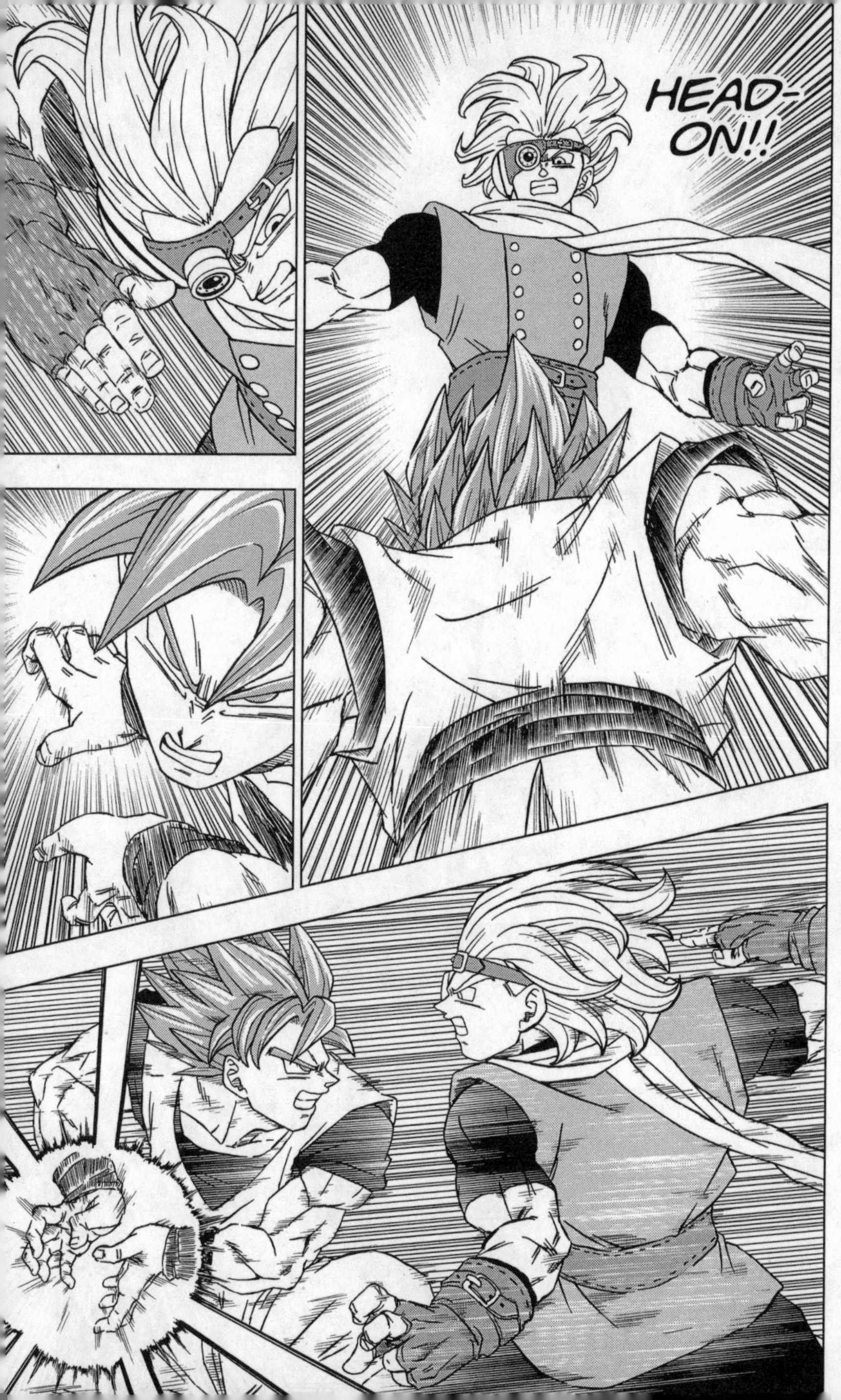
HEAD-ON!!

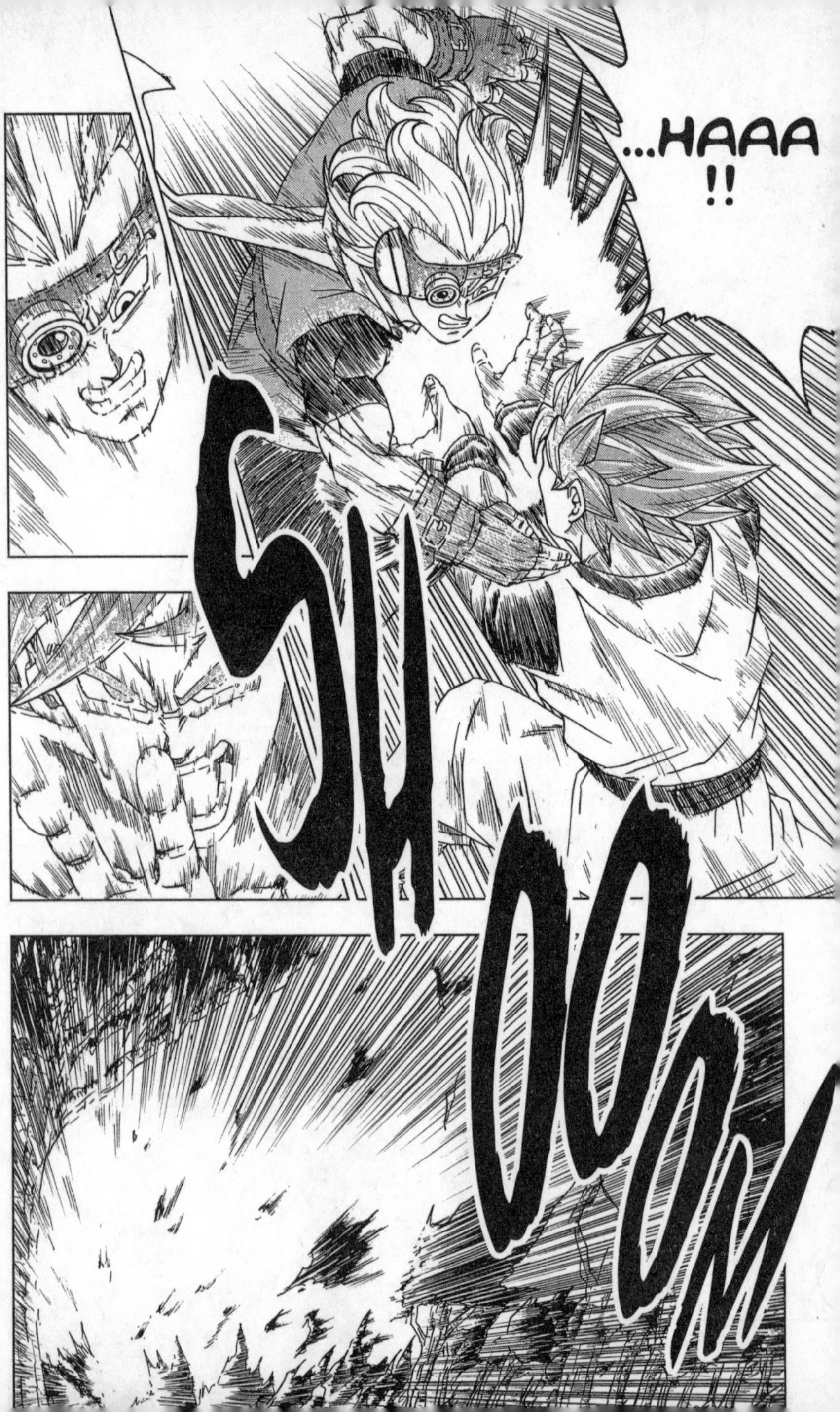
...HAAA!!
SHOOOM

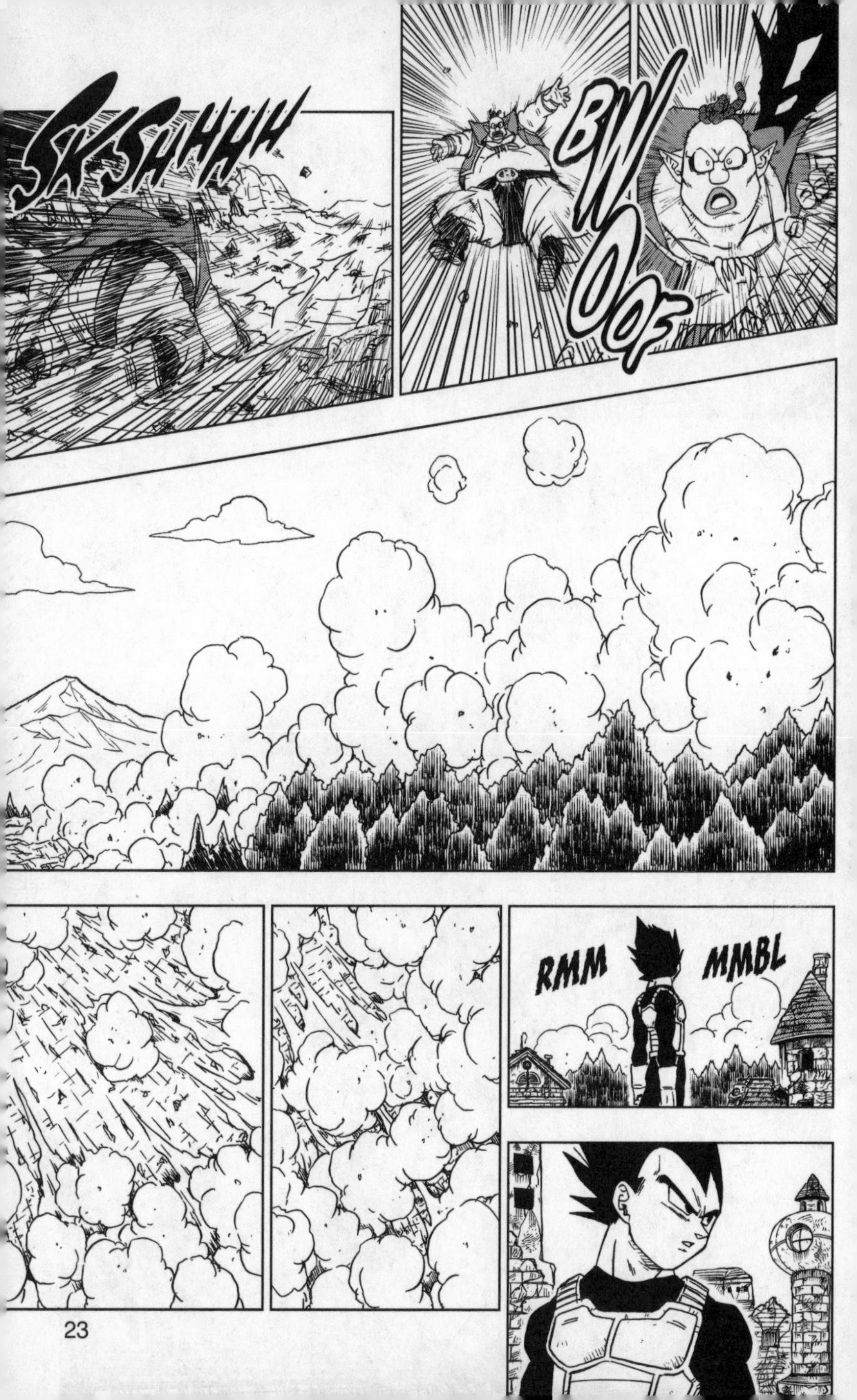
BWOOF
SKSHHHH
RMM
MMBL

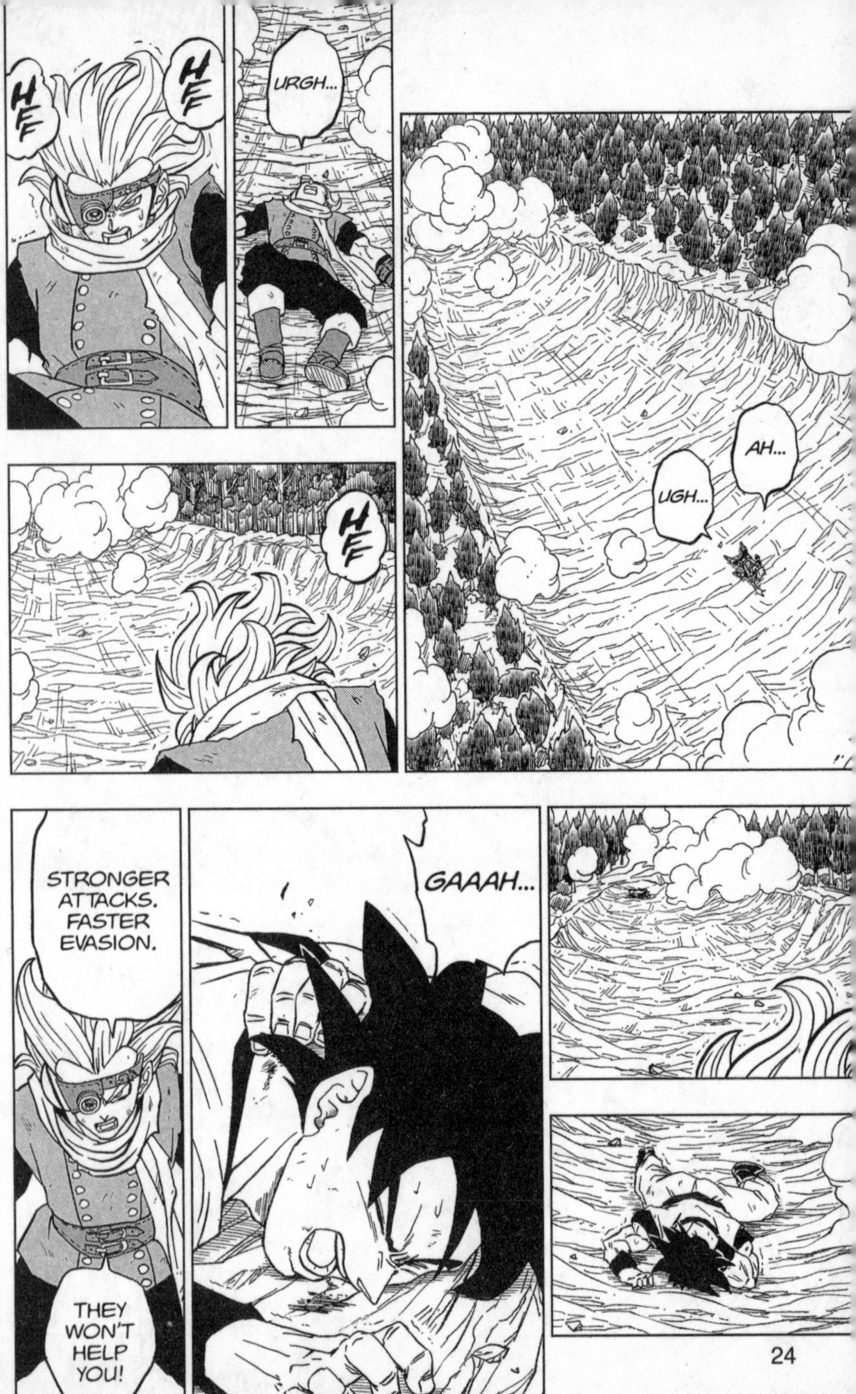
AH...
UGH...
URGH...
HEF
HEF
HEF
GAAAH...
STRONGER ATTACKS. FASTER EVASION.
THEY WON'T HELP YOU!

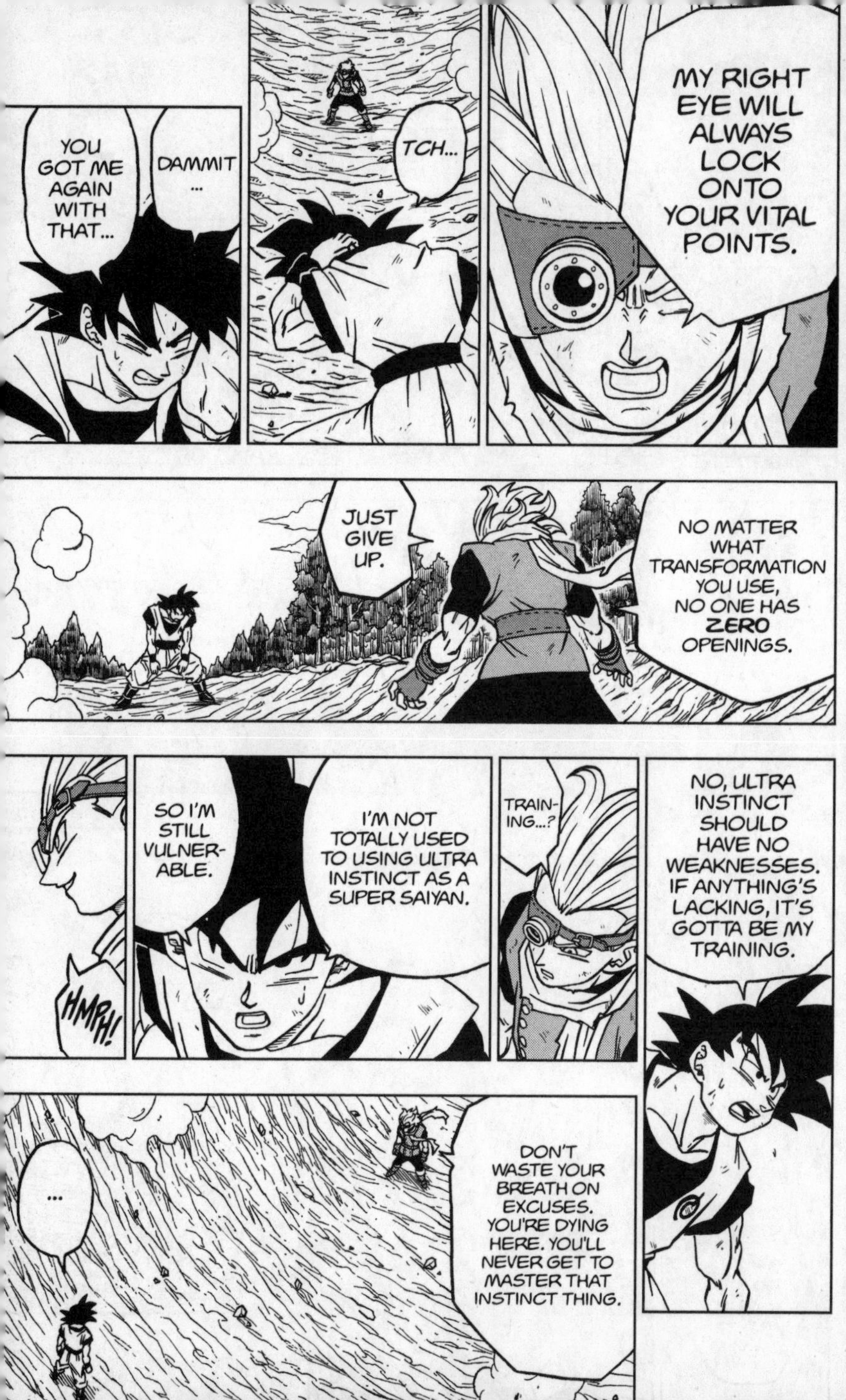
MY RIGHT EYE WILL ALWAYS LOCK ONTO YOUR VITAL POINTS.
TCH...
DAMMIT ...
YOU GOT ME AGAIN WITH THAT...
NO MATTER WHAT TRANSFORMATION YOU USE, NO ONE HAS **ZERO** OPENINGS.
JUST GIVE UP.
NO, ULTRA INSTINCT SHOULD HAVE NO WEAKNESSES. IF ANYTHING'S LACKING, IT'S GOTTA BE MY TRAINING.
TRAIN-ING...?
I'M NOT TOTALLY USED TO USING ULTRA INSTINCT AS A SUPER SAIYAN.
SO I'M STILL VULNER-ABLE.
HMPH!
DON'T WASTE YOUR BREATH ON EXCUSES. YOU'RE DYING HERE. YOU'LL NEVER GET TO MASTER THAT INSTINCT THING.
...

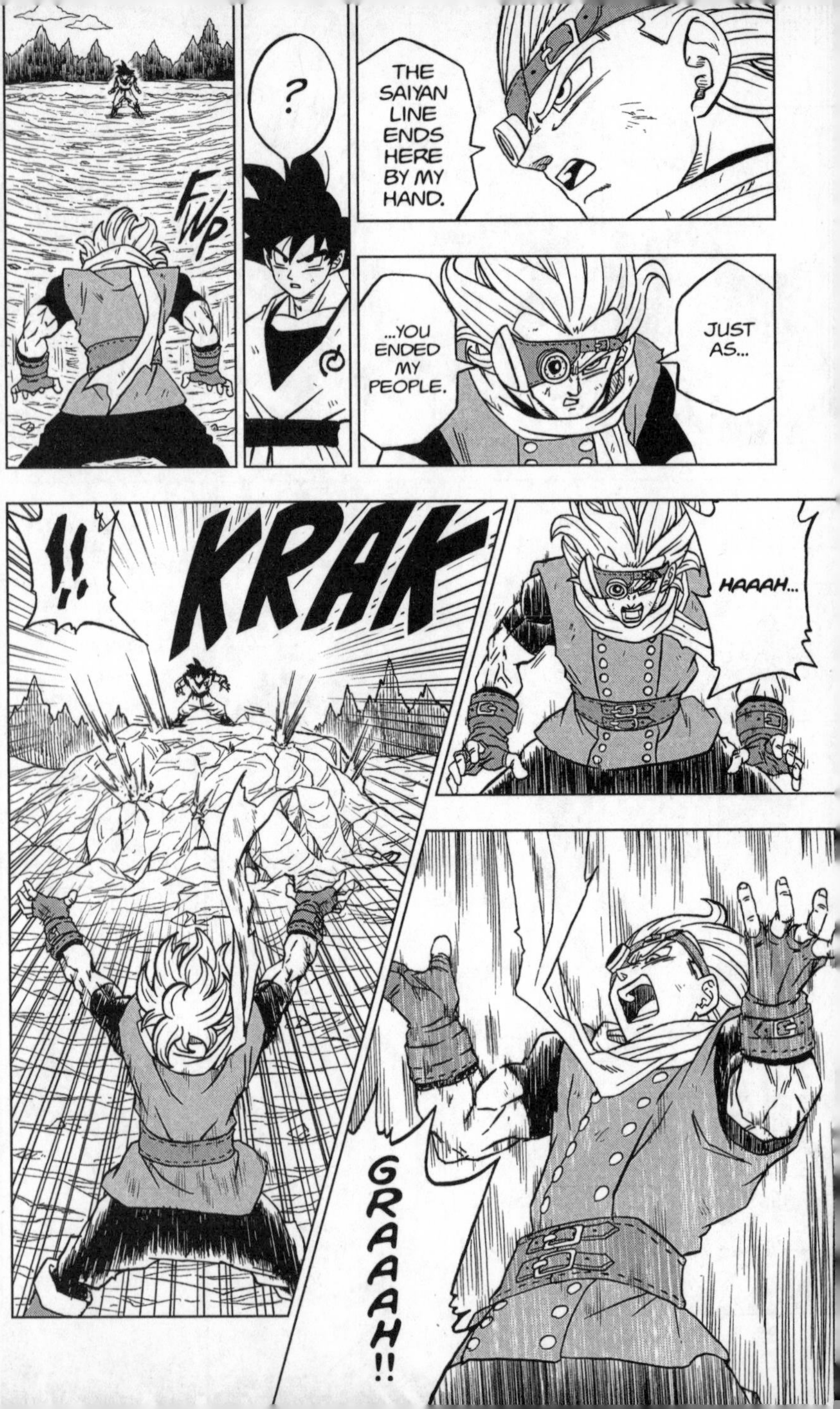
THE SAIYAN LINE ENDS HERE BY MY HAND.
JUST AS...
...YOU ENDED MY PEOPLE.
?
FWP
HAAAH...
GRAAAAH!!
KRAK
!!

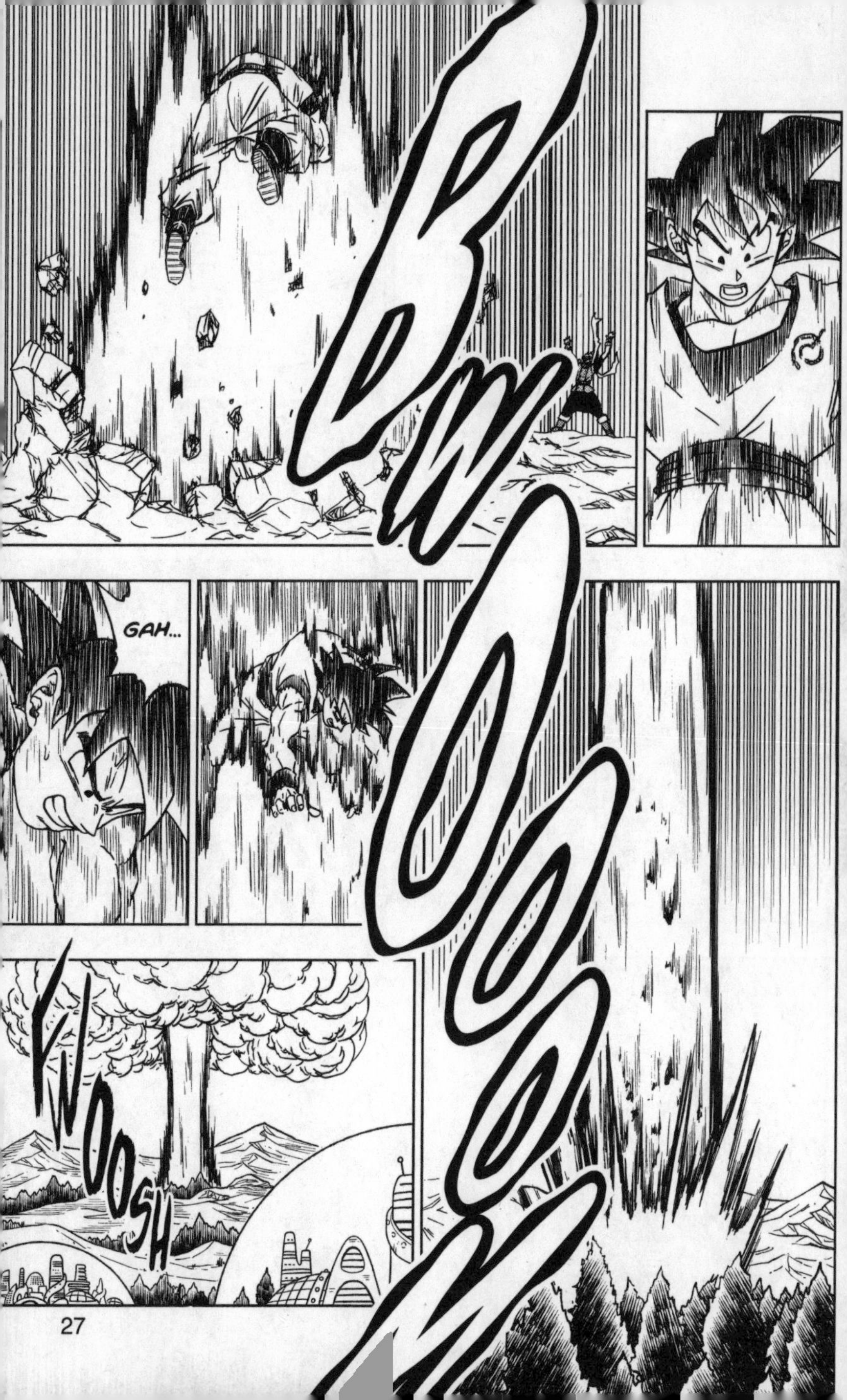
GAH...
FWOOSH

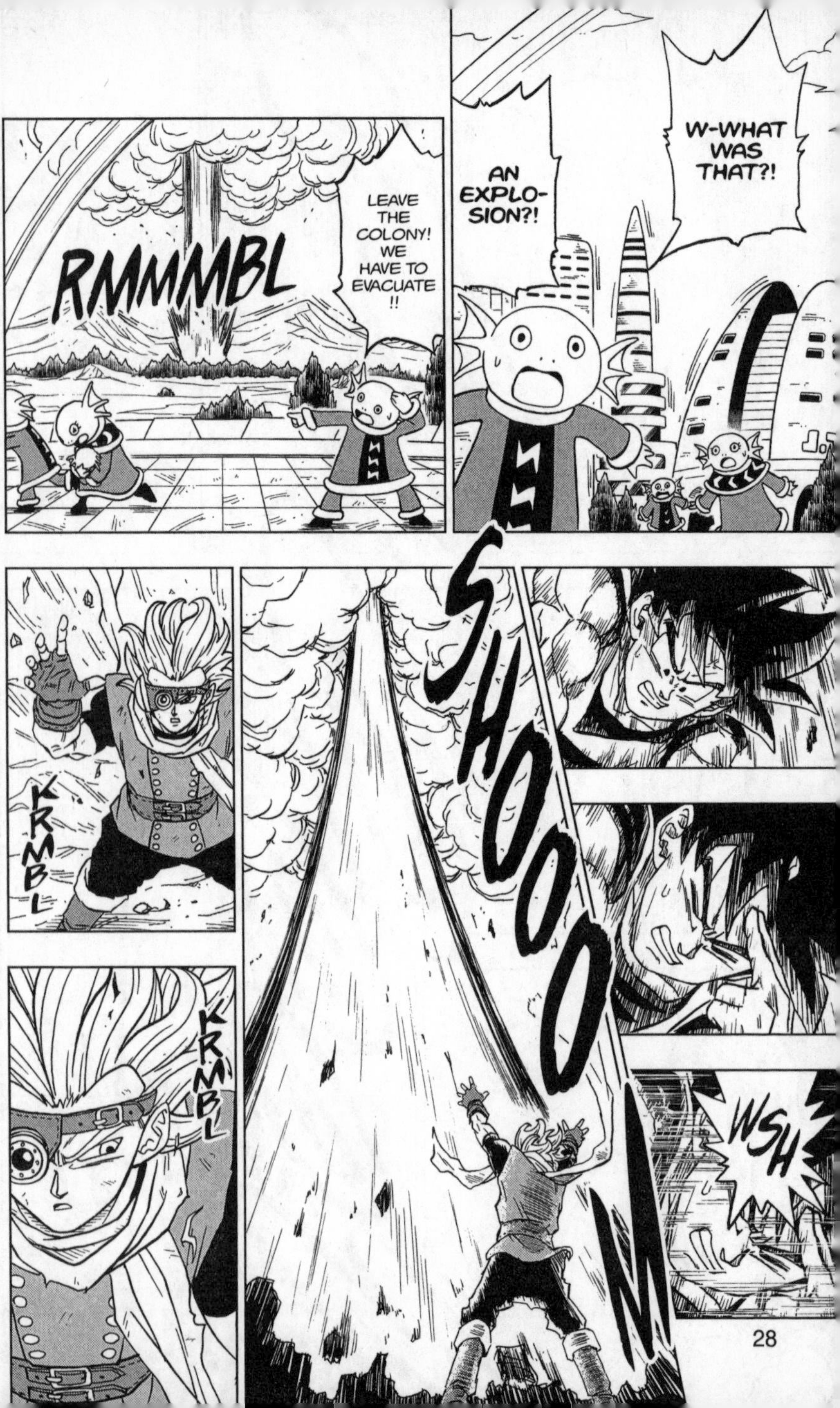
W-WHAT WAS THAT?!
AN EXPLOSION?!
RMMMBL
LEAVE THE COLONY! WE HAVE TO EVACUATE!!
SHOOOOM
WSH
KRMBL
KRMBL

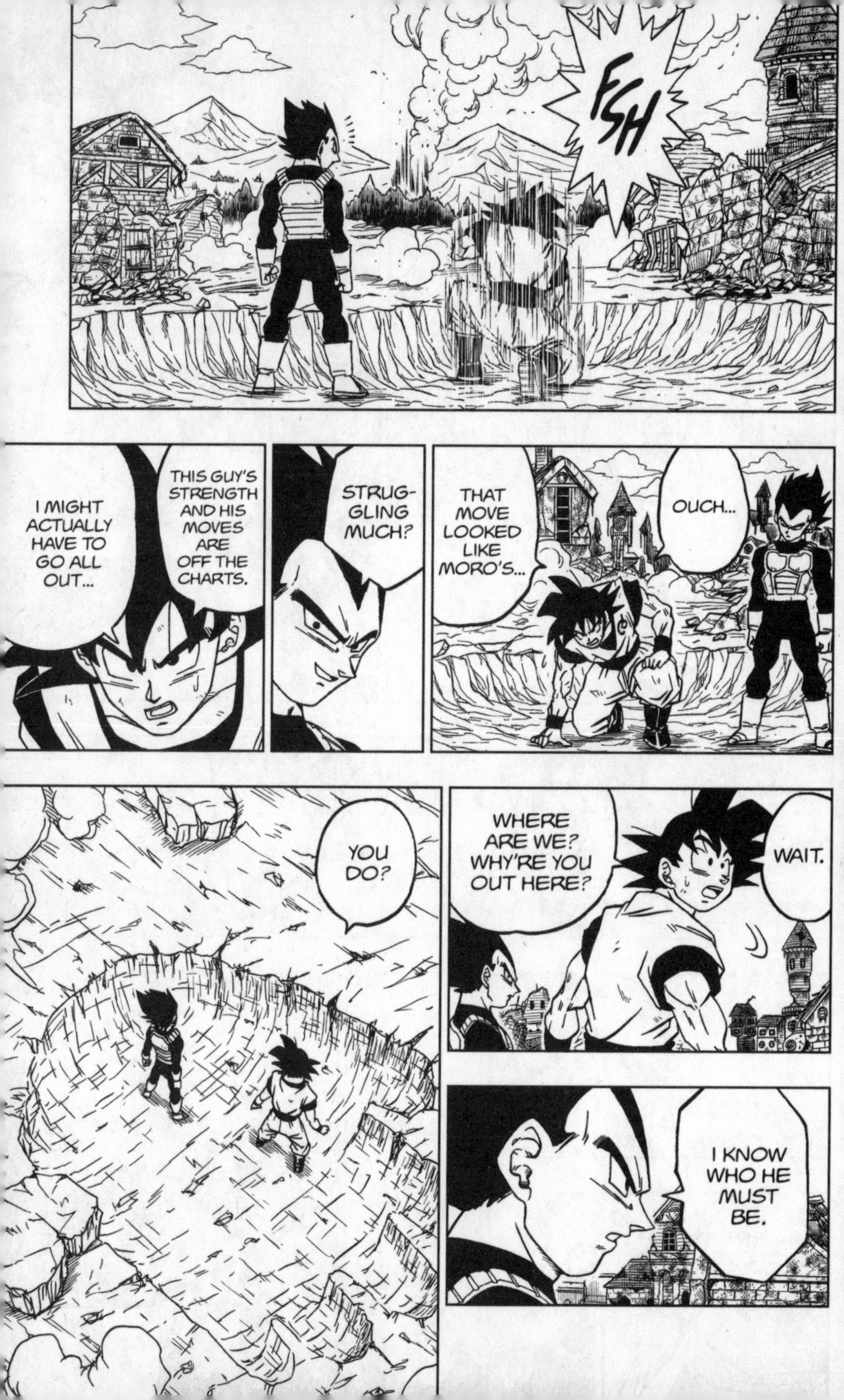
FSH
OUCH...
THAT MOVE LOOKED LIKE MORO'S...
STRUG-GLING MUCH?
THIS GUY'S STRENGTH AND HIS MOVES ARE OFF THE CHARTS.
I MIGHT ACTUALLY HAVE TO GO ALL OUT...
WAIT.
WHERE ARE WE? WHY'RE YOU OUT HERE?
I KNOW WHO HE MUST BE.
YOU DO?

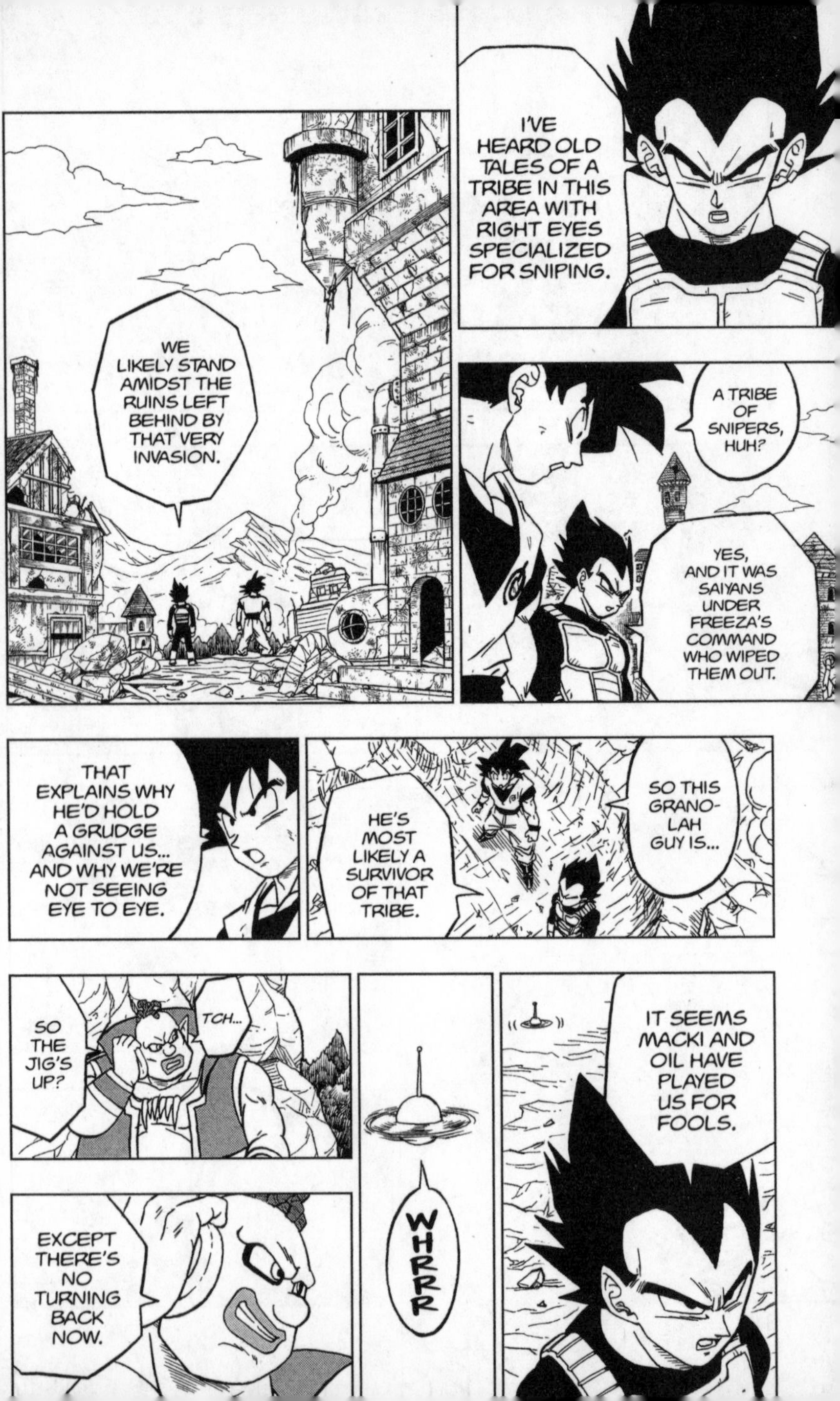
I'VE HEARD OLD TALES OF A TRIBE IN THIS AREA WITH RIGHT EYES SPECIALIZED FOR SNIPING.
A TRIBE OF SNIPERS, HUH?
YES, AND IT WAS SAIYANS UNDER FREEZA'S COMMAND WHO WIPED THEM OUT.
WE LIKELY STAND AMIDST THE RUINS LEFT BEHIND BY THAT VERY INVASION.
SO THIS GRANO-LAH GUY IS...
HE'S MOST LIKELY A SURVIVOR OF THAT TRIBE.
THAT EXPLAINS WHY HE'D HOLD A GRUDGE AGAINST US... AND WHY WE'RE NOT SEEING EYE TO EYE.
IT SEEMS MACKI AND OIL HAVE PLAYED US FOR FOOLS.
WHRRR
TCH...
SO THE JIG'S UP?
EXCEPT THERE'S NO TURNING BACK NOW.

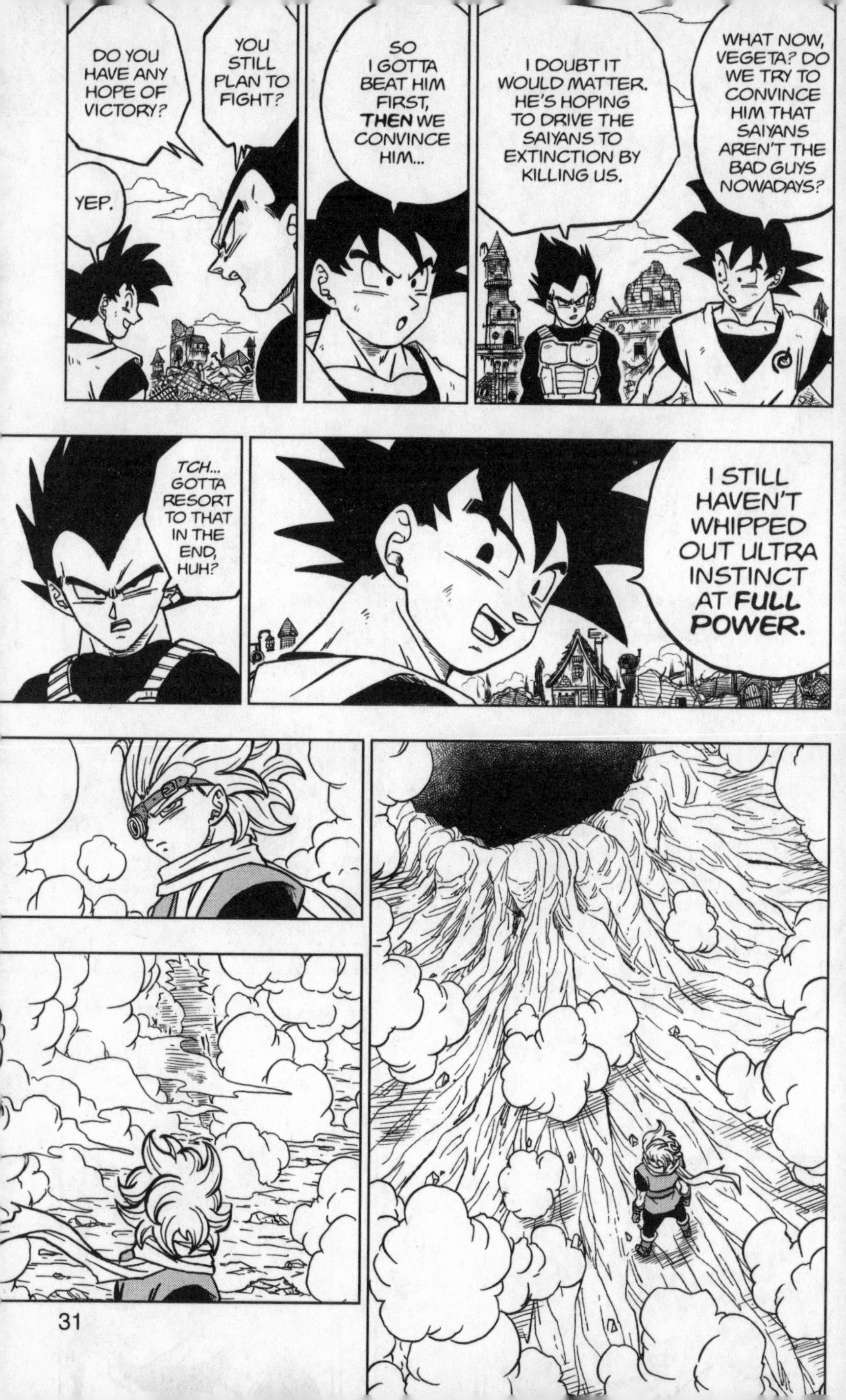
WHAT NOW, VEGETA? DO WE TRY TO CONVINCE HIM THAT SAIYANS AREN'T THE BAD GUYS NOWADAYS?
I DOUBT IT WOULD MATTER. HE'S HOPING TO DRIVE THE SAIYANS TO EXTINCTION BY KILLING US.
SO I GOTTA BEAT HIM FIRST, **THEN** WE CONVINCE HIM...
YOU STILL PLAN TO FIGHT?
DO YOU HAVE ANY HOPE OF VICTORY?
YEP.
I STILL HAVEN'T WHIPPED OUT ULTRA INSTINCT AT **FULL POWER.**
TCH... GOTTA RESORT TO THAT IN THE END, HUH?

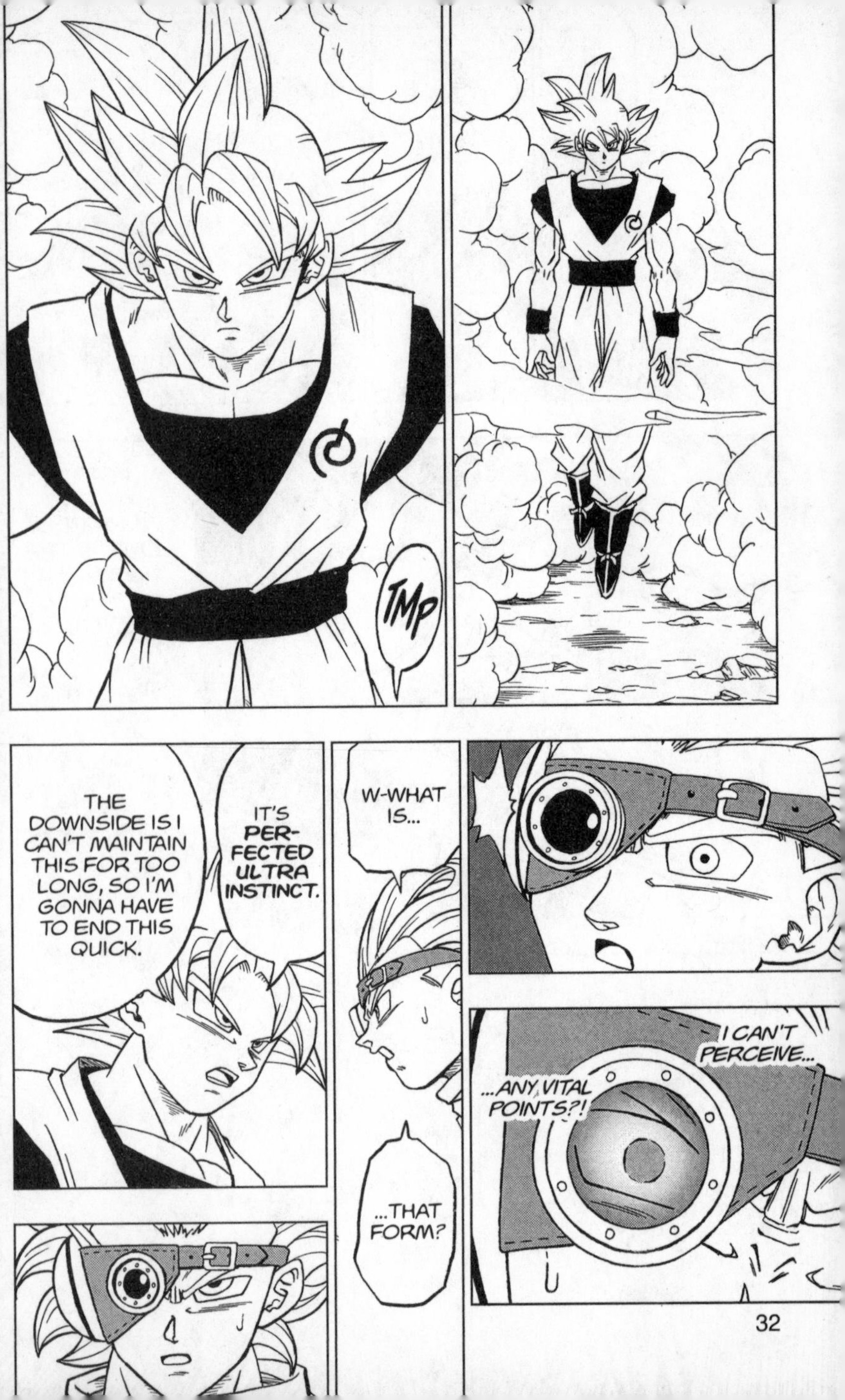
TMP
I CAN'T PERCEIVE...
...ANY VITAL POINTS?!
W-WHAT IS...
...THAT FORM?
IT'S PERFECTED ULTRA INSTINCT.
THE DOWNSIDE IS I CAN'T MAINTAIN THIS FOR TOO LONG, SO I'M GONNA HAVE TO END THIS QUICK.

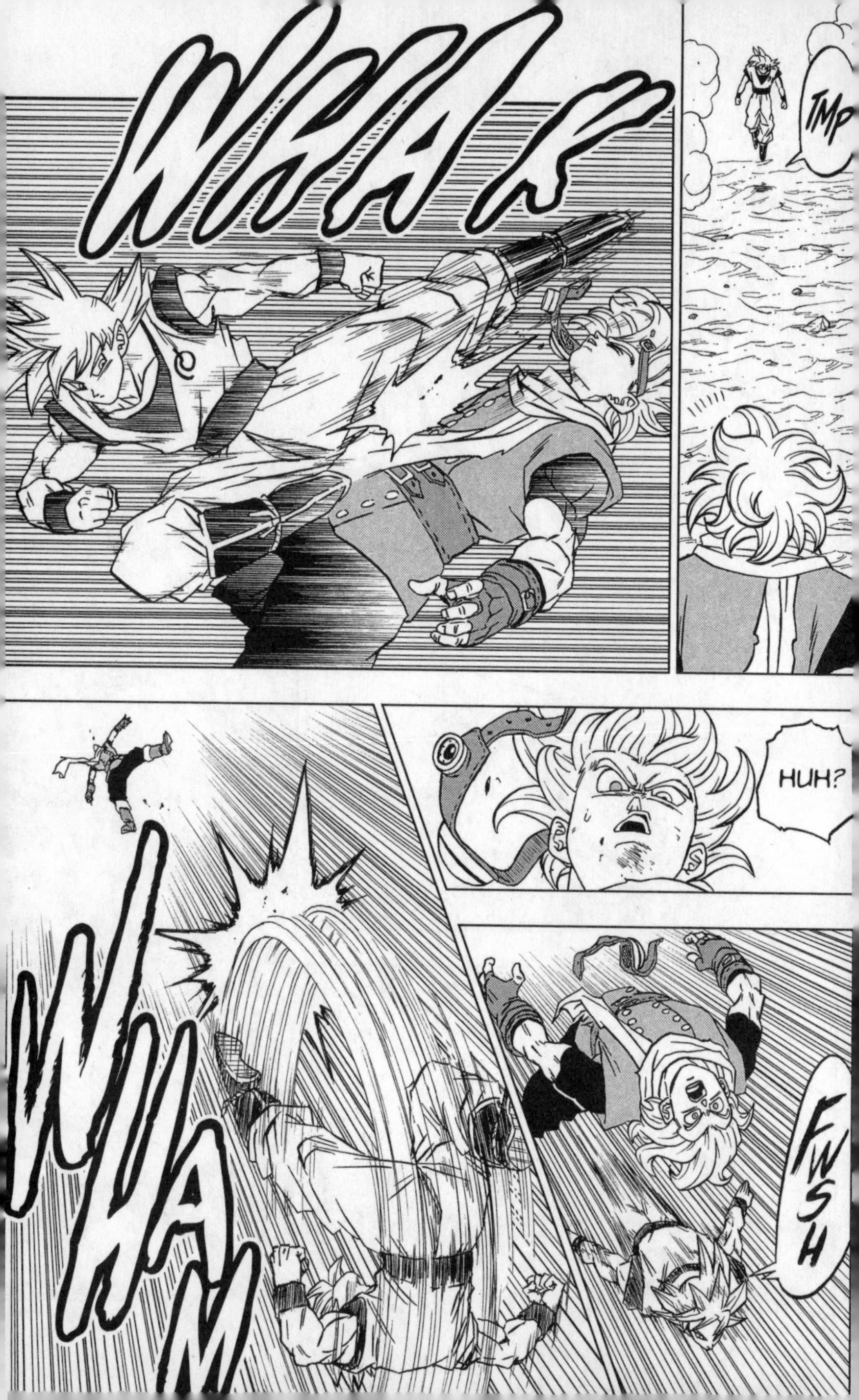
TMP
HUH?
FWSH

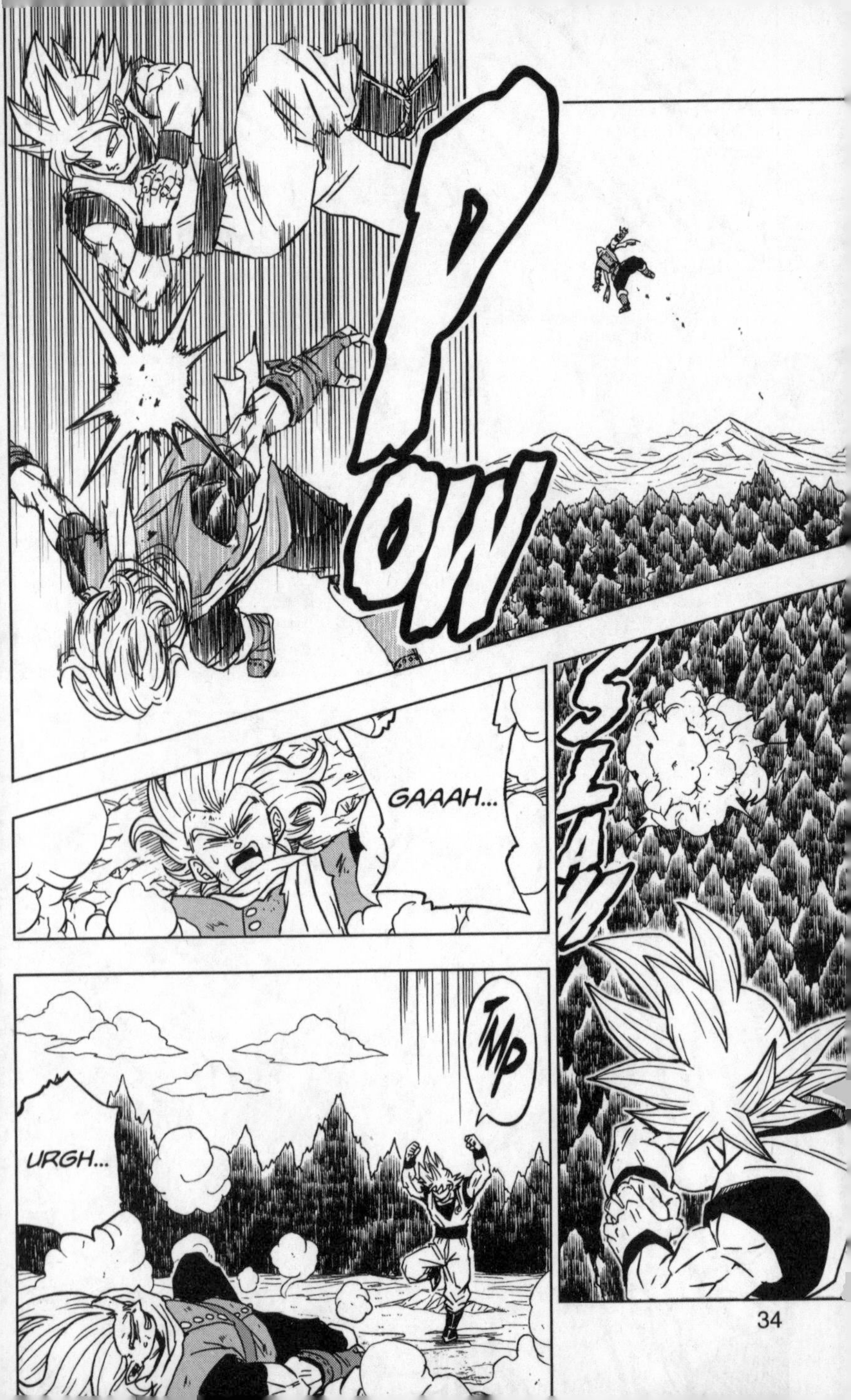
POW
SLAM
GAAAH...
TMP
URGH...

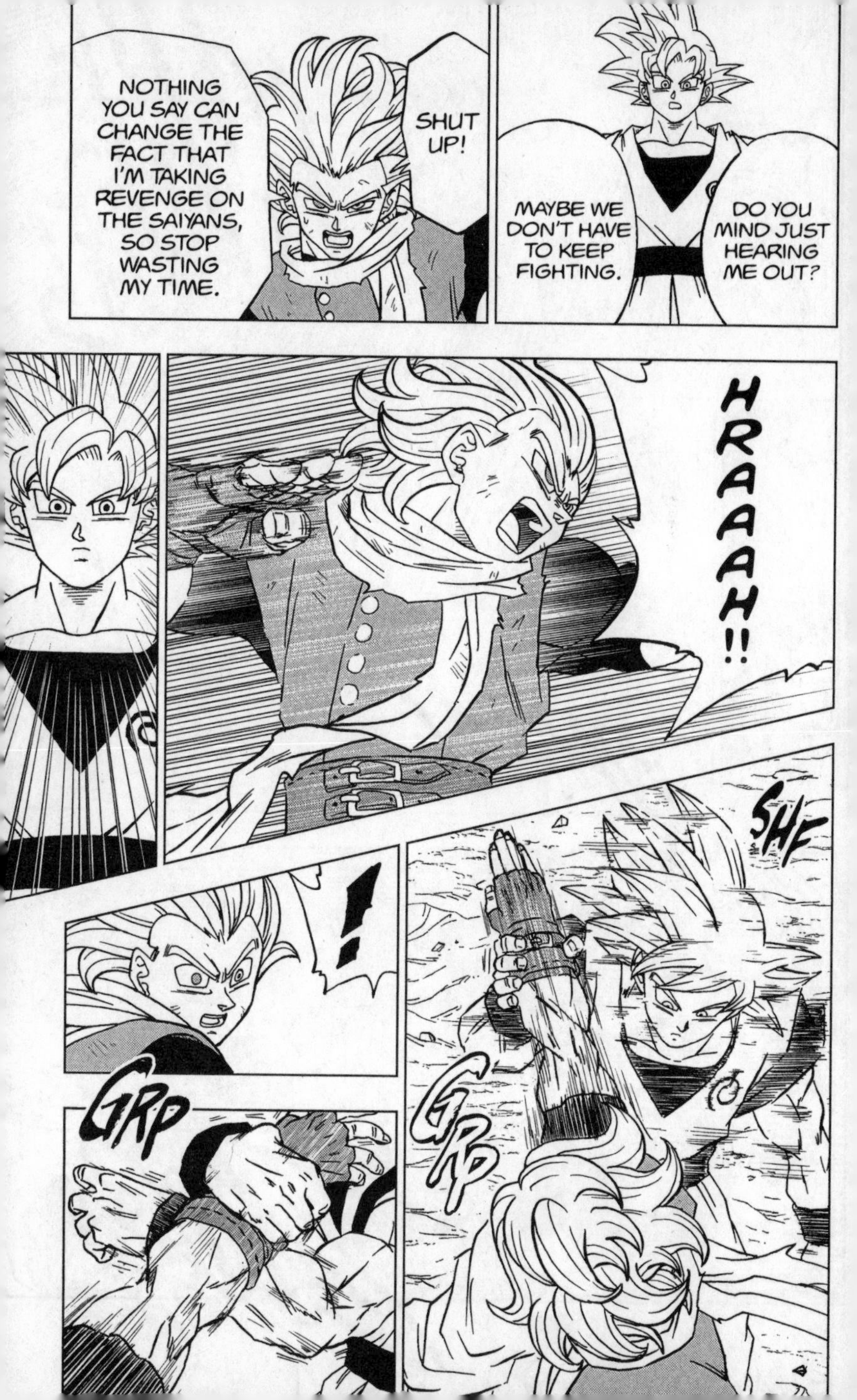
DO YOU MIND JUST HEARING ME OUT?
MAYBE WE DON'T HAVE TO KEEP FIGHTING.
SHUT UP!
NOTHING YOU SAY CAN CHANGE THE FACT THAT I'M TAKING REVENGE ON THE SAIYANS, SO STOP WASTING MY TIME.
HRAAAAH!!
SHF
GRP
!
GRP

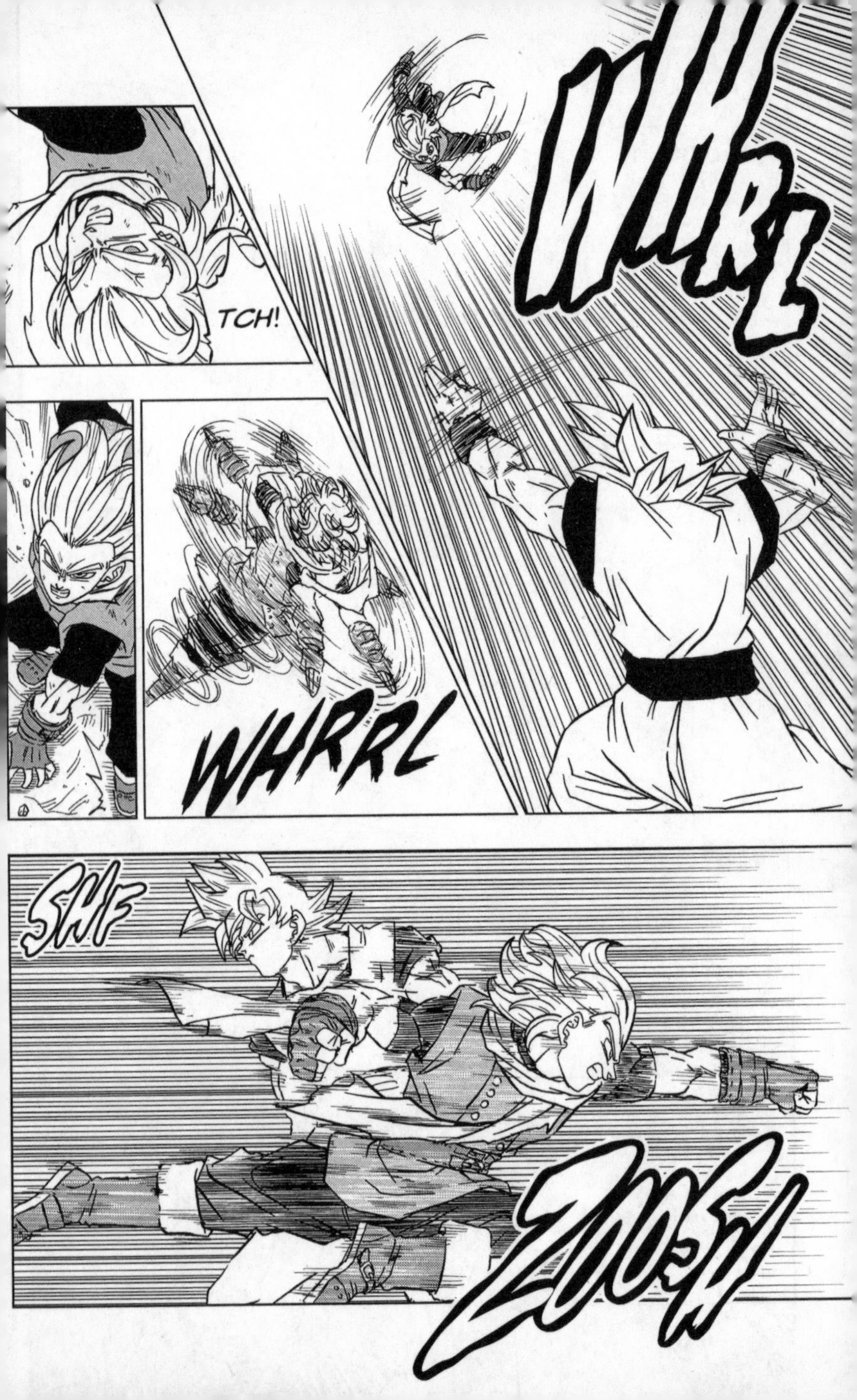
WHRL
TCH!
WHRRL
SHF

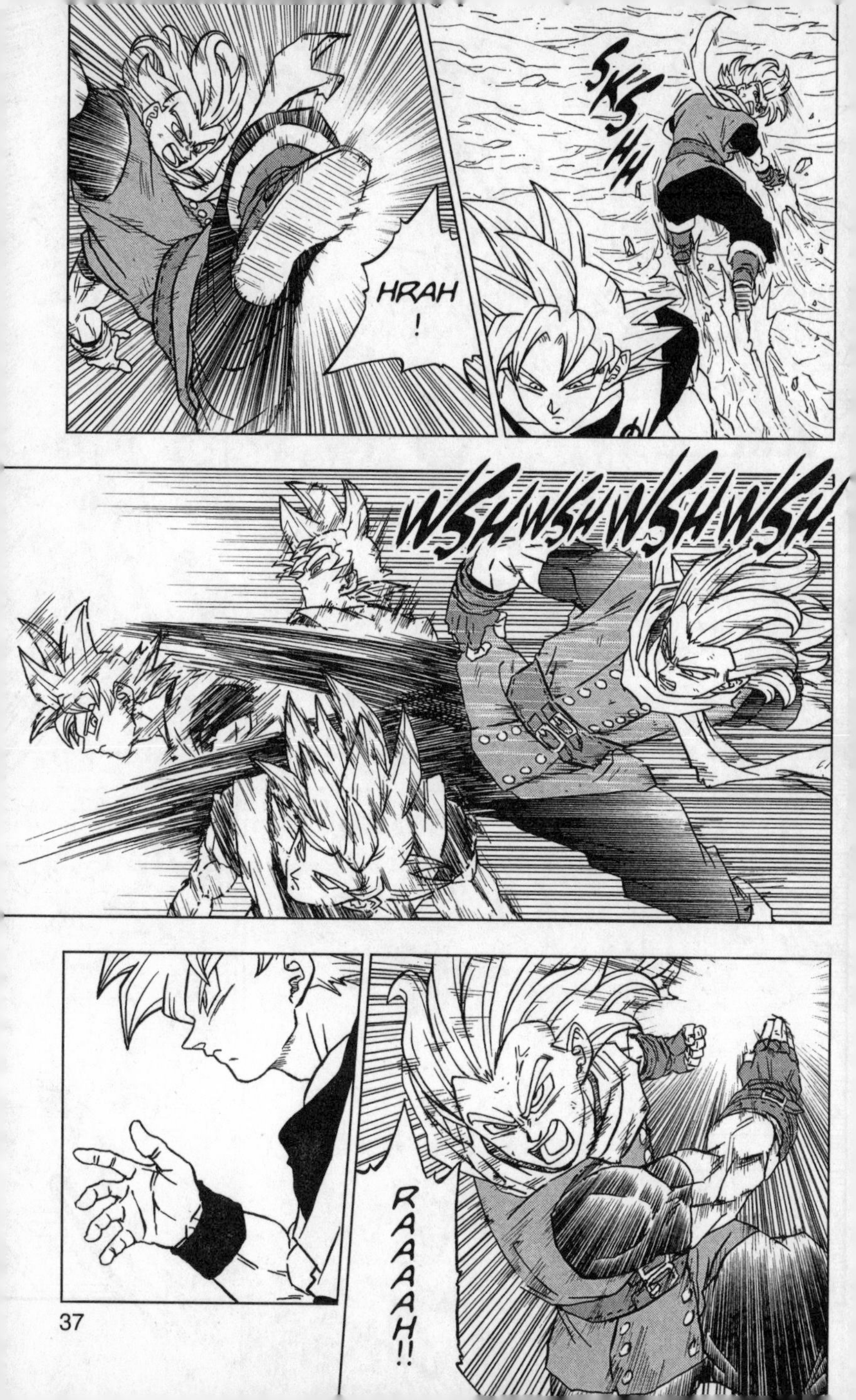
SKSHHH
HRAH!
WSHWSHWSHWSH
RAAAAAH!!

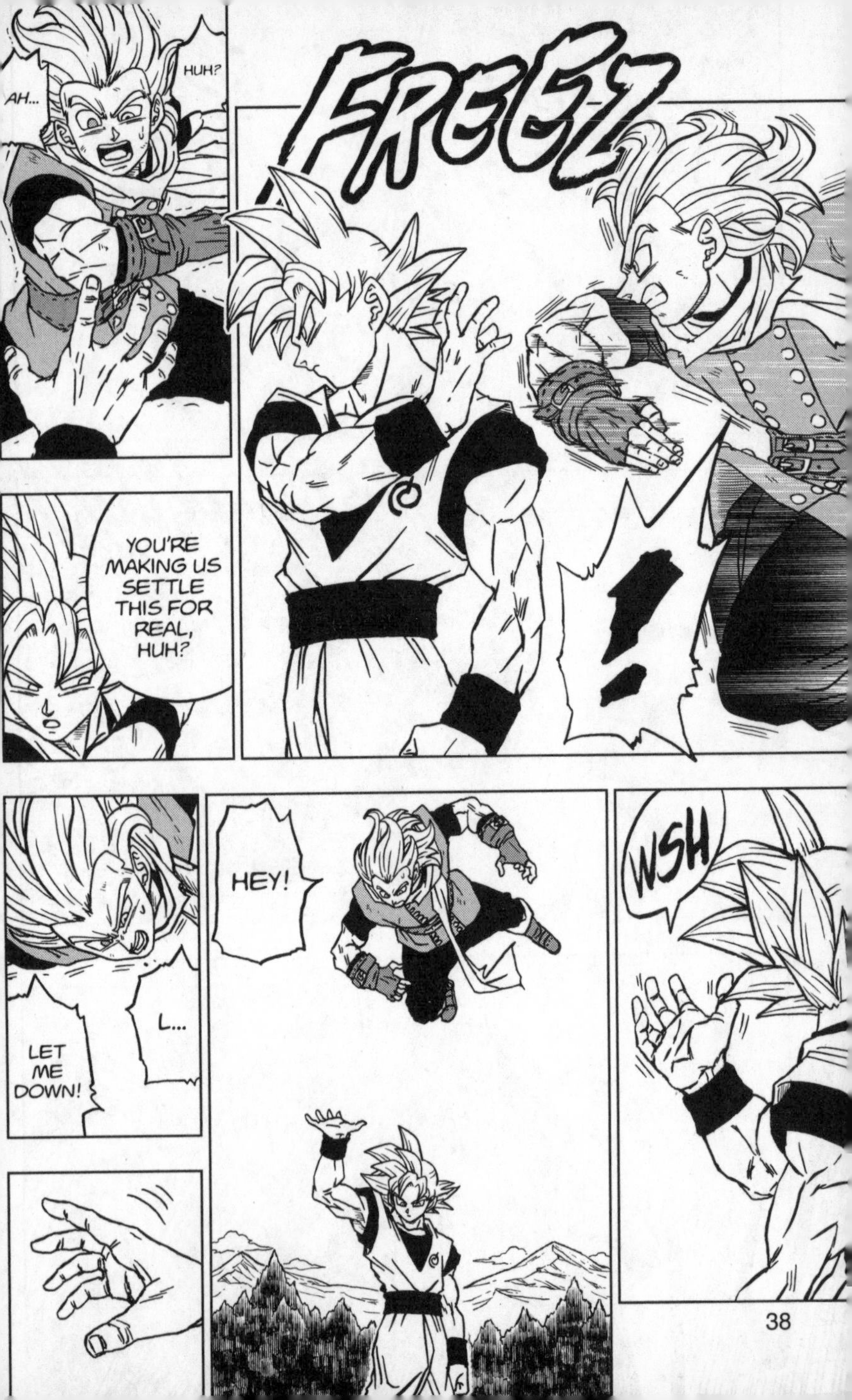
FRGGZ
HUH?
AH...
YOU'RE MAKING US SETTLE THIS FOR REAL, HUH?
WSH
HEY!
L...
LET ME DOWN!

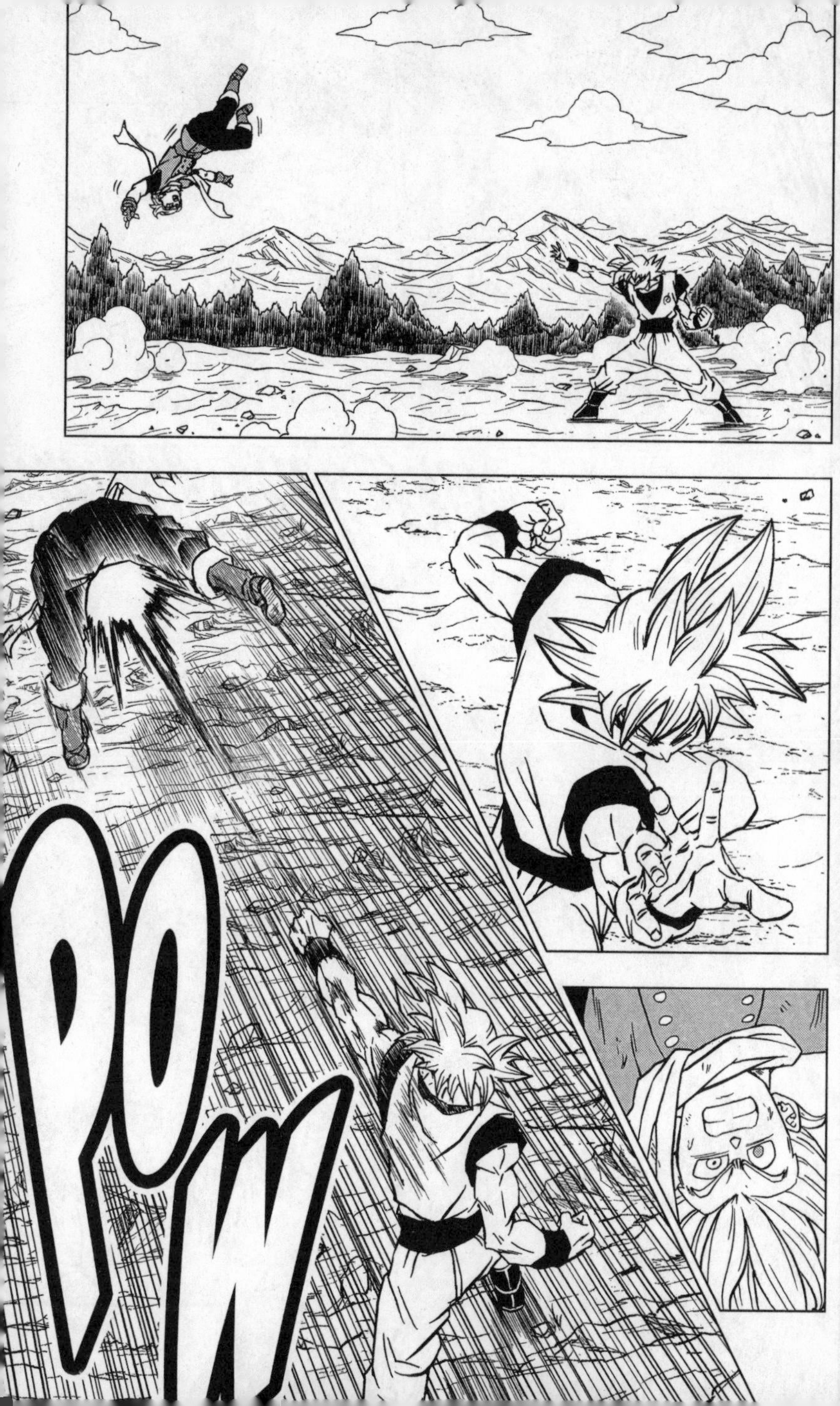
POW

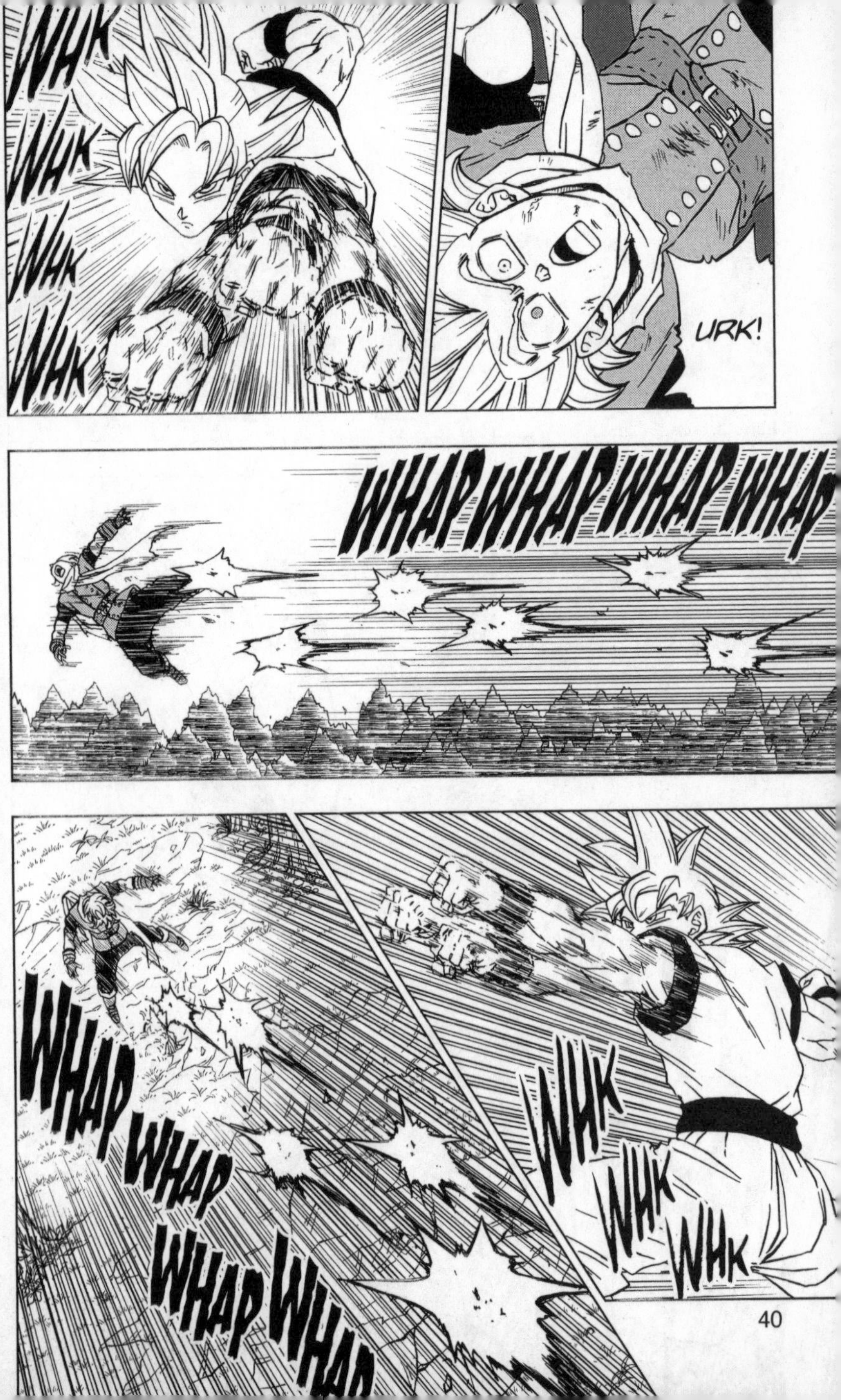
URK!
WHK
WHK
WHK
WHK
WHAP WHAP WHAP WHAP
WHK
WHK
WHK
WHAP
WHAP
WHAP
WHAP

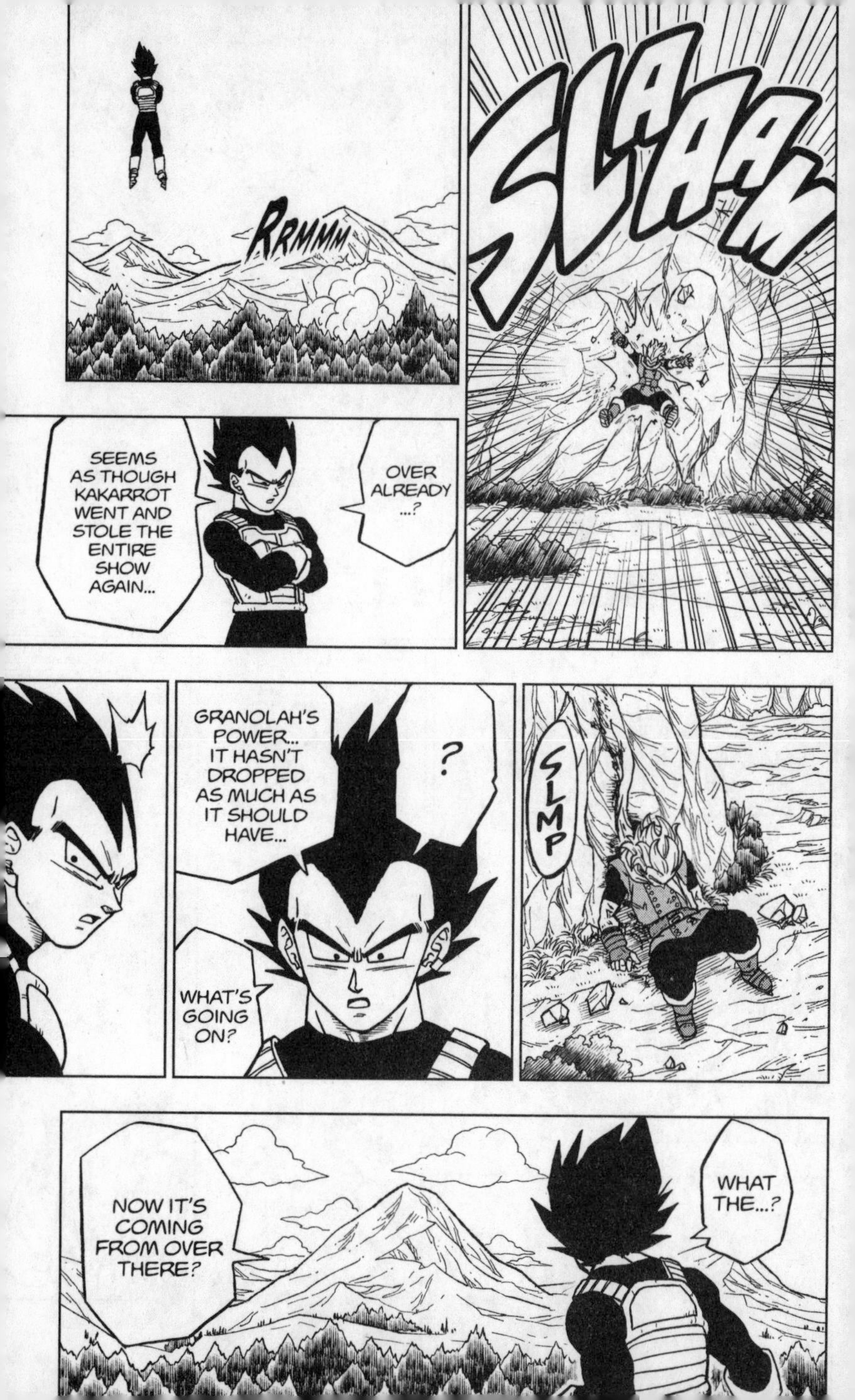
SLAAAM
RRMMM
OVER ALREADY ...?
SEEMS AS THOUGH KAKARROT WENT AND STOLE THE ENTIRE SHOW AGAIN...
SLMP
?
GRANOLAH'S POWER... IT HASN'T DROPPED AS MUCH AS IT SHOULD HAVE...
WHAT'S GOING ON?
WHAT THE...?
NOW IT'S COMING FROM OVER THERE?

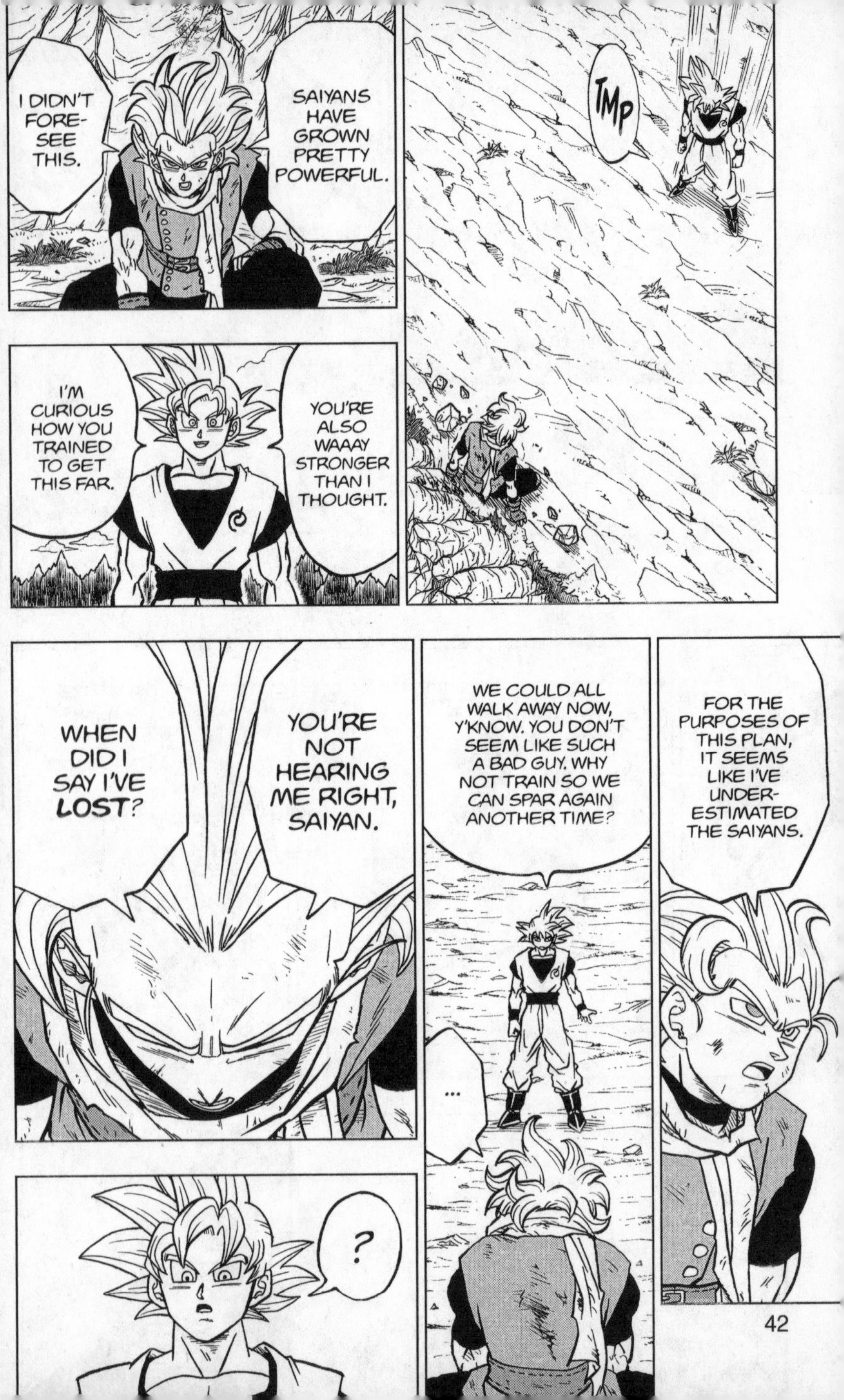
TMP
SAIYANS HAVE GROWN PRETTY POWERFUL.
I DIDN'T FORE-SEE THIS.
YOU'RE ALSO WAAAY STRONGER THAN I THOUGHT.
I'M CURIOUS HOW YOU TRAINED TO GET THIS FAR.
FOR THE PURPOSES OF THIS PLAN, IT SEEMS LIKE I'VE UNDER-ESTIMATED THE SAIYANS.
WE COULD ALL WALK AWAY NOW, Y'KNOW. YOU DON'T SEEM LIKE SUCH A BAD GUY. WHY NOT TRAIN SO WE CAN SPAR AGAIN ANOTHER TIME?
...
YOU'RE NOT HEARING ME RIGHT, SAIYAN.
WHEN DID I SAY I'VE **LOST**?
?

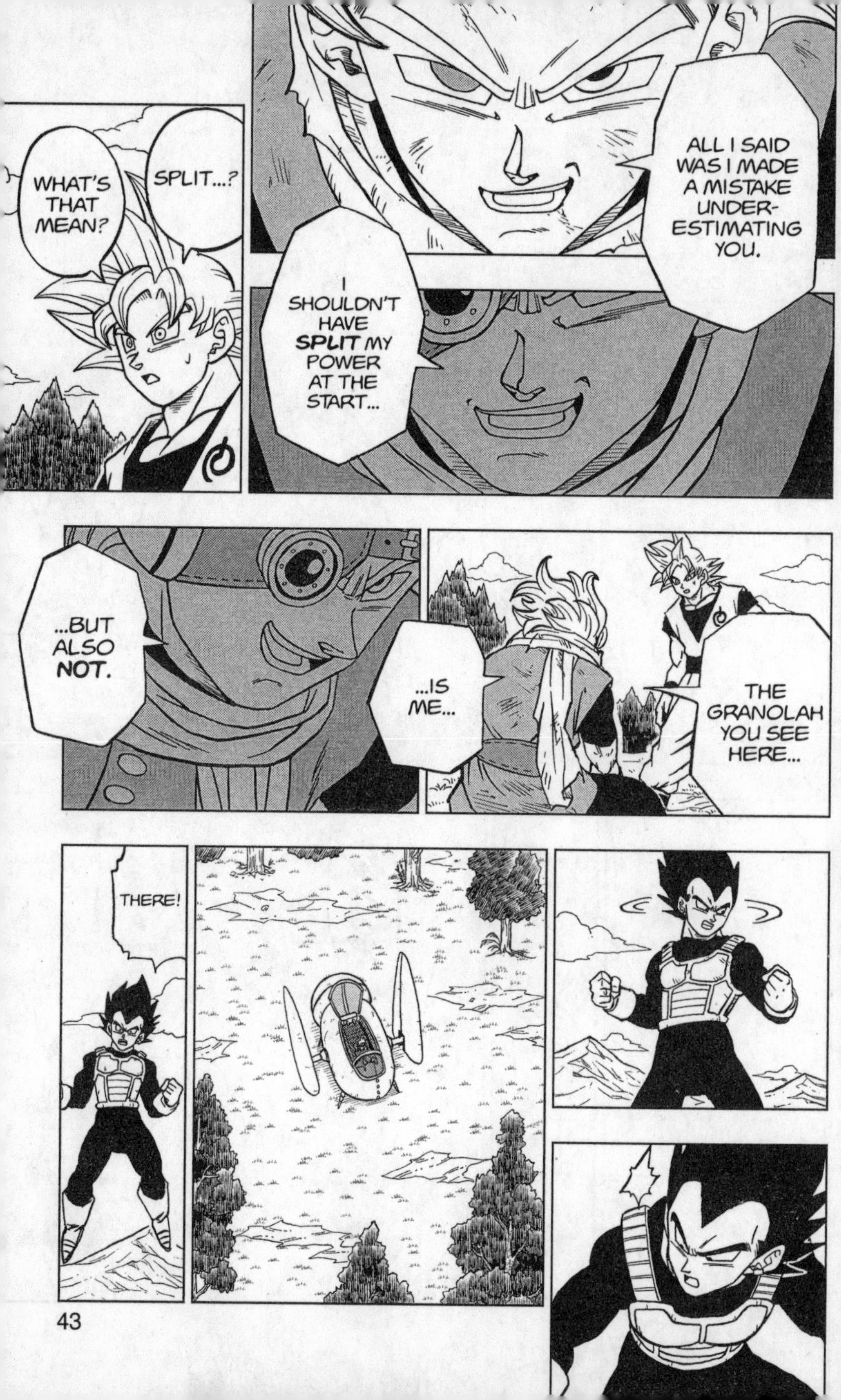
ALL I SAID WAS I MADE A MISTAKE UNDER-ESTIMATING YOU.
I SHOULDN'T HAVE SPLIT MY POWER AT THE START...
SPLIT...?
WHAT'S THAT MEAN?
THE GRANOLAH YOU SEE HERE...
...IS ME...
...BUT ALSO NOT.
THERE!

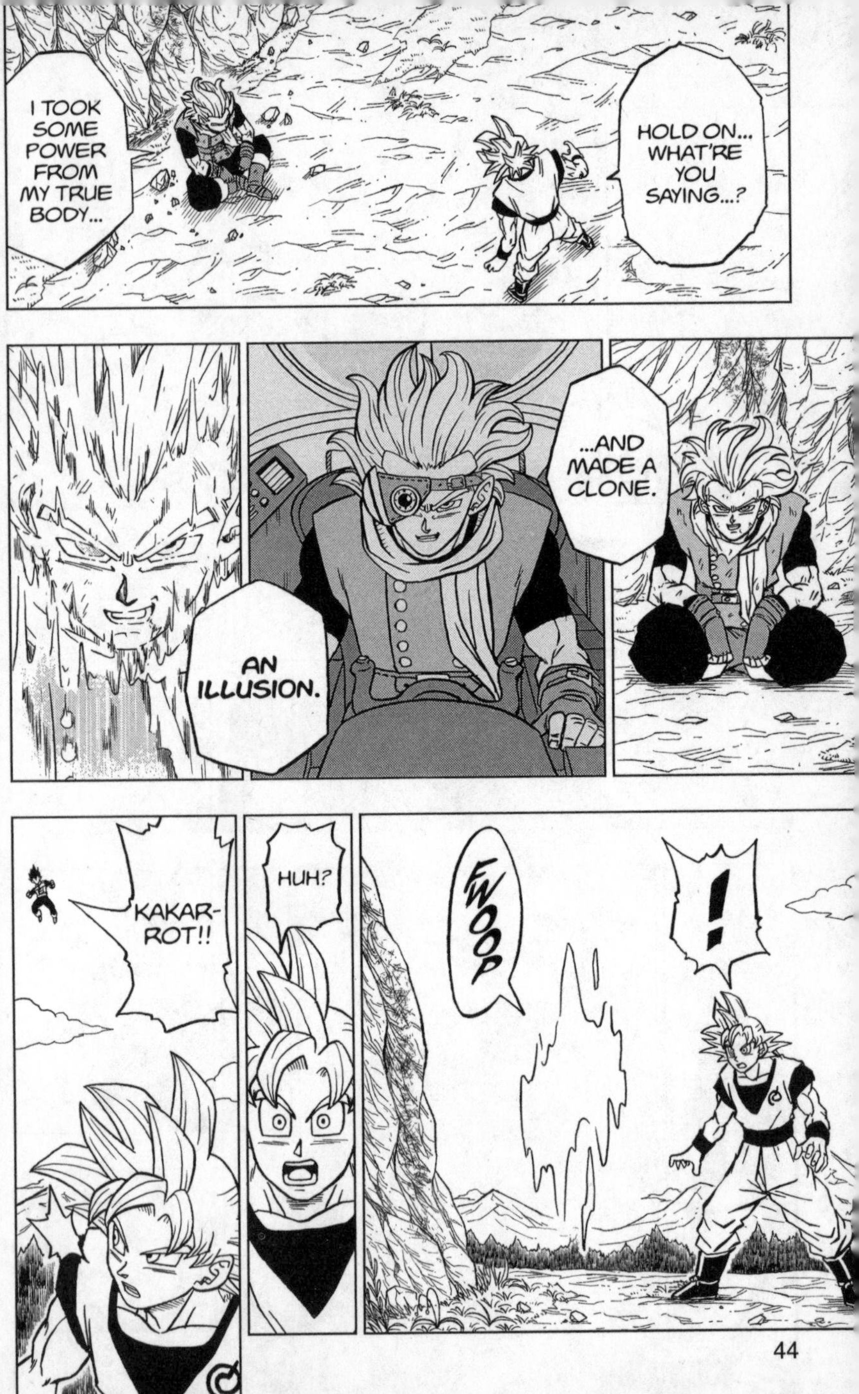
I TOOK SOME POWER FROM MY TRUE BODY...
HOLD ON... WHAT'RE YOU SAYING...?
...AND MADE A CLONE.
AN ILLUSION.
!
FWOOP
HUH?
KAKAR-ROT!!

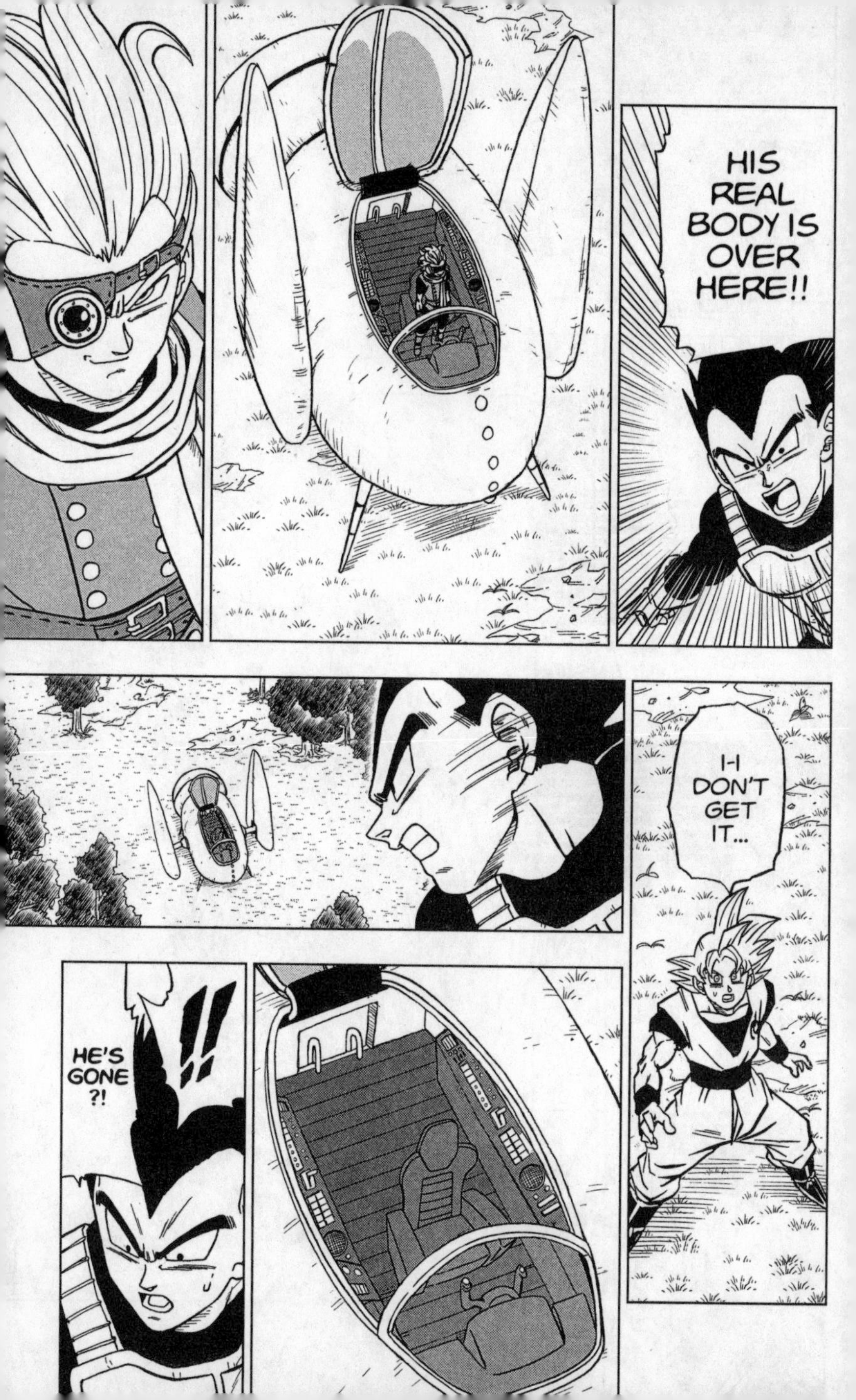
HIS REAL BODY IS OVER HERE!!
I-I DON'T GET IT...
HE'S GONE?!

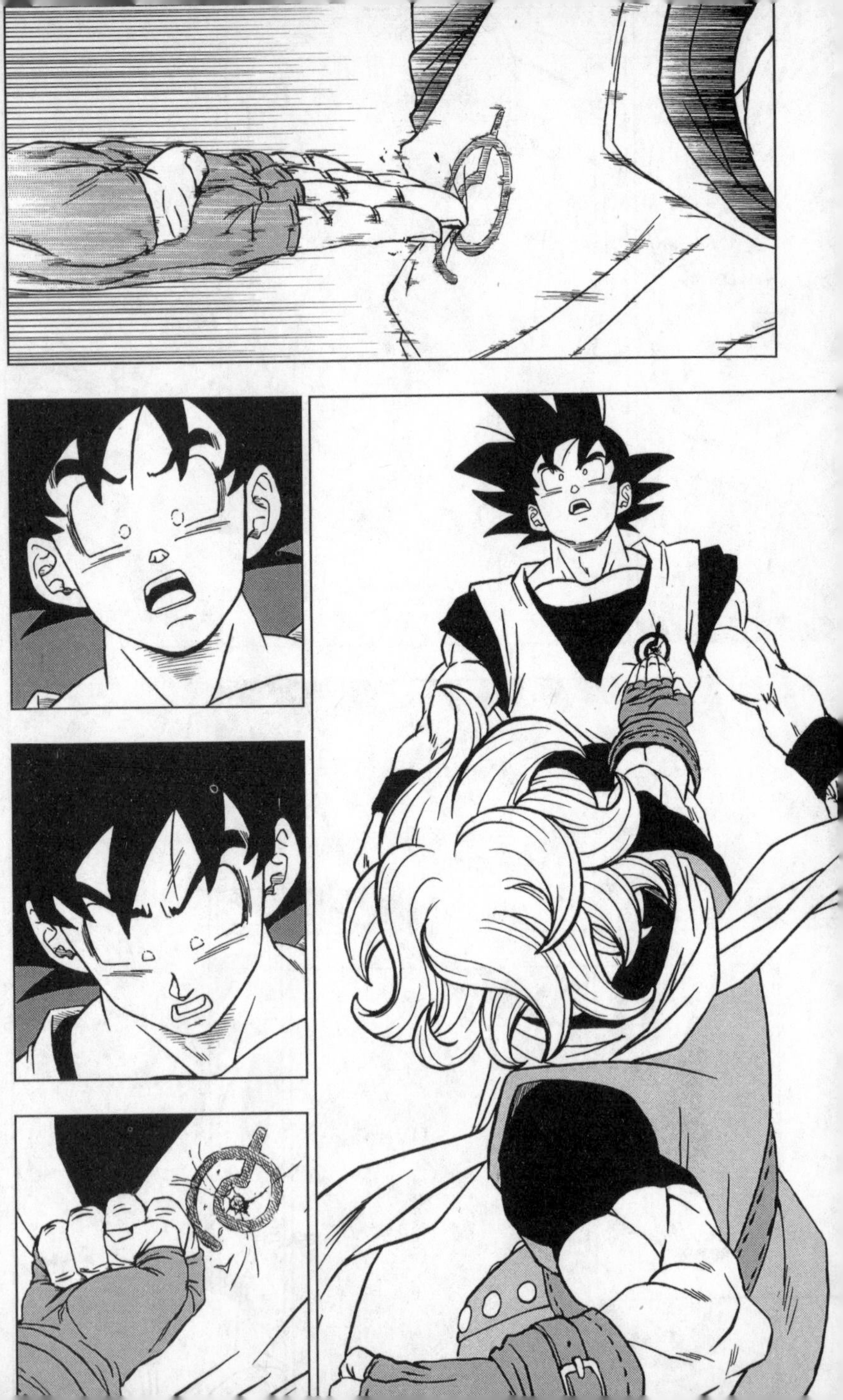

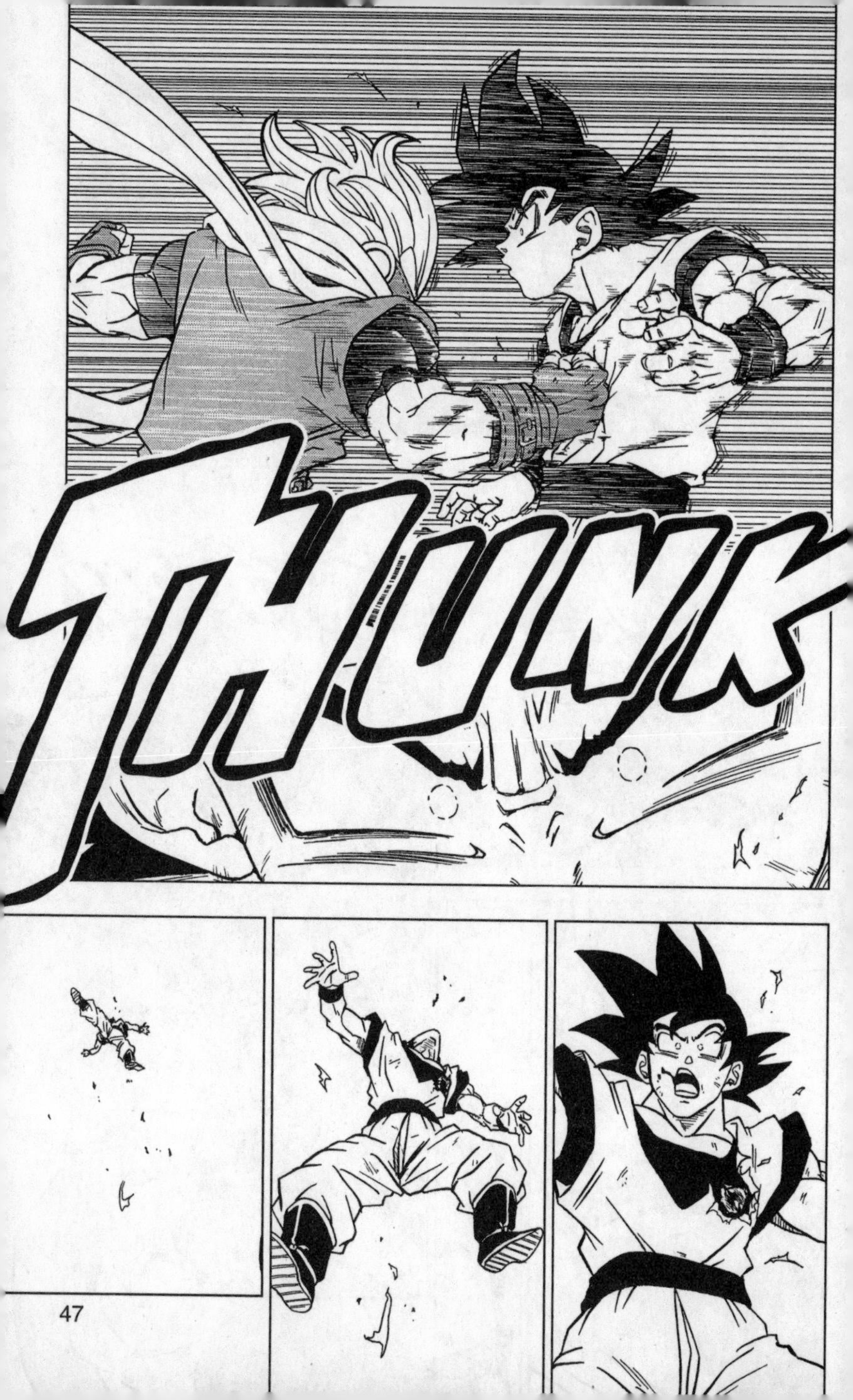
THUNK

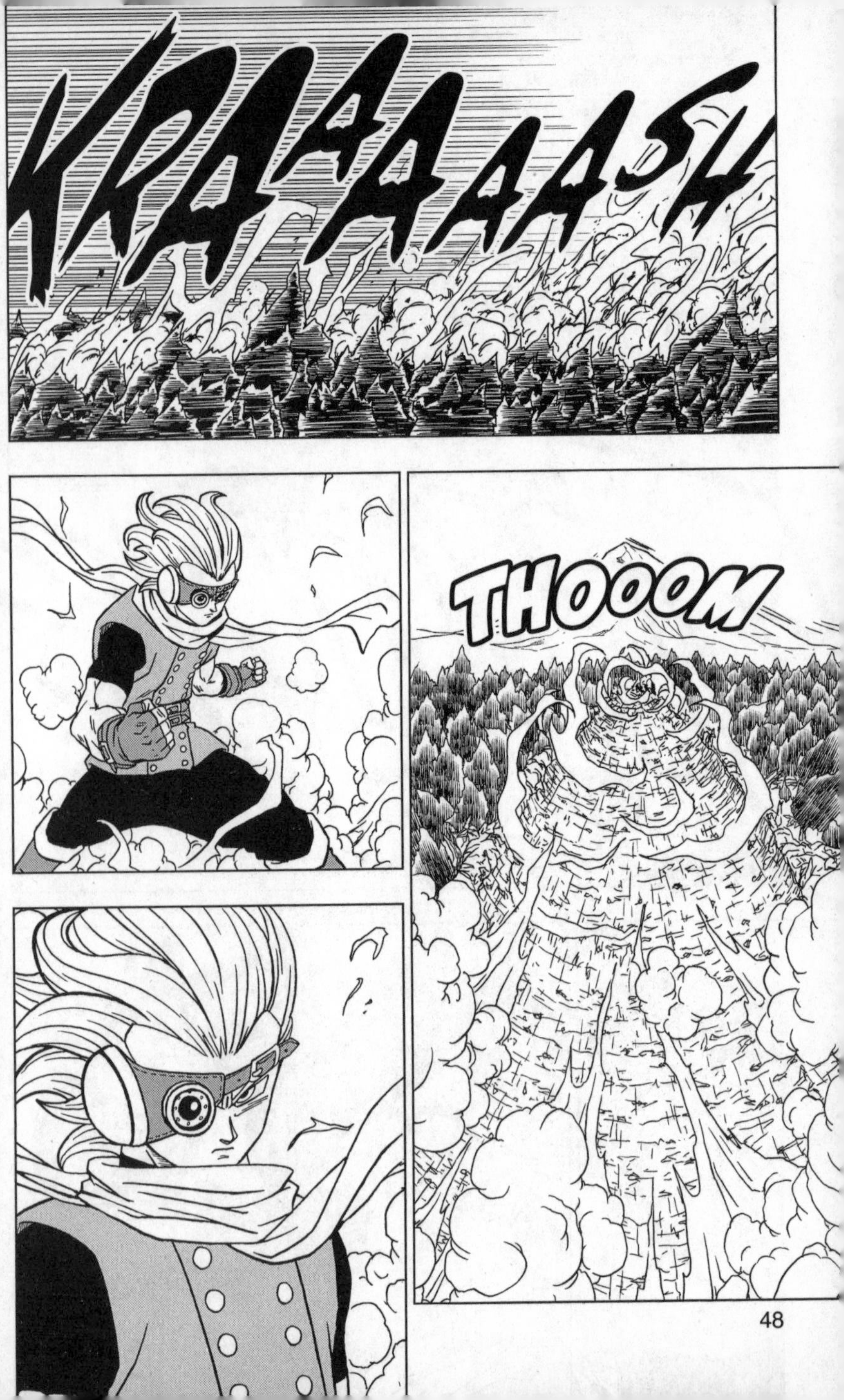
KRAAAASH
THOOOM

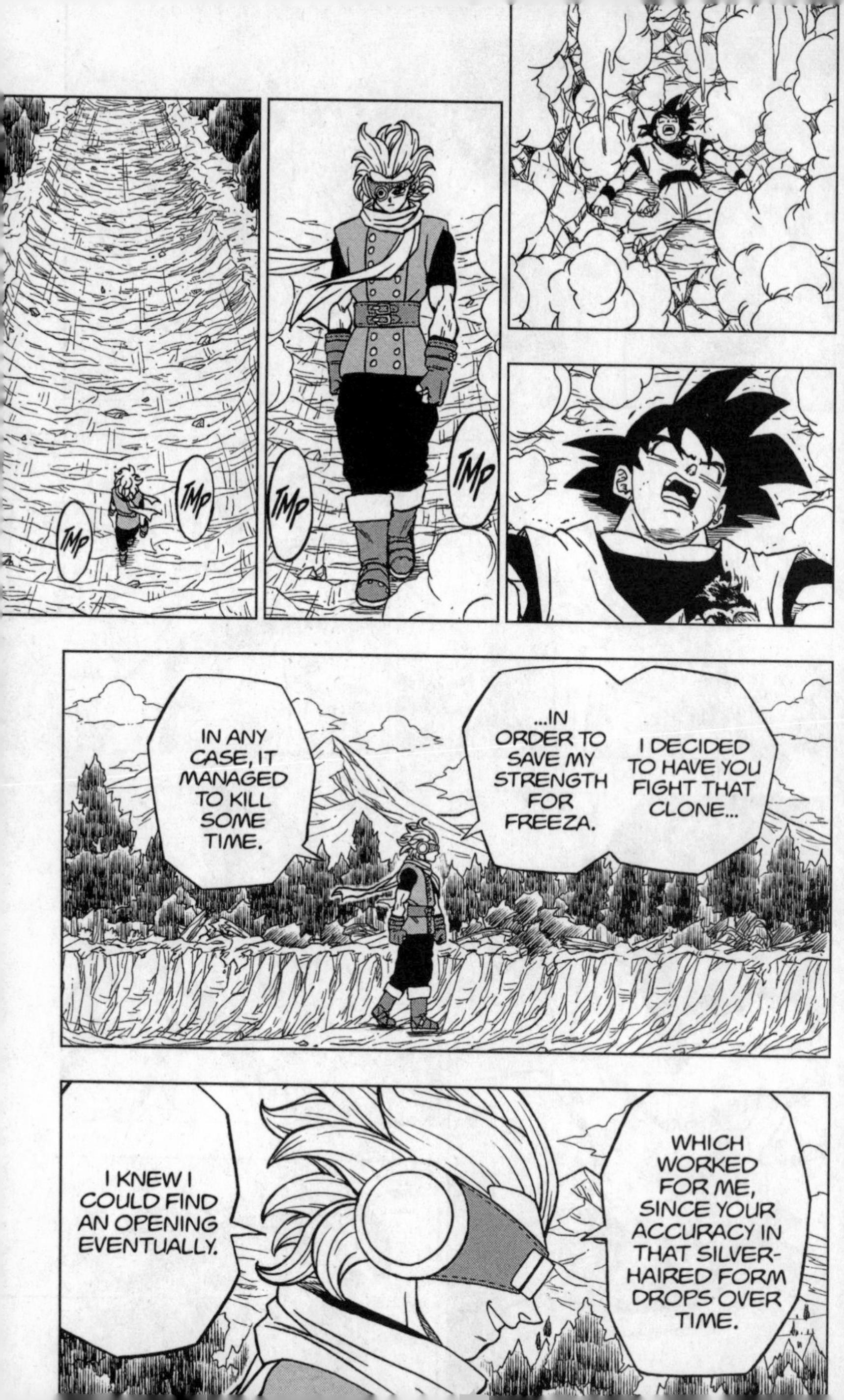
TMP
TMP
TMP
TMP
...IN ORDER TO SAVE MY STRENGTH FOR FREEZA.
I DECIDED TO HAVE YOU FIGHT THAT CLONE...
IN ANY CASE, IT MANAGED TO KILL SOME TIME.
WHICH WORKED FOR ME, SINCE YOUR ACCURACY IN THAT SILVER-HAIRED FORM DROPS OVER TIME.
I KNEW I COULD FIND AN OPENING EVENTUALLY.

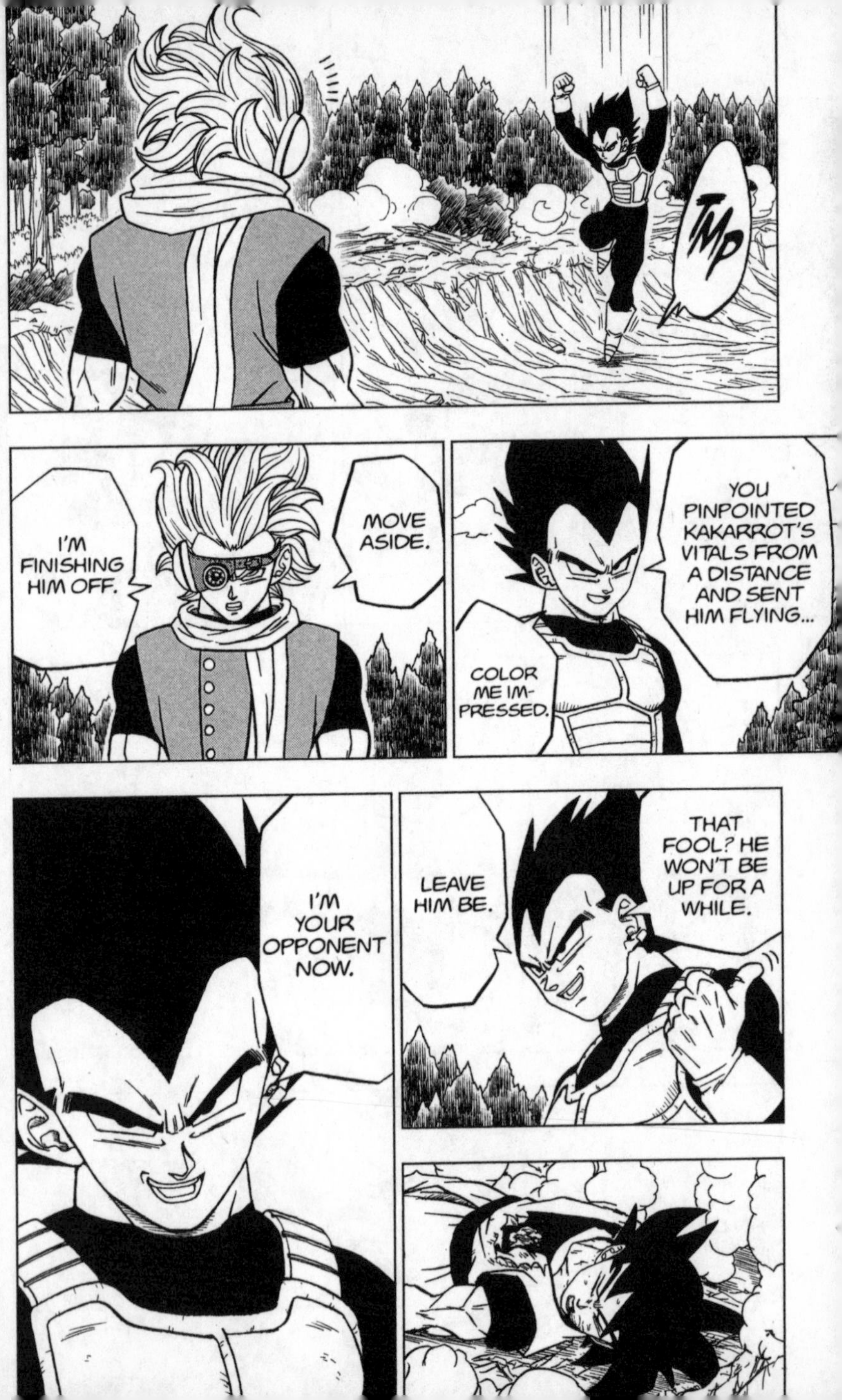
TMP
YOU PINPOINTED KAKARROT'S VITALS FROM A DISTANCE AND SENT HIM FLYING...
COLOR ME IMPRESSED.
MOVE ASIDE.
I'M FINISHING HIM OFF.
THAT FOOL? HE WON'T BE UP FOR A WHILE.
LEAVE HIM BE.
I'M YOUR OPPONENT NOW.

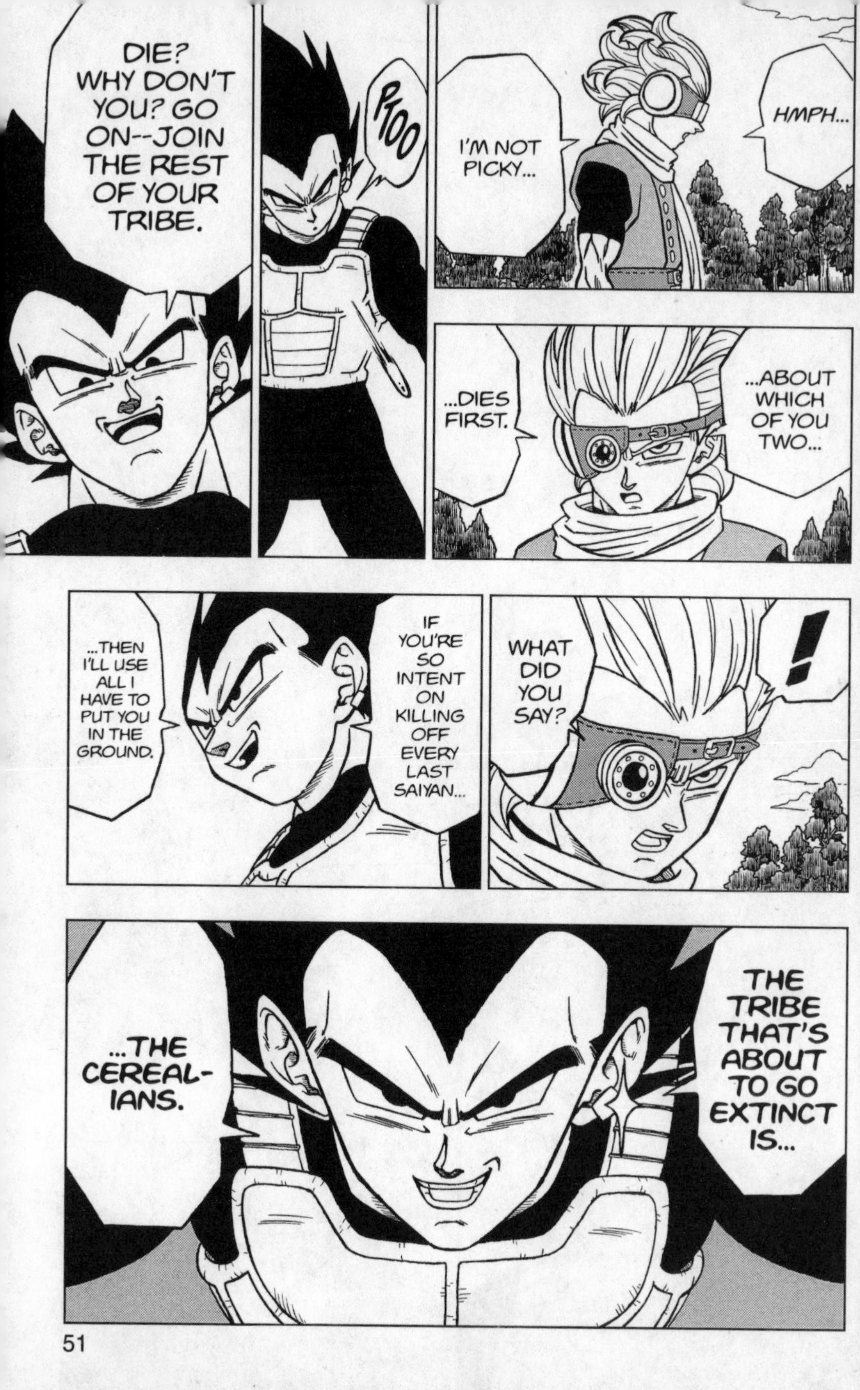
HMPH...
I'M NOT PICKY...
...ABOUT WHICH OF YOU TWO...
...DIES FIRST.
PIOO
DIE? WHY DON'T YOU? GO ON--JOIN THE REST OF YOUR TRIBE.
!
WHAT DID YOU SAY?
IF YOU'RE SO INTENT ON KILLING OFF EVERY LAST SAIYAN...
...THEN I'LL USE ALL I HAVE TO PUT YOU IN THE GROUND.
THE TRIBE THAT'S ABOUT TO GO EXTINCT IS...
...THE CEREAL-IANS.

DRAGON BALL SUPER

CHAPTER 74: VEGETA VS. GRANOLAH

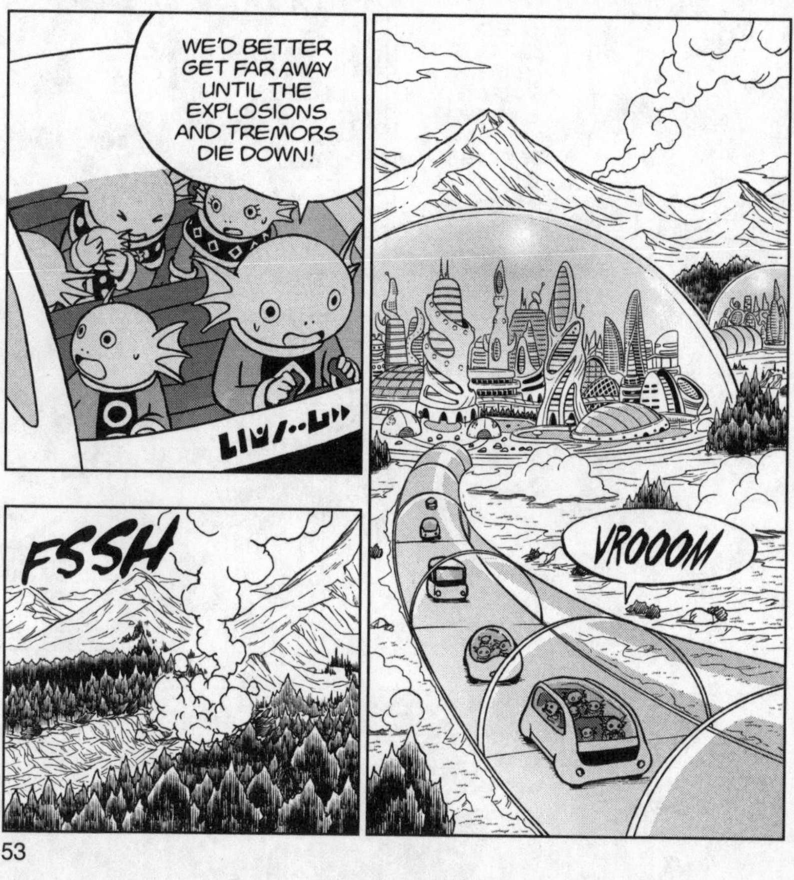

VROOOM
WE'D BETTER GET FAR AWAY UNTIL THE EXPLOSIONS AND TREMORS DIE DOWN!
FSSH

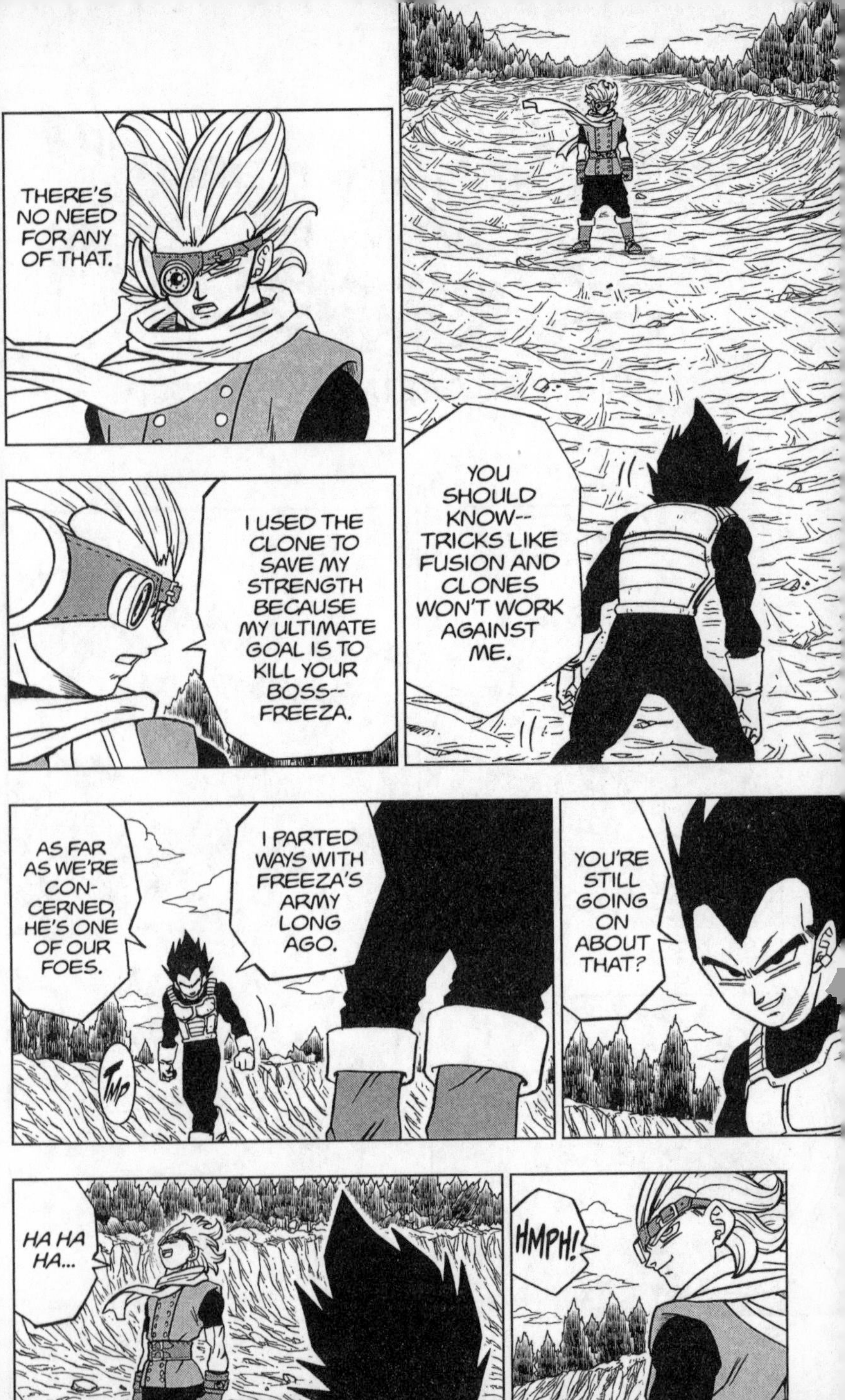
YOU SHOULD KNOW-- TRICKS LIKE FUSION AND CLONES WON'T WORK AGAINST ME.
THERE'S NO NEED FOR ANY OF THAT.
I USED THE CLONE TO SAVE MY STRENGTH BECAUSE MY ULTIMATE GOAL IS TO KILL YOUR BOSS-- FREEZA.
YOU'RE STILL GOING ON ABOUT THAT?
I PARTED WAYS WITH FREEZA'S ARMY LONG AGO.
AS FAR AS WE'RE CON-CERNED, HE'S ONE OF OUR FOES.
TMP
HMPH!
HA HA HA...

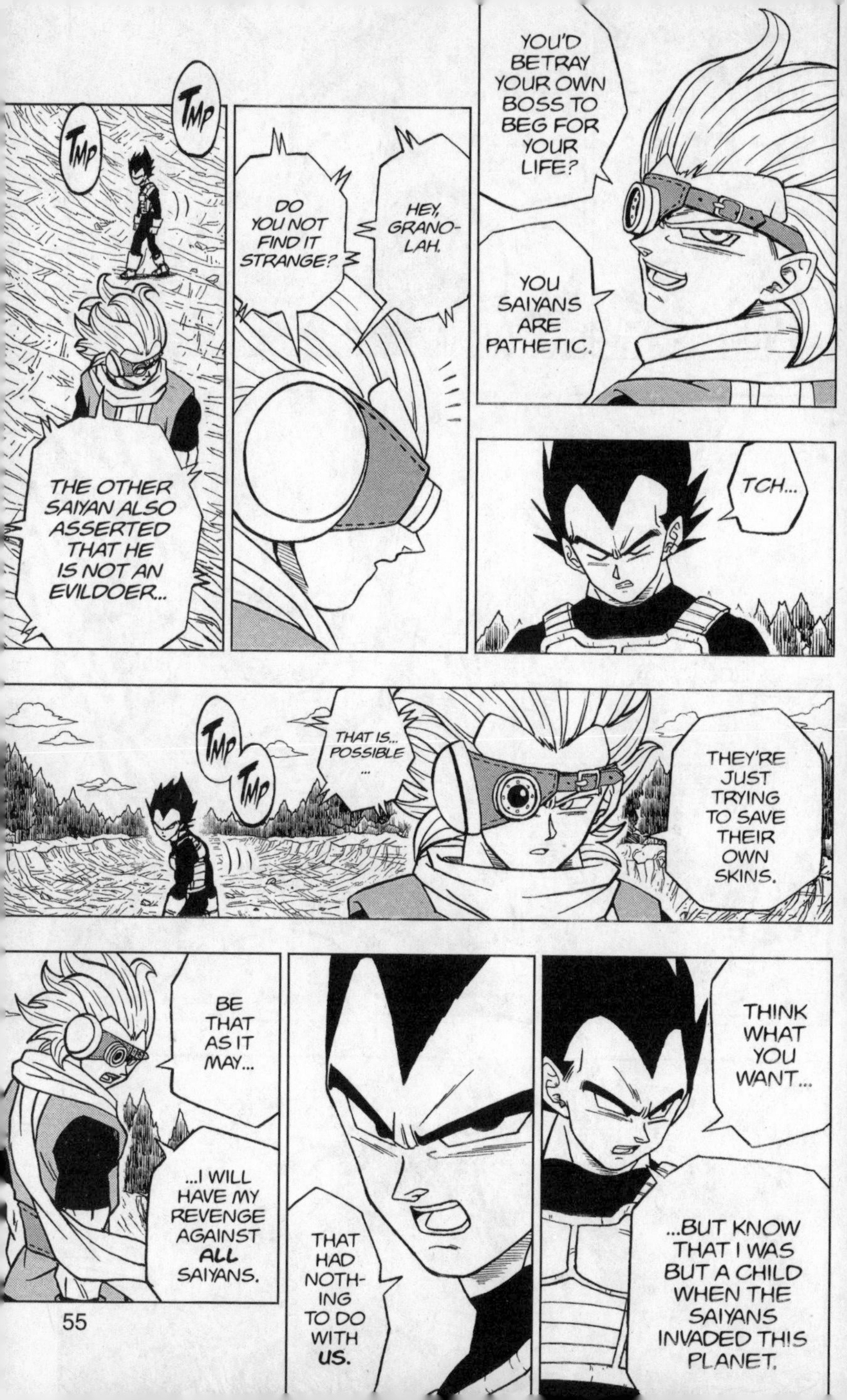
YOU'D BETRAY YOUR OWN BOSS TO BEG FOR YOUR LIFE?
YOU SAIYANS ARE PATHETIC.
TCH...
HEY, GRANOLAH.
DO YOU NOT FIND IT STRANGE?
TMP
TMP
THE OTHER SAIYAN ALSO ASSERTED THAT HE IS NOT AN EVILDOER...
THEY'RE JUST TRYING TO SAVE THEIR OWN SKINS.
THAT IS... POSSIBLE ...
TMP
TMP
THINK WHAT YOU WANT...
...BUT KNOW THAT I WAS BUT A CHILD WHEN THE SAIYANS INVADED THIS PLANET.
THAT HAD NOTHING TO DO WITH **US**.
BE THAT AS IT MAY...
...I WILL HAVE MY REVENGE AGAINST **ALL** SAIYANS.

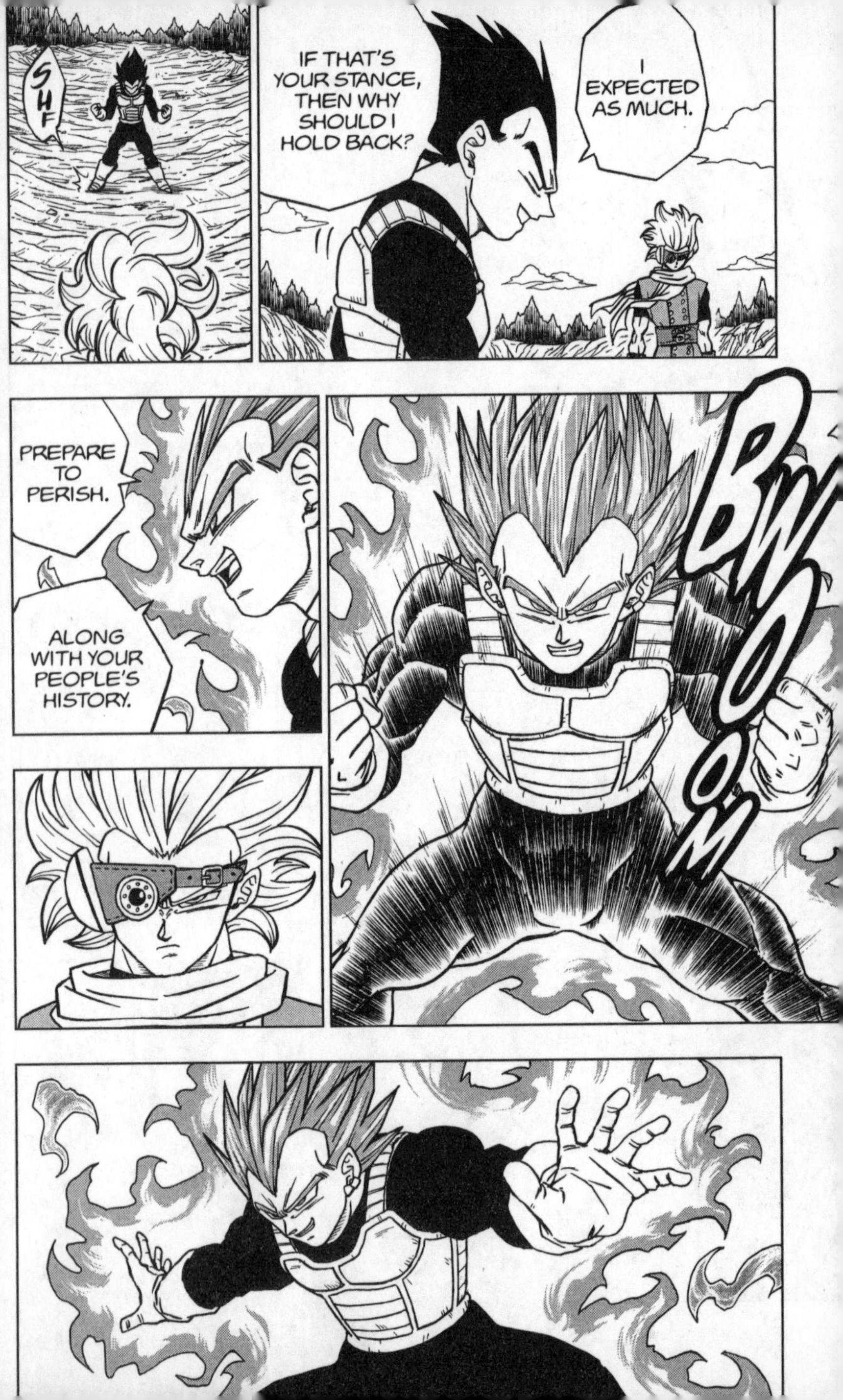
I EXPECTED AS MUCH.
IF THAT'S YOUR STANCE, THEN WHY SHOULD I HOLD BACK?
SHF
BWOOOM
PREPARE TO PERISH.
ALONG WITH YOUR PEOPLE'S HISTORY.

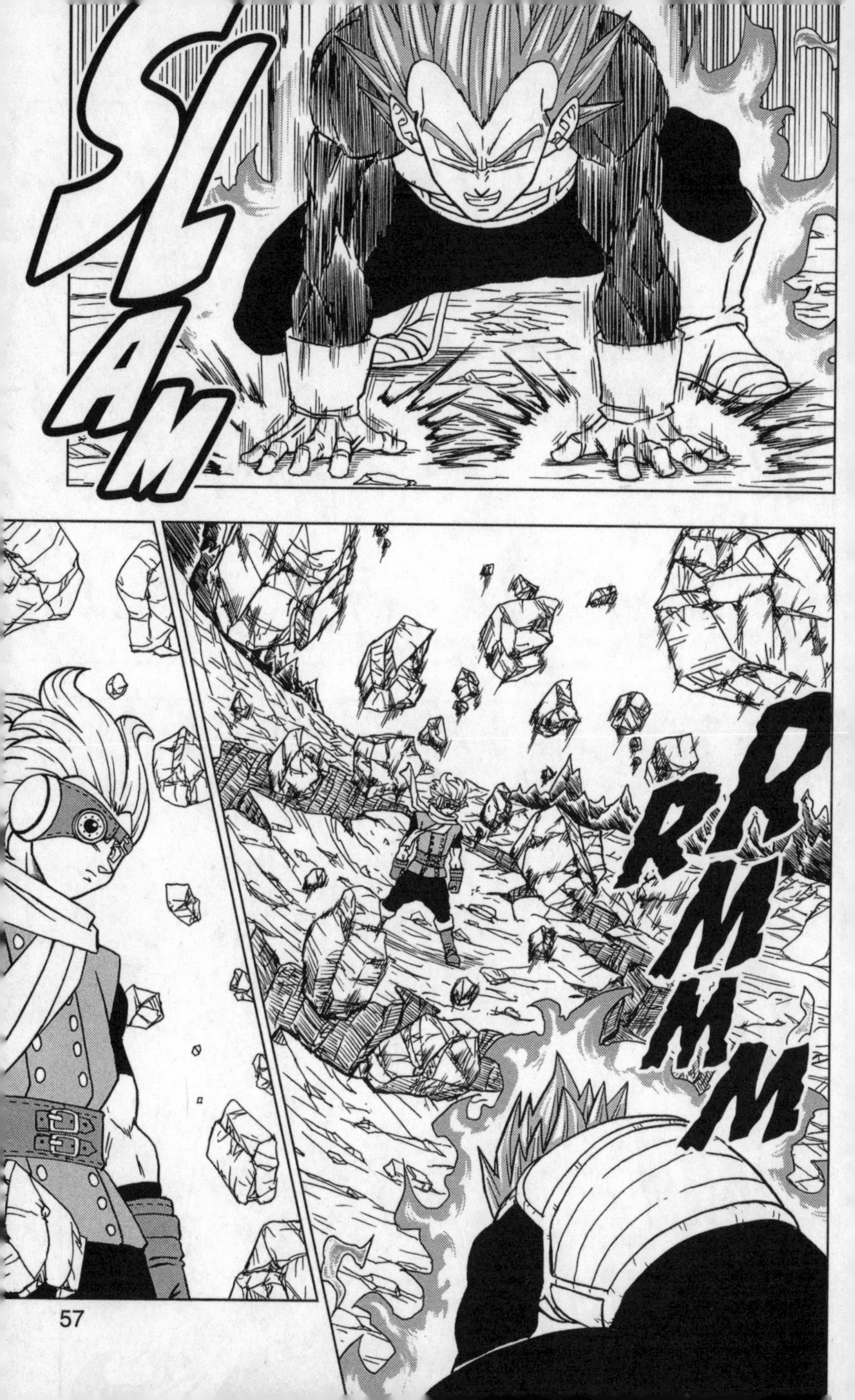
SLAM
RRMMM

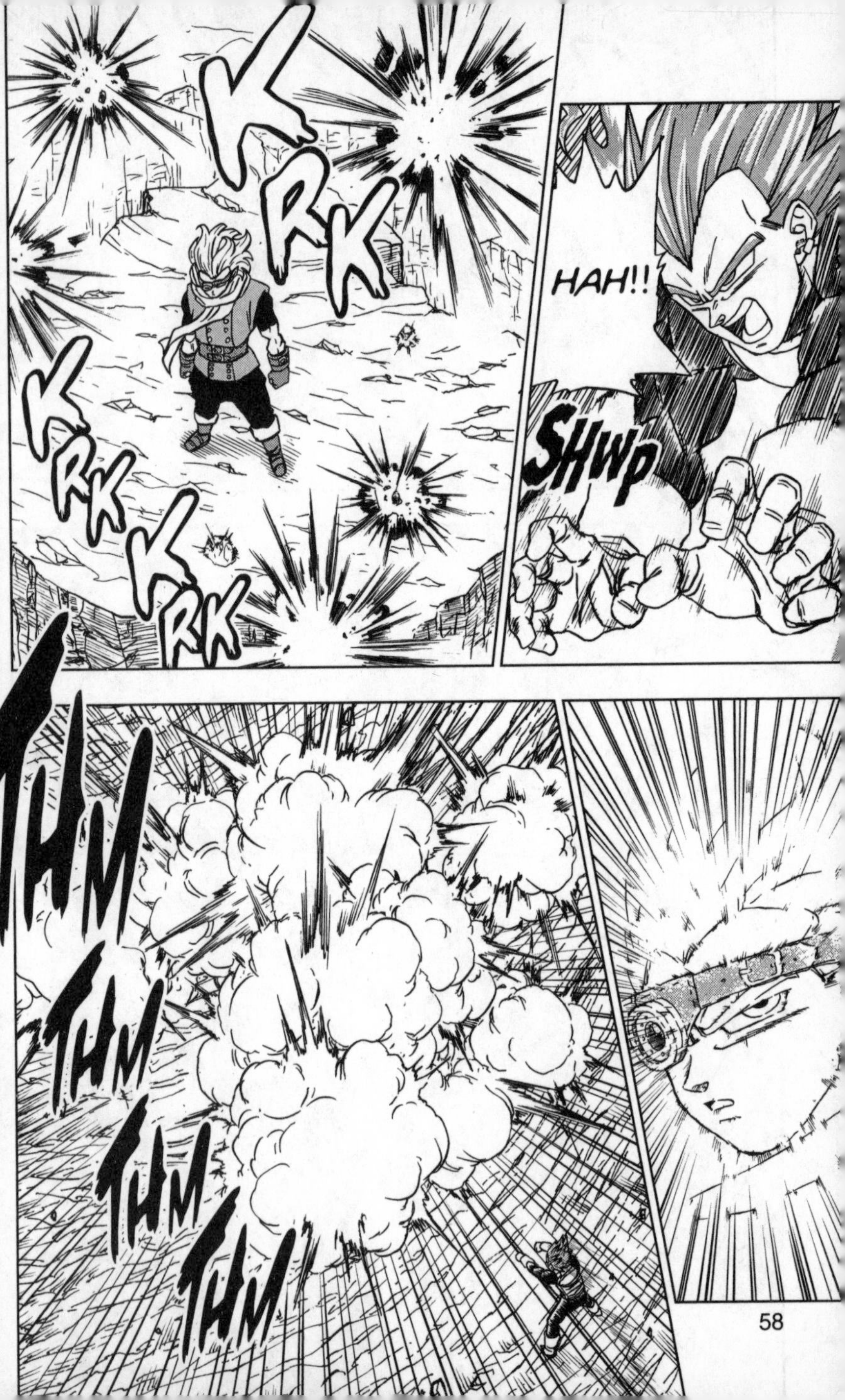
HAH!!
SHWP
KRK
KRK
KRK
THM
THM
THM
THM

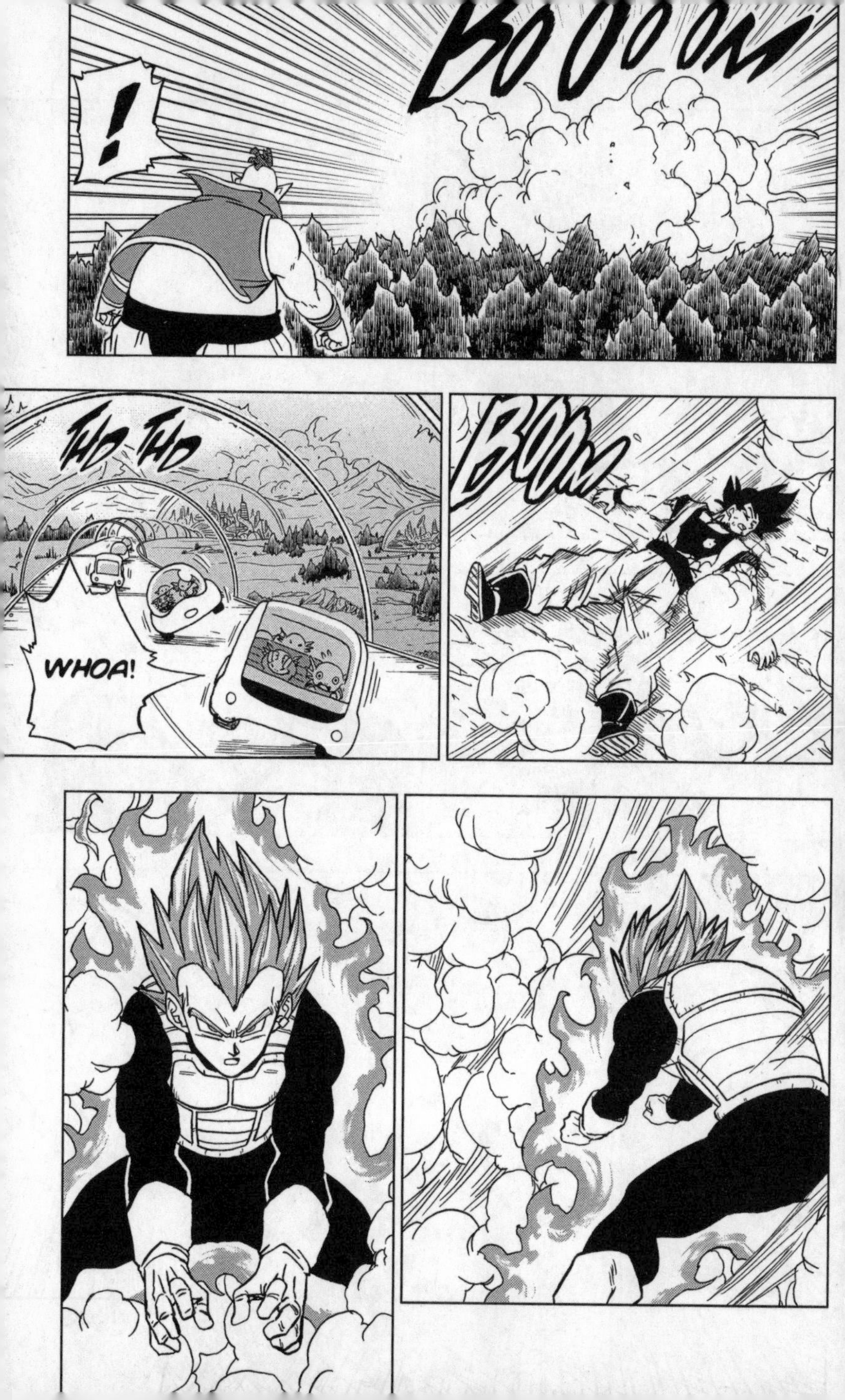
BOOOOM
!
BOOM
THD THD
WHOA!

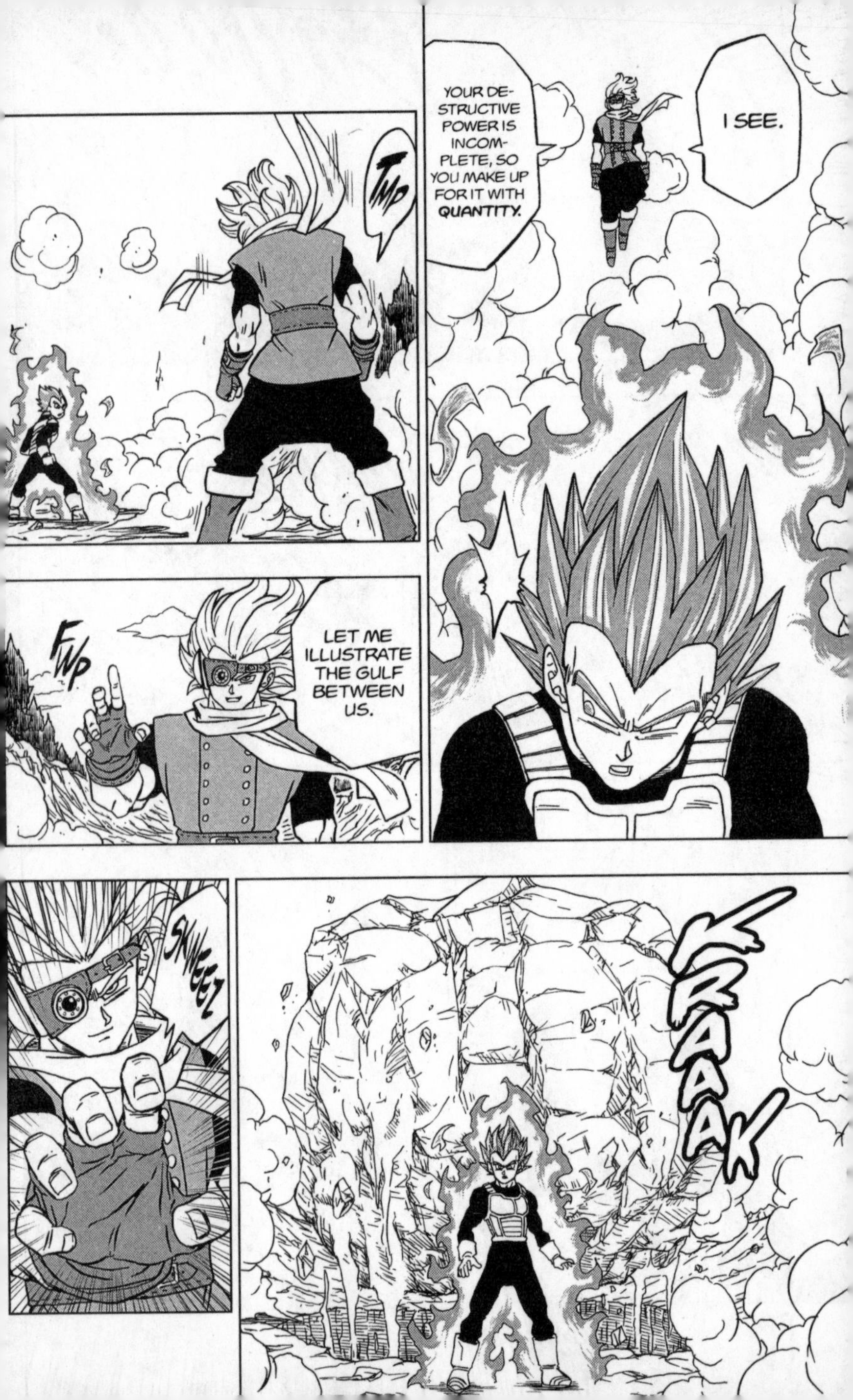

I SEE.
YOUR DE-STRUCTIVE POWER IS INCOMPLETE, SO YOU MAKE UP FOR IT WITH **QUANTITY.**
TMP
FWP
LET ME ILLUSTRATE THE GULF BETWEEN US.
KRAAAK
SKWEEZ

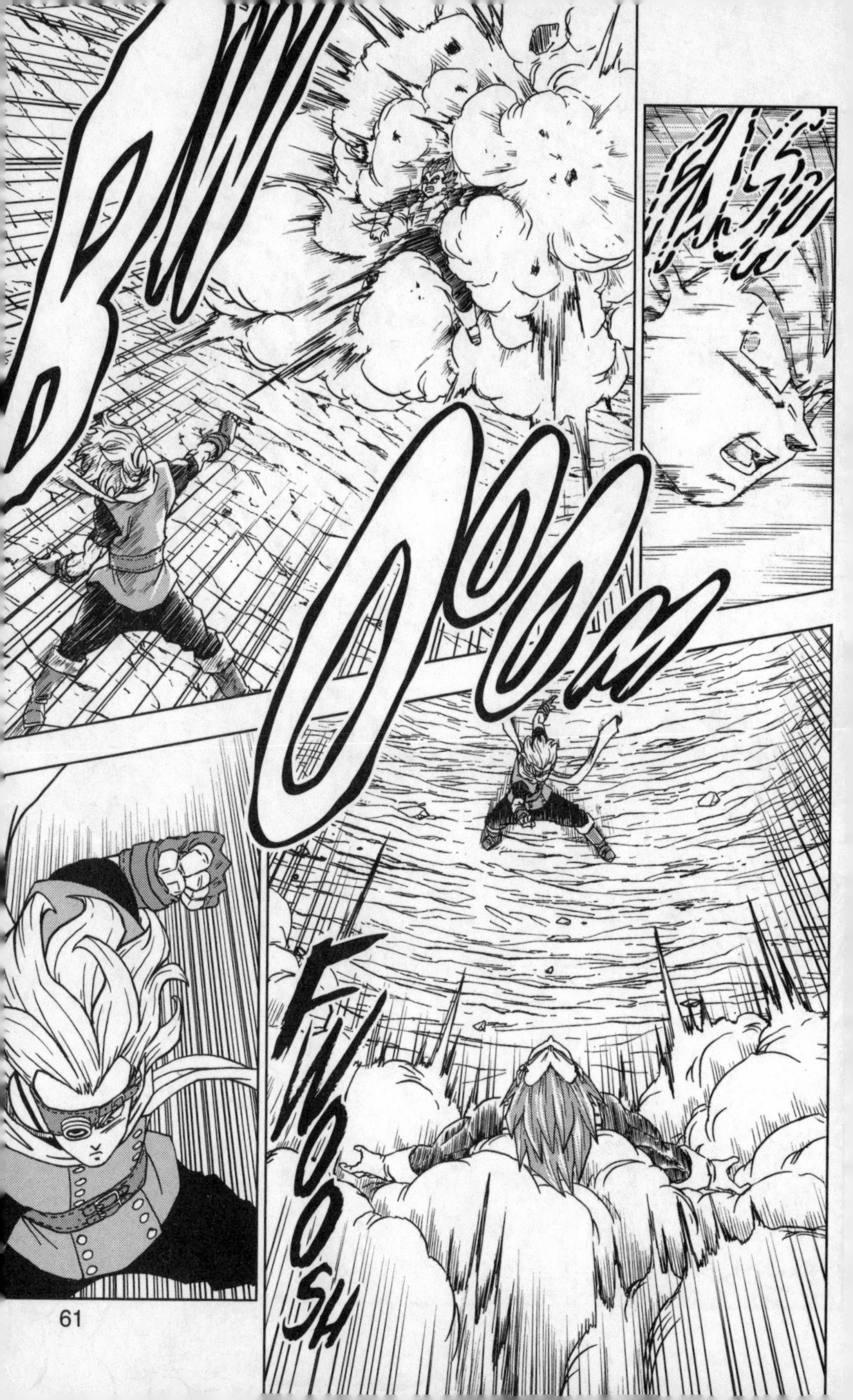
BOOM
FWOOSH

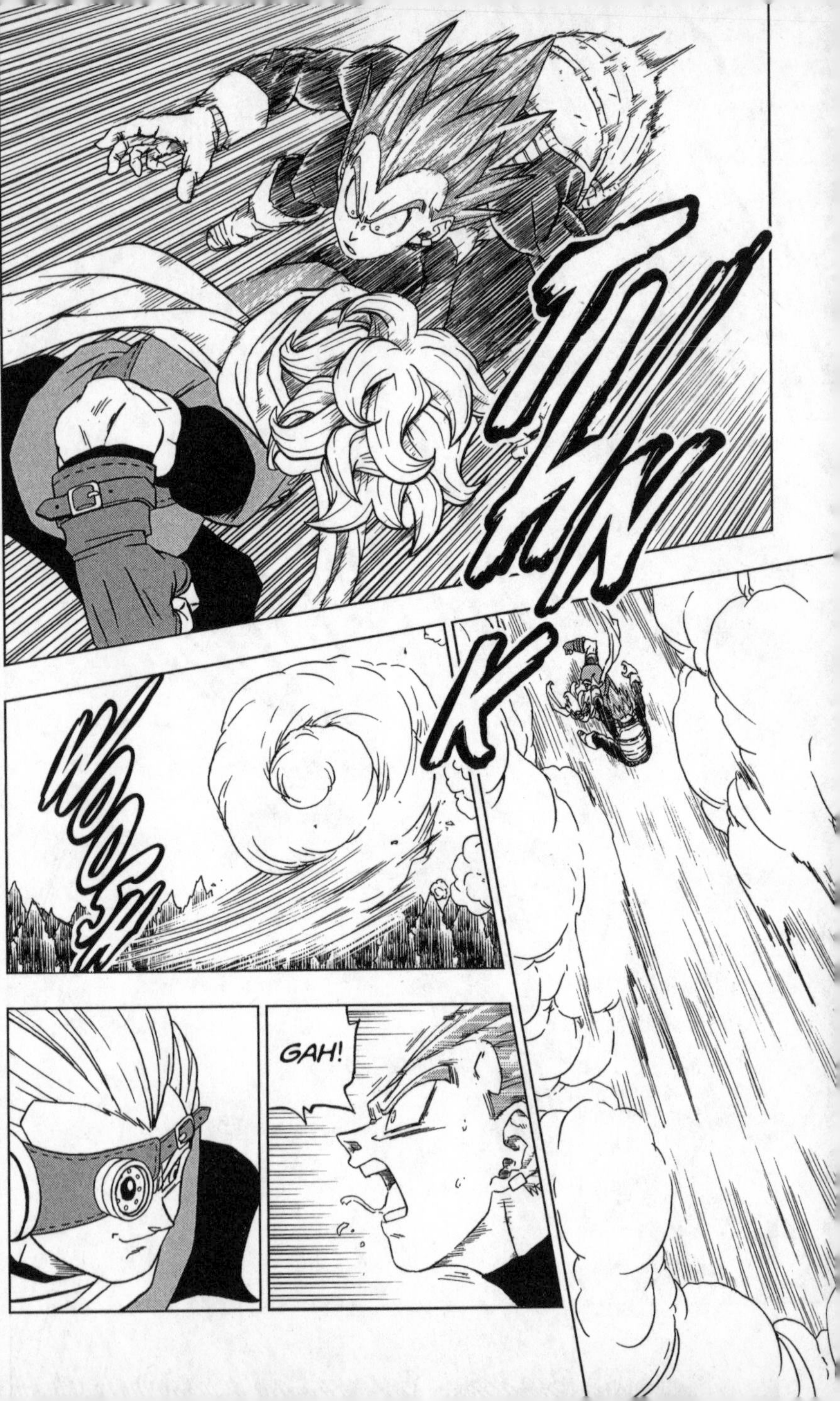
WHOOSH
GAH!

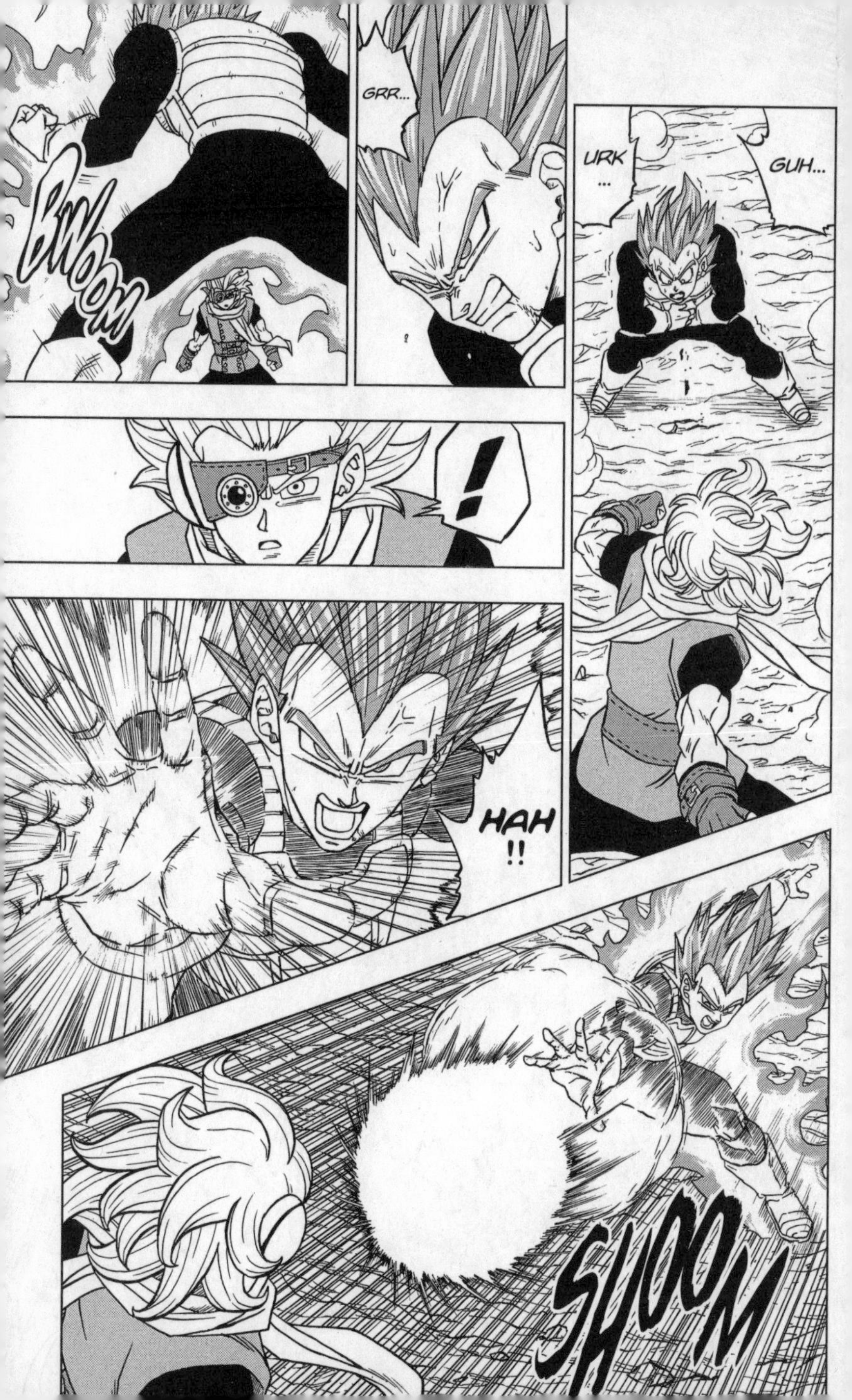
GUH...
URK...
GRR...
BWOOM
!
HAH!!
SHOOM

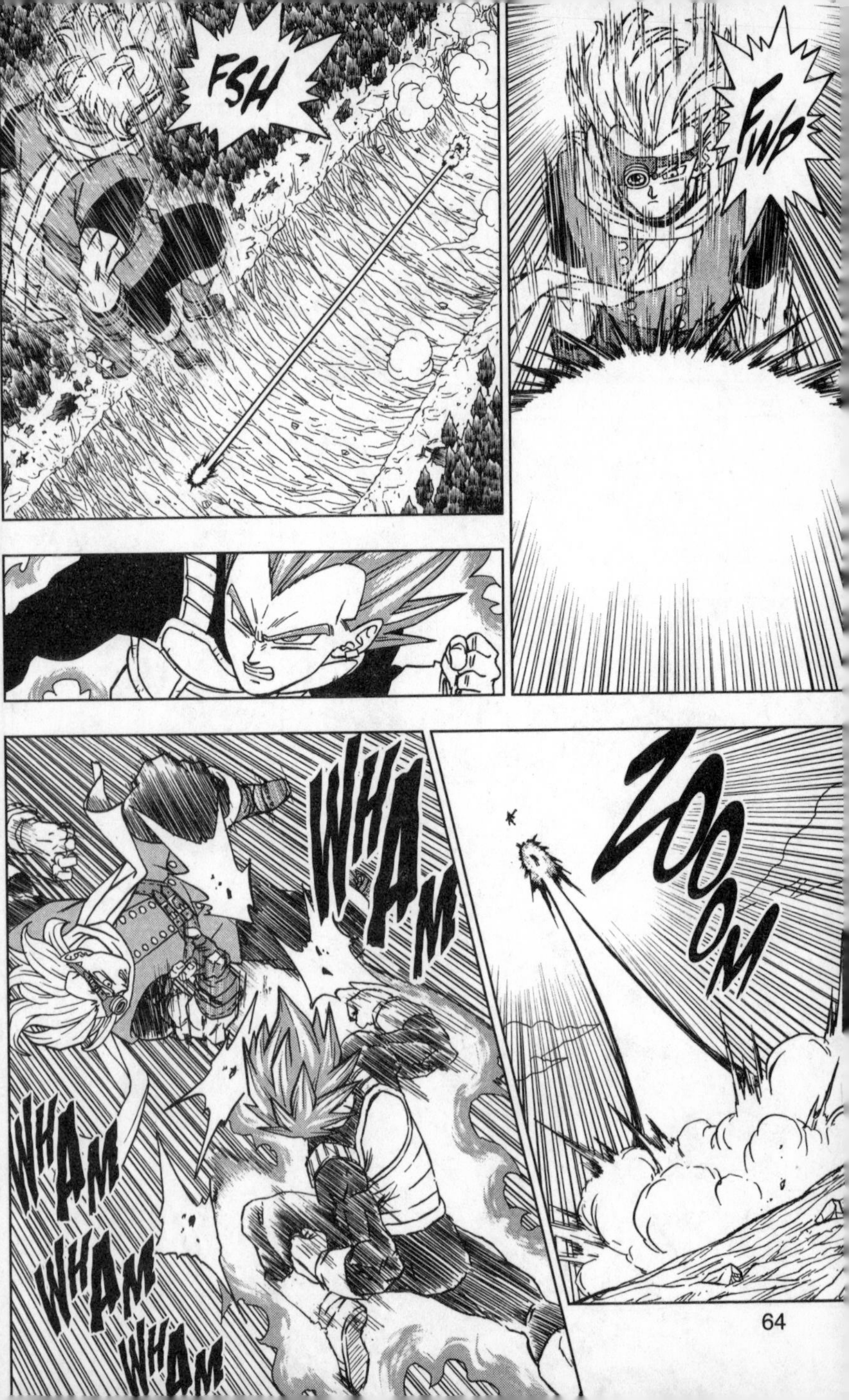
FWP
FSH
ZOOOM
WHAM
WHAM
WHAM
WHAM

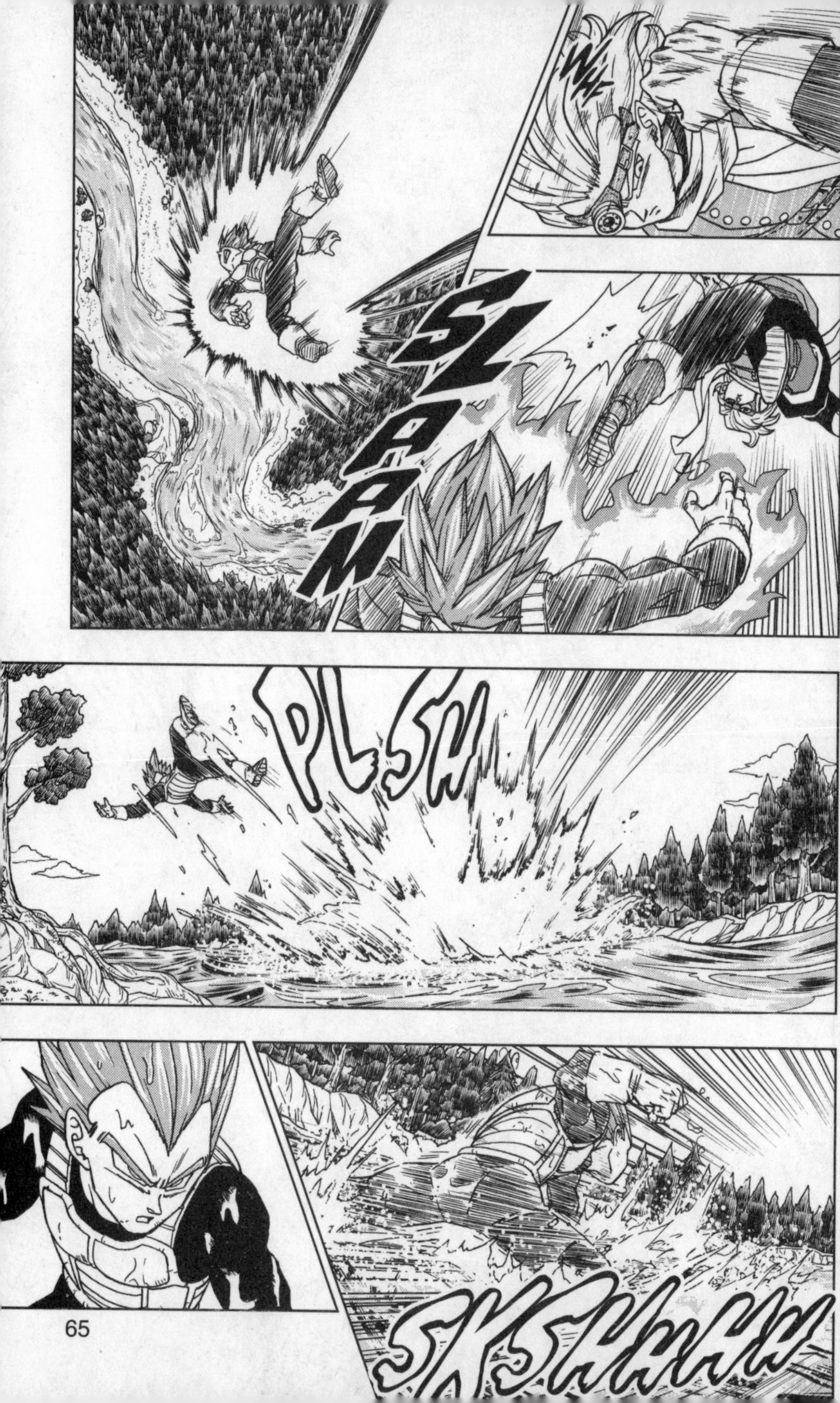
WHF
SLAAM
PLSH
SKSHHHH

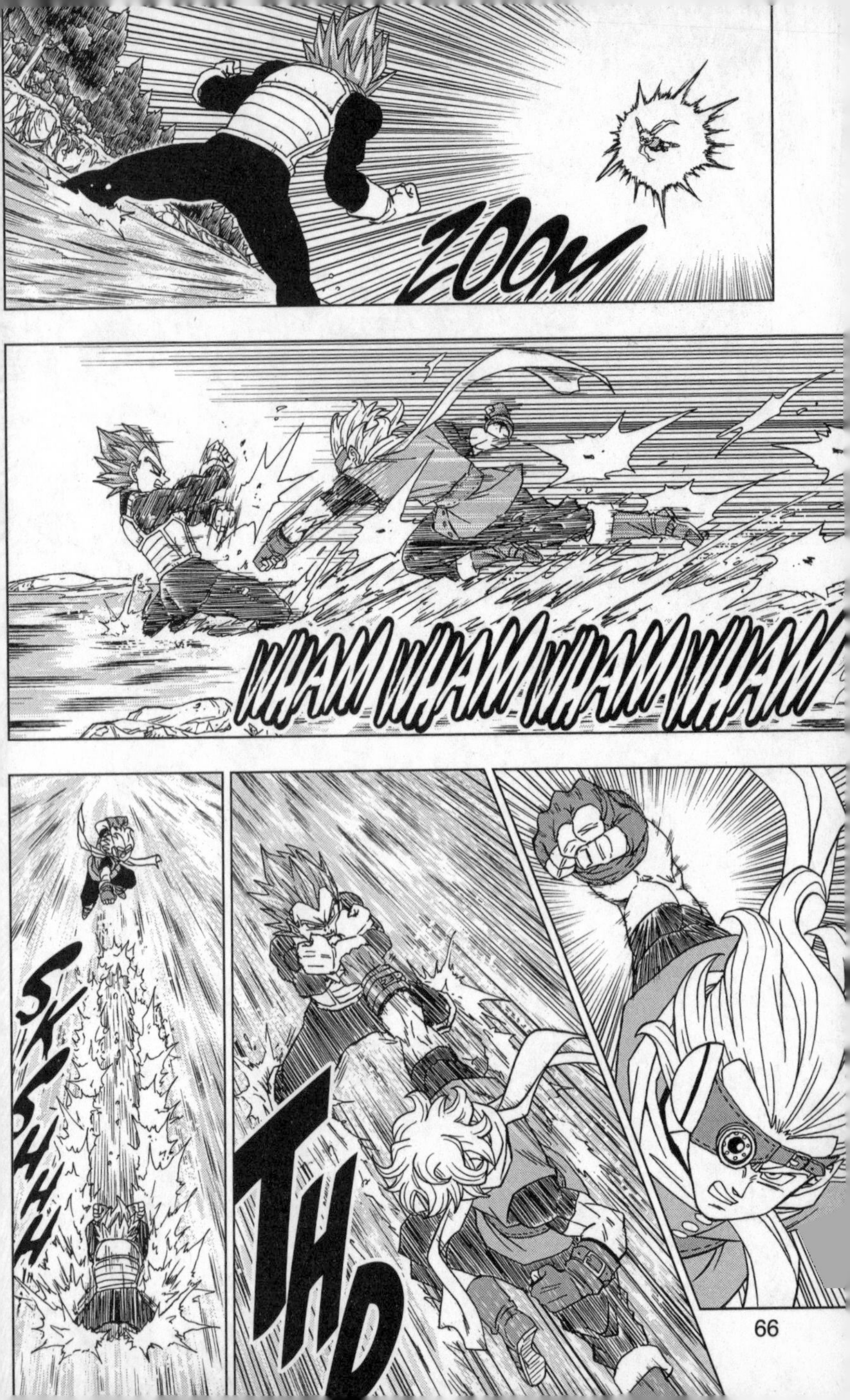
ZOOM
WHAM WHAM WHAM WHAM
THD
SHHHHHH

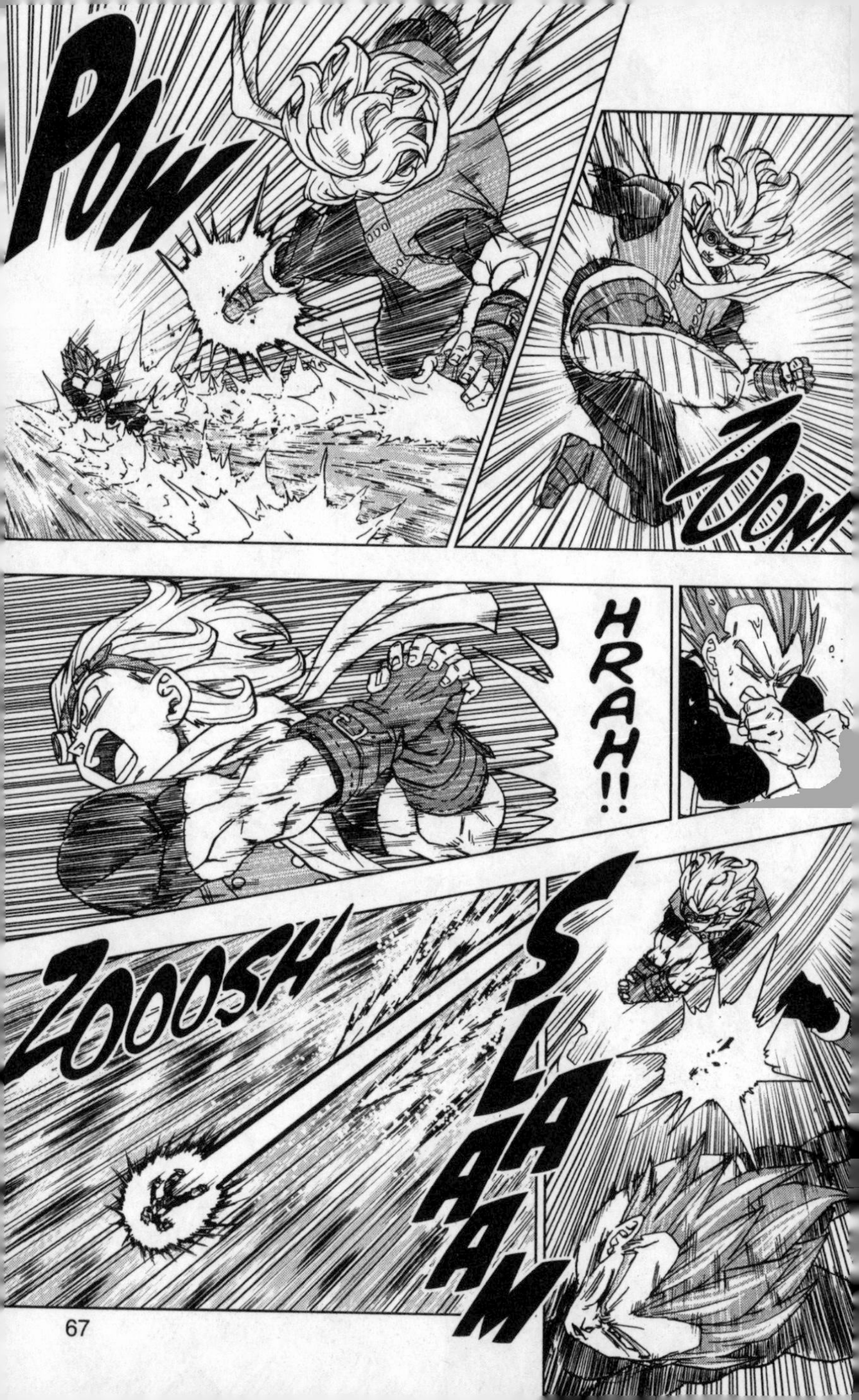
ZOOM
POW
HRAH!!
SLAAAM
ZOOOSH

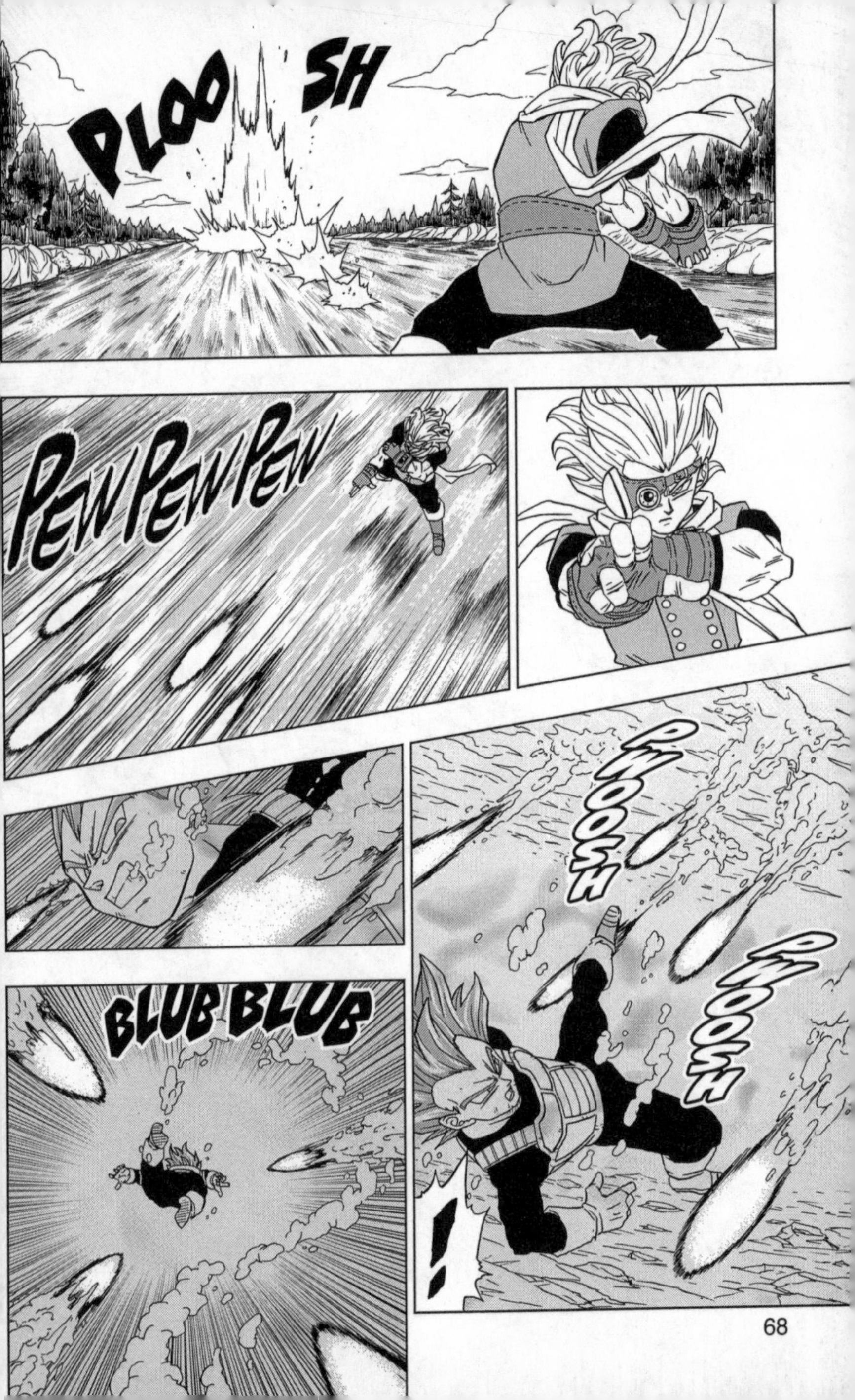
PLOO SH
PEW PEW PEW
PWOOOSH
PWOOOSH
!!
BLUB BLUB

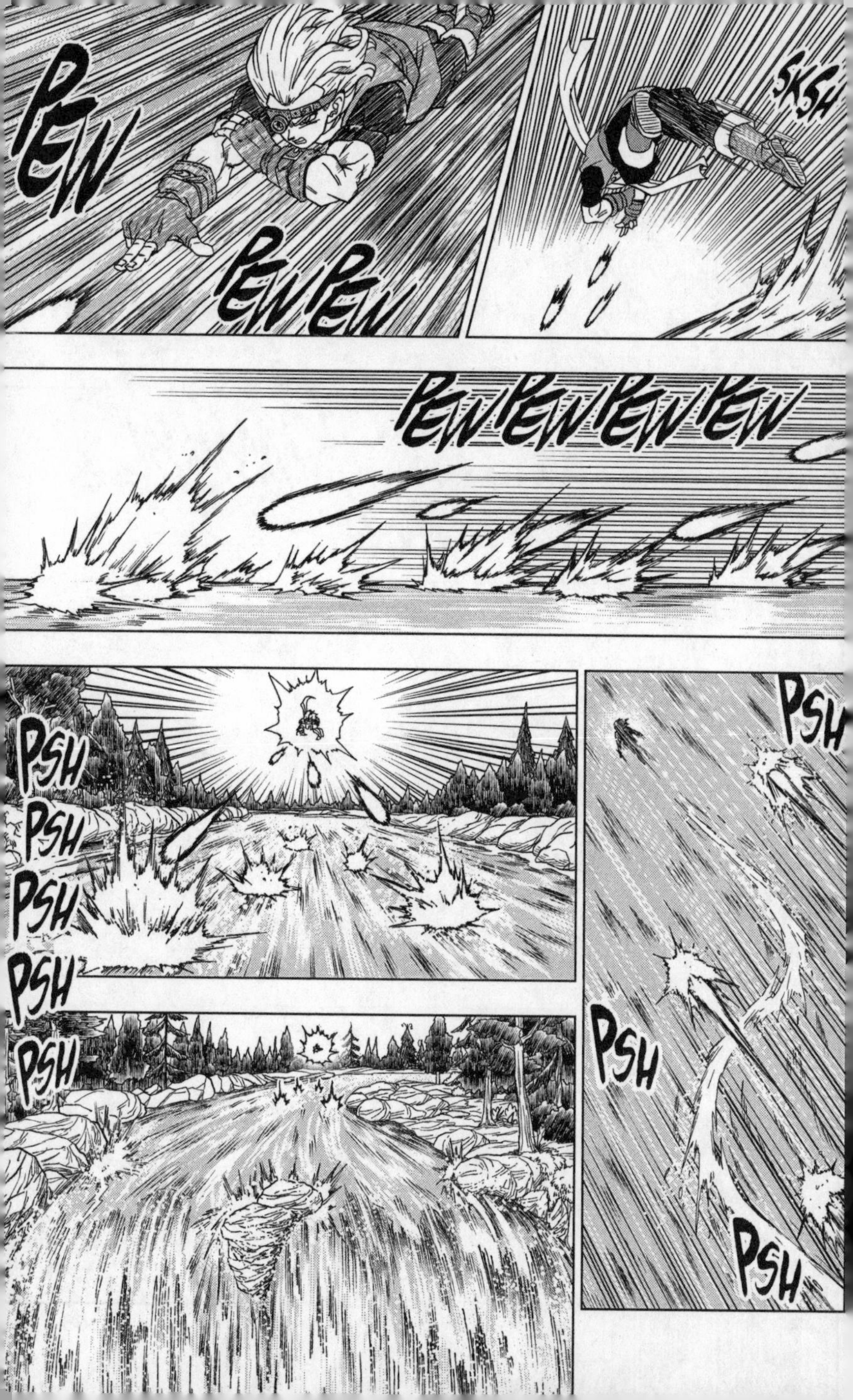
SKSH
PEW
PEW PEW
PEW PEW PEW PEW
PSH
PSH
PSH
PSH
PSH PSH PSH PSH PSH

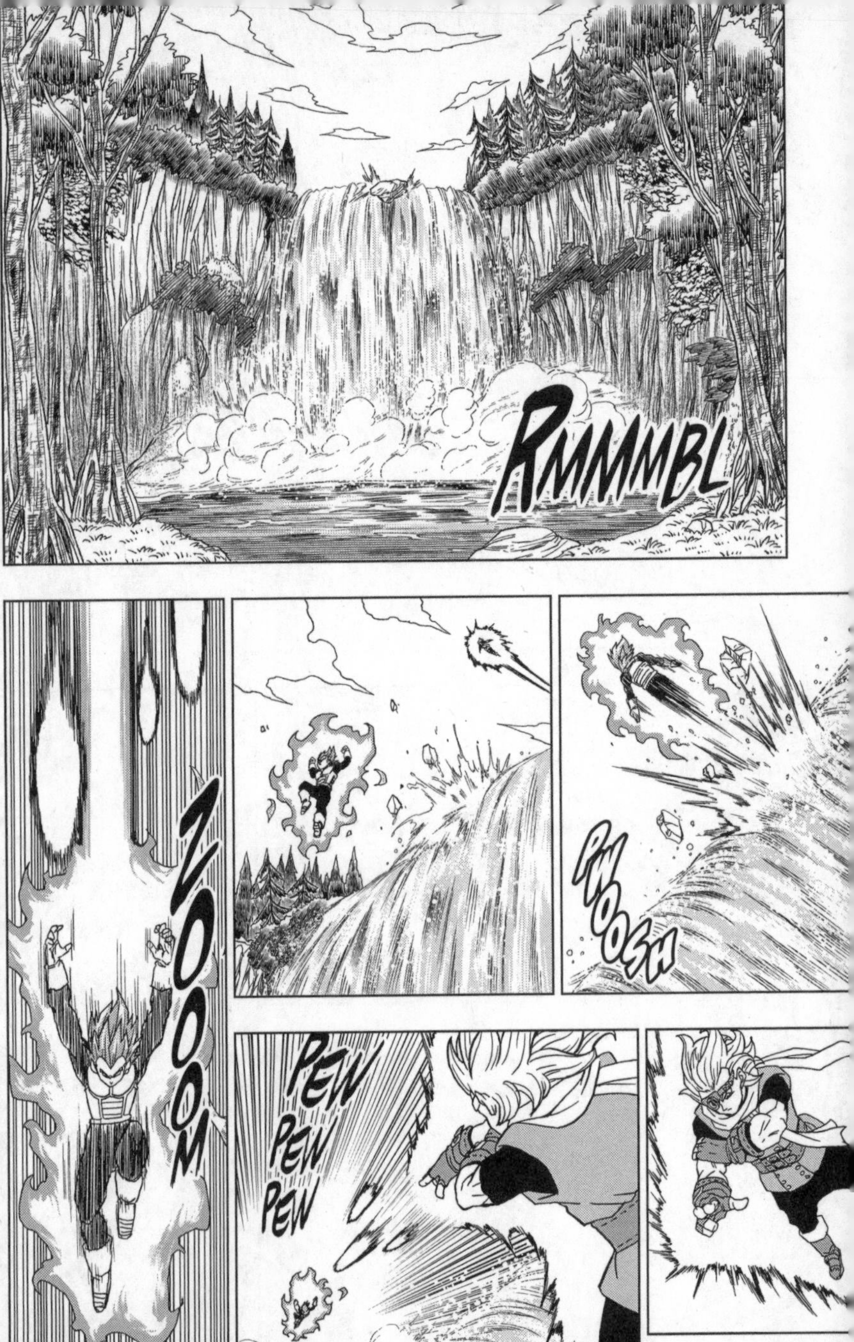
RMMMBL
PWOOSH
PEW PEW PEW
ZOOOOM

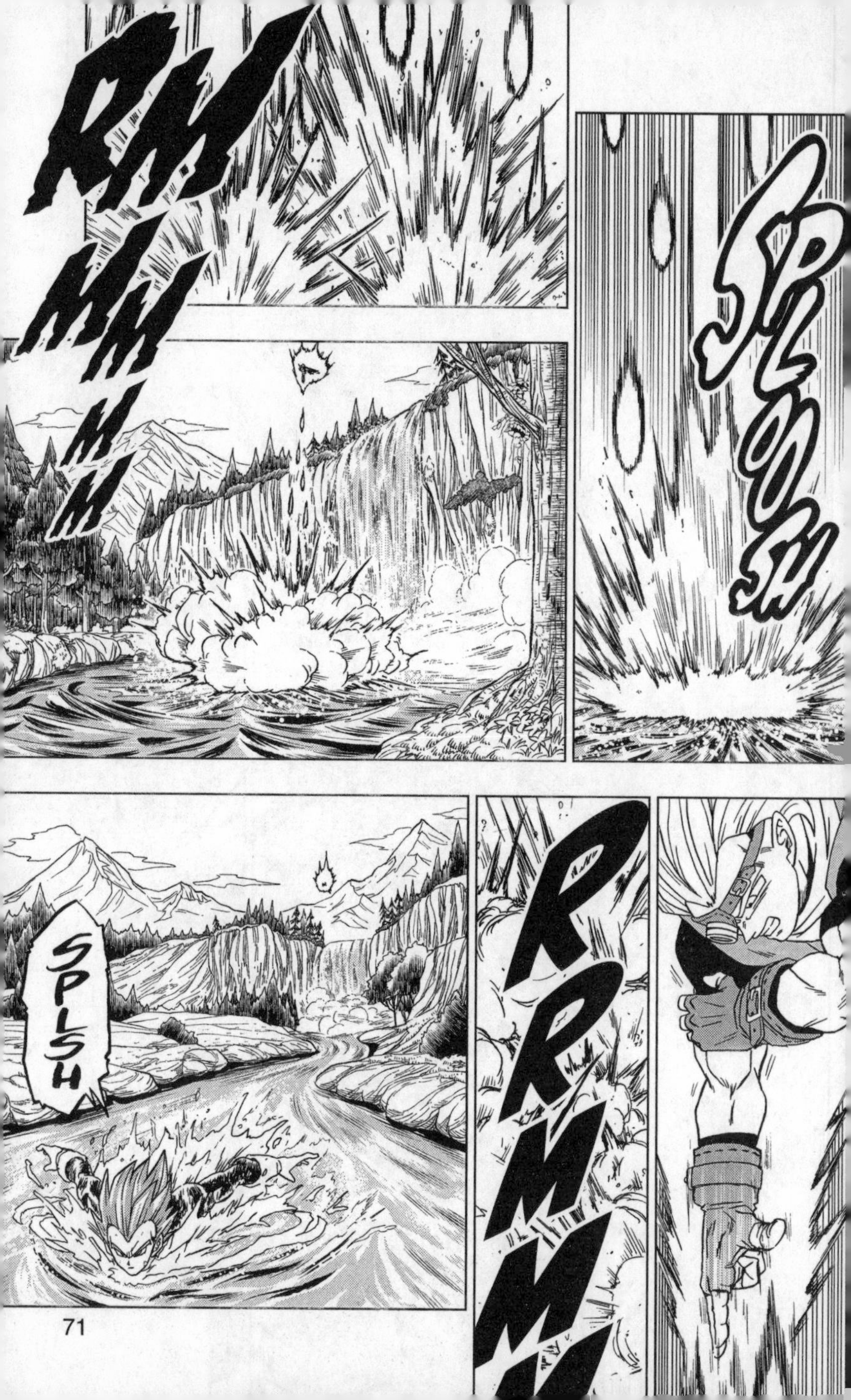
SPLOOSH
RAMMMM
RRMMM
SPLSH

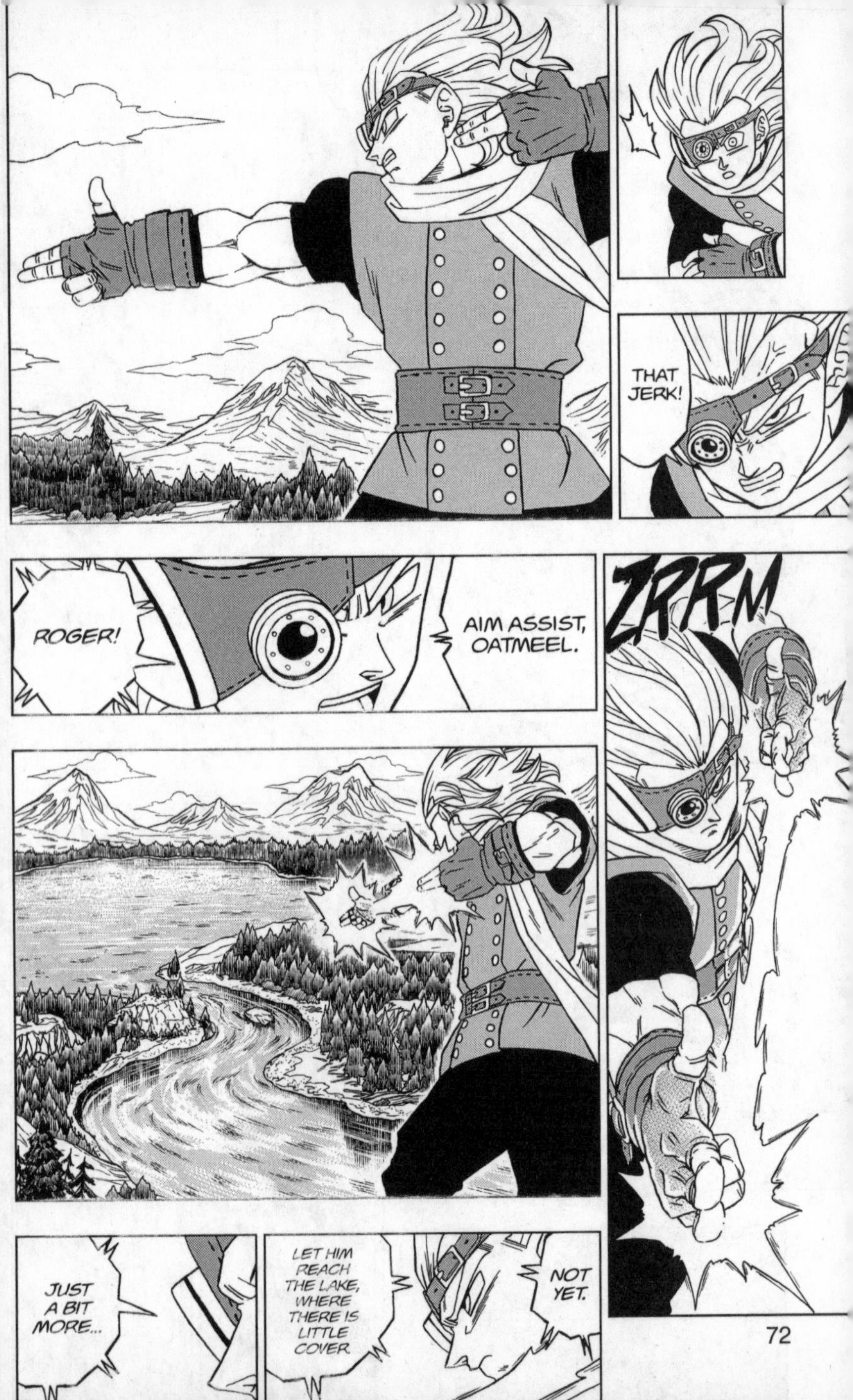
THAT JERK!
ZRRM
AIM ASSIST, OATMEEL.
ROGER!
NOT YET.
LET HIM REACH THE LAKE, WHERE THERE IS LITTLE COVER
JUST A BIT MORE...

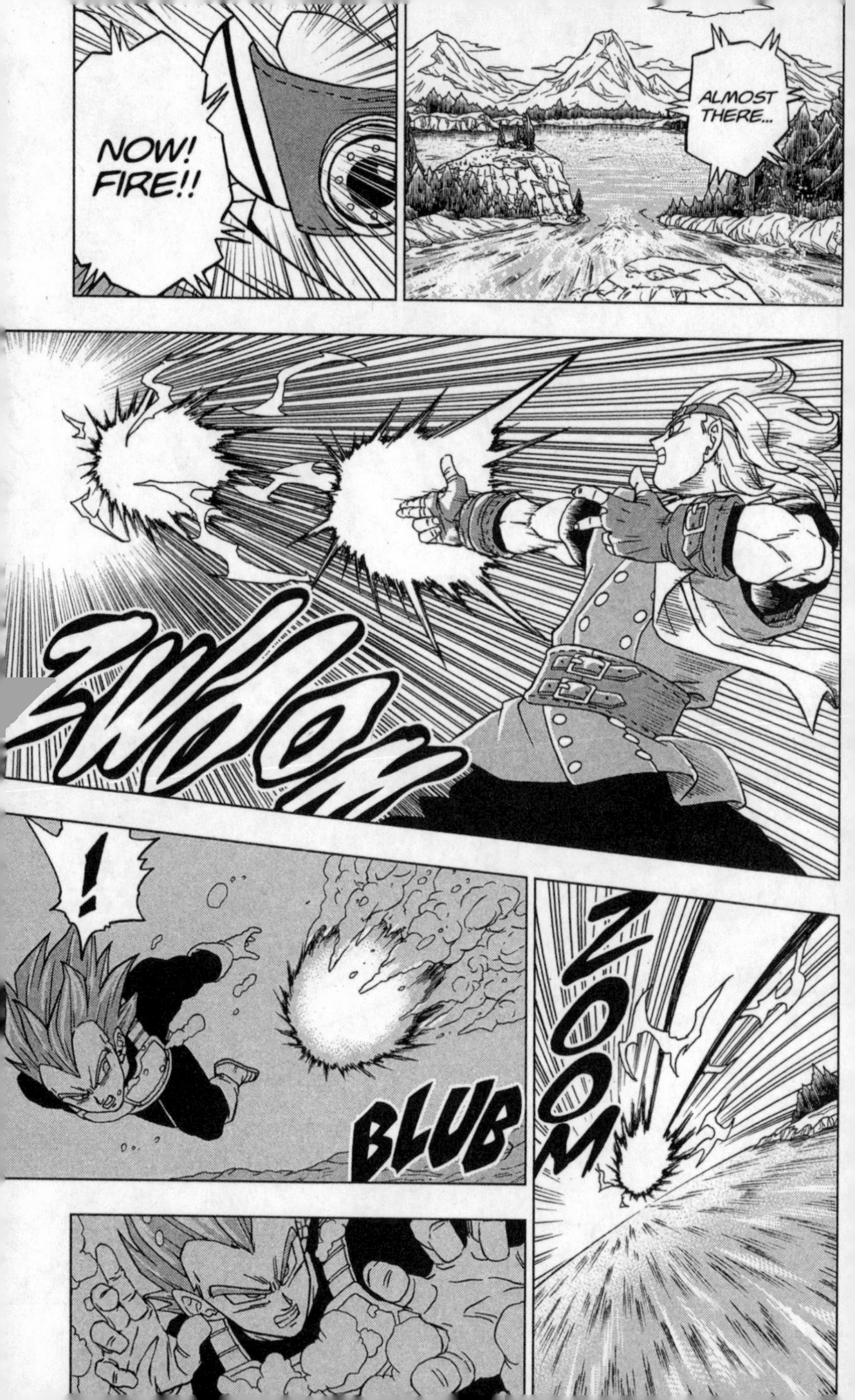
ALMOST THERE...
NOW! FIRE!!
ZWOOM
ZOOM
!
BLUB

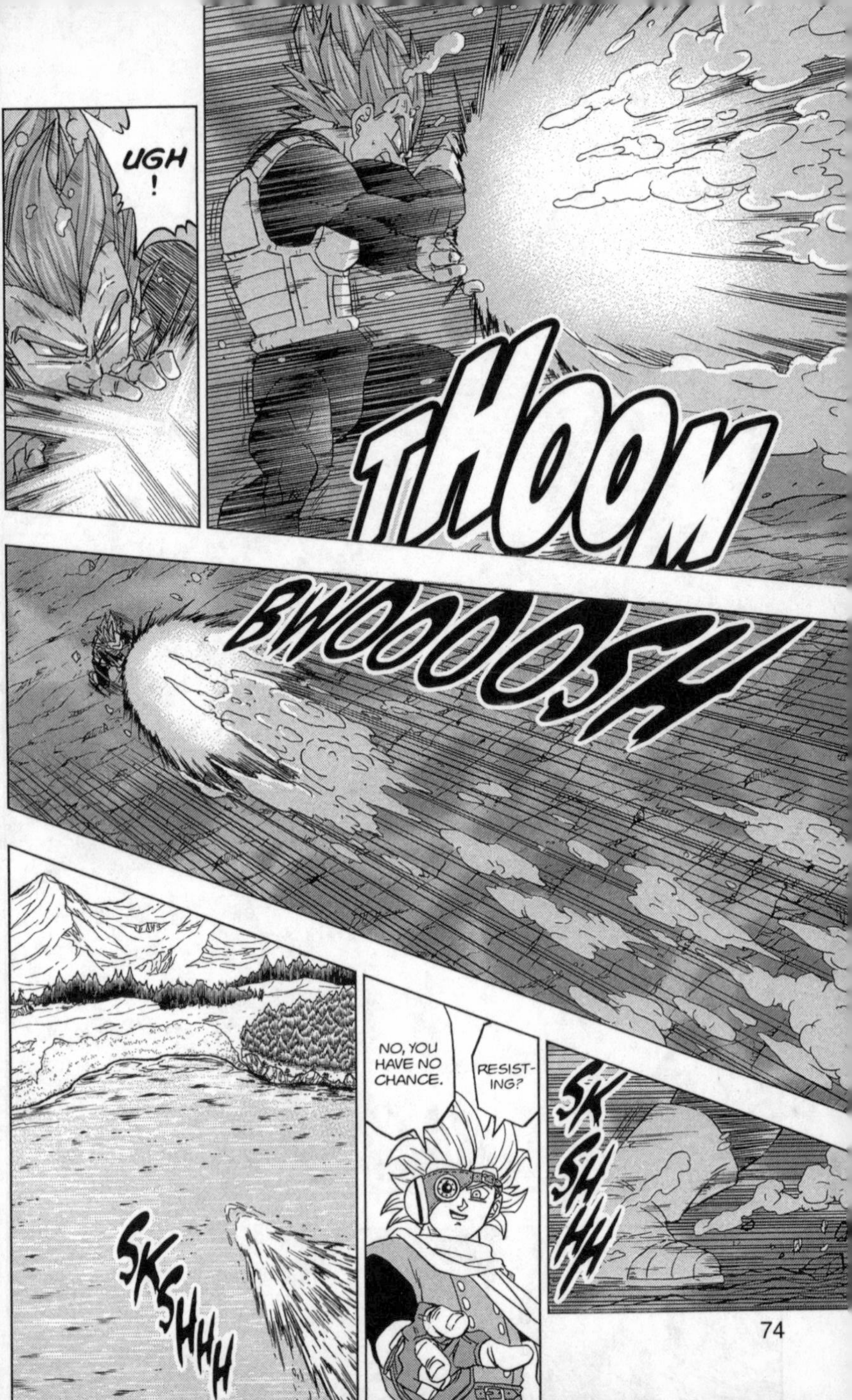
THOOM
UGH!
BWOOOOOSH
SKSHHH
RESISTING?
NO, YOU HAVE NO CHANCE.
SKSHHH

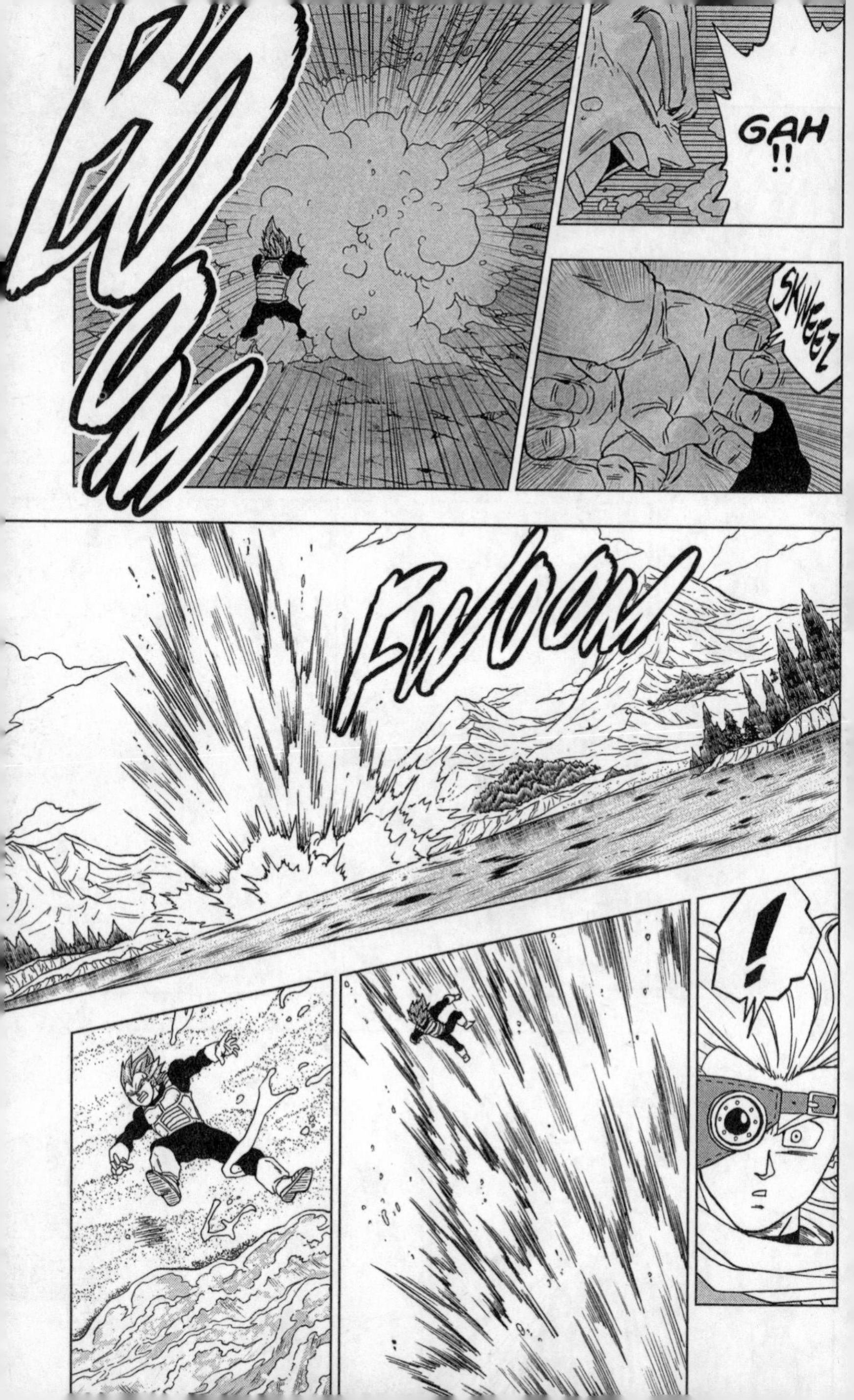
GAH!!
SKWEEZ
FWOOM
!

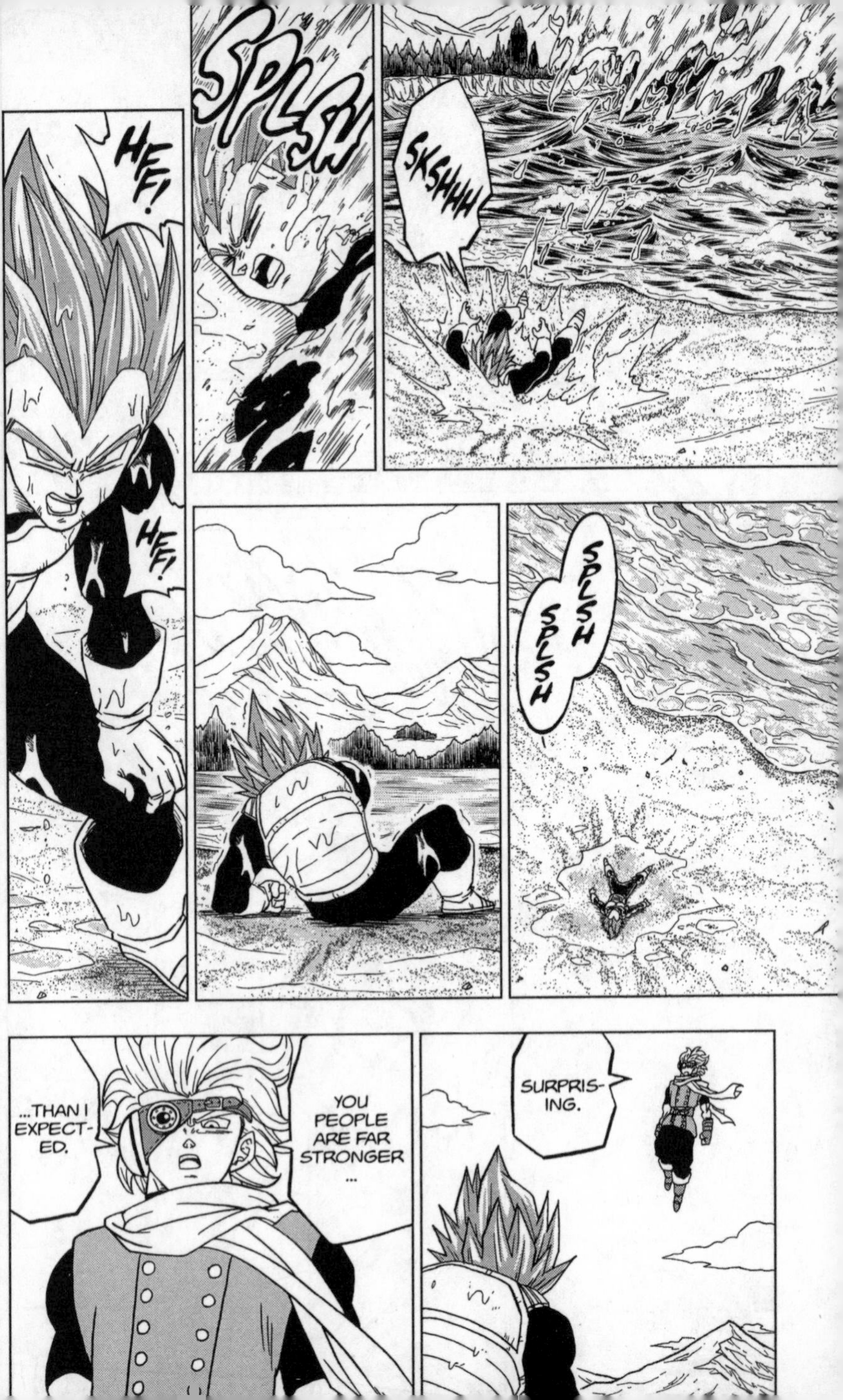

SKSHHH
SPLASH
SPLSH SPLSH
HEF! HEF!
SURPRIS-ING.
YOU PEOPLE ARE FAR STRONGER ...
...THAN I EXPECT-ED.

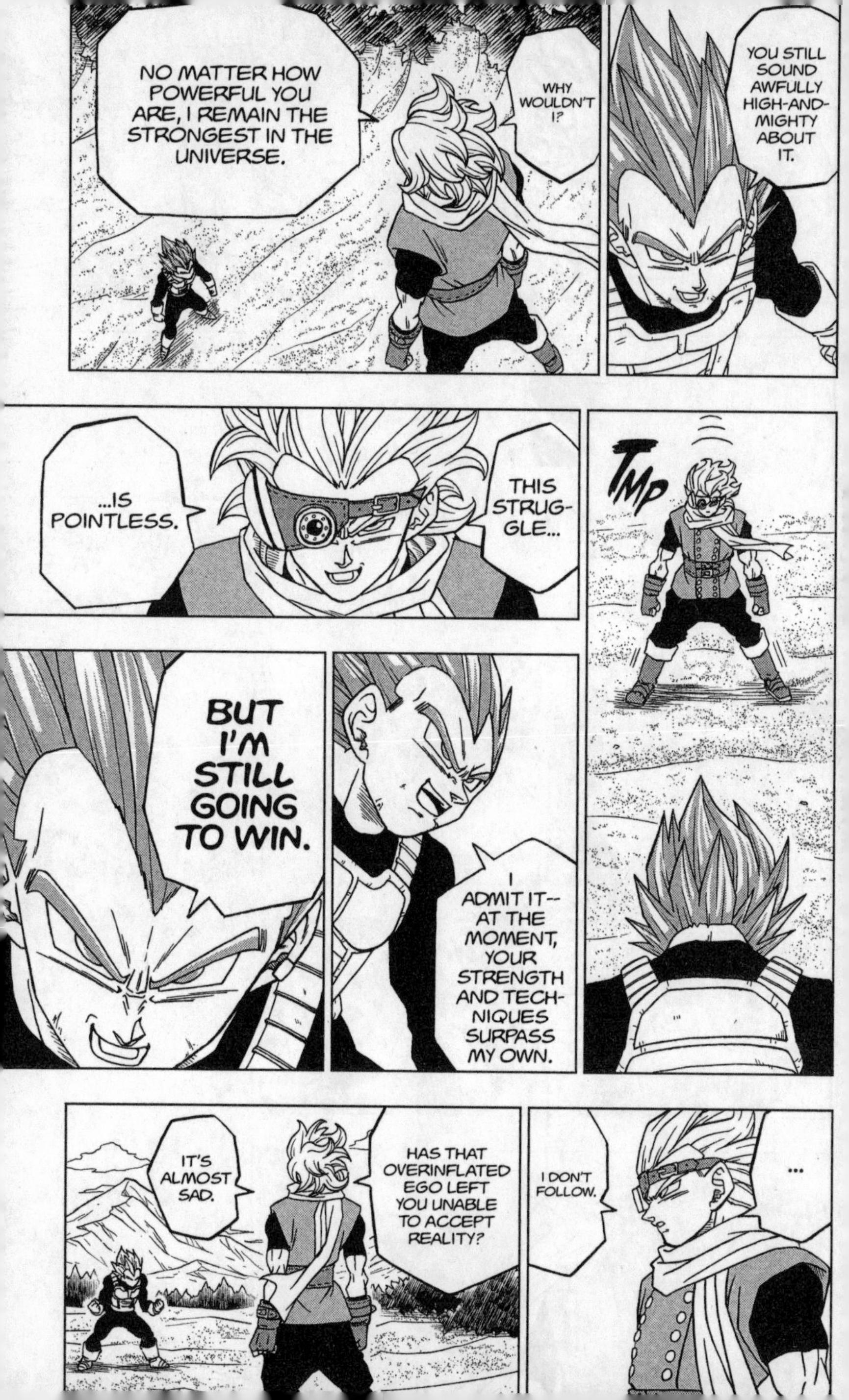
YOU STILL SOUND AWFULLY HIGH-AND-MIGHTY ABOUT IT.
WHY WOULDN'T I?
NO MATTER HOW POWERFUL YOU ARE, I REMAIN THE STRONGEST IN THE UNIVERSE.
TMP
THIS STRUG-GLE...
...IS POINTLESS.
I ADMIT IT--AT THE MOMENT, YOUR STRENGTH AND TECH-NIQUES SURPASS MY OWN.
BUT I'M STILL GOING TO WIN.
...
I DON'T FOLLOW.
HAS THAT OVERINFLATED EGO LEFT YOU UNABLE TO ACCEPT REALITY?
IT'S ALMOST SAD.

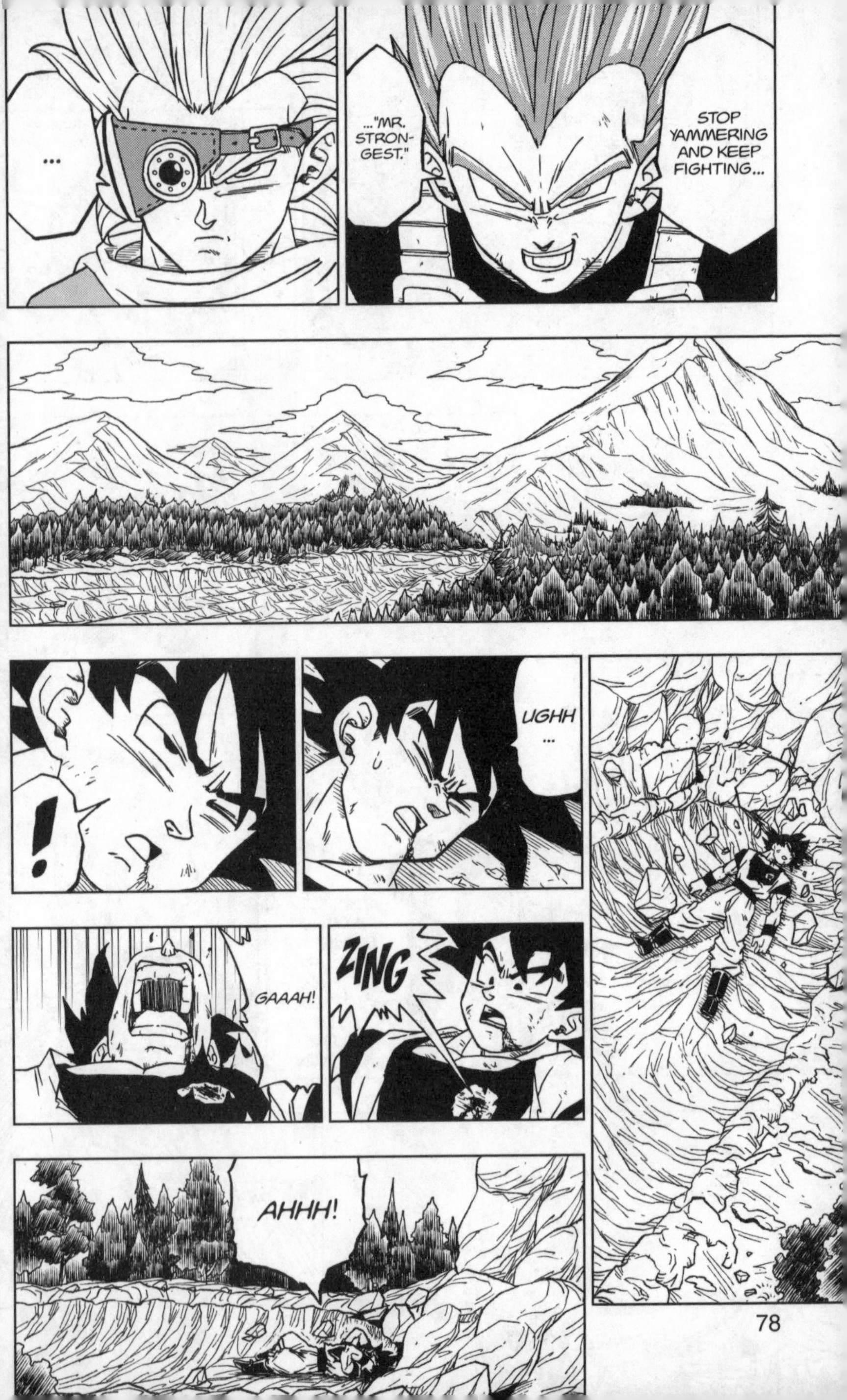
STOP YAMMERING AND KEEP FIGHTING...
..."MR. STRONGEST."
...
UGHH ...
!
ZING
GAAAH!
AHHH!

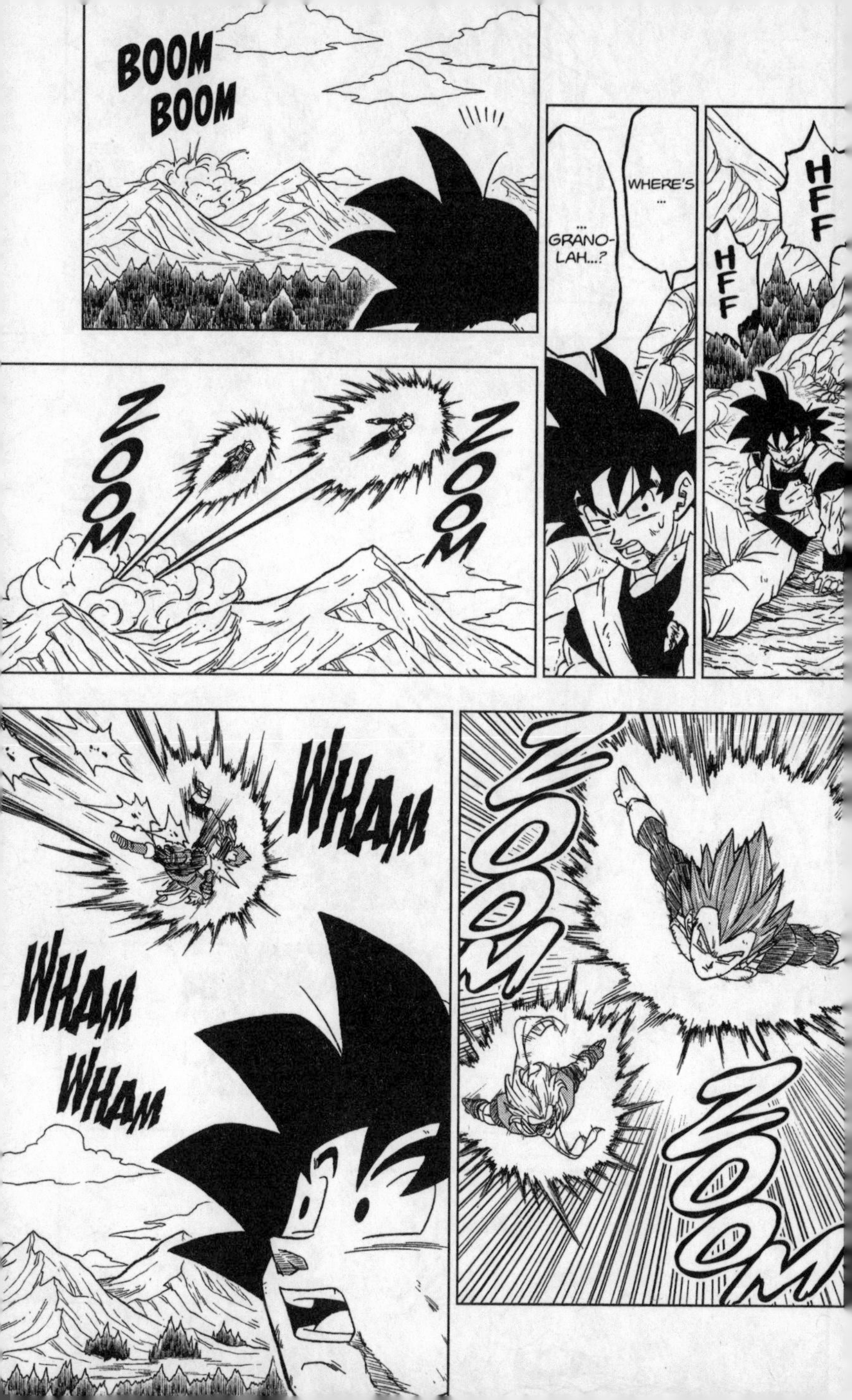
HFF HFF
HFF HFF
WHERE'S ...
... GRANO-LAH...?
BOOM BOOM
ZOOM
ZOOM
ZOOM
ZOOM
WHAM
WHAM
WHAM

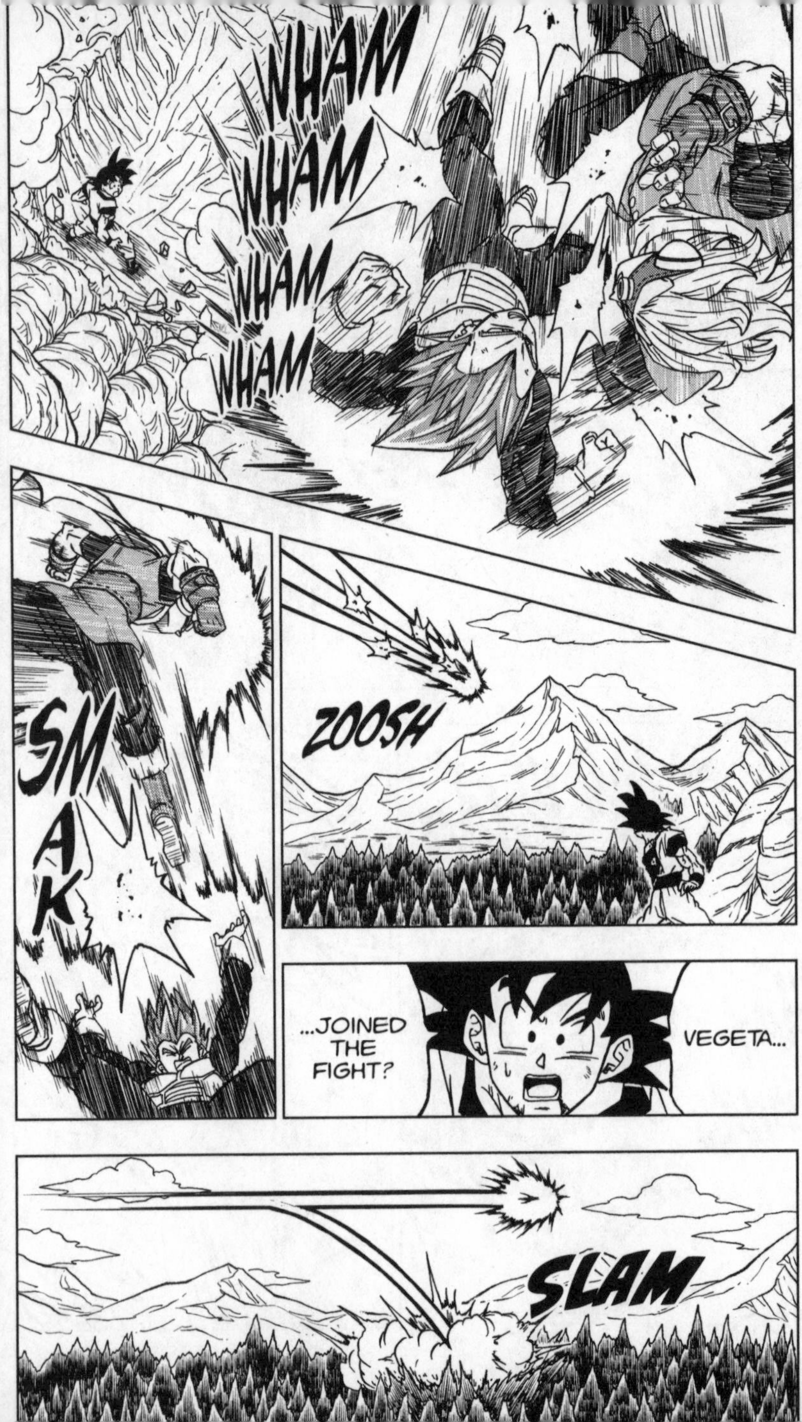
WHAM
WHAM
WHAM
WHAM
ZOOSH
VEGETA...
...JOINED THE FIGHT?
SMAK
SLAM

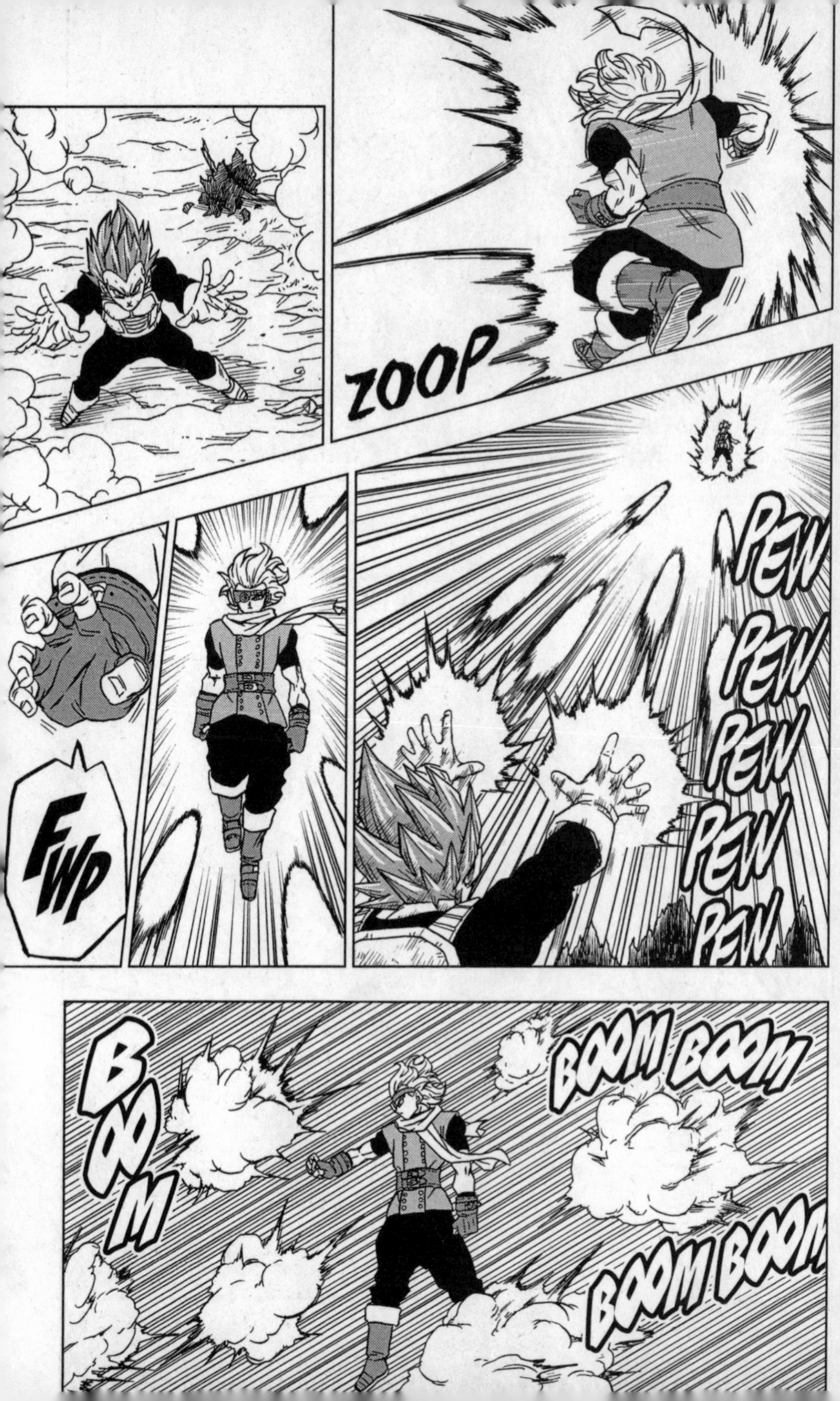
ZOOP
PEW PEW PEW PEW PEW
FWP
BOOM BOOM
BOOM BOOM
BOOM

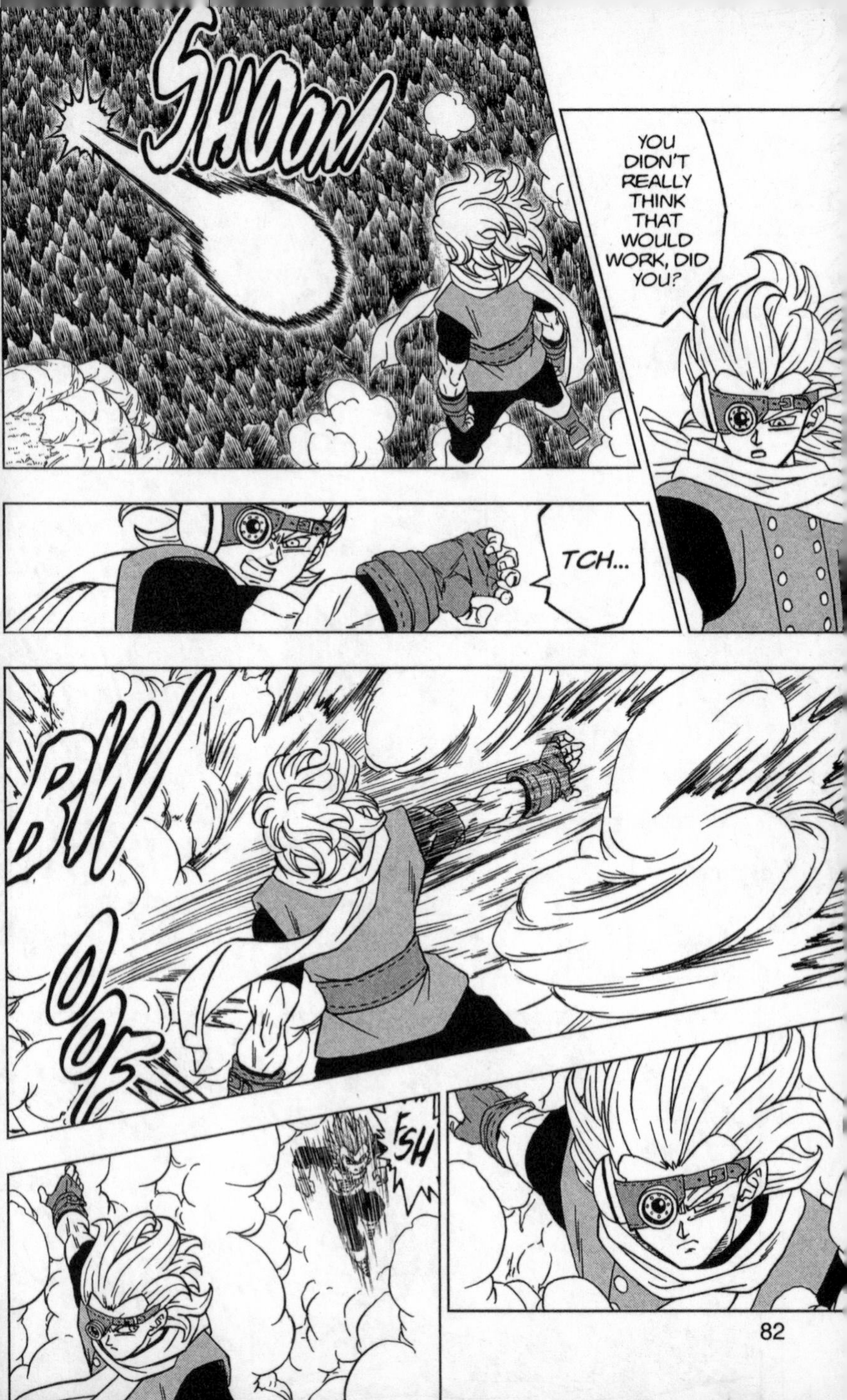
SHOOM
YOU DIDN'T REALLY THINK THAT WOULD WORK, DID YOU?
TCH...
BWOOOM
FSH

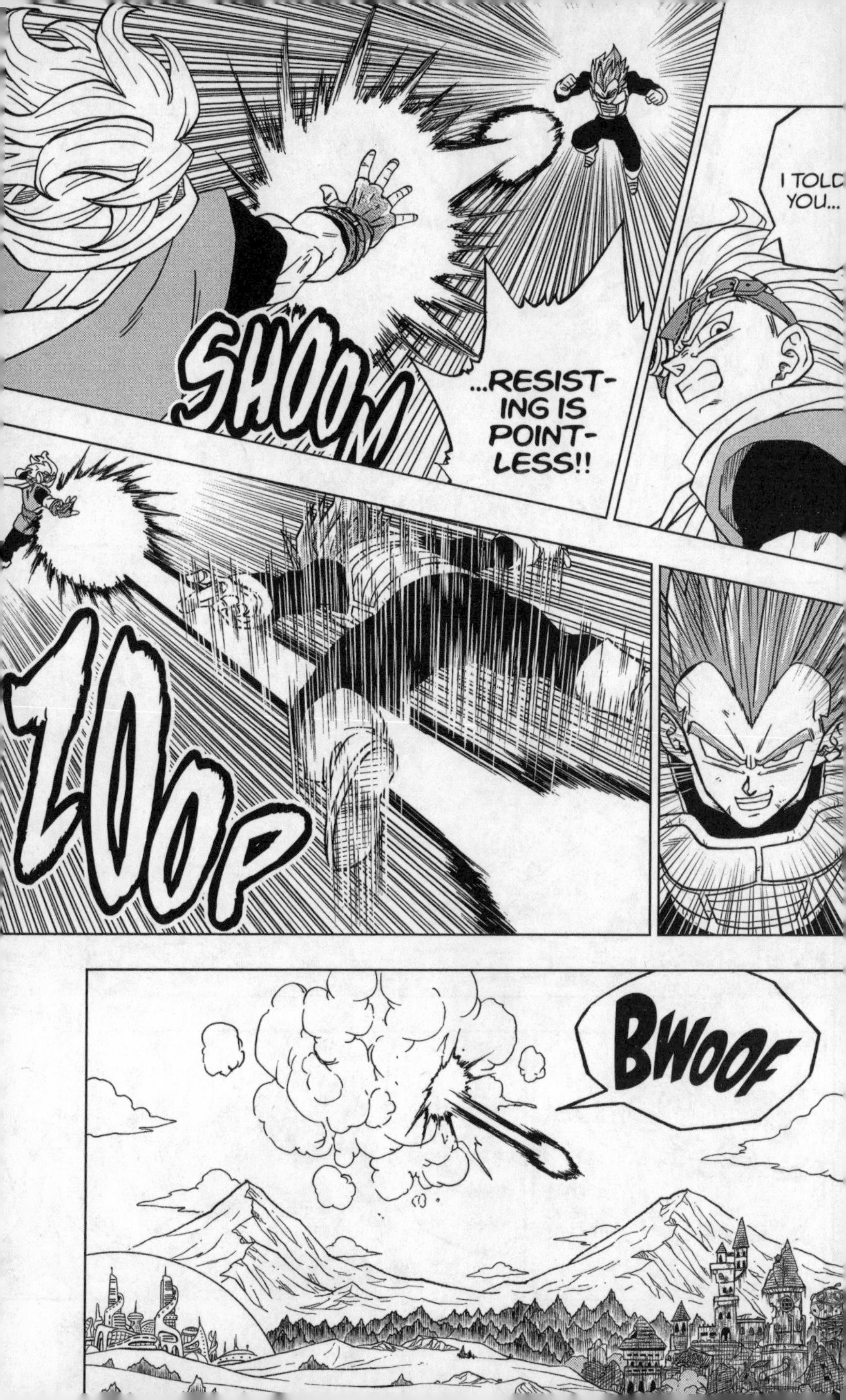
I TOLD YOU...
...RESISTING IS POINTLESS!!
SHOOM
ZOOP
BWOOF

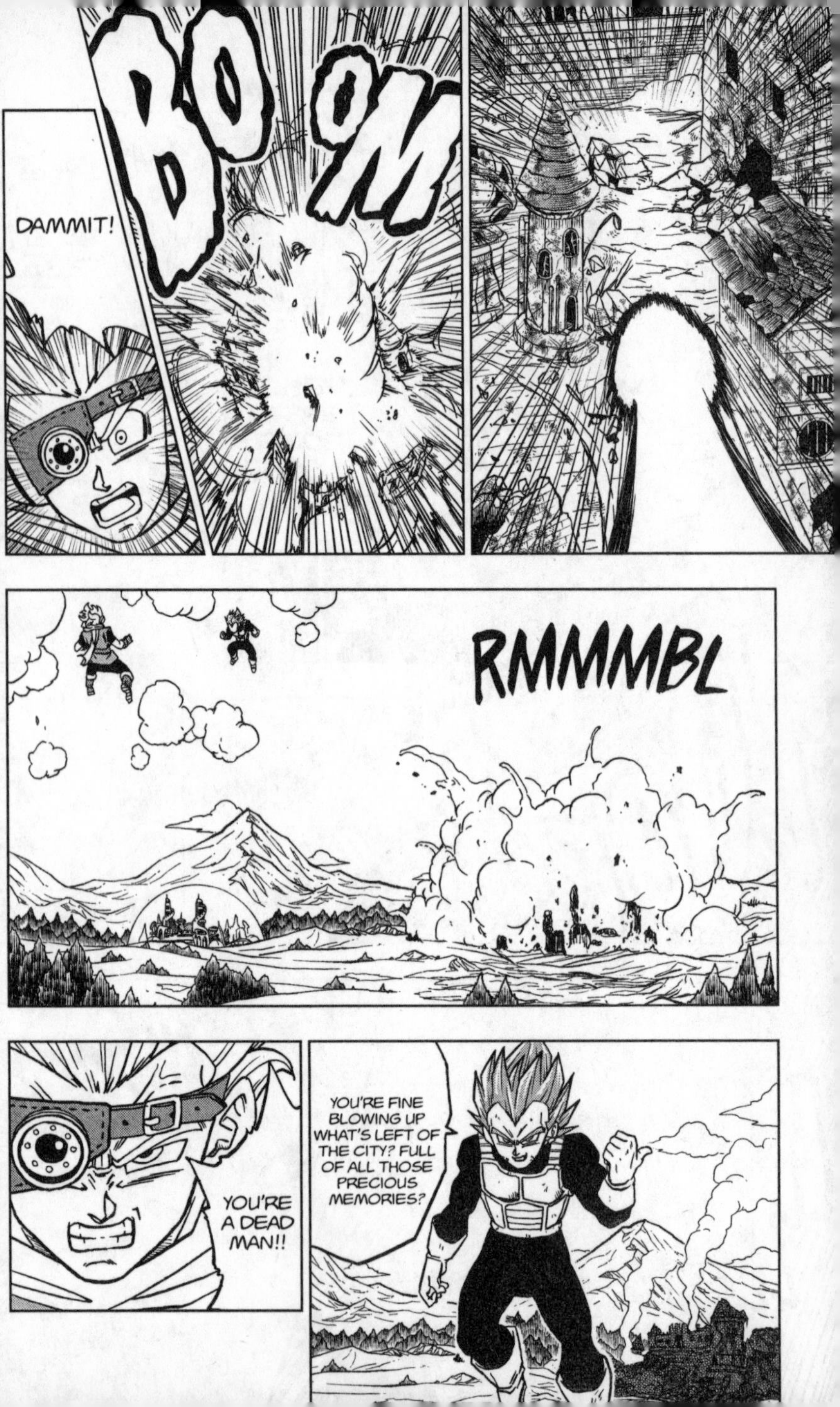
BOOM
DAMMIT!
RMMMBL
YOU'RE FINE BLOWING UP WHAT'S LEFT OF THE CITY? FULL OF ALL THOSE PRECIOUS MEMORIES?
YOU'RE A DEAD MAN!!

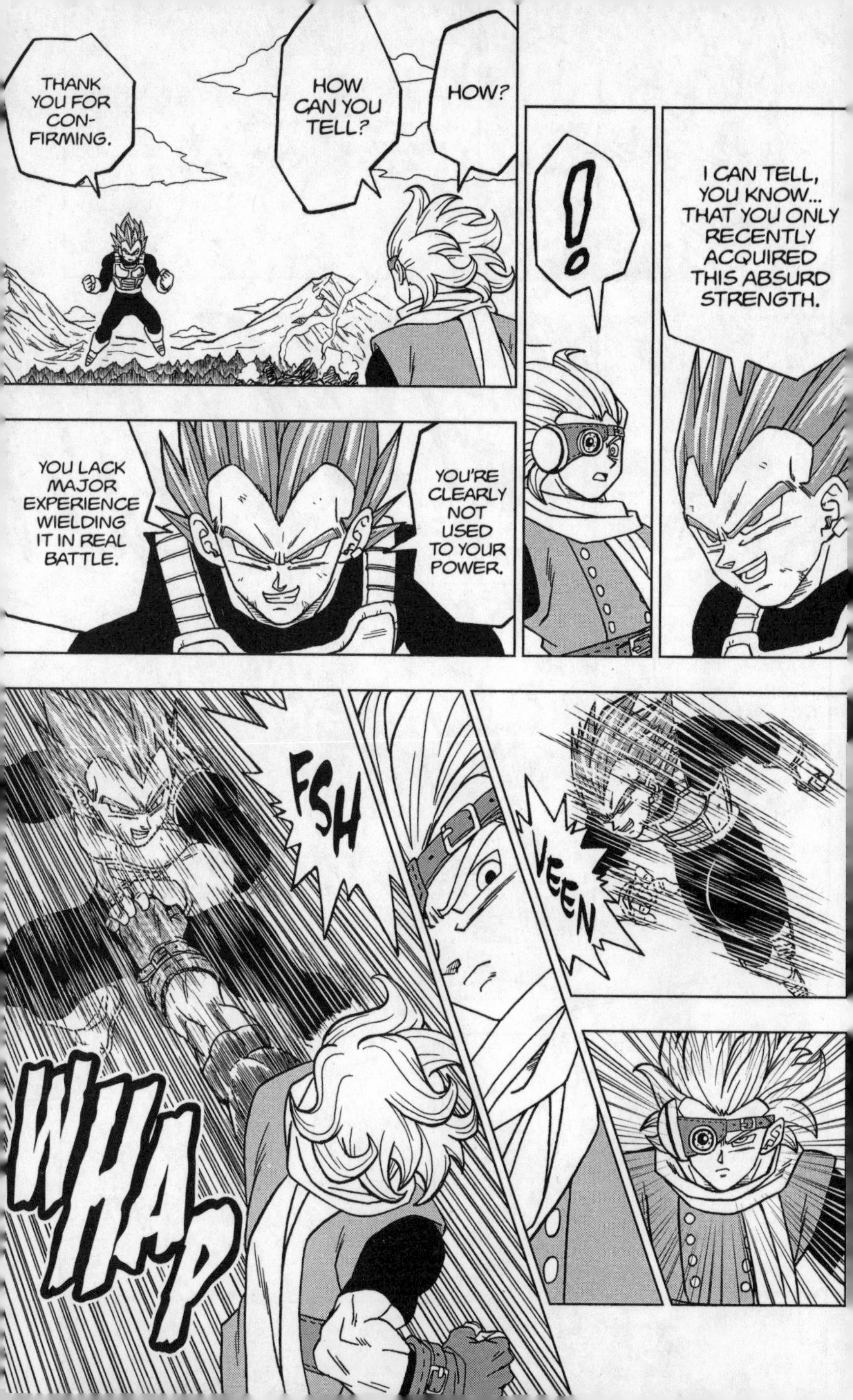

HOW?
HOW CAN YOU TELL?
THANK YOU FOR CON-FIRMING.
I CAN TELL, YOU KNOW... THAT YOU ONLY RECENTLY ACQUIRED THIS ABSURD STRENGTH.
!
YOU'RE CLEARLY NOT USED TO YOUR POWER.
YOU LACK MAJOR EXPERIENCE WIELDING IT IN REAL BATTLE.
VEEN
FSH
WHAP

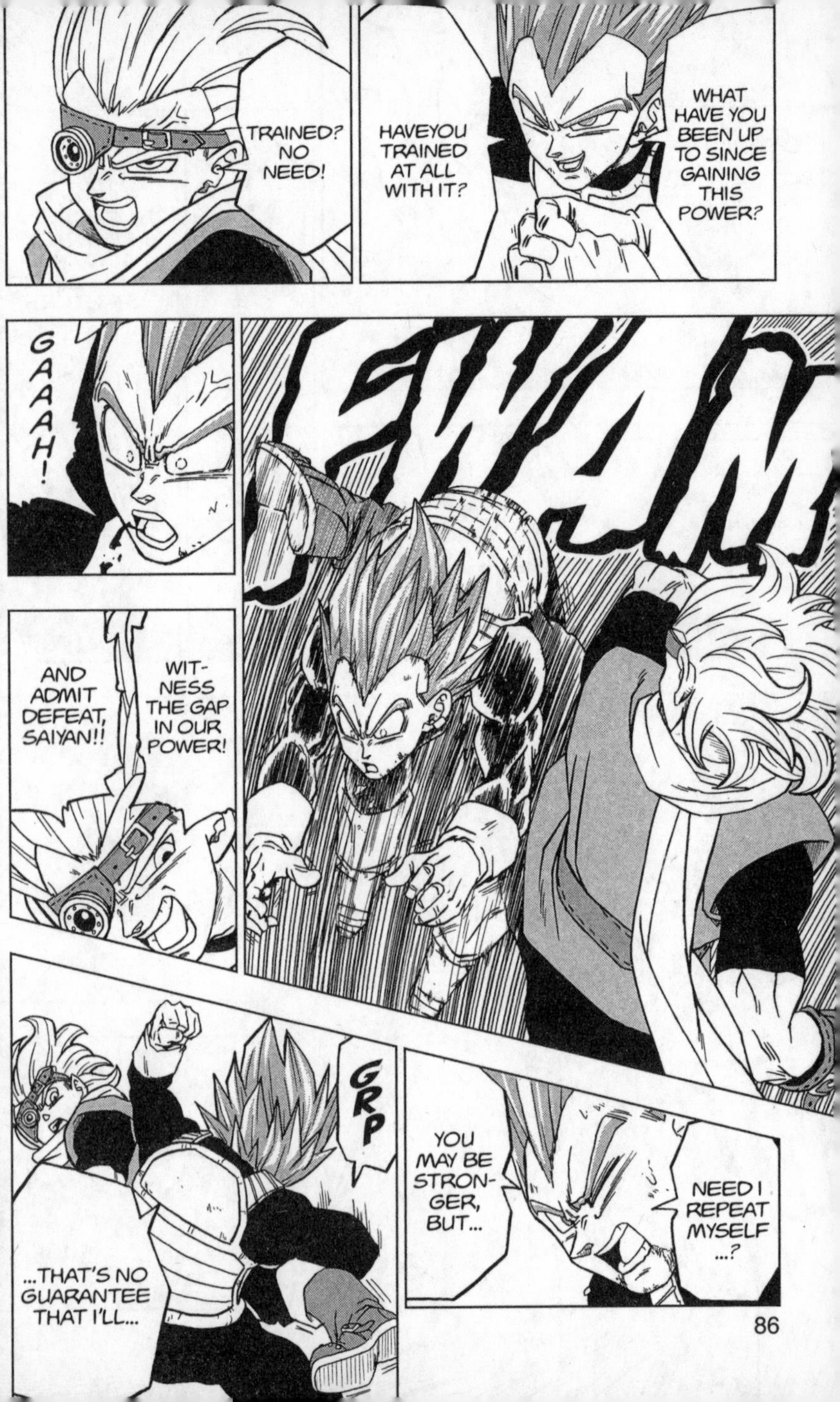
WHAT HAVE YOU BEEN UP TO SINCE GAINING THIS POWER?
HAVEYOU TRAINED AT ALL WITH IT?
TRAINED? NO NEED!
SWAM
GAAAAH!
WIT-NESS THE GAP IN OUR POWER!
AND ADMIT DEFEAT, SAIYAN!!
NEED I REPEAT MYSELF ...?
YOU MAY BE STRON-GER, BUT...
GRP
...THAT'S NO GUARANTEE THAT I'LL...

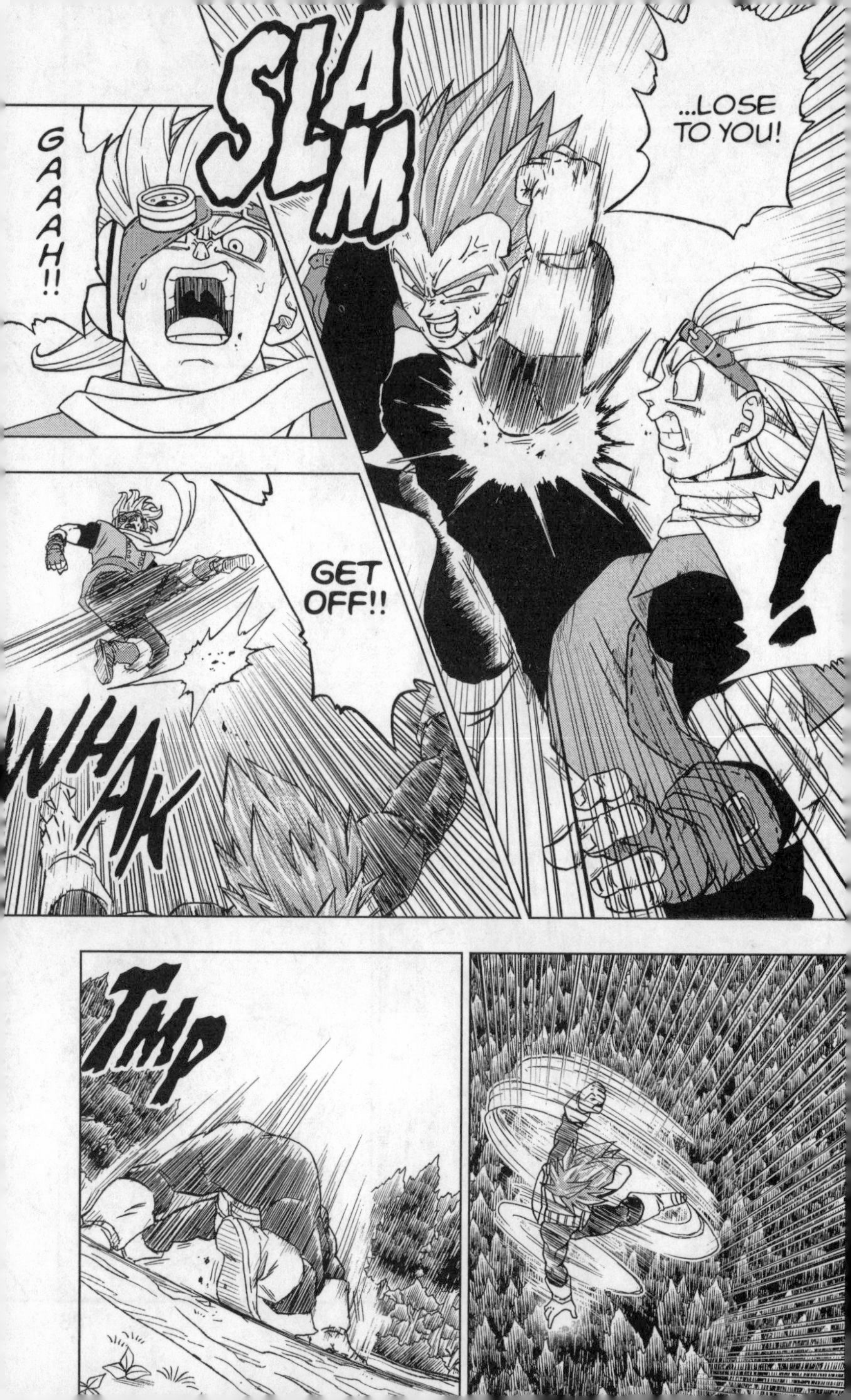
...LOSE TO YOU!
SLAM
!
GAAAAH!!
GET OFF!!
WHAK
TMP

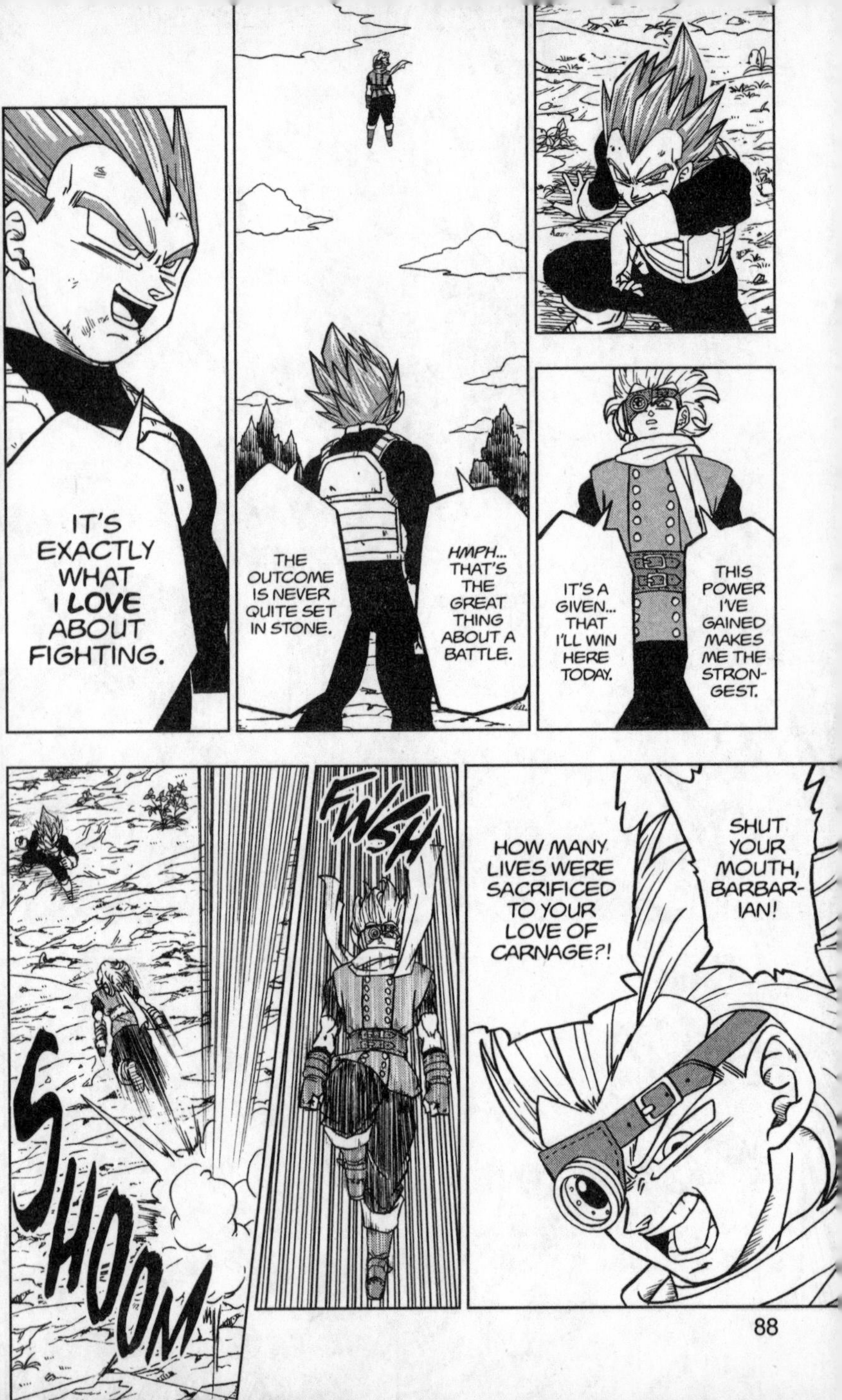
THIS POWER I'VE GAINED MAKES ME THE STRONG-GEST.
IT'S A GIVEN... THAT I'LL WIN HERE TODAY.
HMPH... THAT'S THE GREAT THING ABOUT A BATTLE.
THE OUTCOME IS NEVER QUITE SET IN STONE.
IT'S EXACTLY WHAT I **LOVE** ABOUT FIGHTING.
SHUT YOUR MOUTH, BARBAR-IAN!
HOW MANY LIVES WERE SACRIFICED TO YOUR LOVE OF CARNAGE?!
FWSH
SHOOM

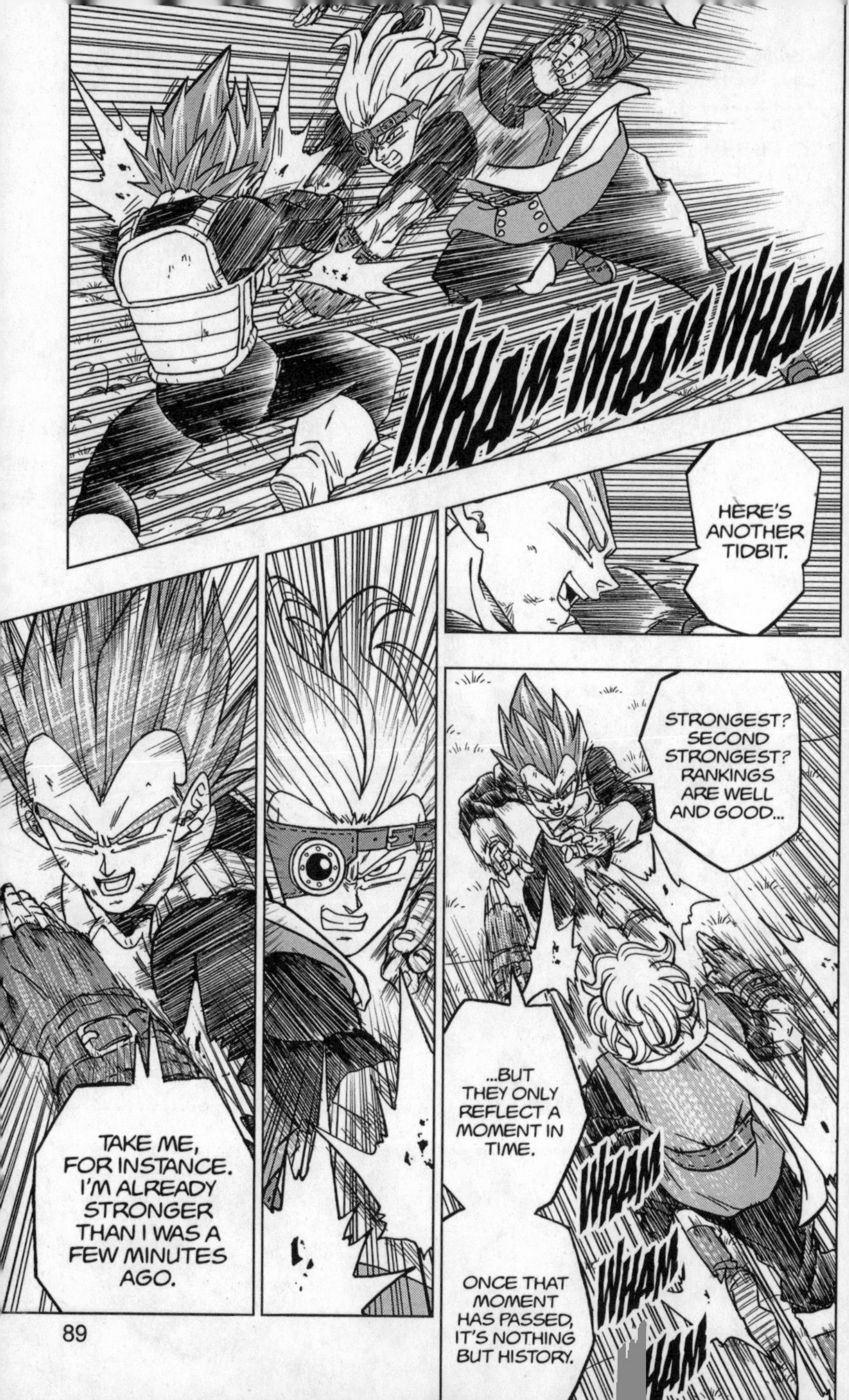
WHAM WHAM WHAM
HERE'S ANOTHER TIDBIT.
STRONGEST? SECOND STRONGEST? RANKINGS ARE WELL AND GOOD...
...BUT THEY ONLY REFLECT A MOMENT IN TIME.
WHAM
WHAM
WHAM
ONCE THAT MOMENT HAS PASSED, IT'S NOTHING BUT HISTORY.
TAKE ME, FOR INSTANCE. I'M ALREADY STRONGER THAN I WAS A FEW MINUTES AGO.

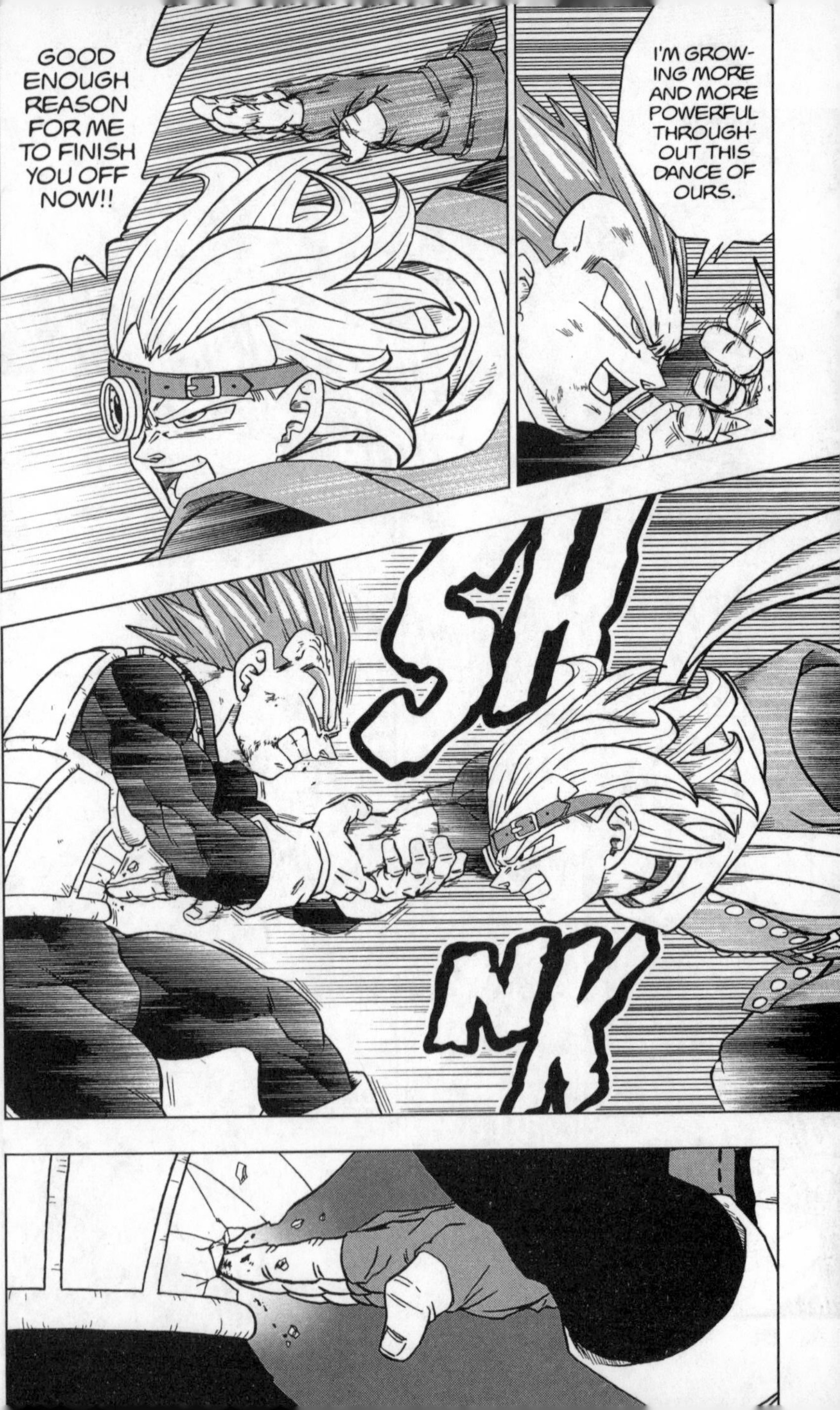
I'M GROWING MORE AND MORE POWERFUL THROUGHOUT THIS DANCE OF OURS.
GOOD ENOUGH REASON FOR ME TO FINISH YOU OFF NOW!!
SHNK

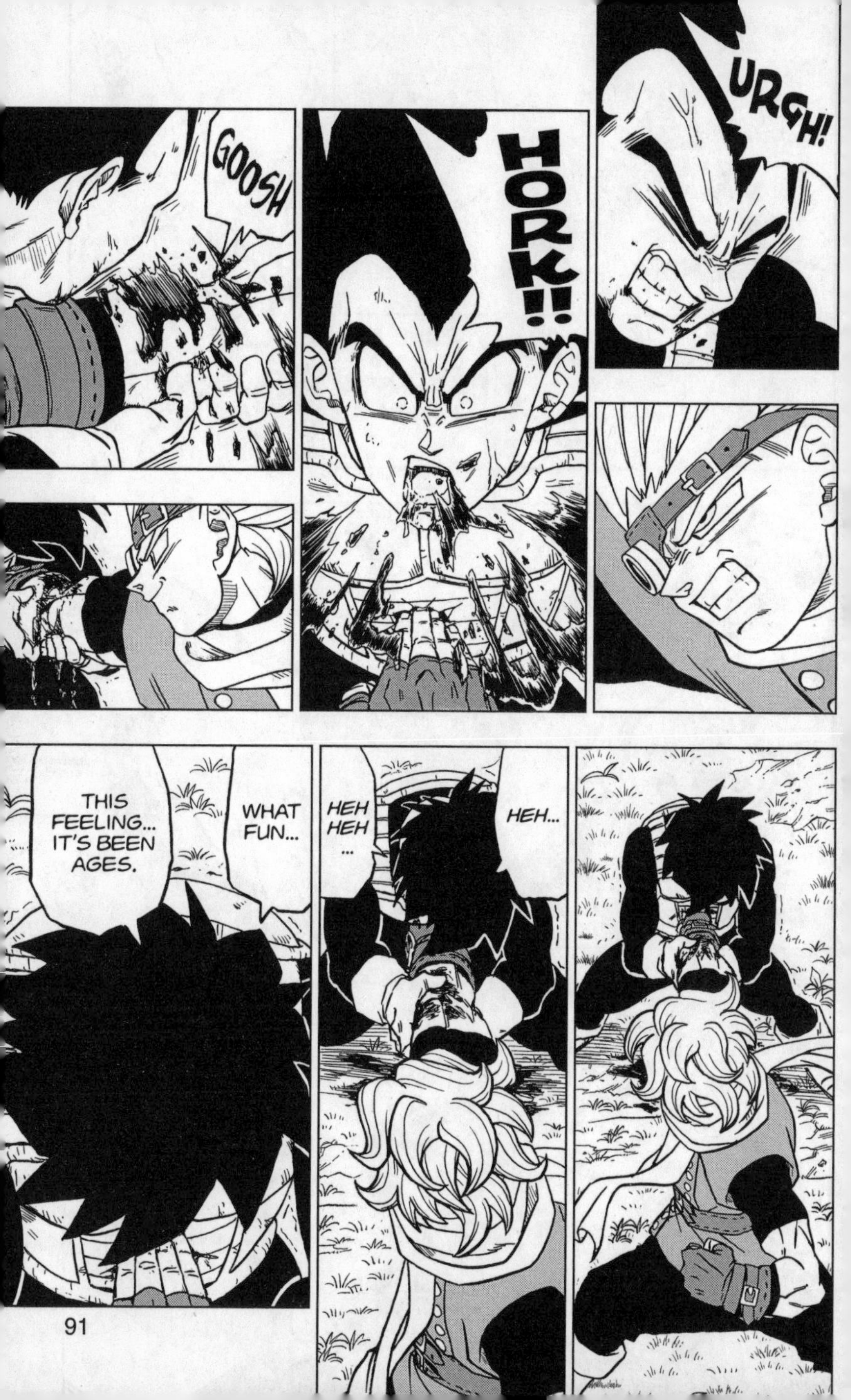
URGH!
HORK!!
GOOSH
HEH...
HEH HEH ...
WHAT FUN...
THIS FEELING... IT'S BEEN AGES.

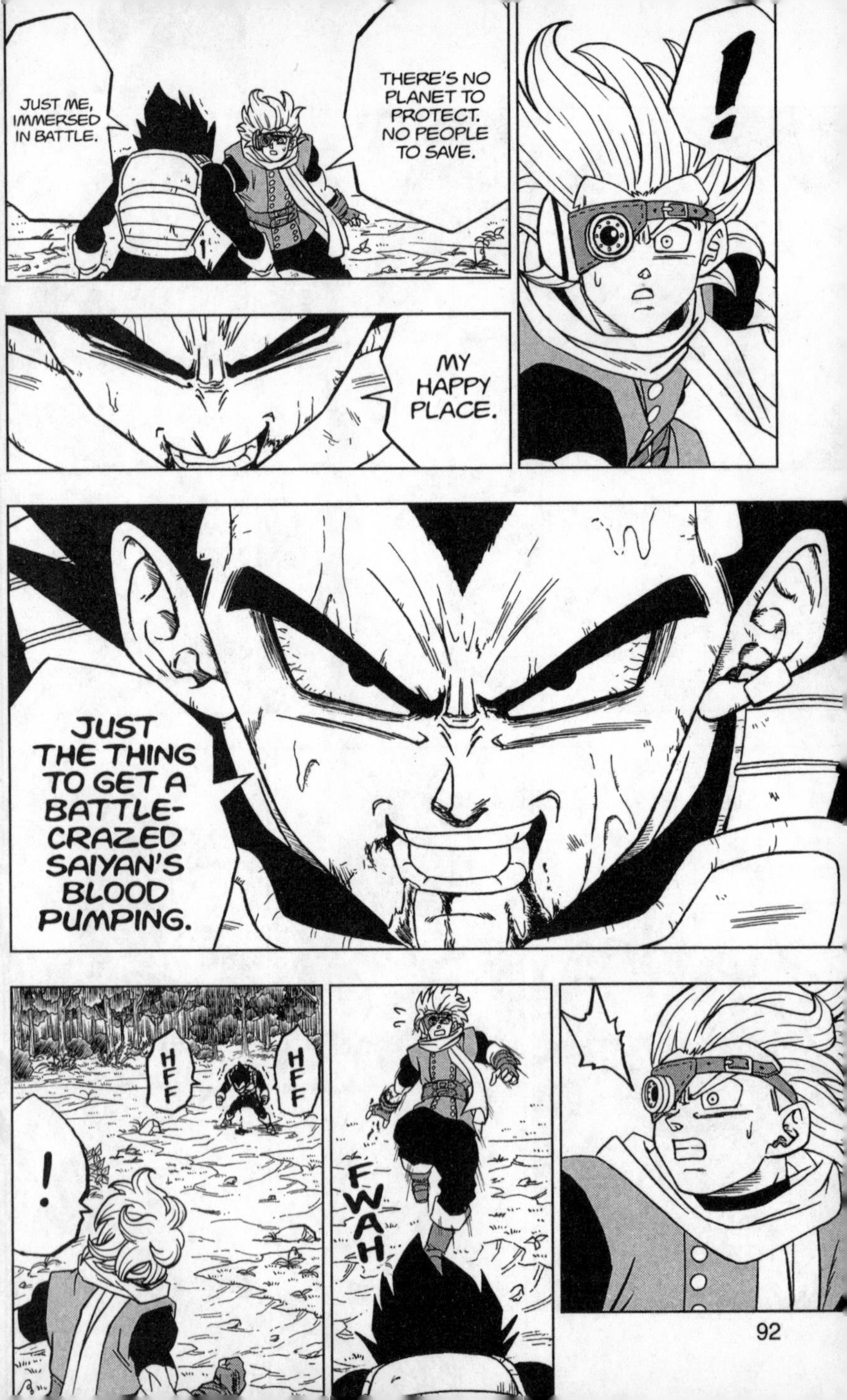
!
THERE'S NO PLANET TO PROTECT. NO PEOPLE TO SAVE.
JUST ME, IMMERSED IN BATTLE.
MY HAPPY PLACE.
JUST THE THING TO GET A BATTLE-CRAZED SAIYAN'S BLOOD PUMPING.
FWAH
HFF
HFF
!

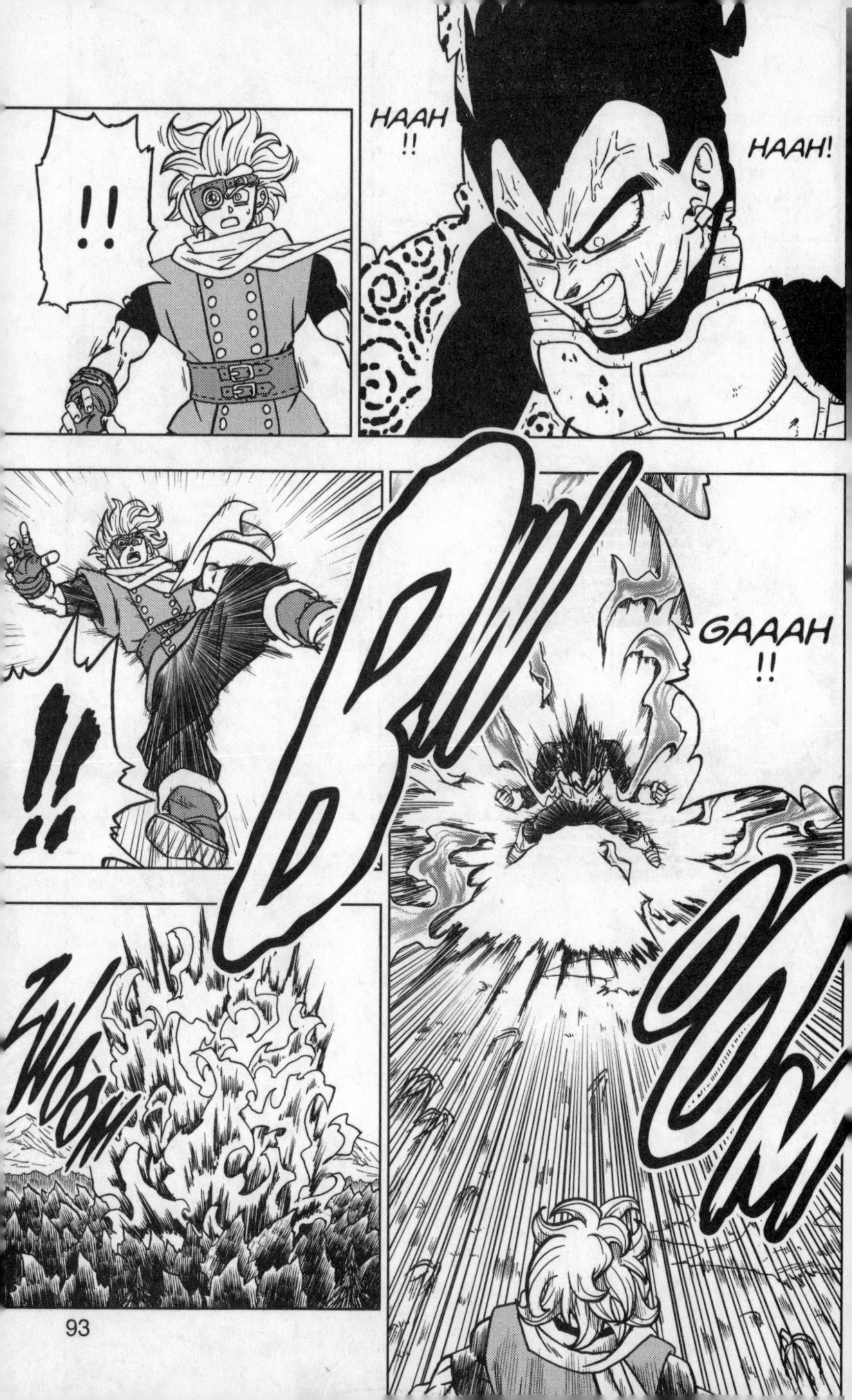
HAAH!
HAAH!!
!!
GAAAH!!
!!

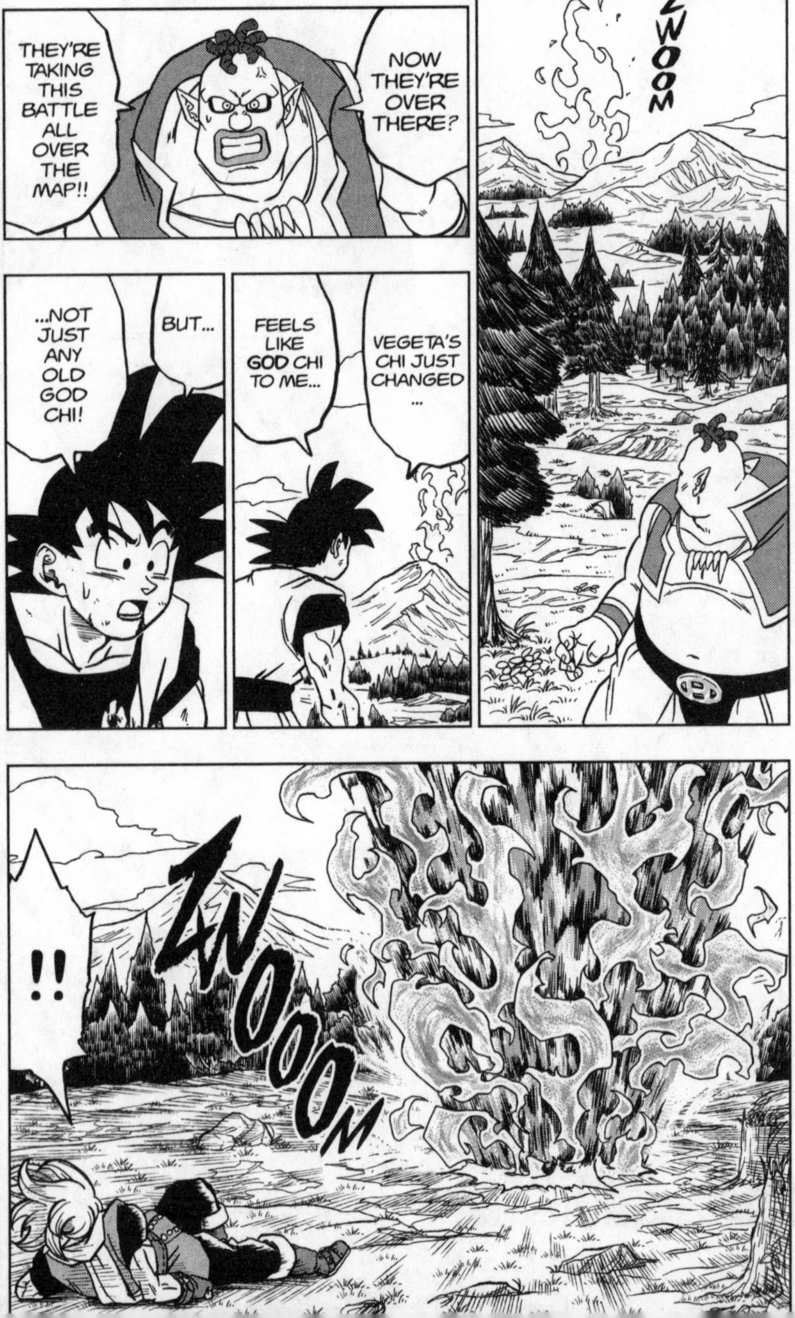
ZWOOOM
NOW THEY'RE OVER THERE?
THEY'RE TAKING THIS BATTLE ALL OVER THE MAP!!
VEGETA'S CHI JUST CHANGED ...
FEELS LIKE GOD CHI TO ME...
BUT...
...NOT JUST ANY OLD GOD CHI!
ZWOOOOM
!!

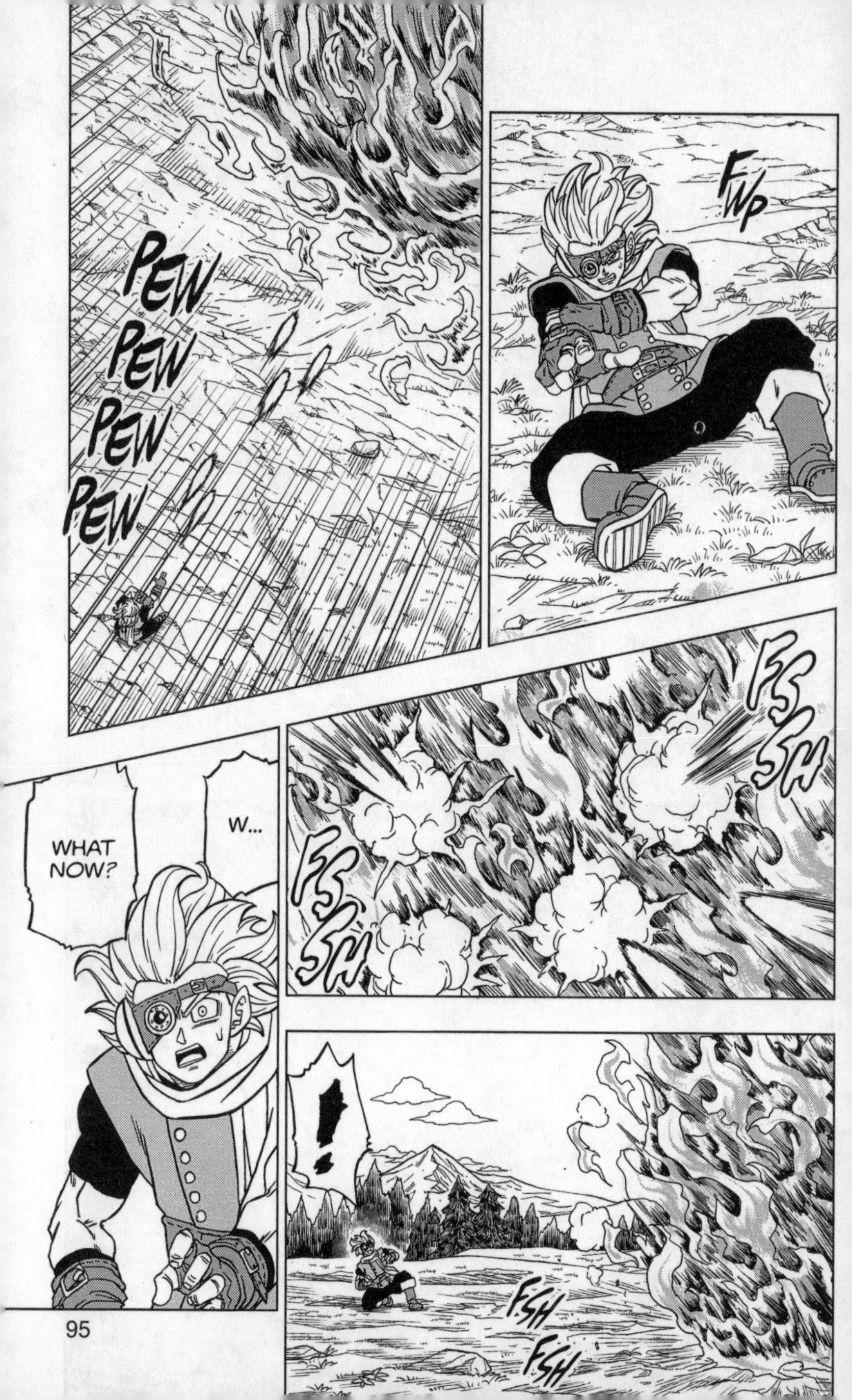
FWP
PEW PEW PEW PEW
FSSH
FSSH
!
FSH
FSH
W...
WHAT NOW?

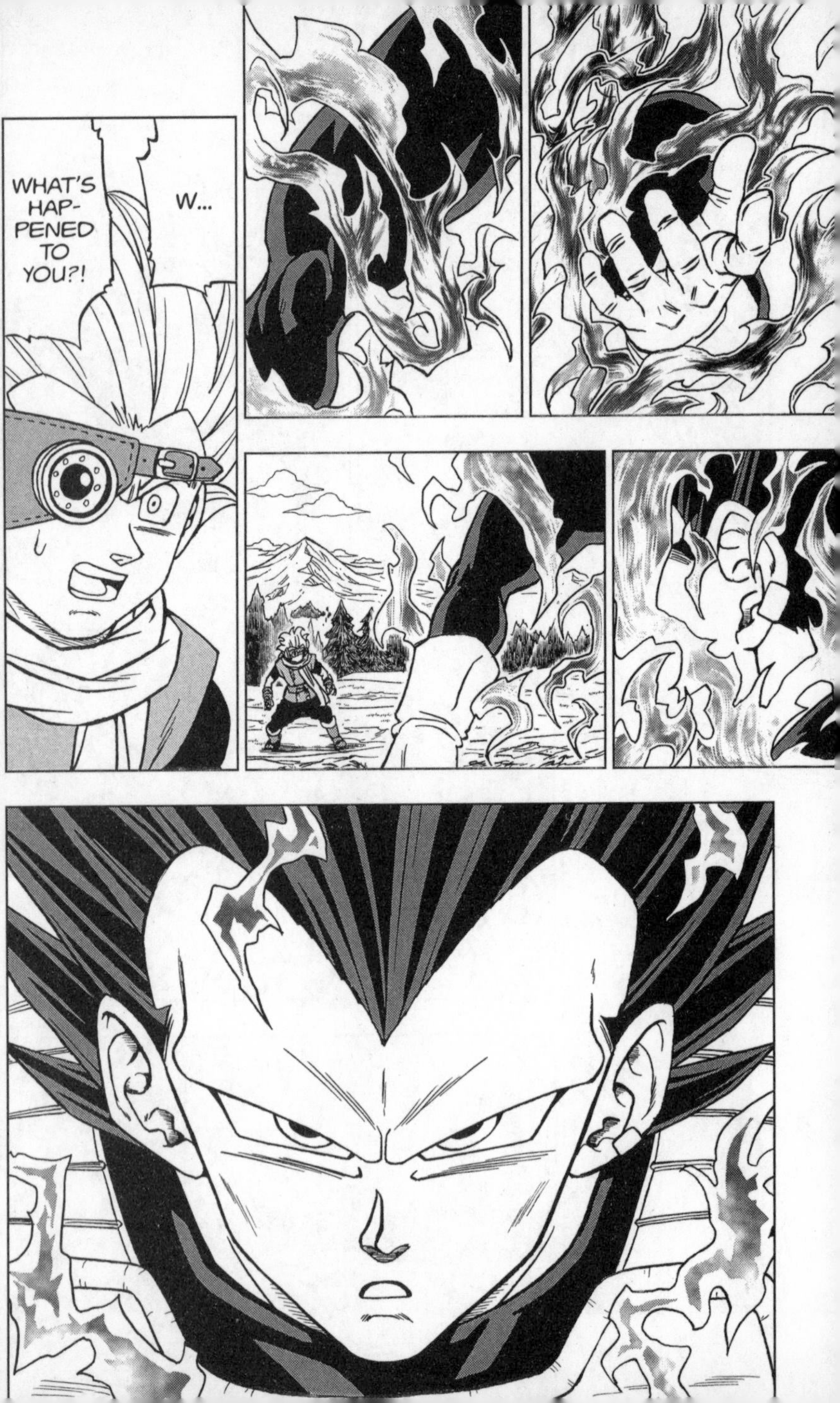
W...
WHAT'S HAPPENED TO YOU?!

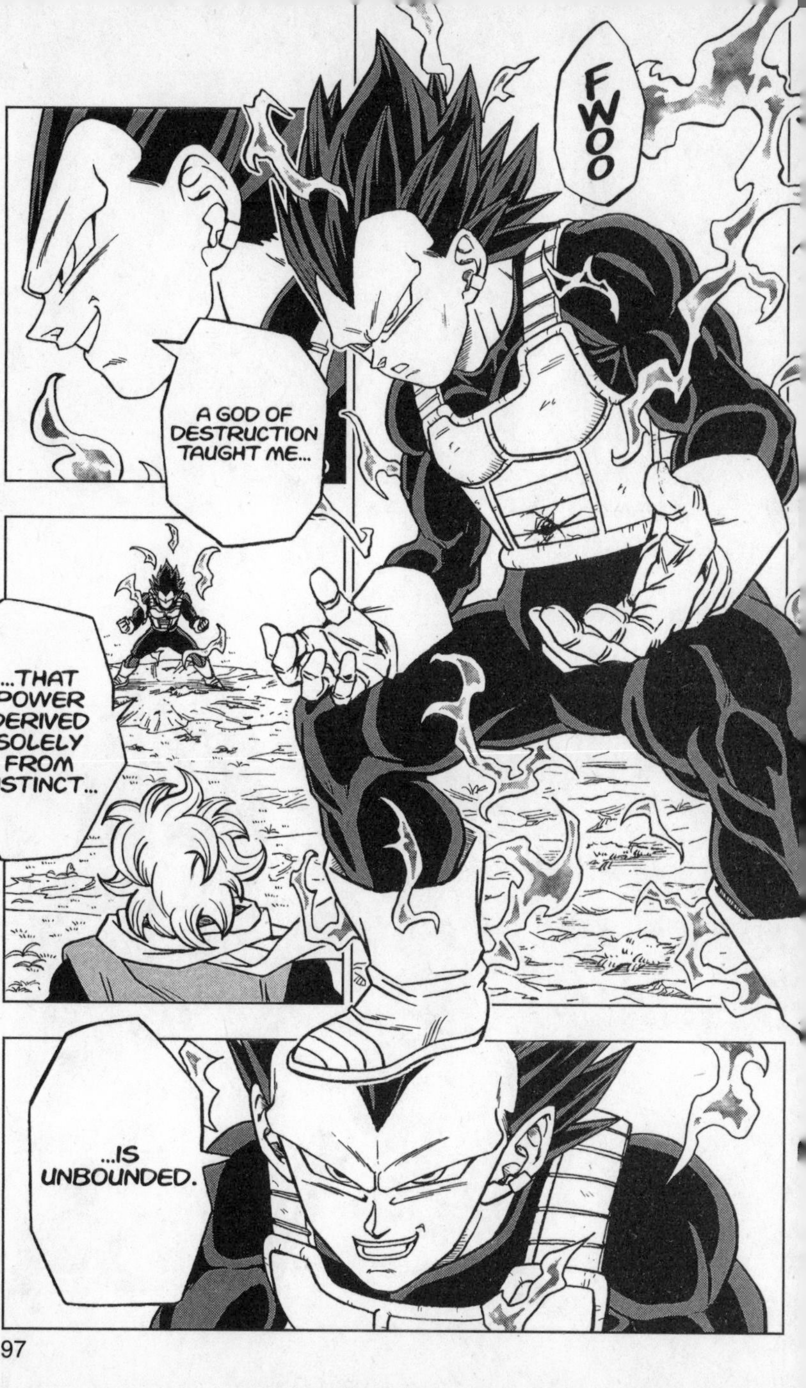
FWOO
A GOD OF DESTRUCTION TAUGHT ME...
...THAT POWER DERIVED SOLELY FROM INSTINCT...
...IS UNBOUNDED.

DRAGON BALL SUPER

CHAPTER 75: GOD OF DESTRUCTION POWER

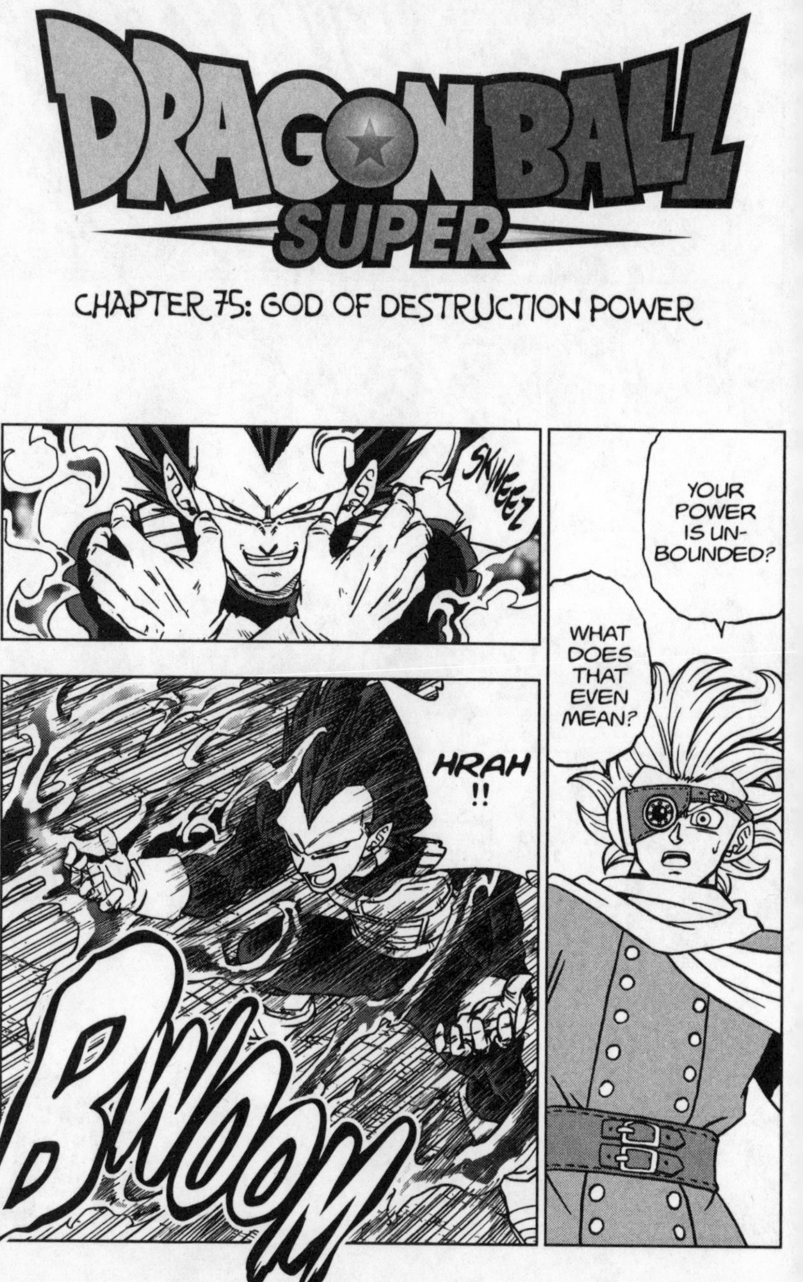
YOUR POWER IS UN-BOUNDED?
WHAT DOES THAT EVEN MEAN?
SKWEEZ
HRAH !!
BWOOM

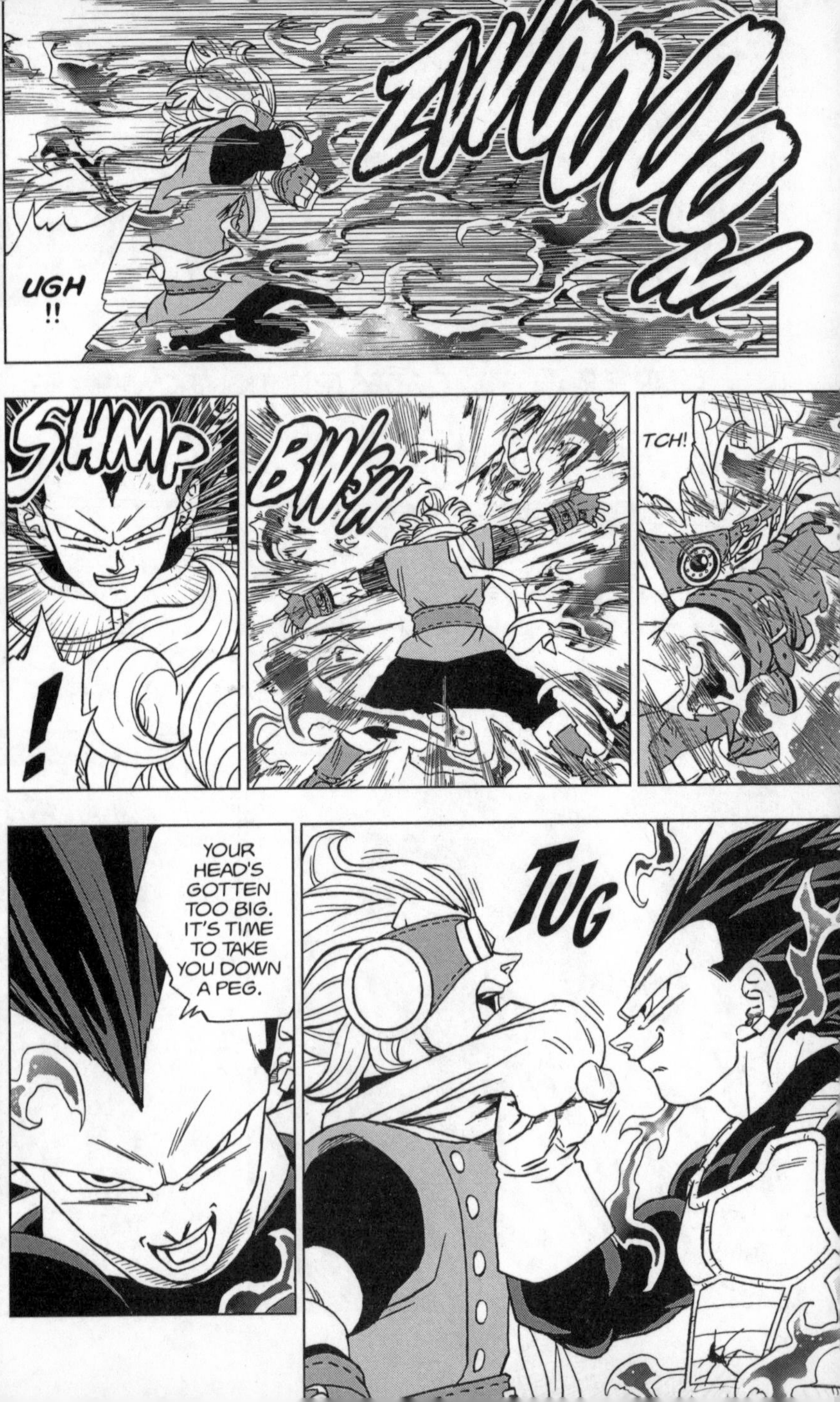
ZWOOOOM
UGH !!
TCH!
BWSH
SHMP
!
TUG
YOUR HEAD'S GOTTEN TOO BIG. IT'S TIME TO TAKE YOU DOWN A PEG.

GET READY FOR A DOSE OF MY **TOUGH** LOVE.

!

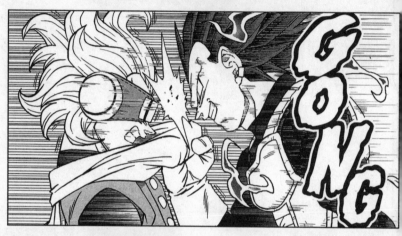

GO NG

WSHH

ACK...

SWF

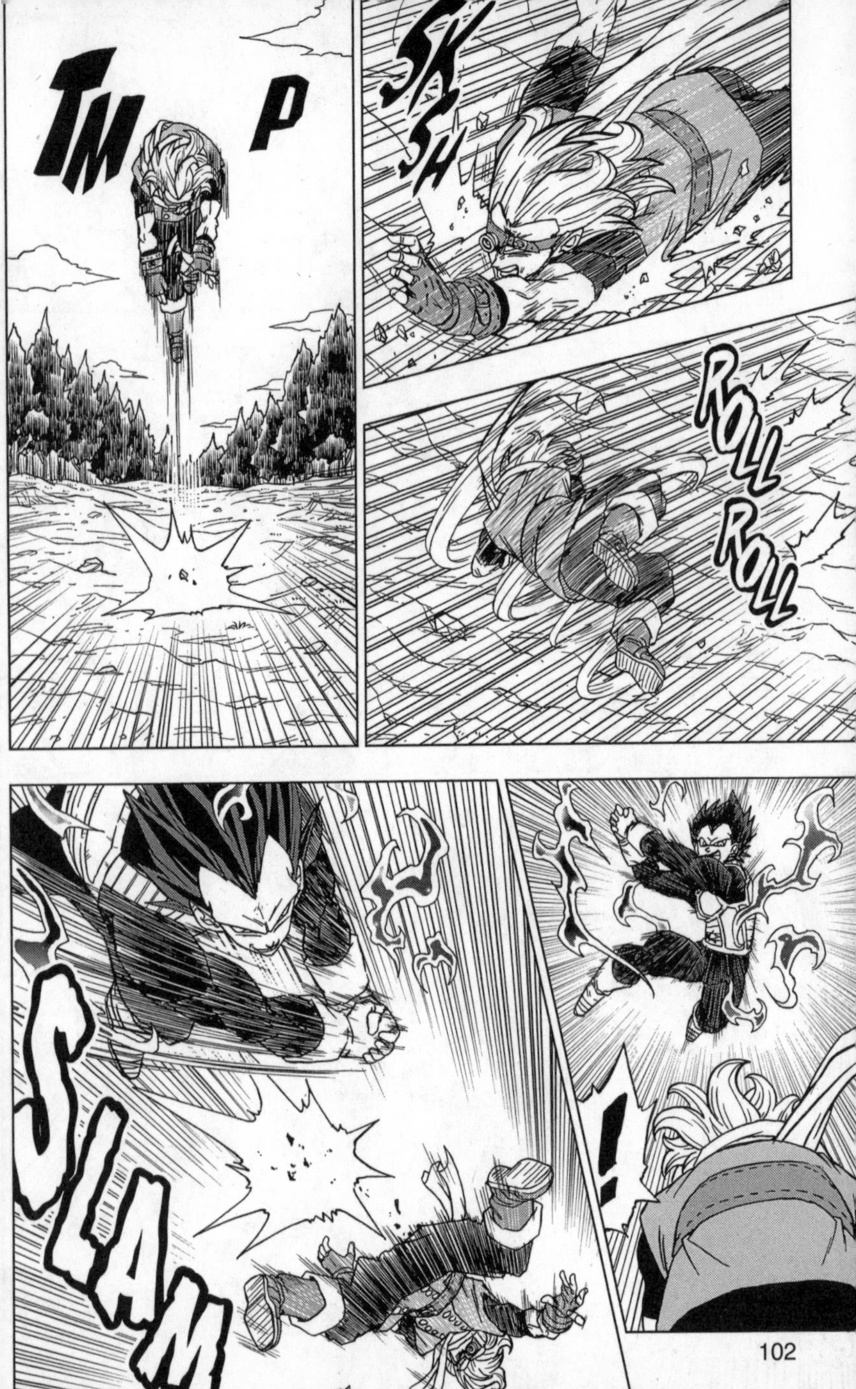
SKASH
ROLL ROLL
TMP
!
SLAM

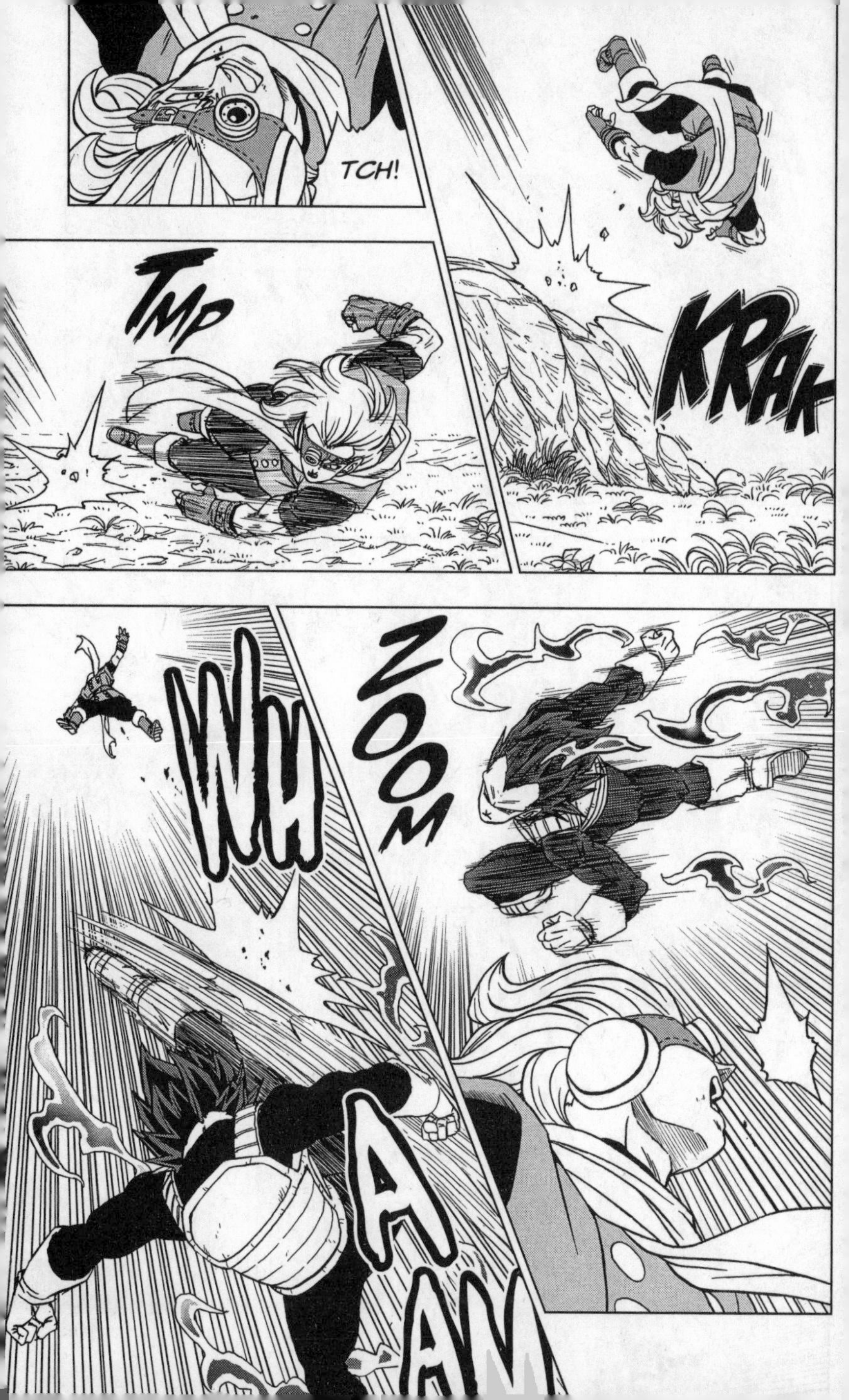
KRAK
TCH!
TMP
ZOOM
WH
A
AN

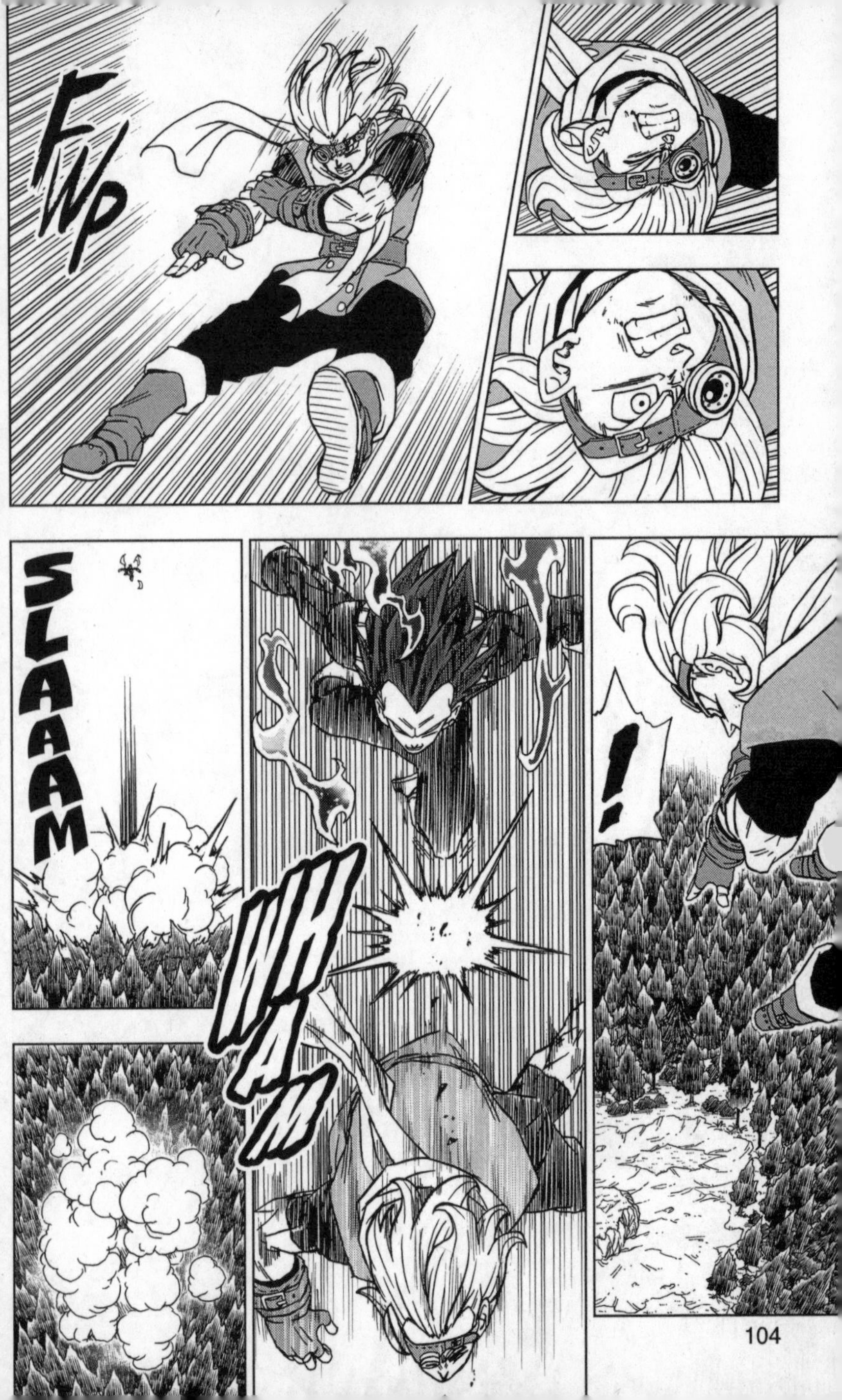
FWP
!
WHAM
SLAAAM

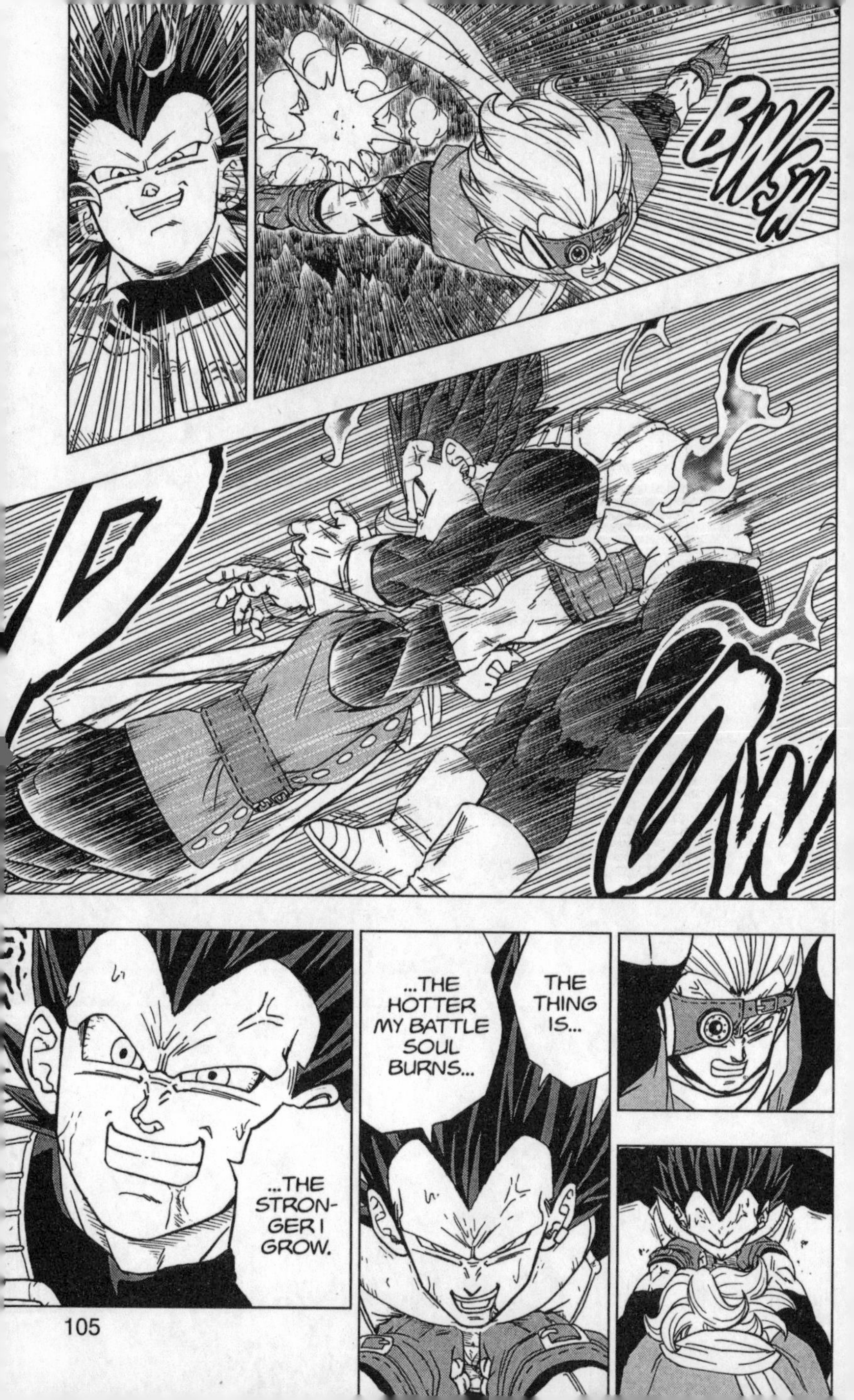
BWSH
THE THING IS...
...THE HOTTER MY BATTLE SOUL BURNS...
...THE STRONGER I GROW.

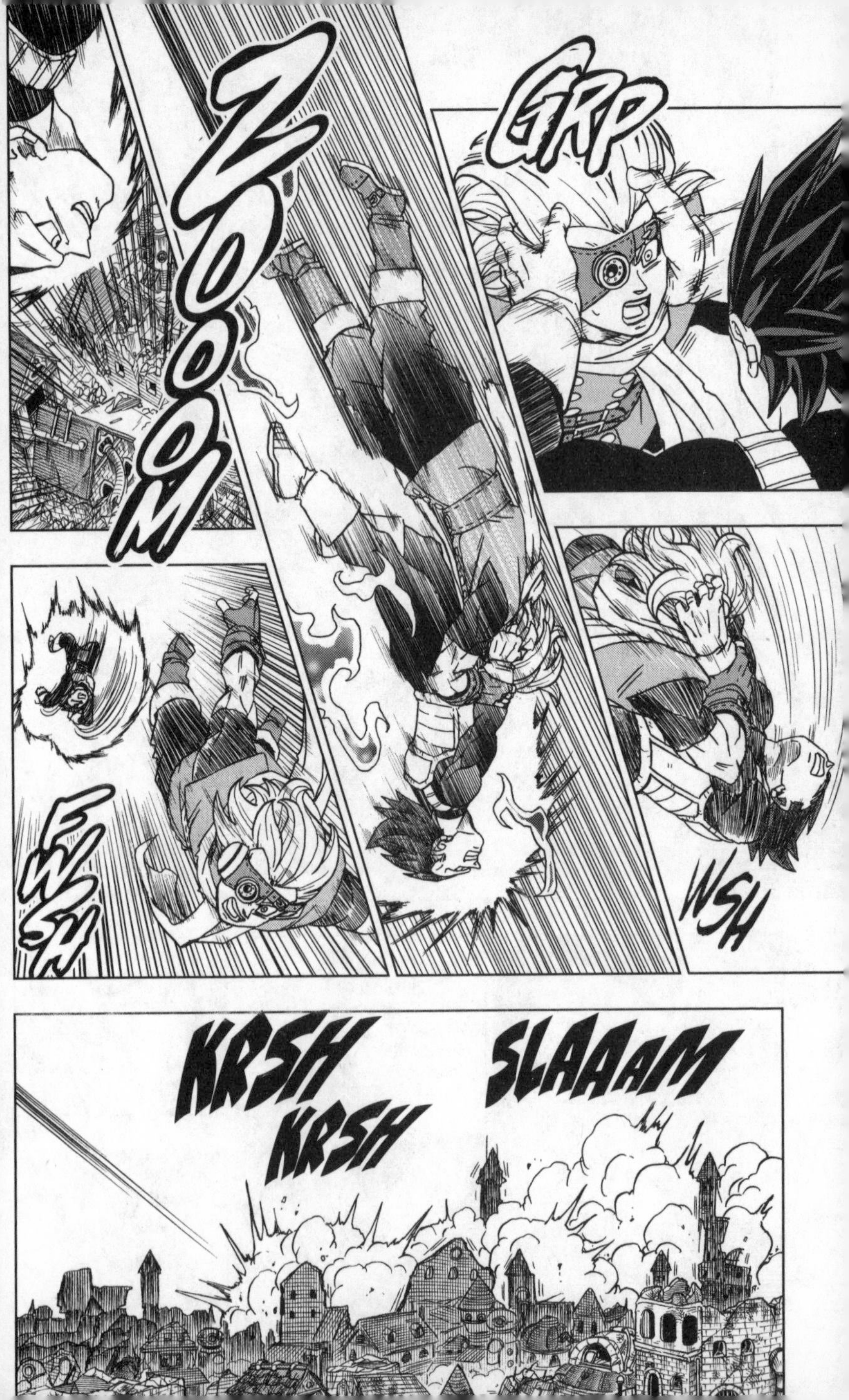
GRP
ZOOOOM
WSH
FWSH
SLAAAM
KRSH
KRSH

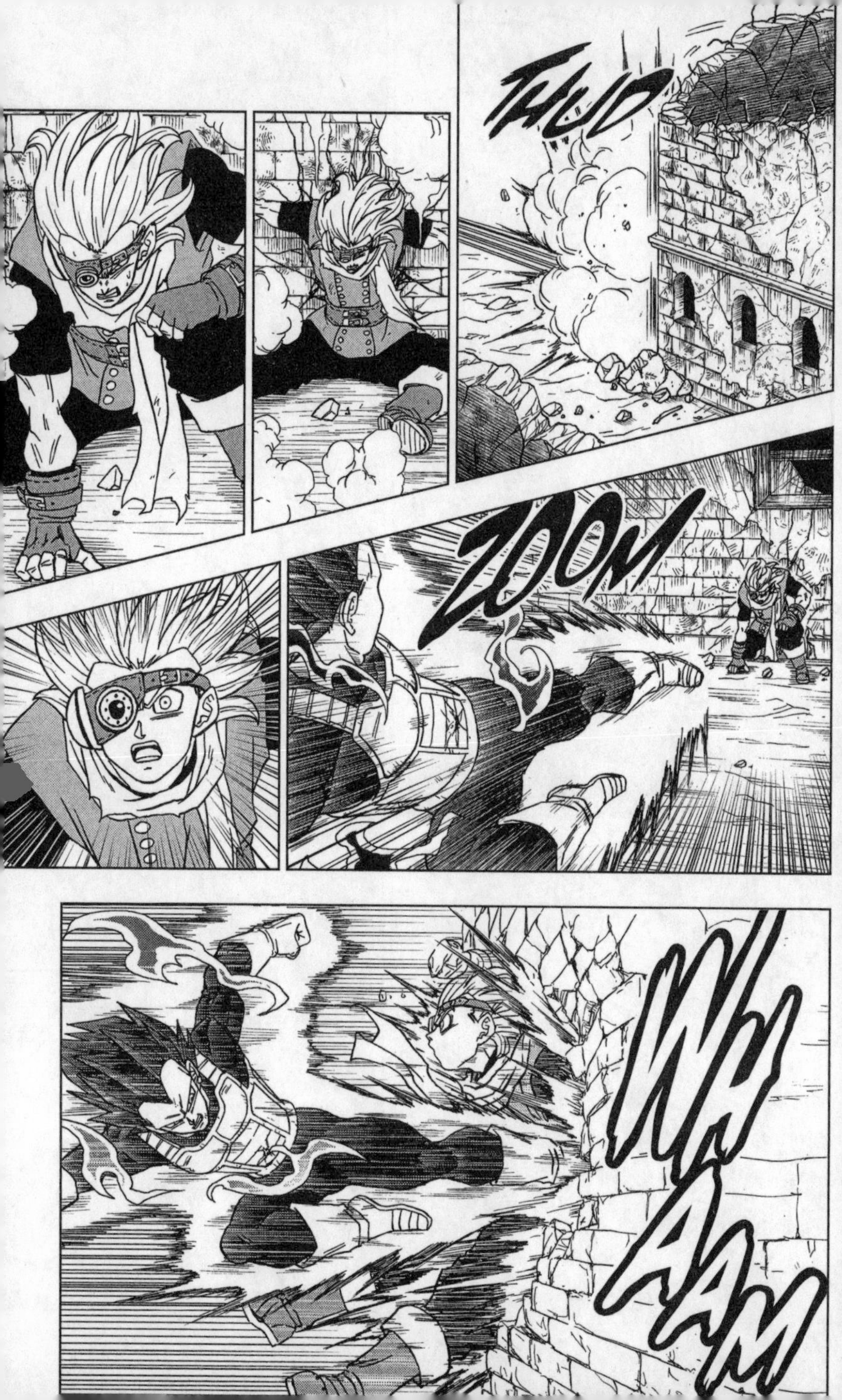
THUD
ZOOM
WHAM

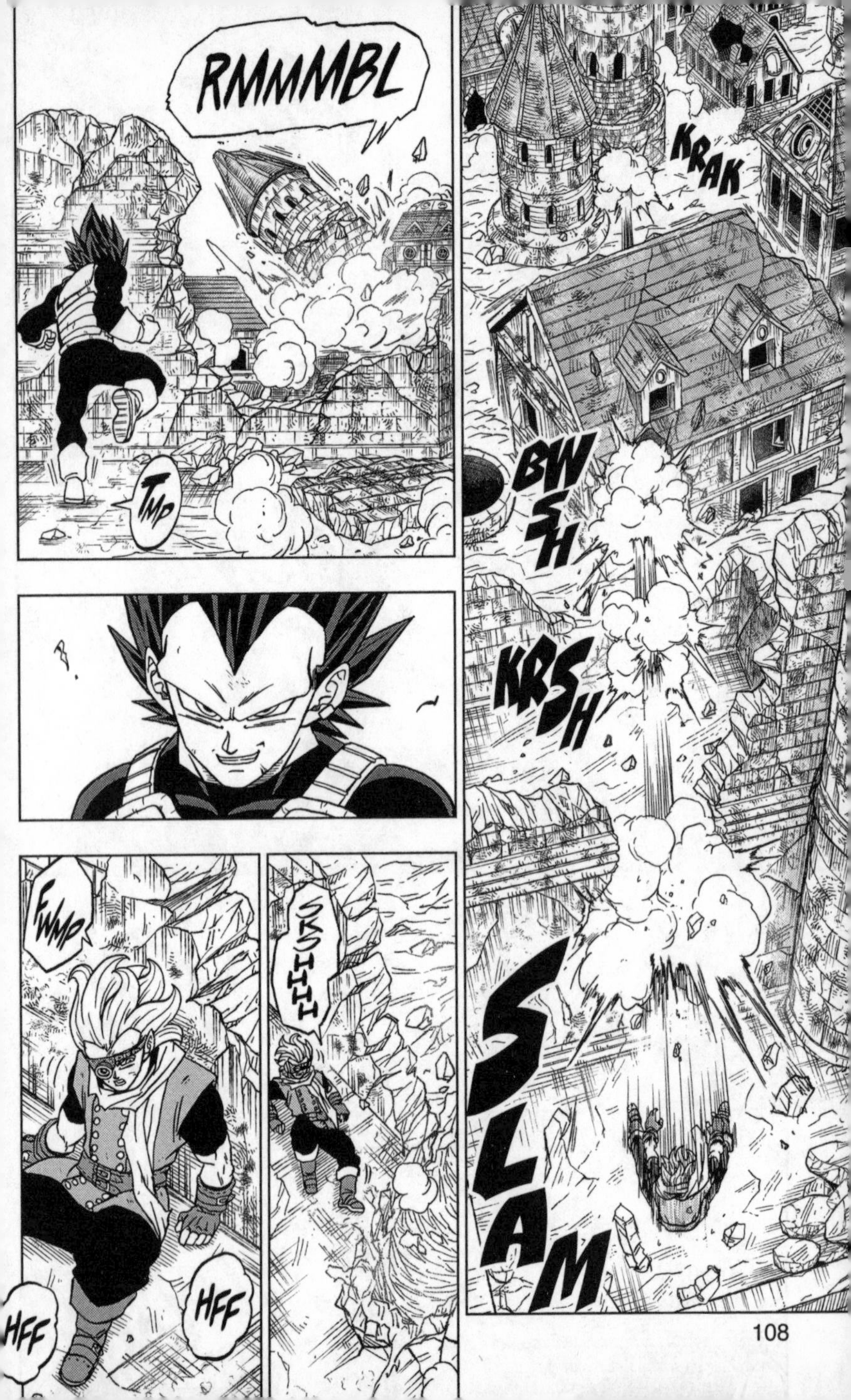
KRAK
BWSH
KRSH
SLAM
RMMMBL
TMP
SKSHHHH
FWMP
HFF
HFF

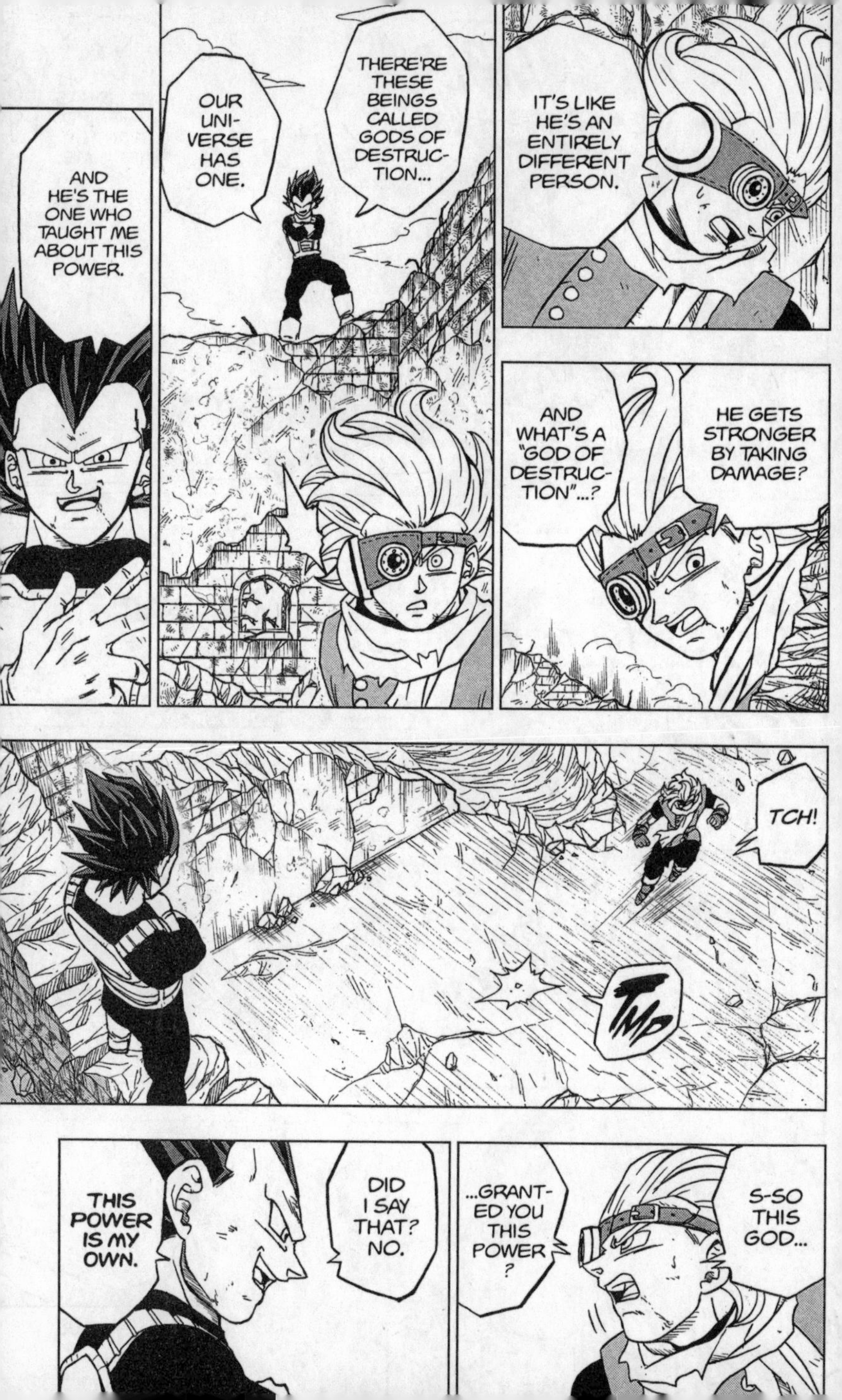
IT'S LIKE HE'S AN ENTIRELY DIFFERENT PERSON.
HE GETS STRONGER BY TAKING DAMAGE?
AND WHAT'S A "GOD OF DESTRUCTION"...?
THERE'RE THESE BEINGS CALLED GODS OF DESTRUCTION...
OUR UNIVERSE HAS ONE.
AND HE'S THE ONE WHO TAUGHT ME ABOUT THIS POWER.
TCH!
TMP
S-SO THIS GOD...
...GRANTED YOU THIS POWER?
DID I SAY THAT? NO.
THIS POWER IS MY OWN.

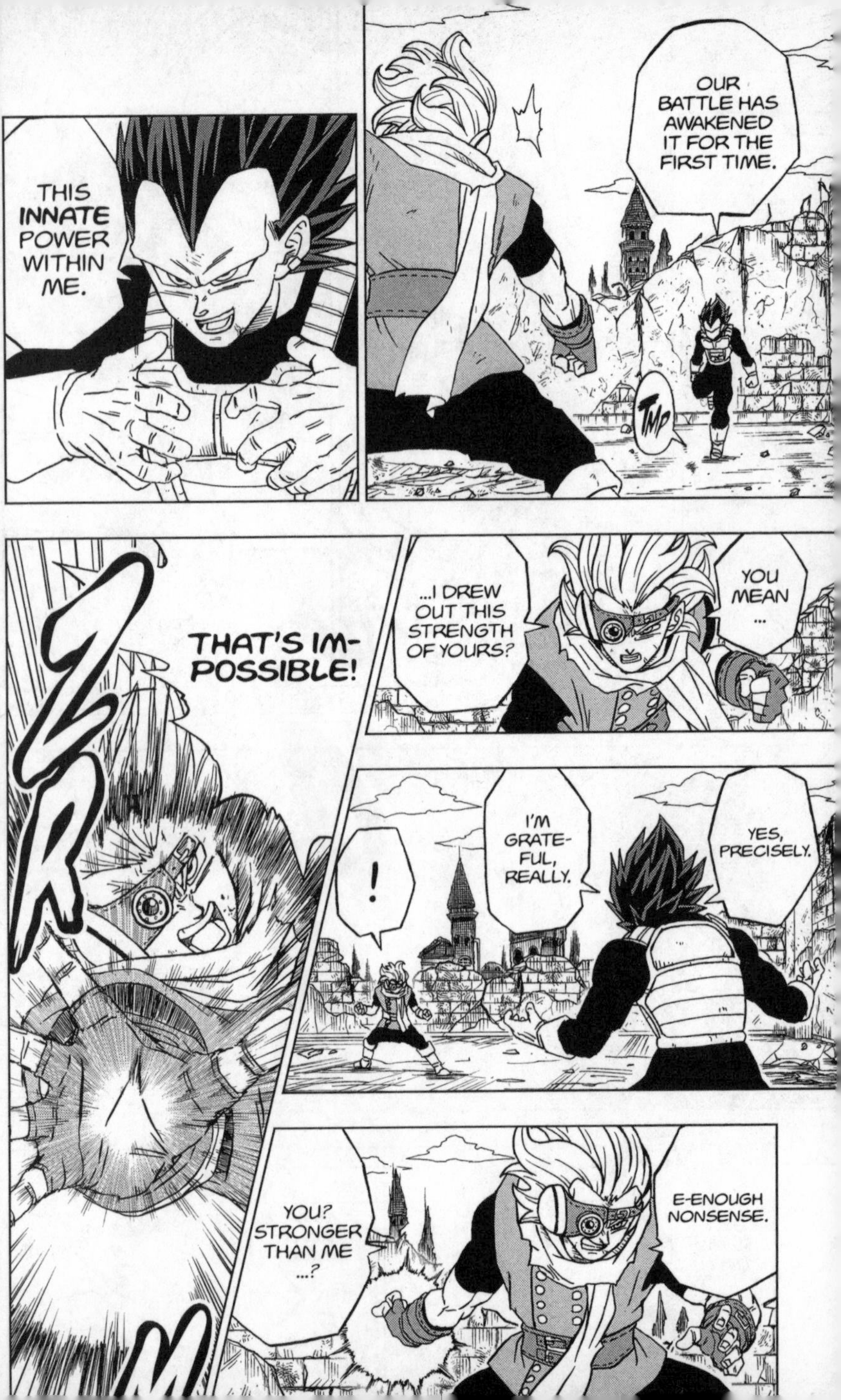

OUR BATTLE HAS AWAKENED IT FOR THE FIRST TIME.
TMP
THIS INNATE POWER WITHIN ME.
YOU MEAN ...
...I DREW OUT THIS STRENGTH OF YOURS?
YES, PRECISELY.
I'M GRATE-FUL, REALLY.
!
E-ENOUGH NONSENSE.
YOU? STRONGER THAN ME ...?
THAT'S IM-POSSIBLE!

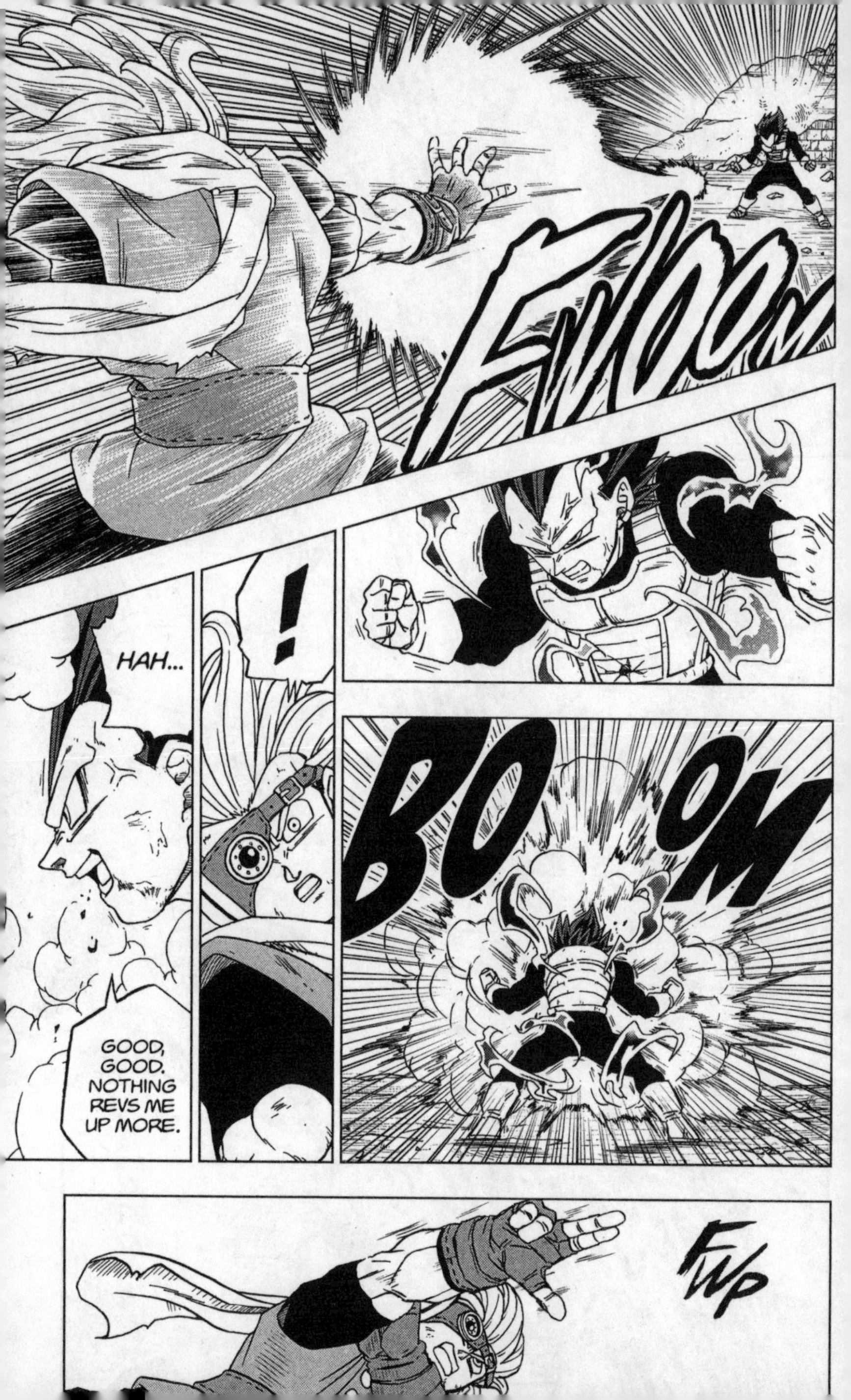
FWOOM
BOOM
!
HAH...
GOOD, GOOD. NOTHING REVS ME UP MORE.
FWP

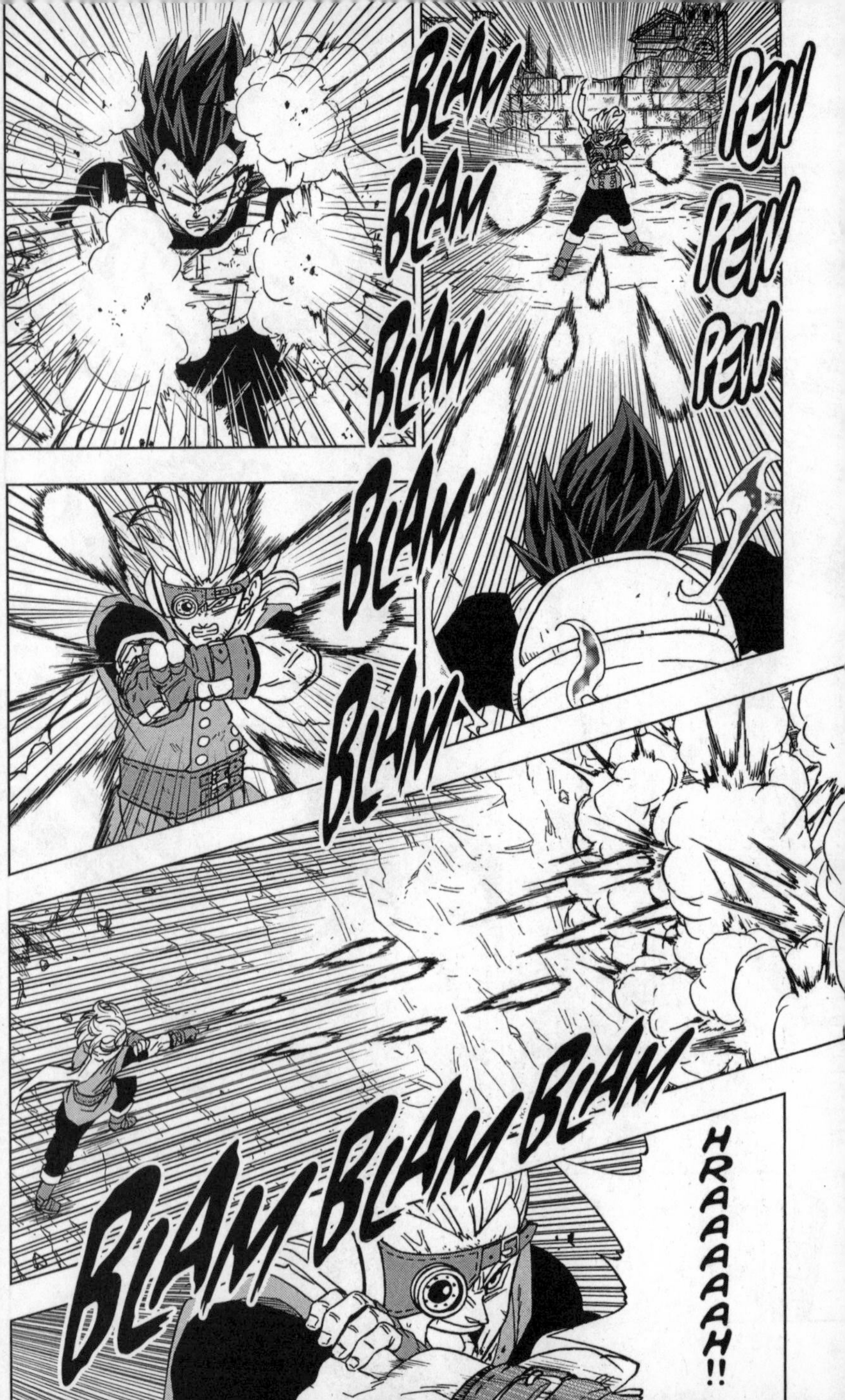
PEW PEW PEW
BLAM BLAM BLAM
BLAM
BLAM
BLAM BLAM BLAM
HRAAAAAAH!!

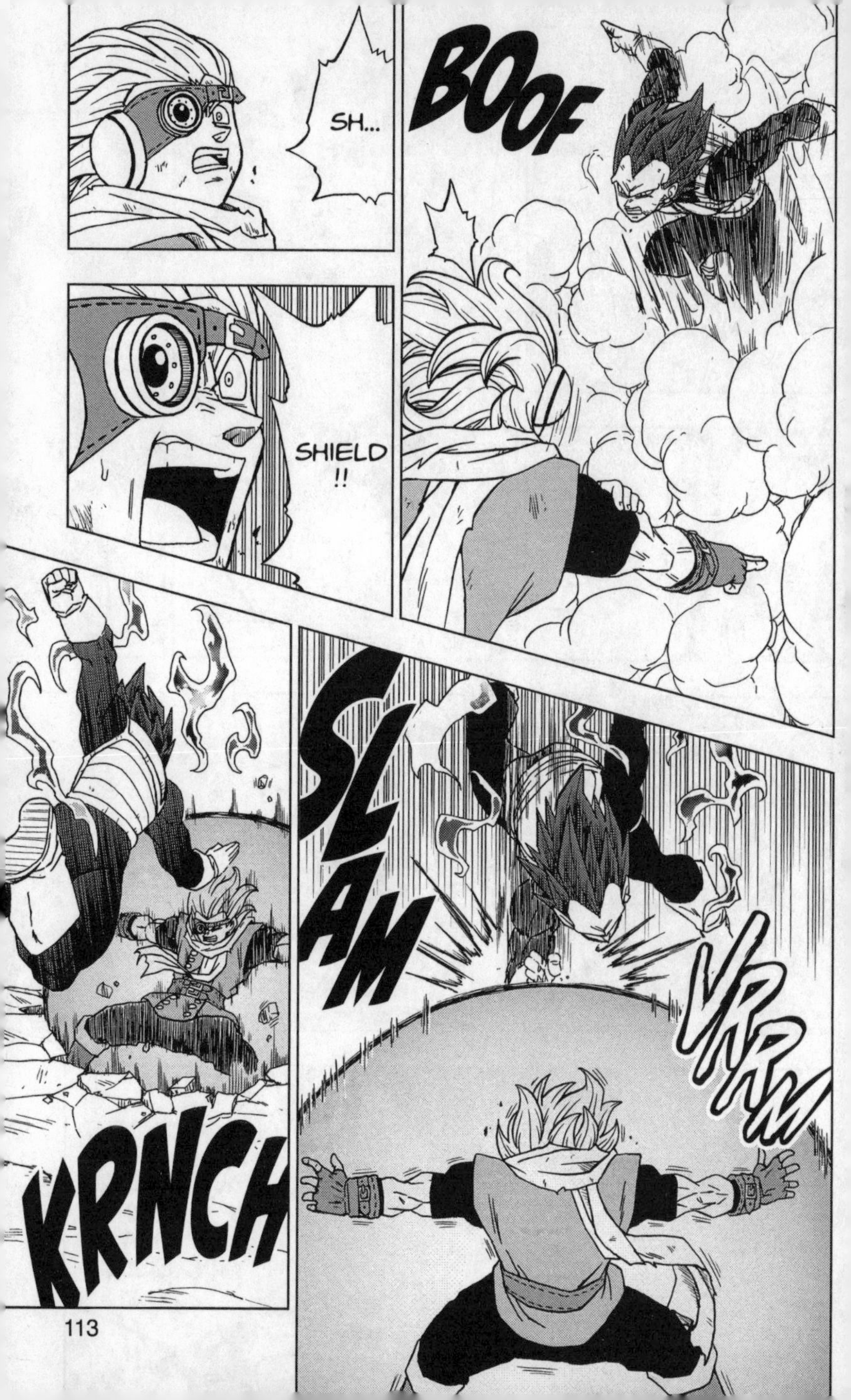
BOOF
SH...
SHIELD !!
SLAM
VRRM
KRNCH

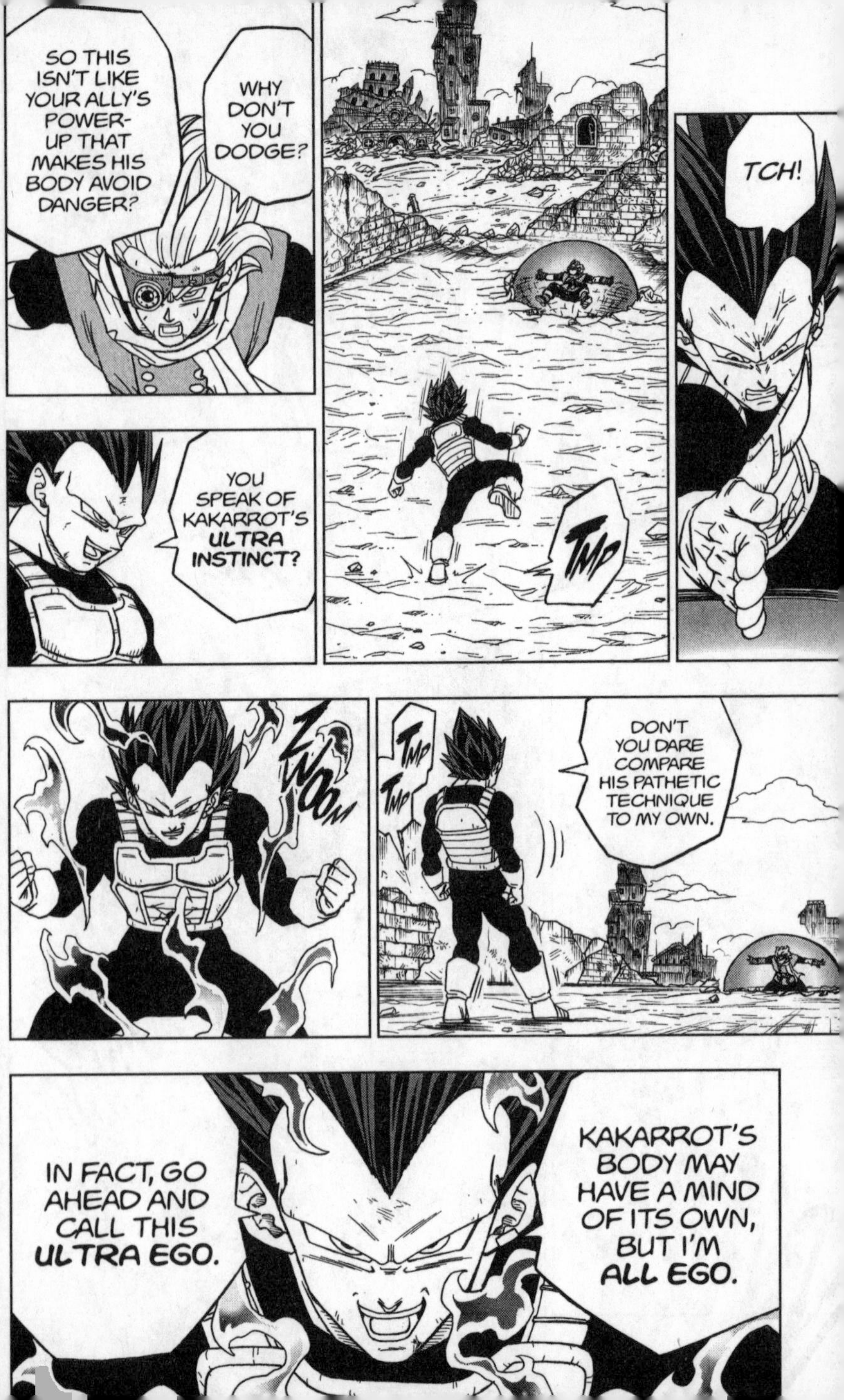
TCH!
TMP
WHY DON'T YOU DODGE?
SO THIS ISN'T LIKE YOUR ALLY'S POWER-UP THAT MAKES HIS BODY AVOID DANGER?
YOU SPEAK OF KAKARROT'S **ULTRA INSTINCT**?
DON'T YOU DARE COMPARE HIS PATHETIC TECHNIQUE TO MY OWN.
TMP
TMP
ZWOOM
KAKARROT'S BODY MAY HAVE A MIND OF ITS OWN, BUT I'M **ALL EGO**.
IN FACT, GO AHEAD AND CALL THIS **ULTRA EGO**.

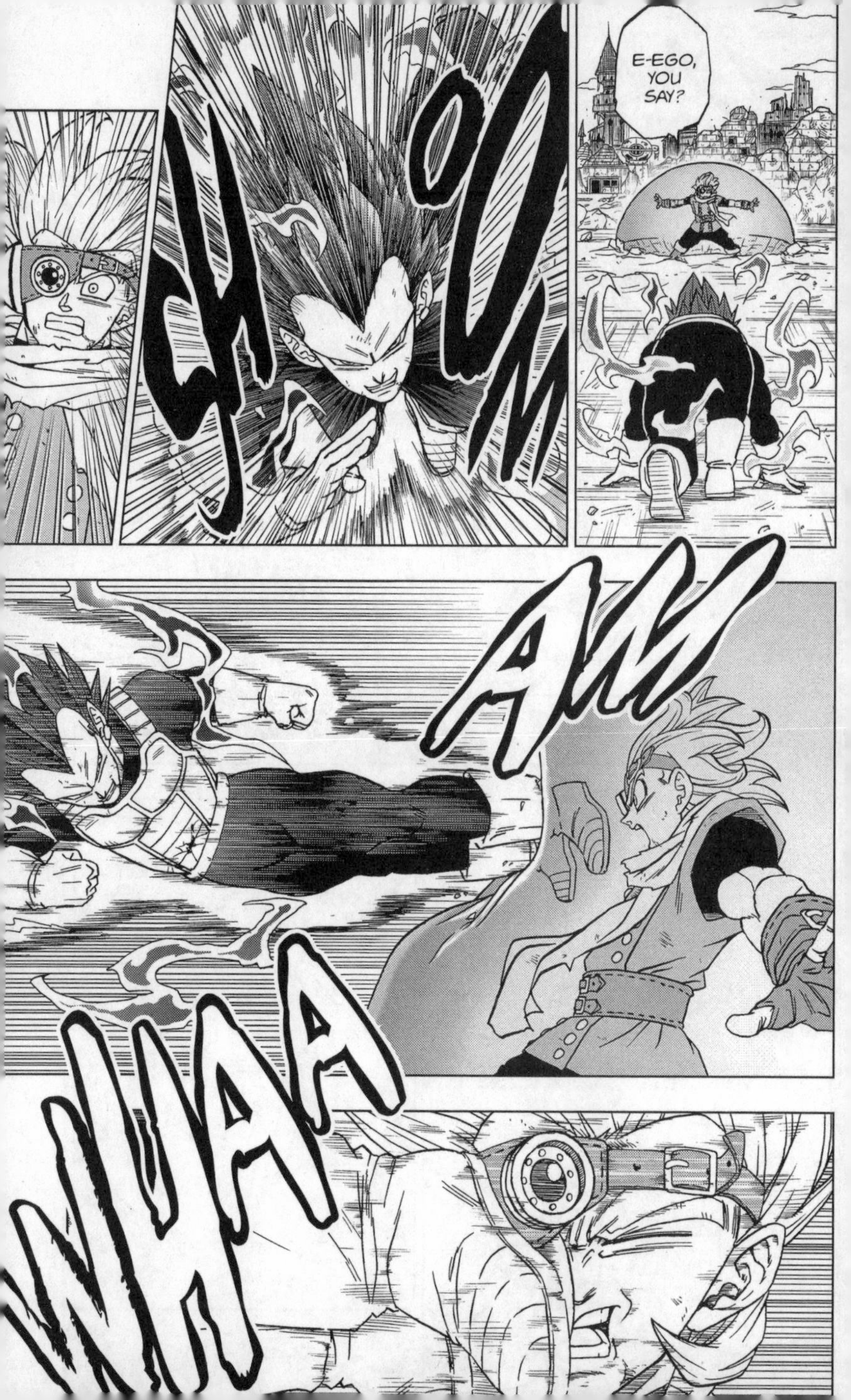
E-EGO, YOU SAY?
WHAAAM

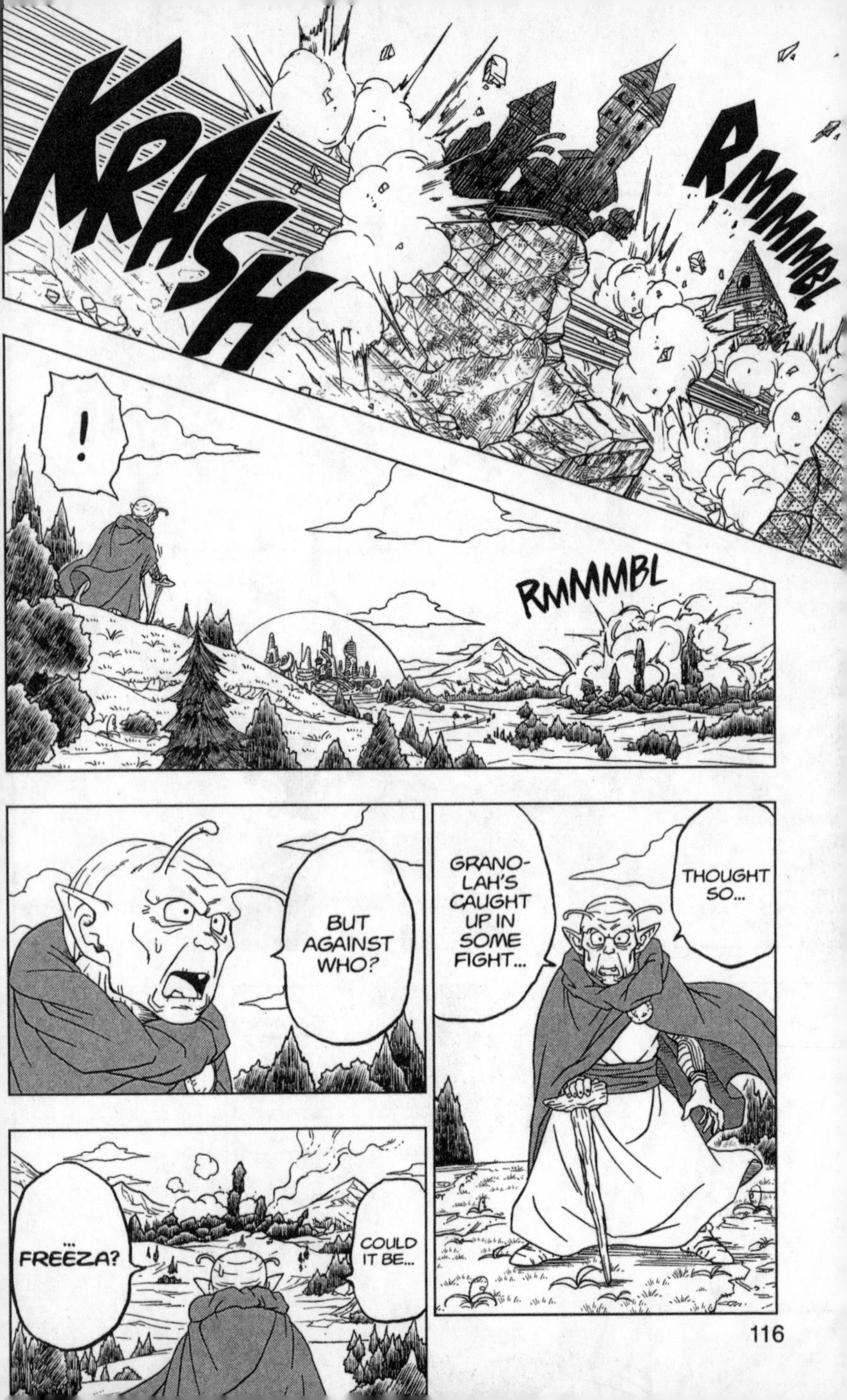
RMMMMBL!
KRASH
!
RMMMBL
THOUGHT SO...
GRANO-LAH'S CAUGHT UP IN SOME FIGHT...
BUT AGAINST WHO?
COULD IT BE...
...FREEZA?

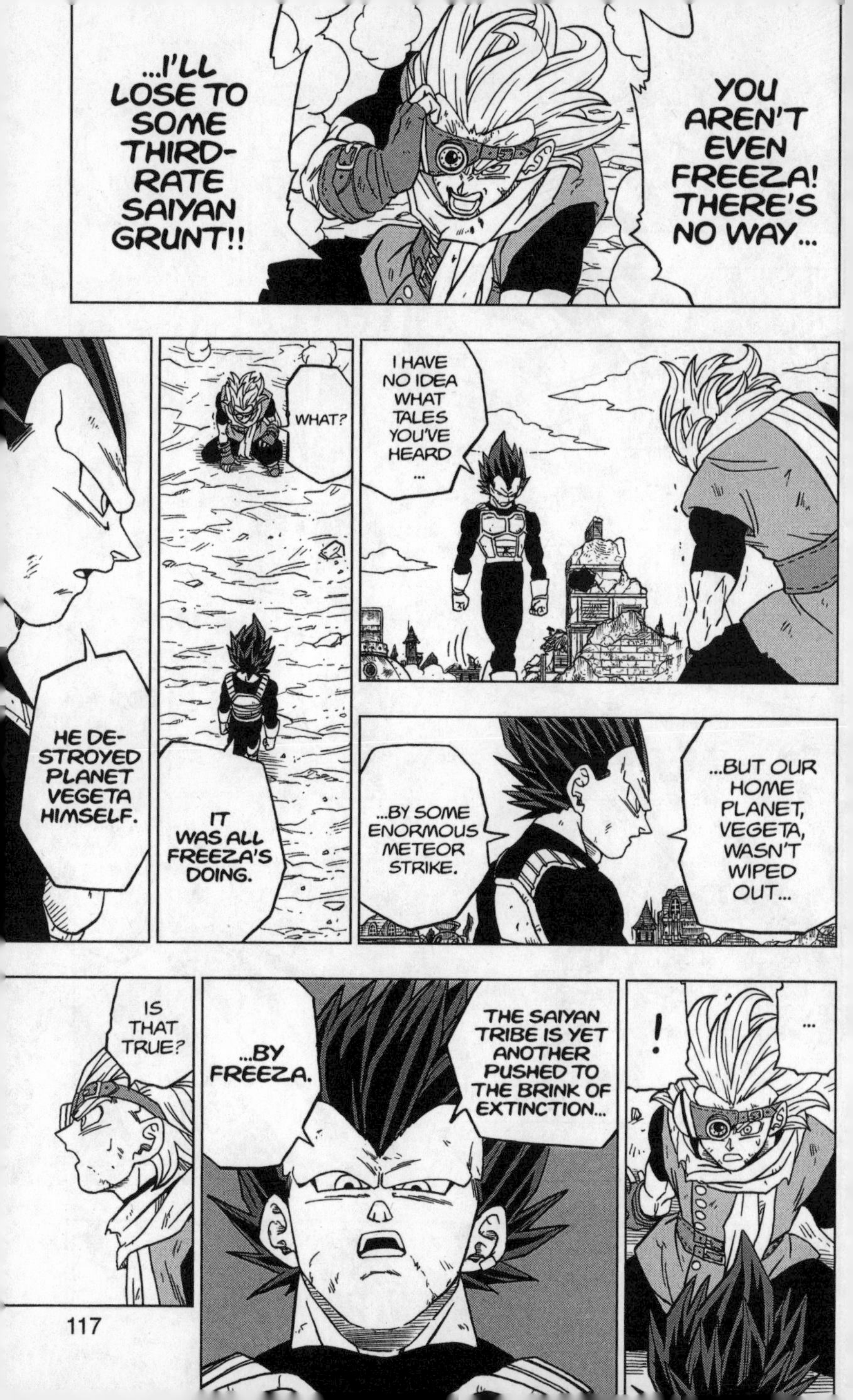
YOU AREN'T EVEN FREEZA! THERE'S NO WAY...
...I'LL LOSE TO SOME THIRD-RATE SAIYAN GRUNT!!
I HAVE NO IDEA WHAT TALES YOU'VE HEARD...
...BUT OUR HOME PLANET, VEGETA, WASN'T WIPED OUT...
...BY SOME ENORMOUS METEOR STRIKE.
WHAT?
IT WAS ALL FREEZA'S DOING.
HE DE-STROYED PLANET VEGETA HIMSELF.
...
!
THE SAIYAN TRIBE IS YET ANOTHER PUSHED TO THE BRINK OF EXTINCTION...
...BY FREEZA.
IS THAT TRUE?

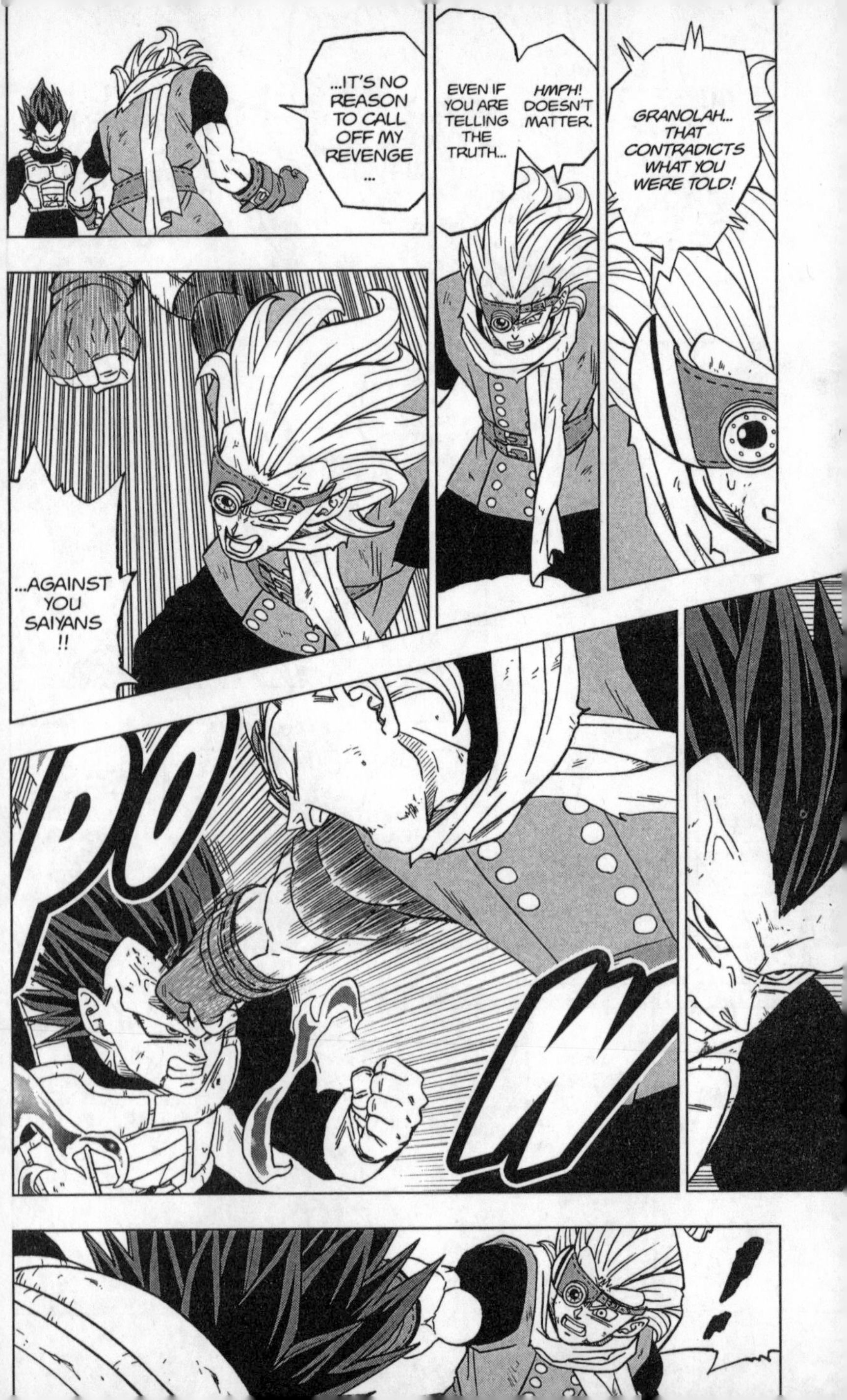
GRANOLAH... THAT CONTRADICTS WHAT YOU WERE TOLD!
HMPH! DOESN'T MATTER.
EVEN IF YOU ARE TELLING THE TRUTH...
...IT'S NO REASON TO CALL OFF MY REVENGE ...
...AGAINST YOU SAIYANS !!
!

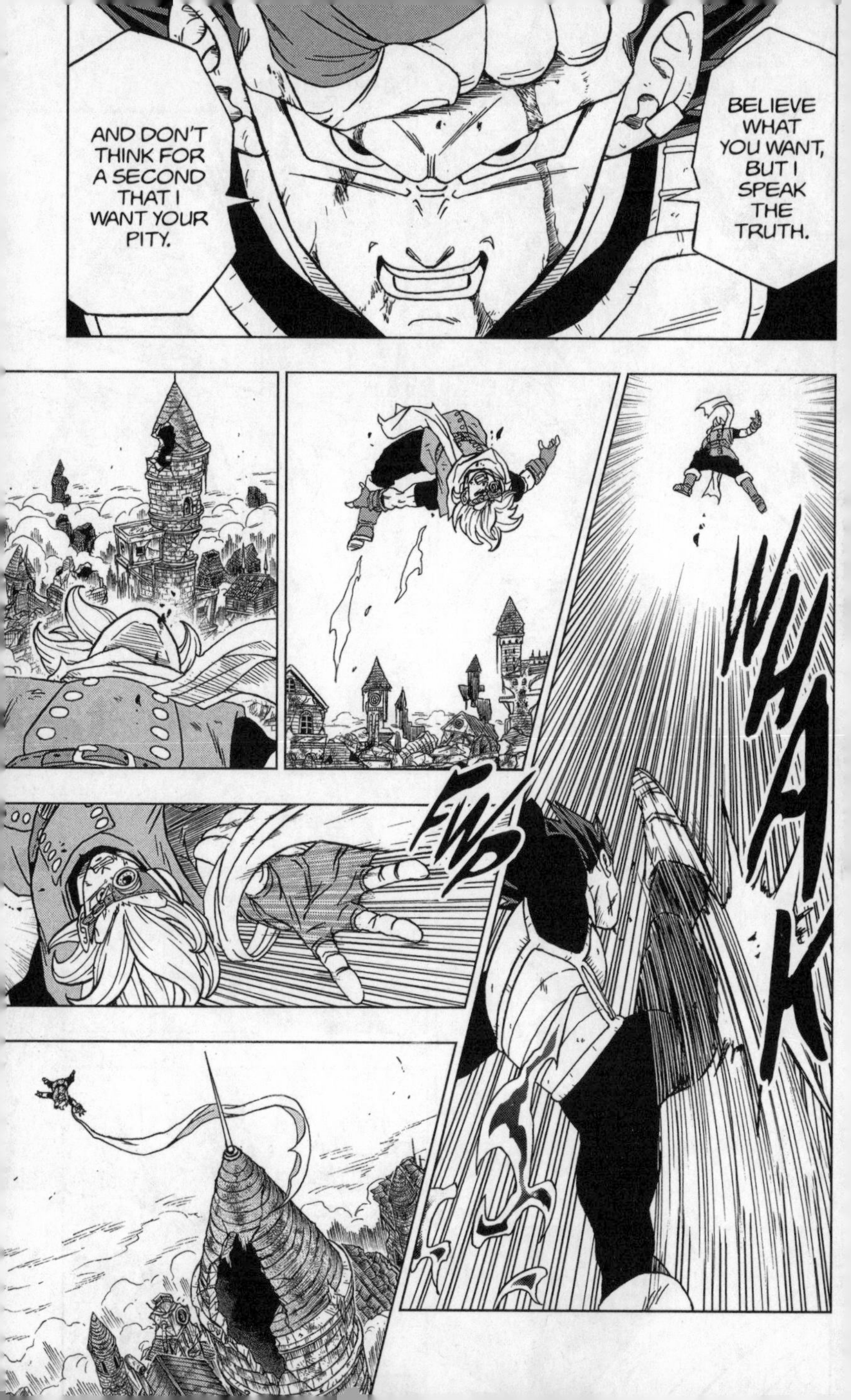
BELIEVE WHAT YOU WANT, BUT I SPEAK THE TRUTH.
AND DON'T THINK FOR A SECOND THAT I WANT YOUR PITY.
WHAK
FWP

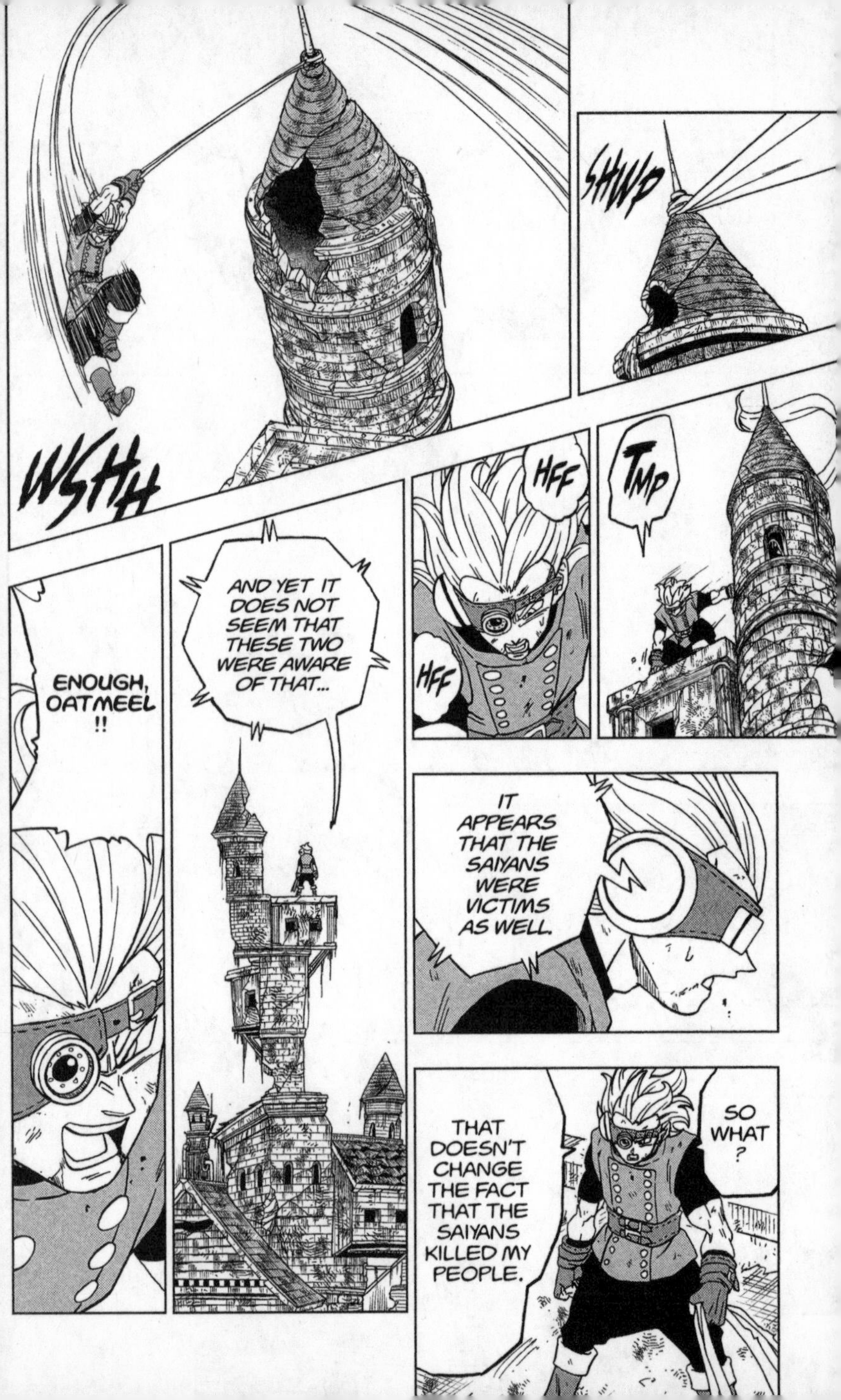
SHWP
WSHH
TMP
HFF
HFF
IT APPEARS THAT THE SAIYANS WERE VICTIMS AS WELL.
AND YET IT DOES NOT SEEM THAT THESE TWO WERE AWARE OF THAT...
SO WHAT?
THAT DOESN'T CHANGE THE FACT THAT THE SAIYANS KILLED MY PEOPLE.
ENOUGH, OATMEEL!!

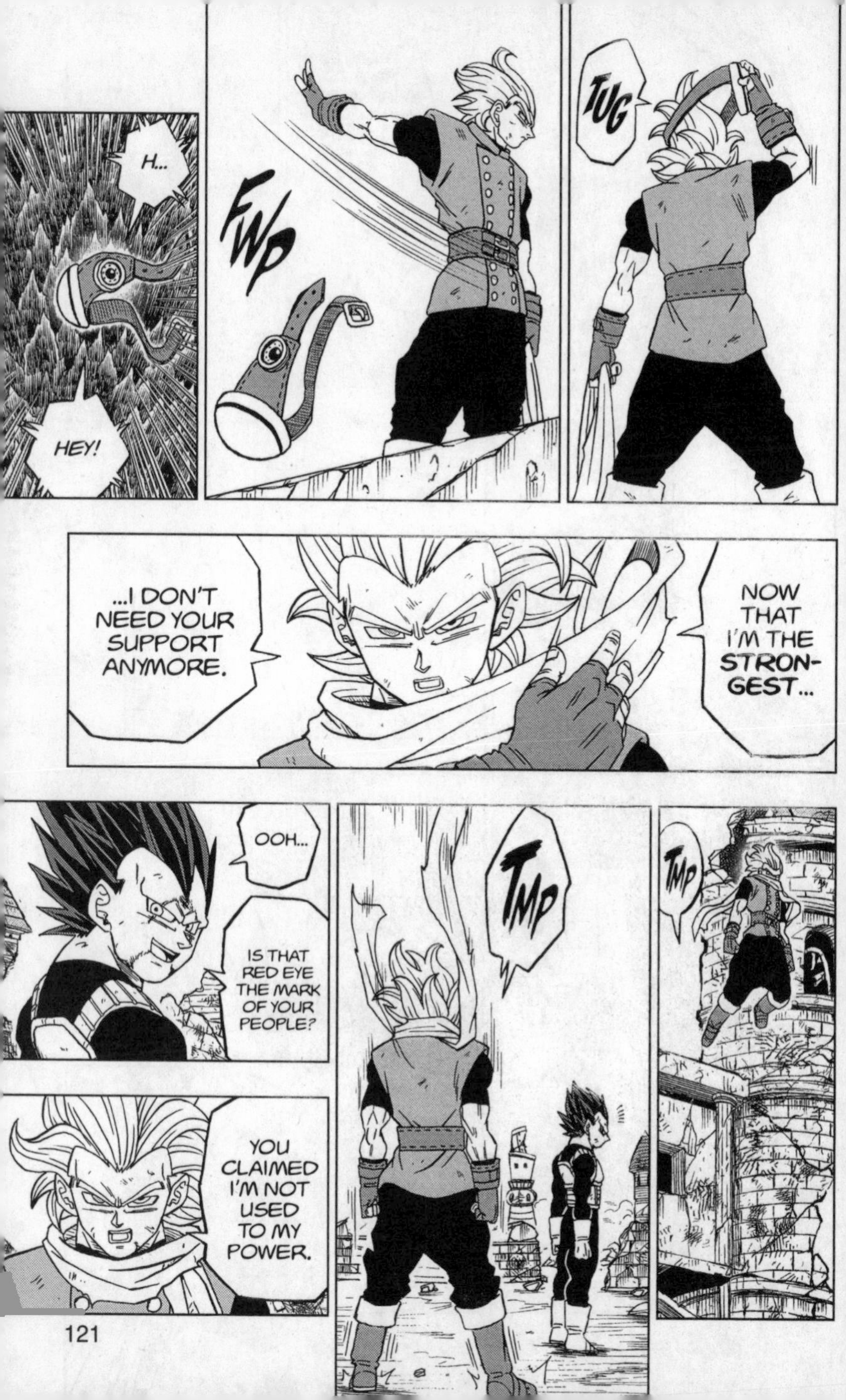

TUG
FWP
H...
HEY!
NOW THAT I'M THE STRONG-GEST...
...I DON'T NEED YOUR SUPPORT ANYMORE.
TMP
TMP
OOH...
IS THAT RED EYE THE MARK OF YOUR PEOPLE?
YOU CLAIMED I'M NOT USED TO MY POWER.

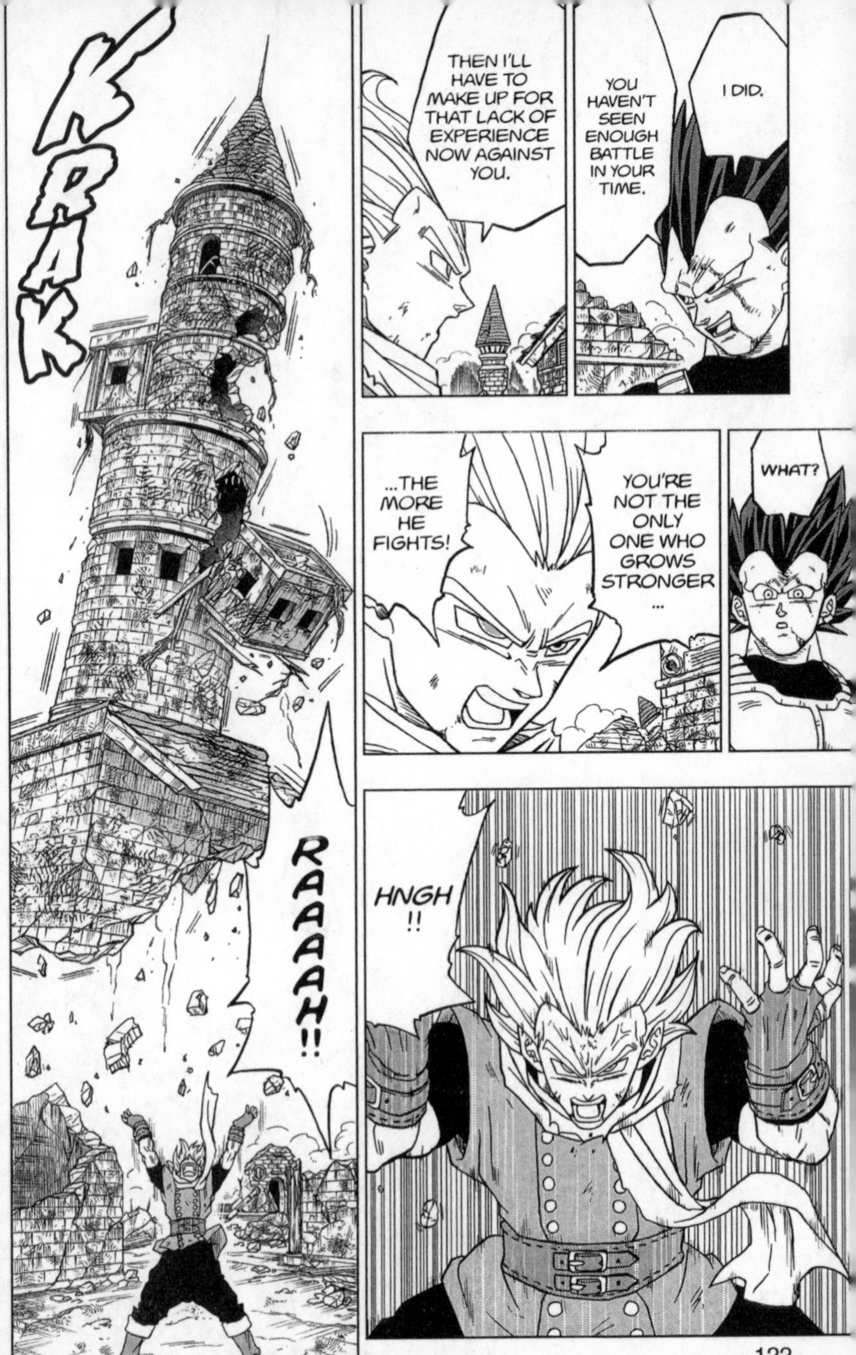
I DID.
YOU HAVEN'T SEEN ENOUGH BATTLE IN YOUR TIME.
THEN I'LL HAVE TO MAKE UP FOR THAT LACK OF EXPERIENCE NOW AGAINST YOU.
WHAT?
YOU'RE NOT THE ONLY ONE WHO GROWS STRONGER ...
...THE MORE HE FIGHTS!
HNGH !!
KRAK
RAAAAAH!!

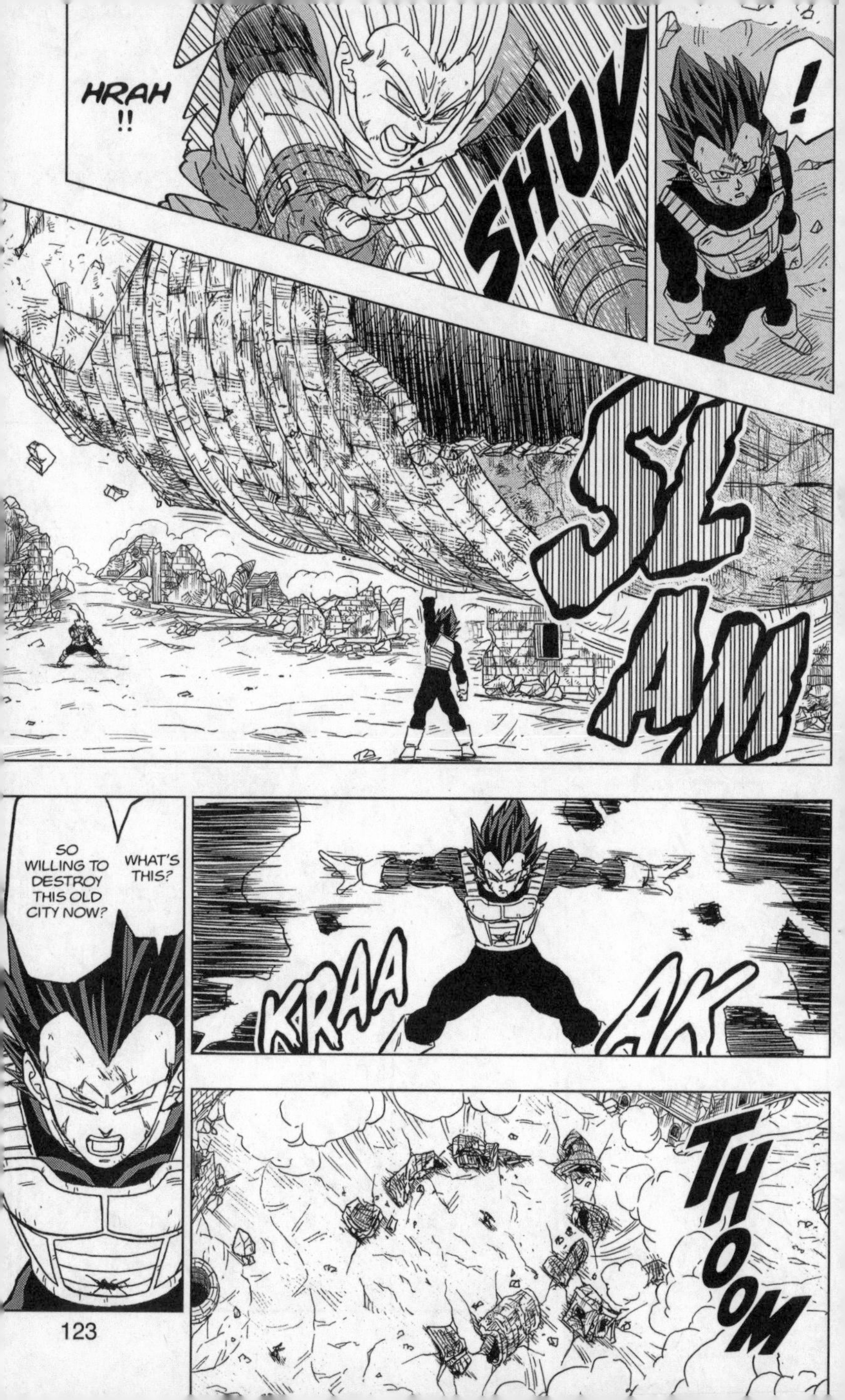
!
HRAH !!
SHUV
SLAM
KRAA AK
THOOM
WHAT'S THIS?
SO WILLING TO DESTROY THIS OLD CITY NOW?

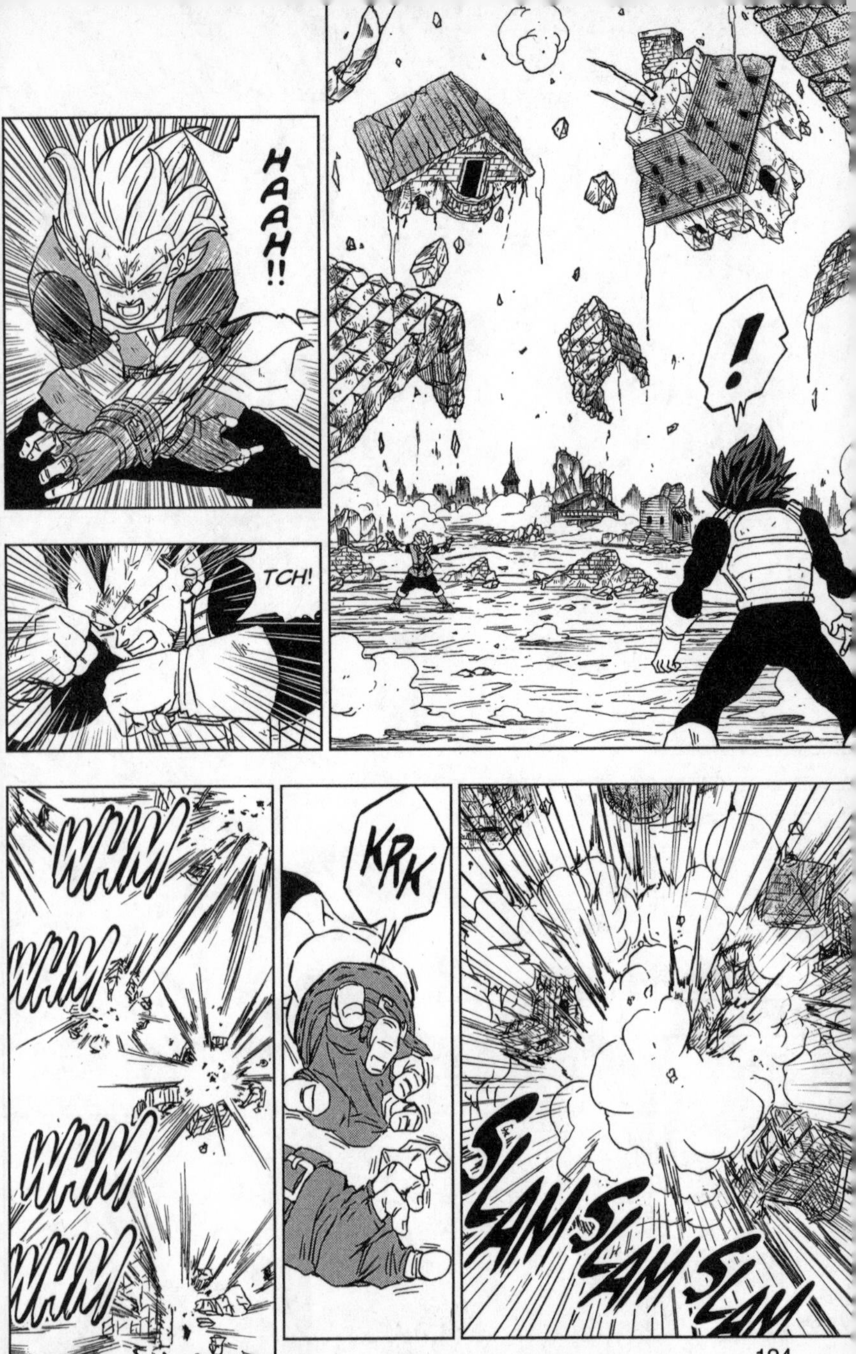
!
HAAAH!!
TCH!
SLAM SLAM SLAM
KRK
WHM
WHM
WHM
WHM

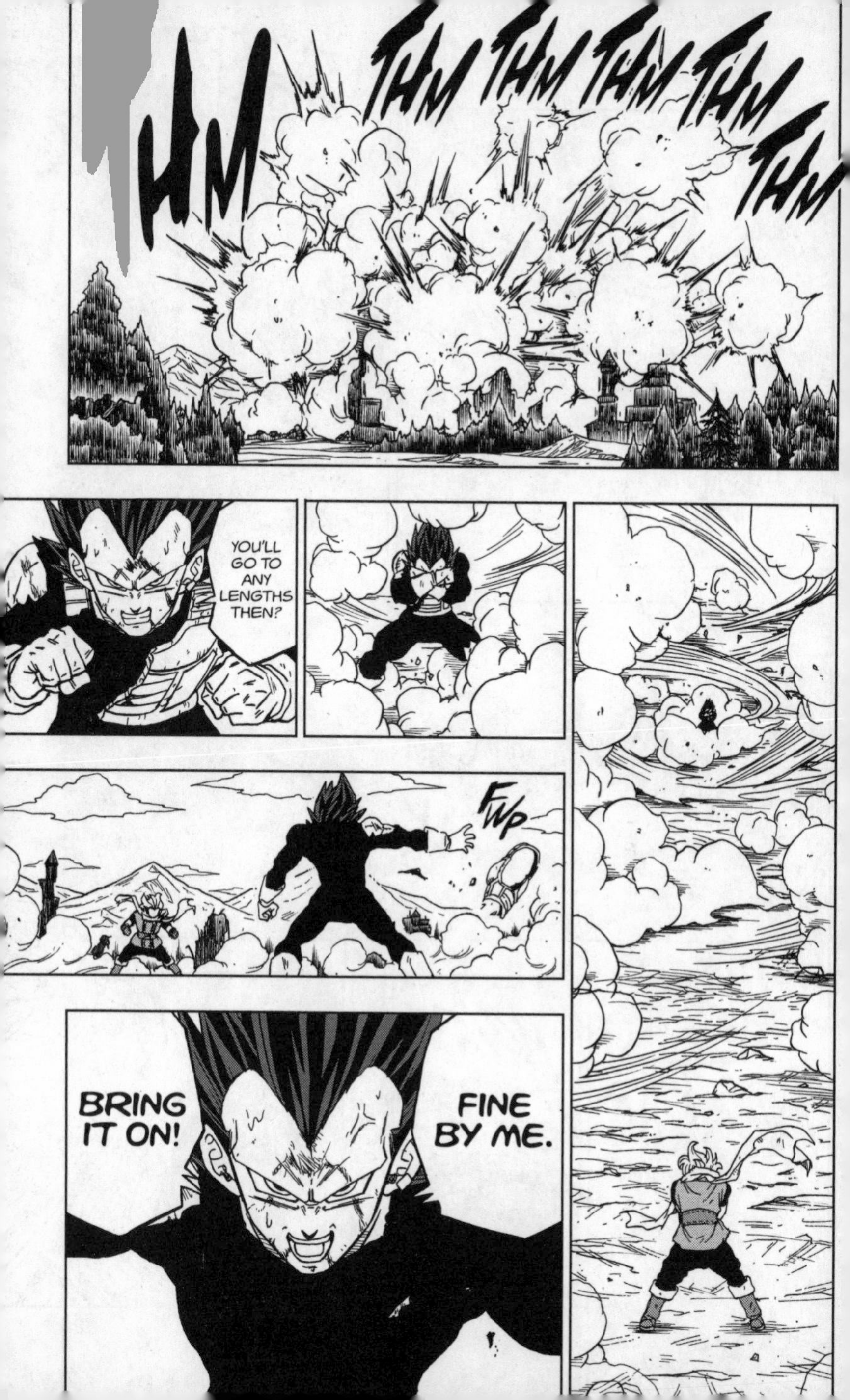

THM THM THM THM THM THM
YOU'LL GO TO ANY LENGTHS THEN?
FWP
FINE BY ME.
BRING IT ON!

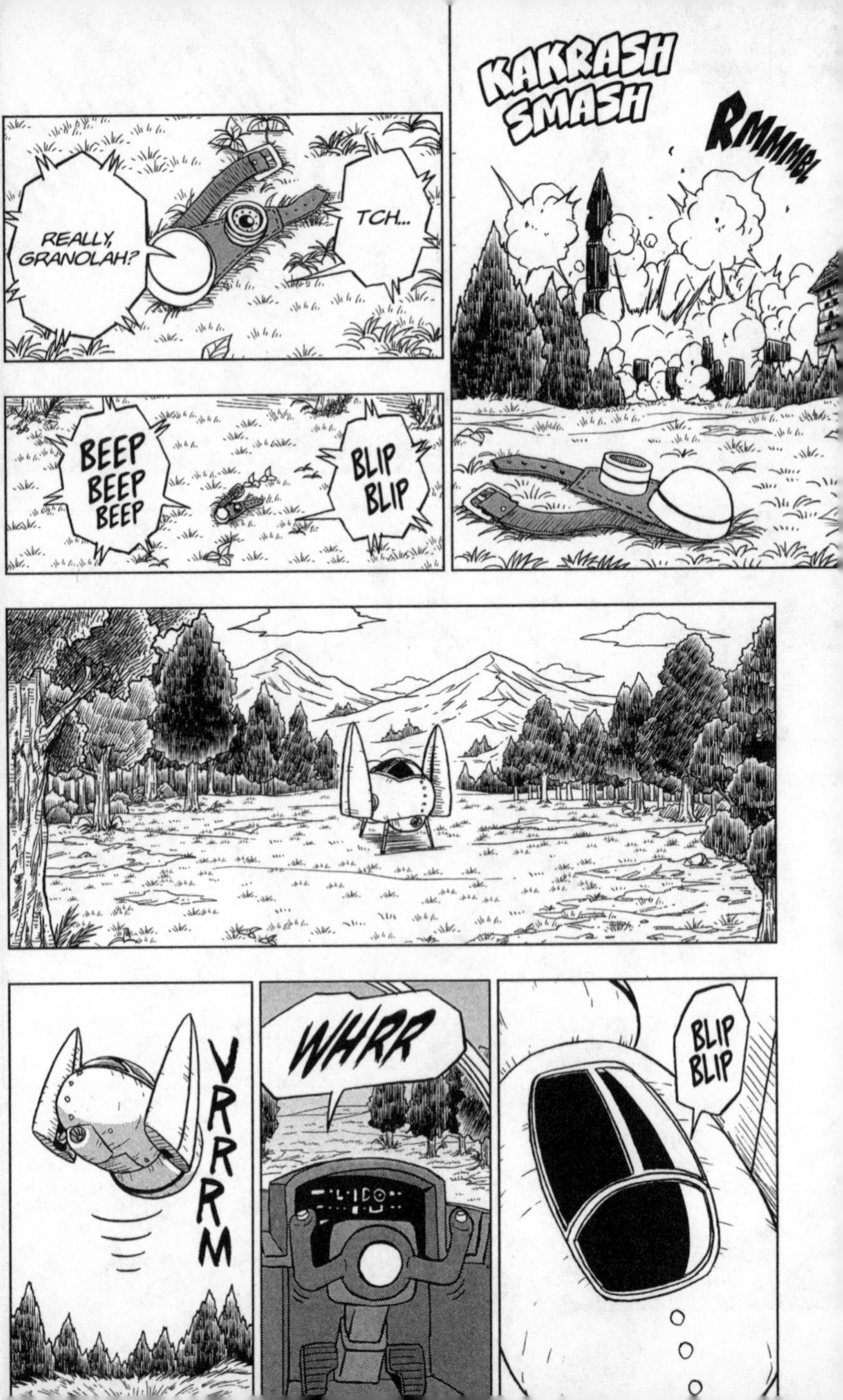
KAKRASH SMASH
RMMMBL
TCH...
REALLY, GRANOLAH?
BLIP BLIP
BEEP BEEP BEEP
BLIP BLIP
WHRR
VRRRM

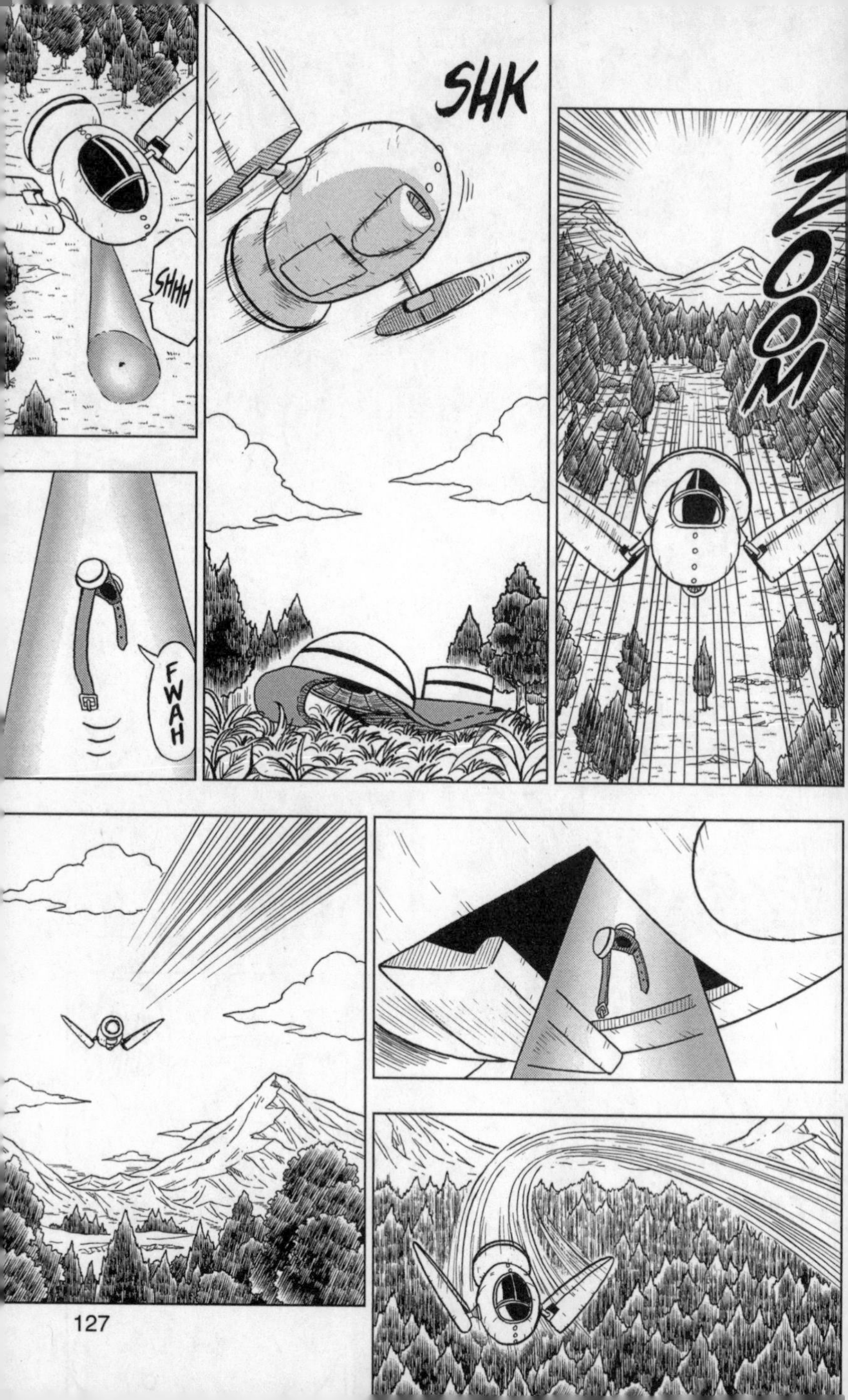
ZOOM
SHK
SHHH
FWAH

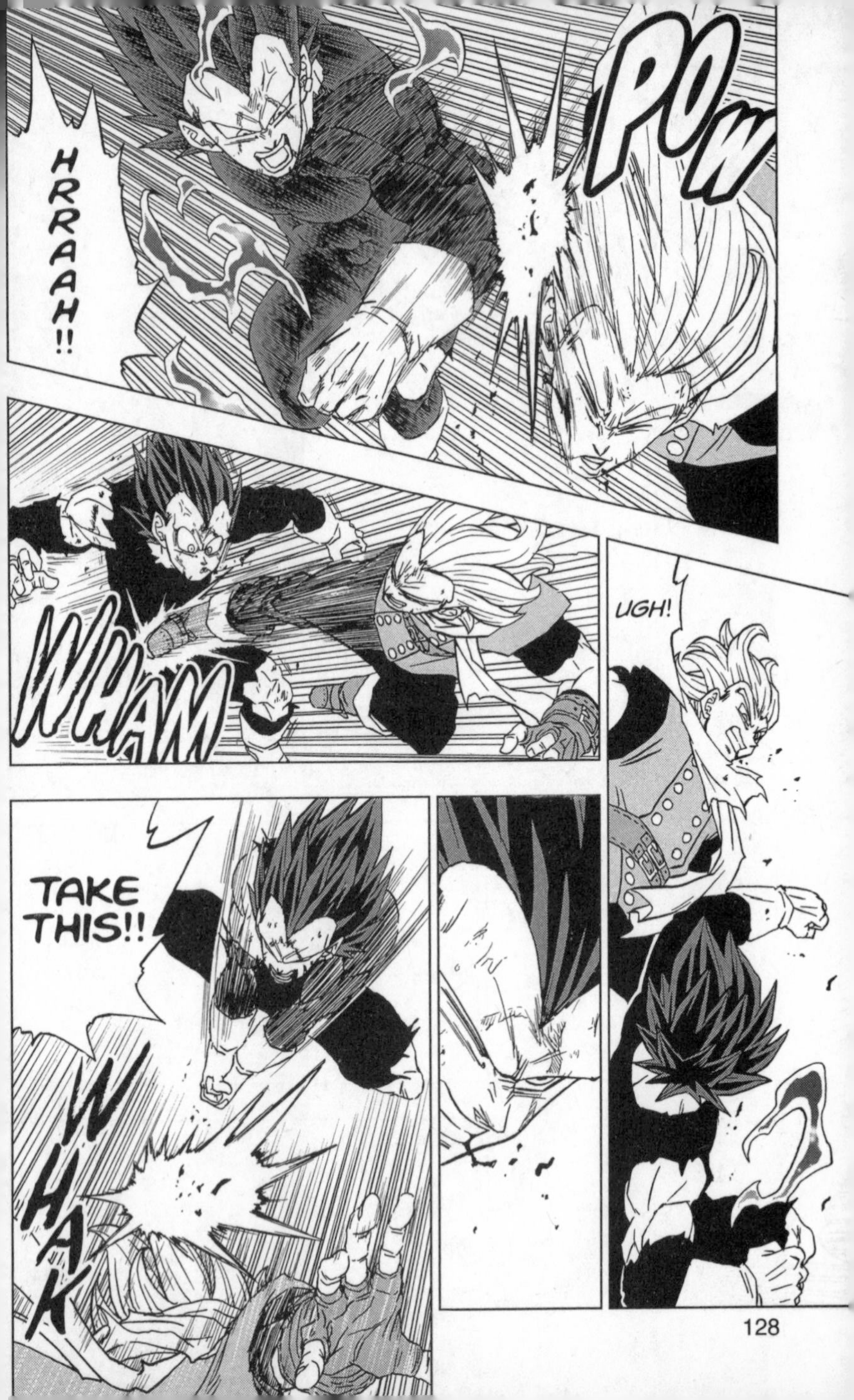
POW
HRRAAAH!!
UGH!
WHAM
TAKE THIS!!
WHAK

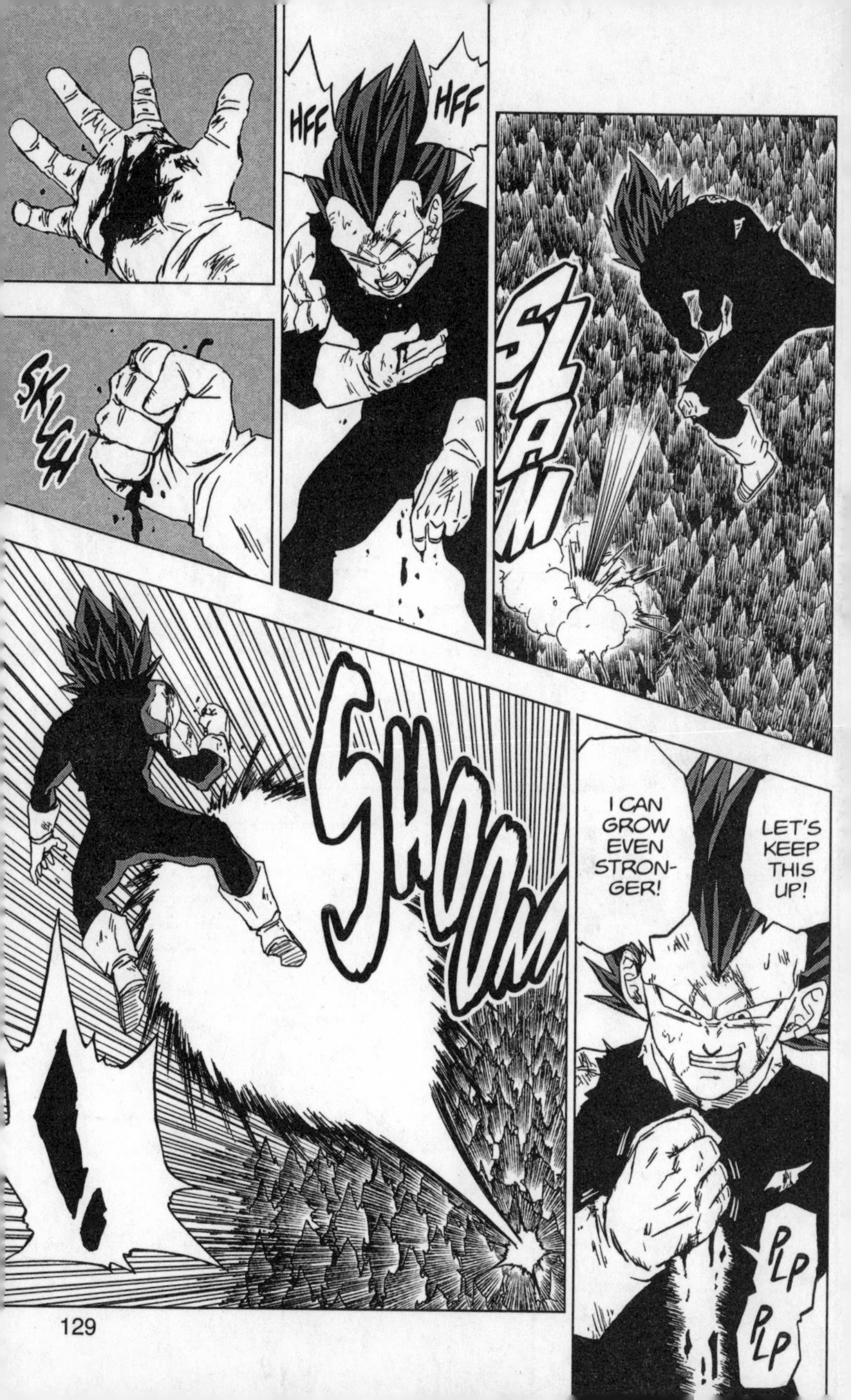
SLAM
HFF
HFF
SKLCH
LET'S KEEP THIS UP!
I CAN GROW EVEN STRONGER!
PLP
PLP
SHOOM

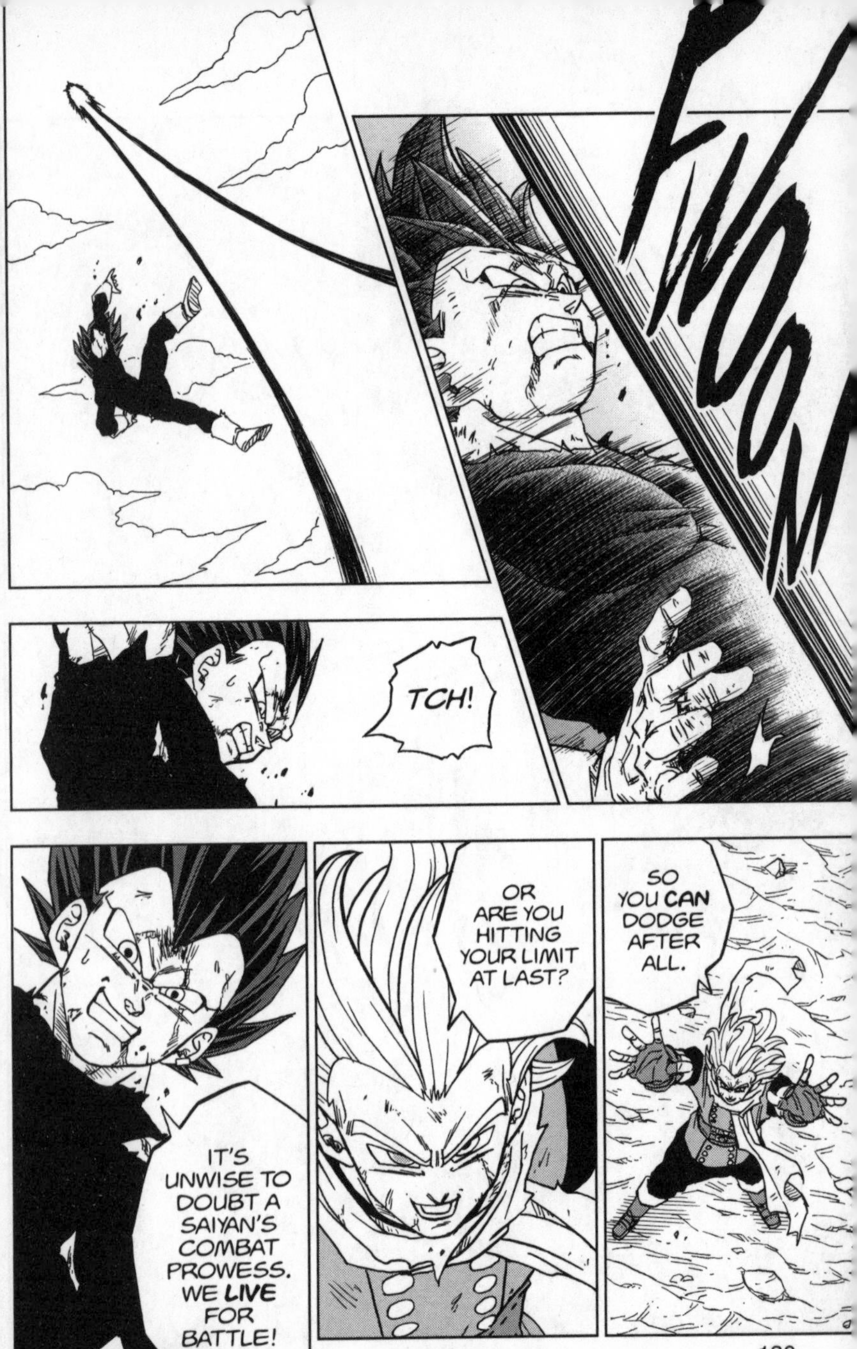
FWOOM
TCH!
SO YOU **CAN** DODGE AFTER ALL.
OR ARE YOU HITTING YOUR LIMIT AT LAST?
IT'S UNWISE TO DOUBT A SAIYAN'S COMBAT PROWESS. WE **LIVE** FOR BATTLE!

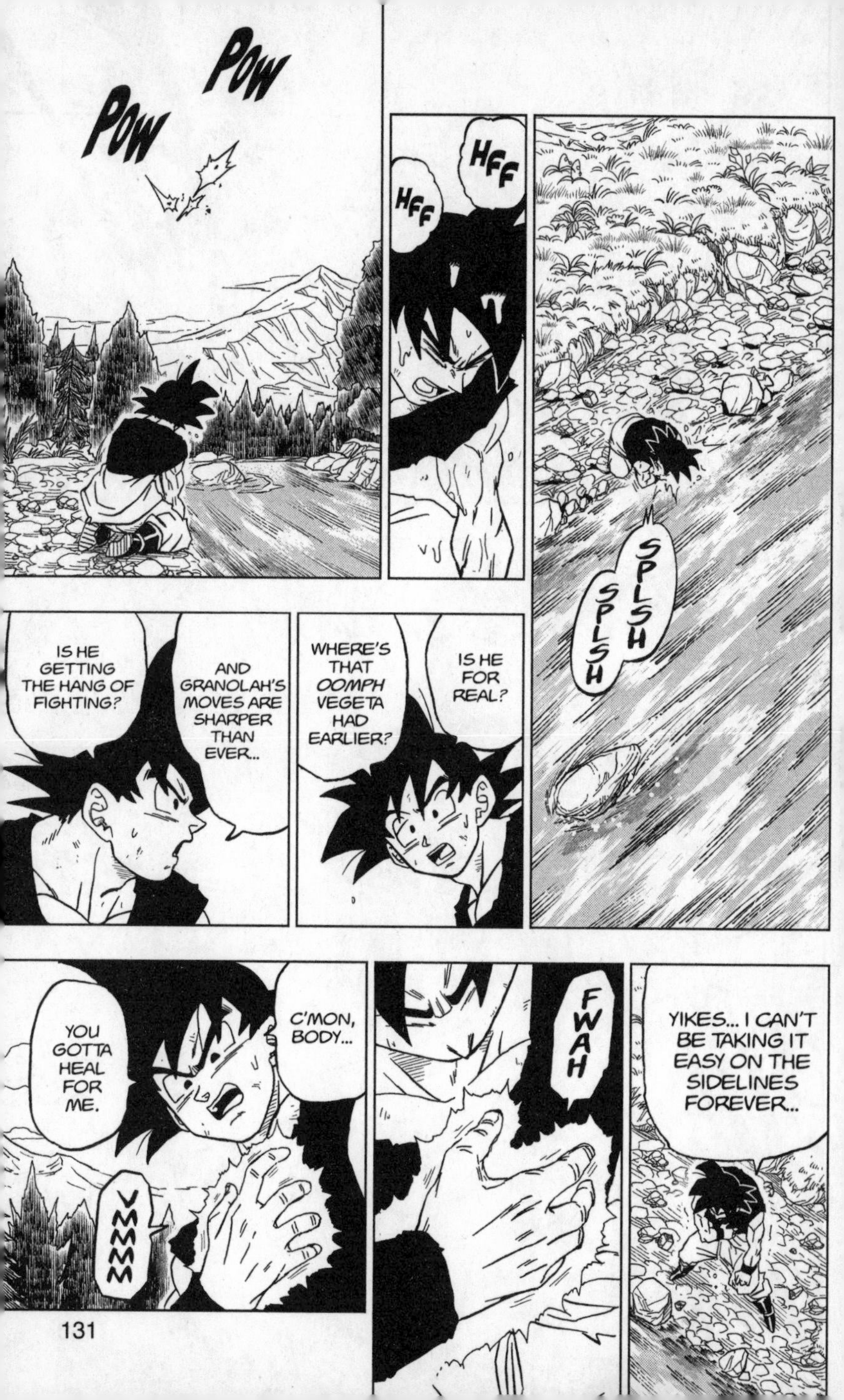
SPLSH
SPLSH
HFF
HFF
POW
POW
IS HE FOR REAL?
WHERE'S THAT *OOMPH* VEGETA HAD EARLIER?
AND GRANOLAH'S MOVES ARE SHARPER THAN EVER...
IS HE GETTING THE HANG OF FIGHTING?
YIKES... I CAN'T BE TAKING IT EASY ON THE SIDELINES FOREVER...
FWAH
C'MON, BODY...
YOU GOTTA HEAL FOR ME.
VMMMM

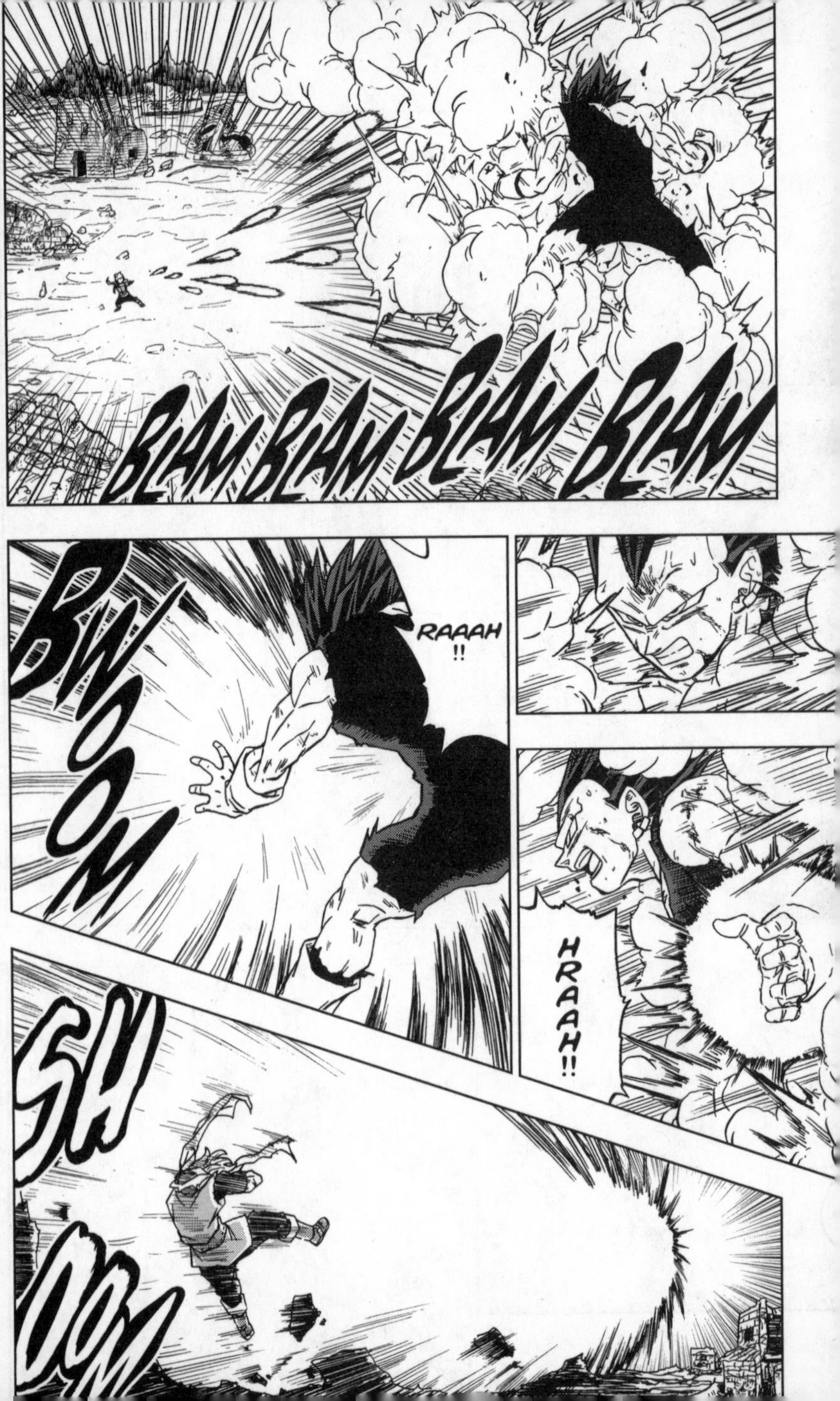
BLAM BLAM BLAM BLAM
HRAAAH!!
RAAAH!!
BWOOOM
SHOOM

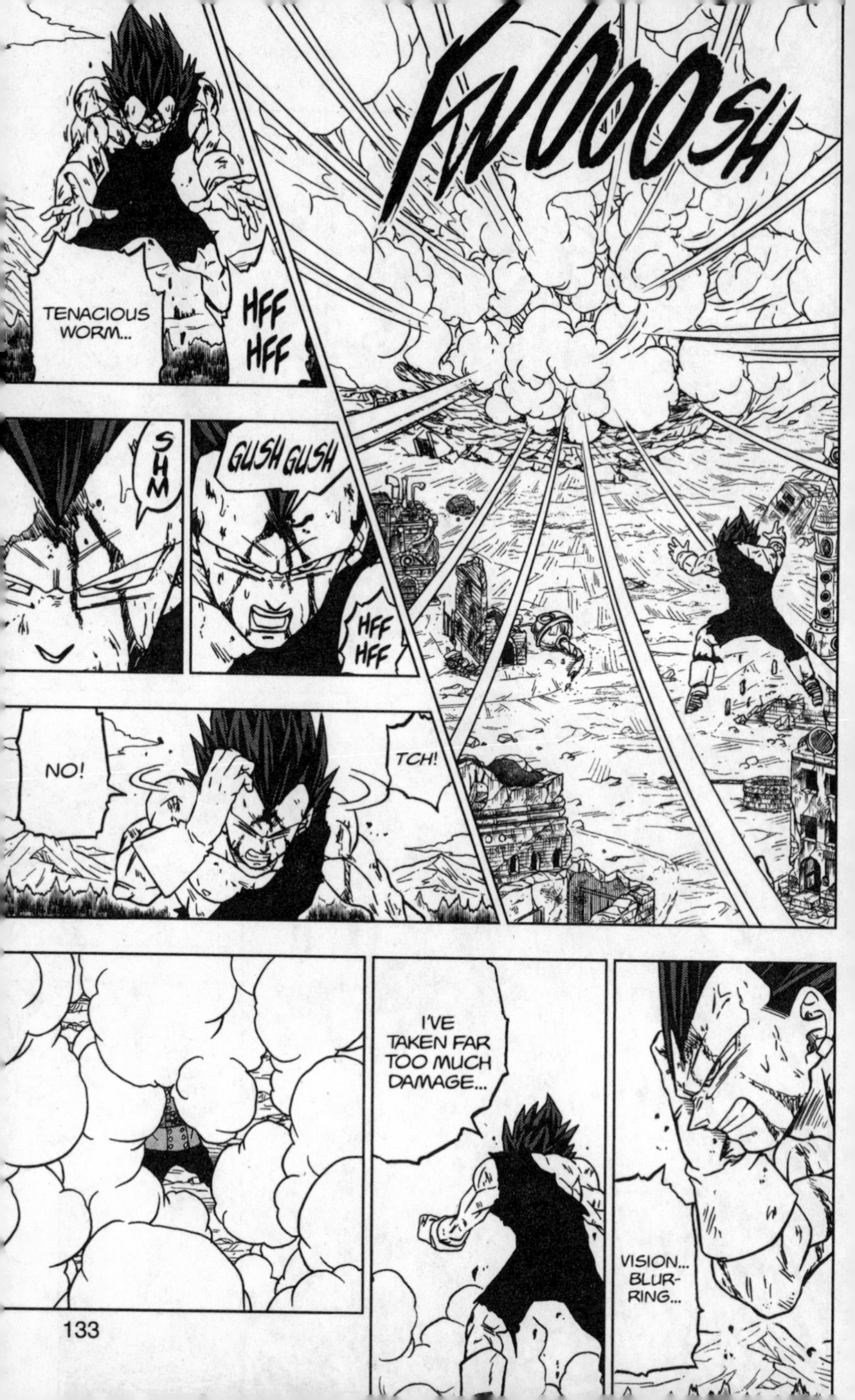
FWOOOSH
TENACIOUS WORM...
HFF HFF
GUSH GUSH
HFF HFF
SHM
TCH!
NO!
VISION... BLUR-RING...
I'VE TAKEN FAR TOO MUCH DAMAGE...

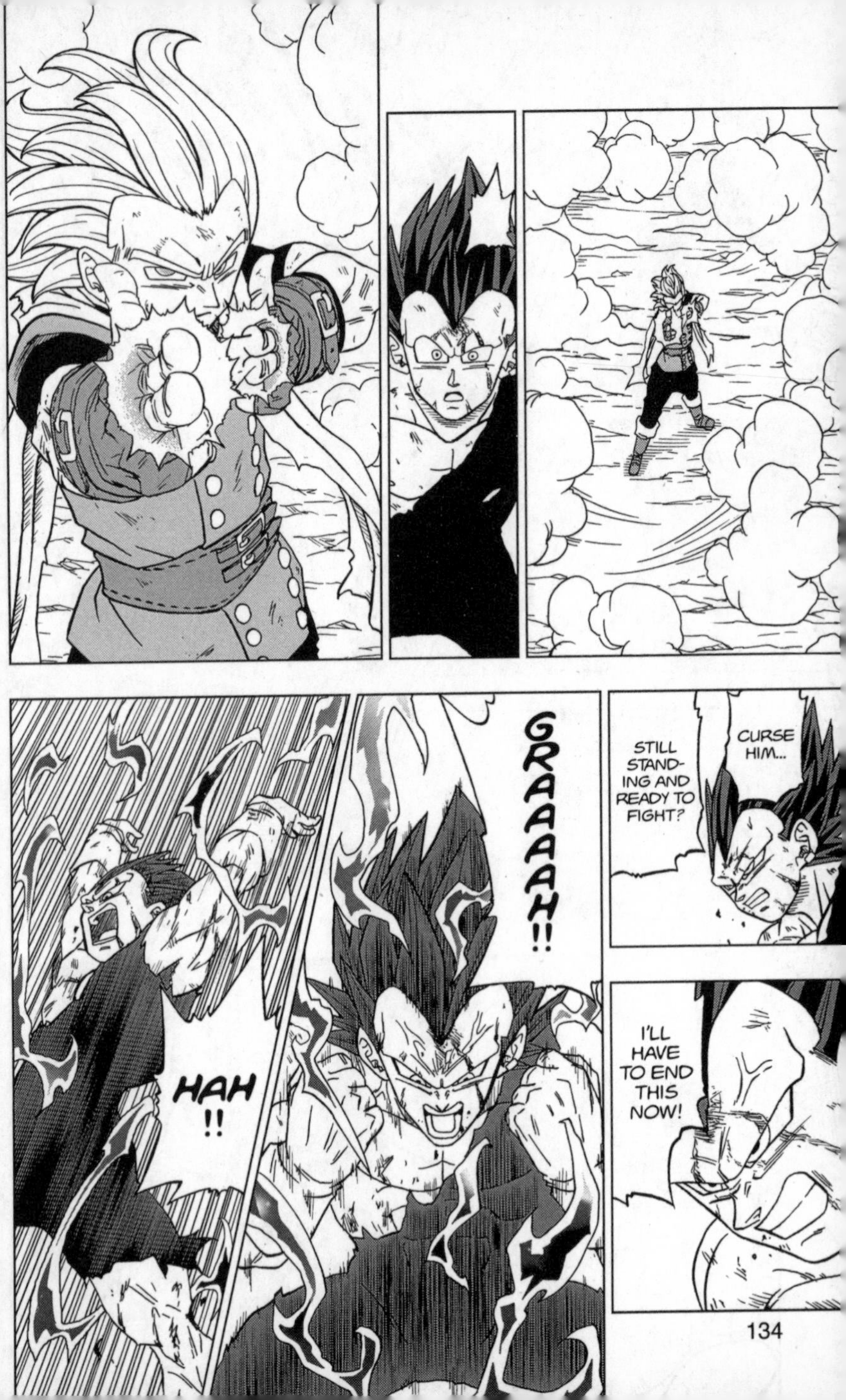
CURSE HIM...
STILL STANDING AND READY TO FIGHT?
I'LL HAVE TO END THIS NOW!
GRAAAAAH!!
HAH!!

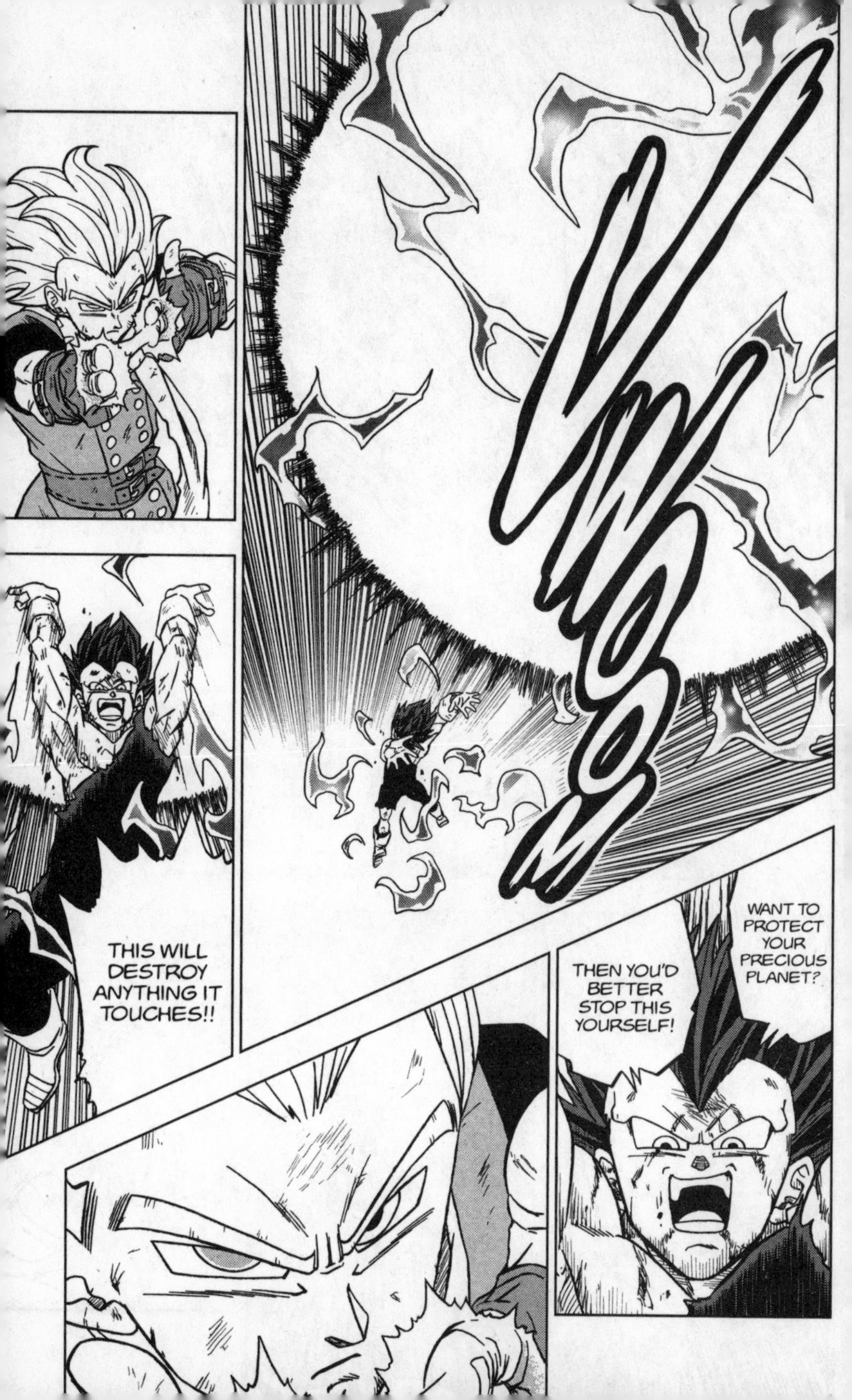
THIS WILL DESTROY ANYTHING IT TOUCHES!!
WANT TO PROTECT YOUR PRECIOUS PLANET?
THEN YOU'D BETTER STOP THIS YOURSELF!

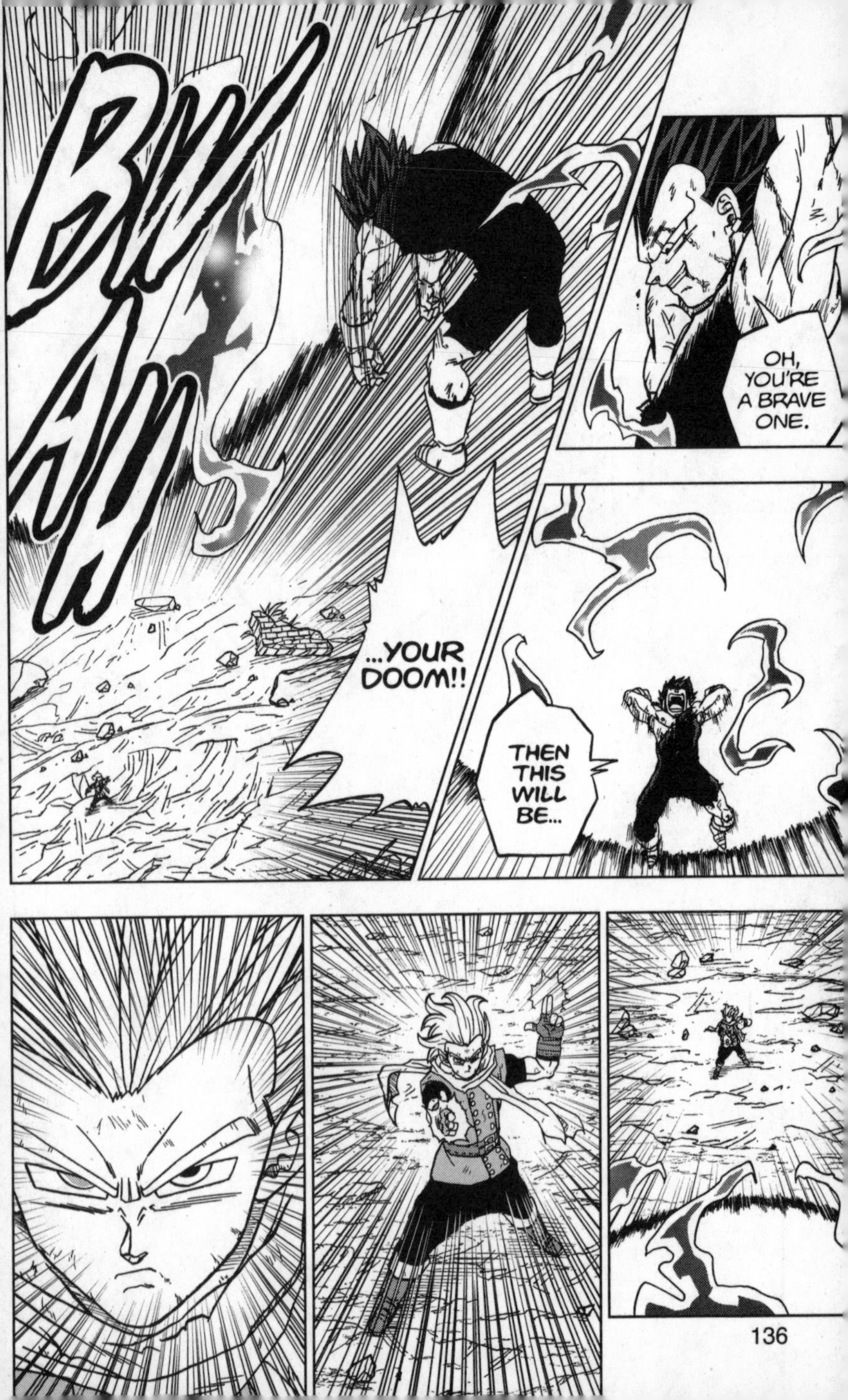
OH, YOU'RE A BRAVE ONE.
THEN THIS WILL BE...
...YOUR DOOM!!
BWAM

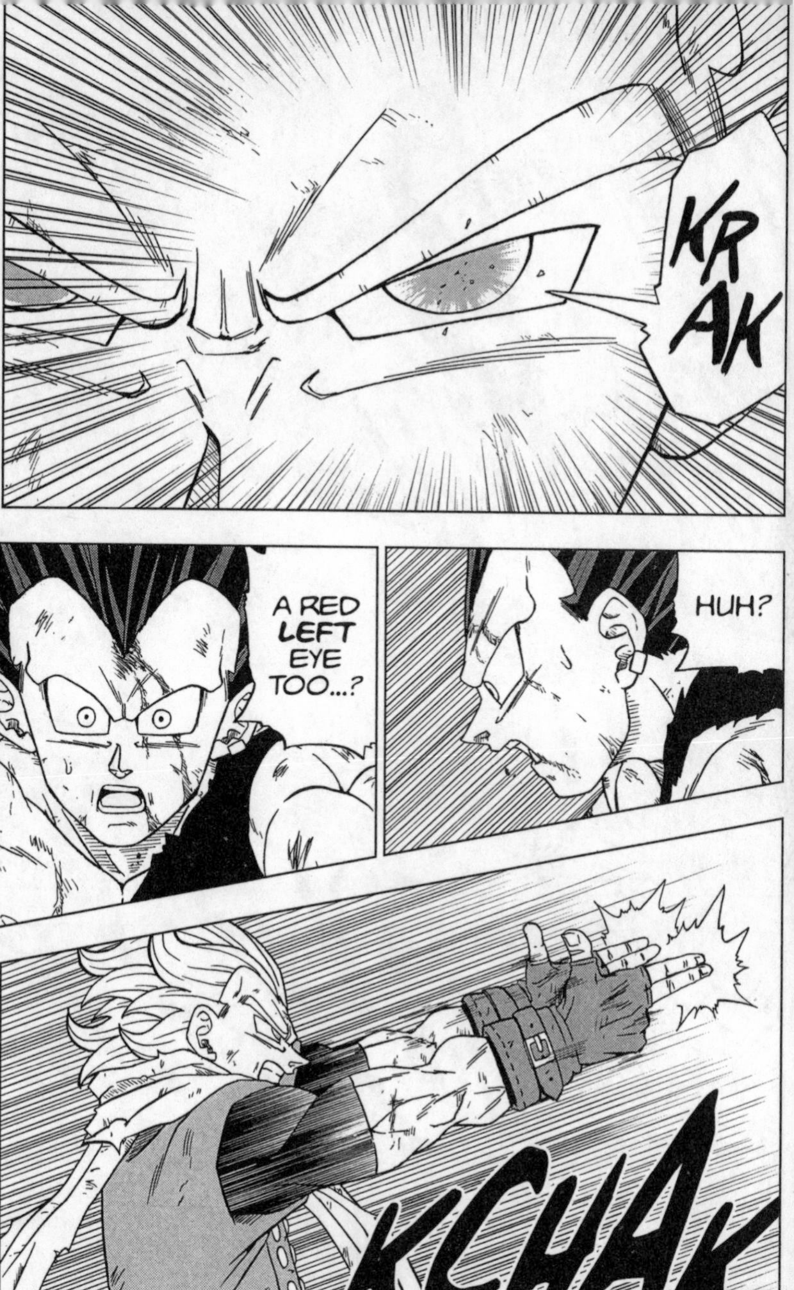
KRAK
HUH?
A RED LEFT EYE TOO...?
KCHAK

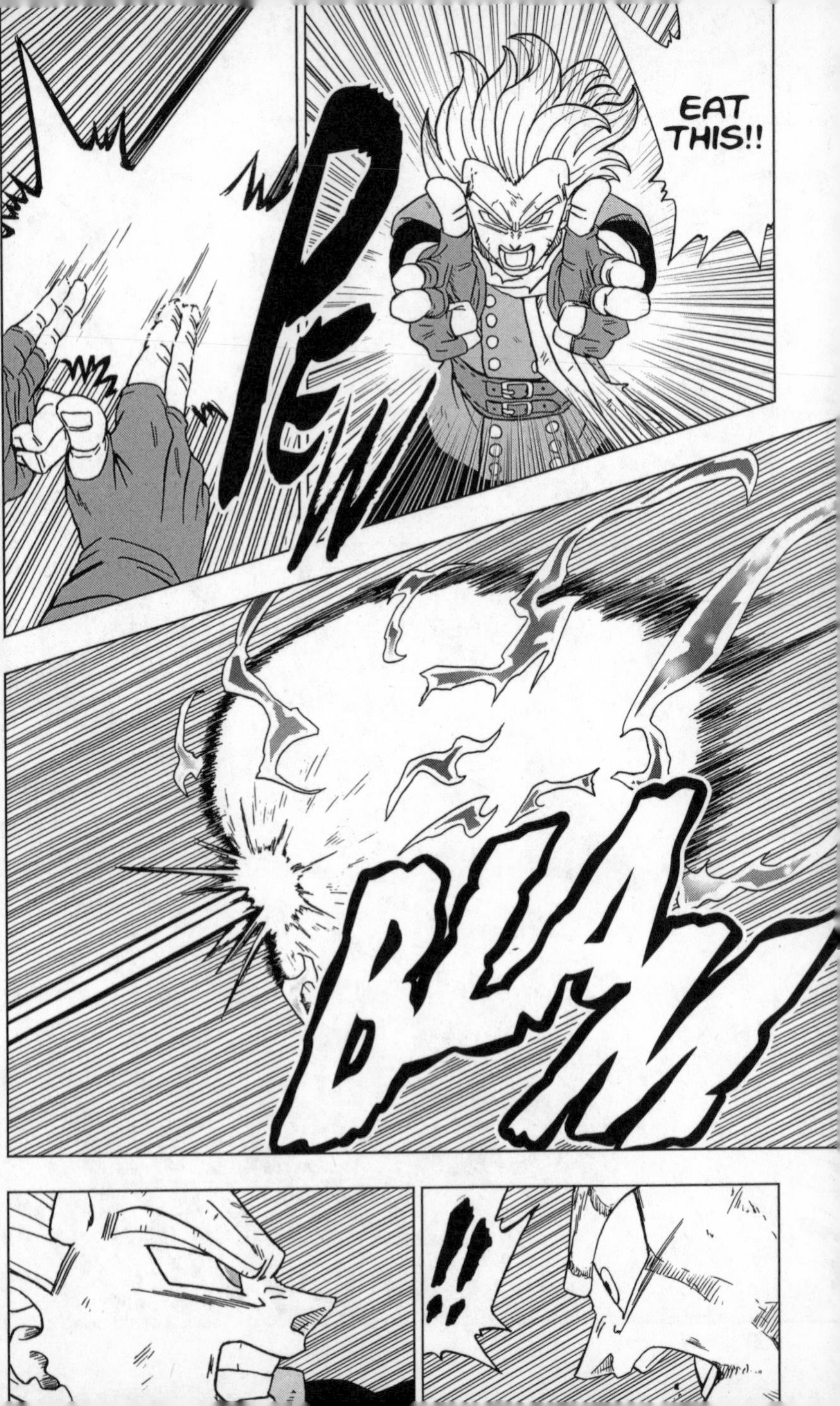
EAT THIS!!
PEW
BLAM
!!

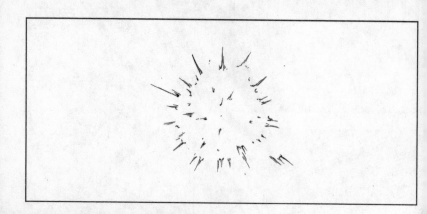

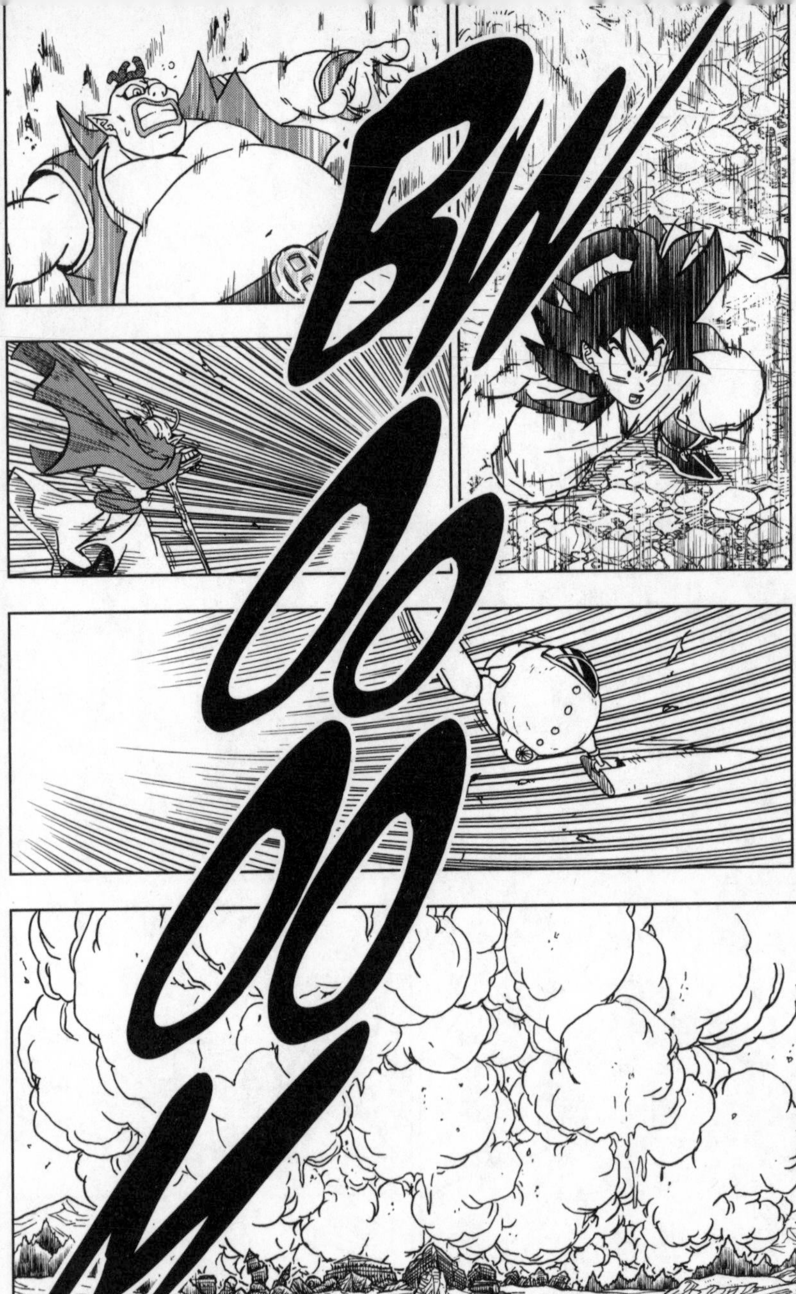
BWOOOOOOM

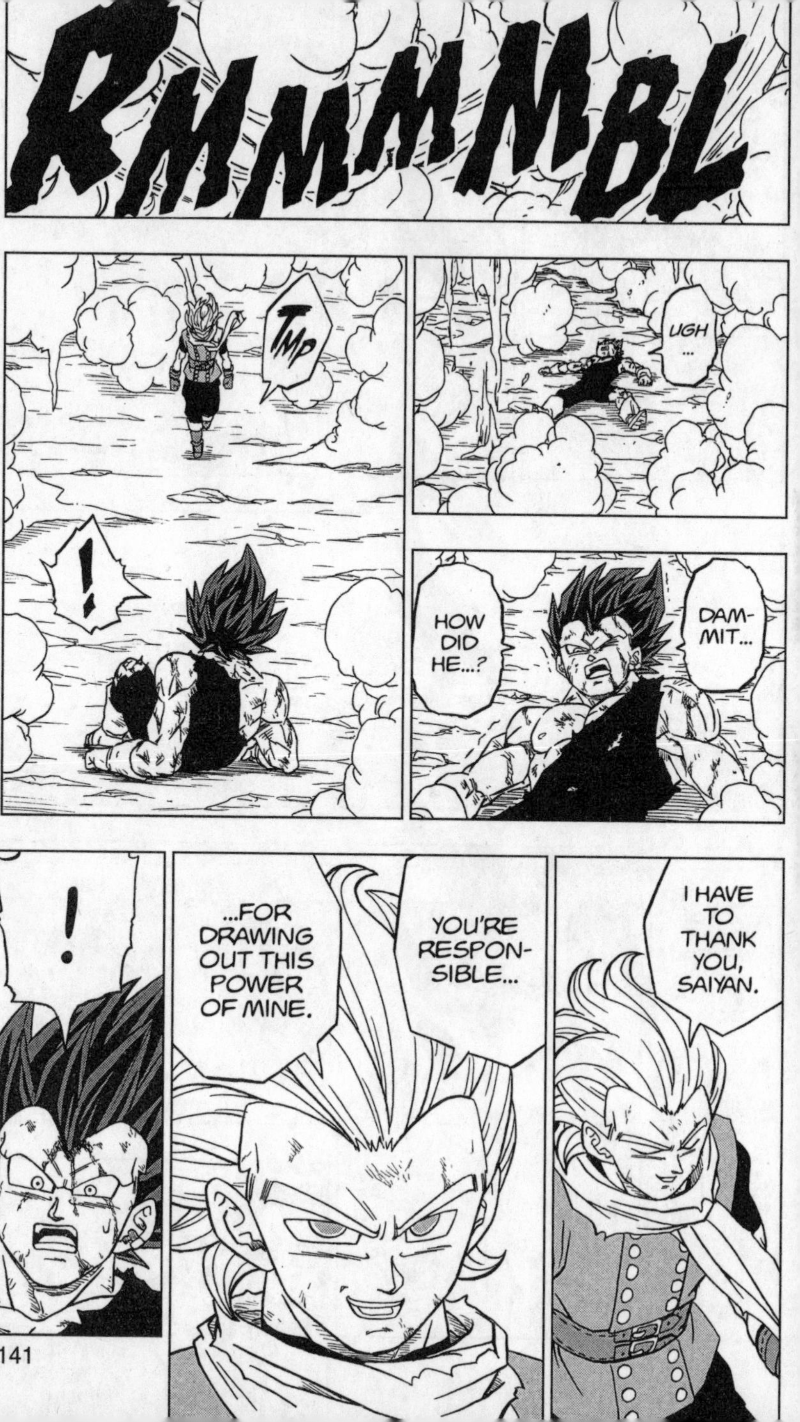
RMMMBL
UGH ...
DAM-MIT...
HOW DID HE...?
TMP
!
I HAVE TO THANK YOU, SAIYAN.
YOU'RE RESPON-SIBLE...
...FOR DRAWING OUT THIS POWER OF MINE.
!

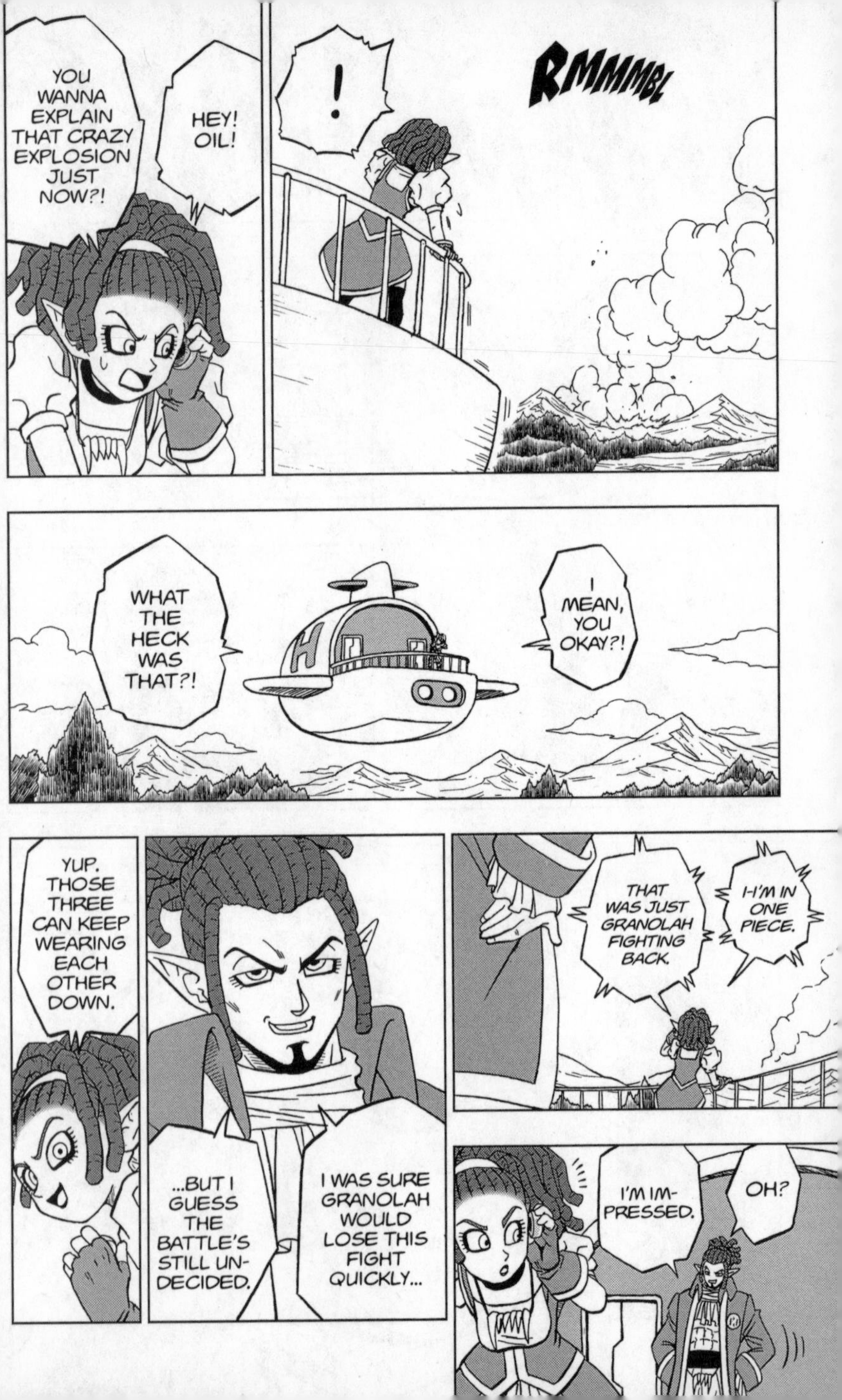
RMMMBL
!
HEY! OIL!
YOU WANNA EXPLAIN THAT CRAZY EXPLOSION JUST NOW?!
WHAT THE HECK WAS THAT?!
I MEAN, YOU OKAY?!
I-I'M IN ONE PIECE.
THAT WAS JUST GRANOLAH FIGHTING BACK.
OH?
I'M IM-PRESSED.
I WAS SURE GRANOLAH WOULD LOSE THIS FIGHT QUICKLY...
...BUT I GUESS THE BATTLE'S STILL UN-DECIDED.
YUP. THOSE THREE CAN KEEP WEARING EACH OTHER DOWN.

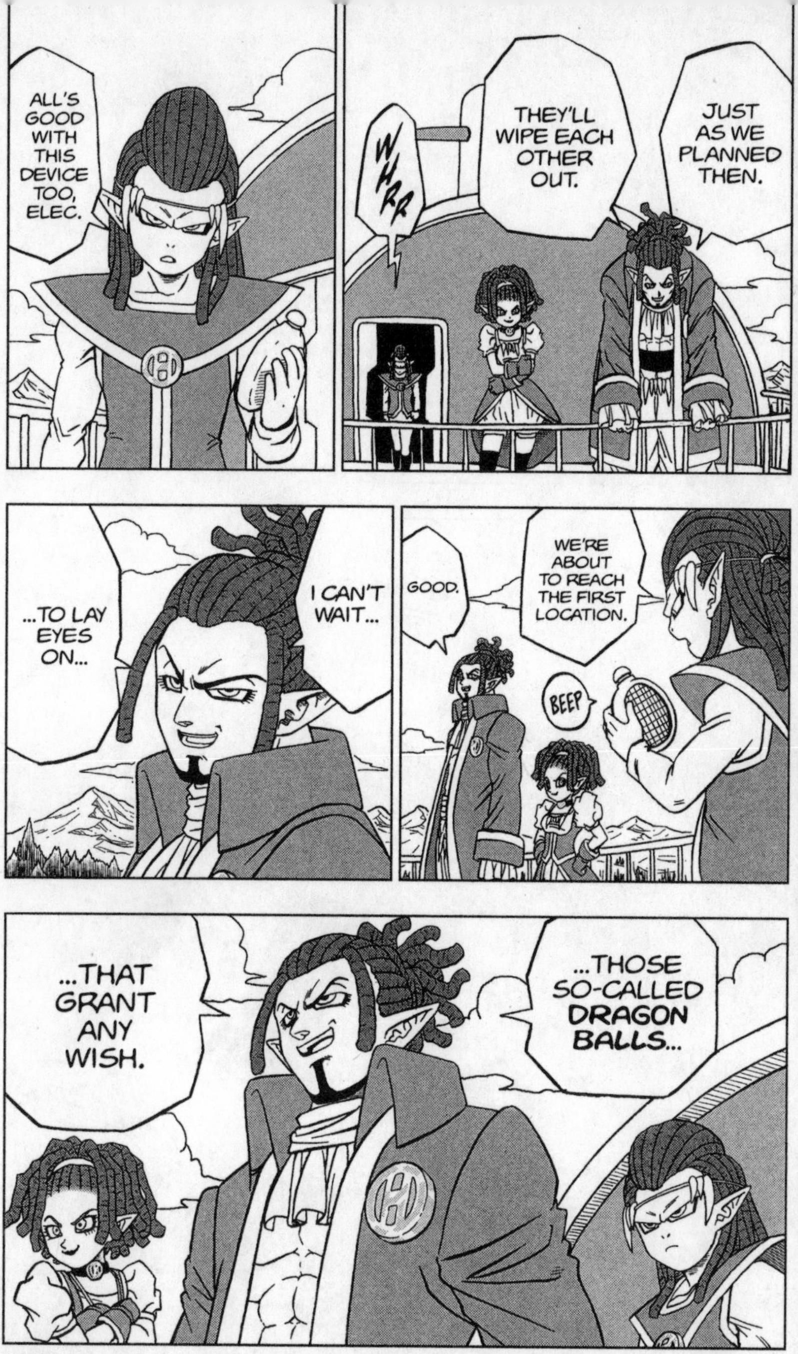
JUST AS WE PLANNED THEN.
THEY'LL WIPE EACH OTHER OUT.
WHRR
ALL'S GOOD WITH THIS DEVICE TOO, ELEC.
WE'RE ABOUT TO REACH THE FIRST LOCATION.
GOOD.
BEEP
I CAN'T WAIT...
...TO LAY EYES ON...
...THOSE SO-CALLED DRAGON BALLS...
...THAT GRANT ANY WISH.

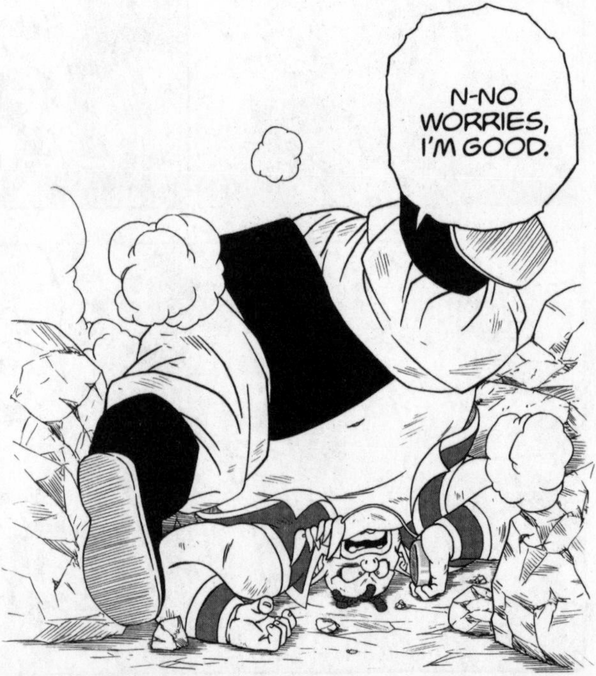
N-NO WORRIES, I'M GOOD.

DRAGON BALL SUPER

CHAPTER 76: THE FATE OF THE SAIYANS

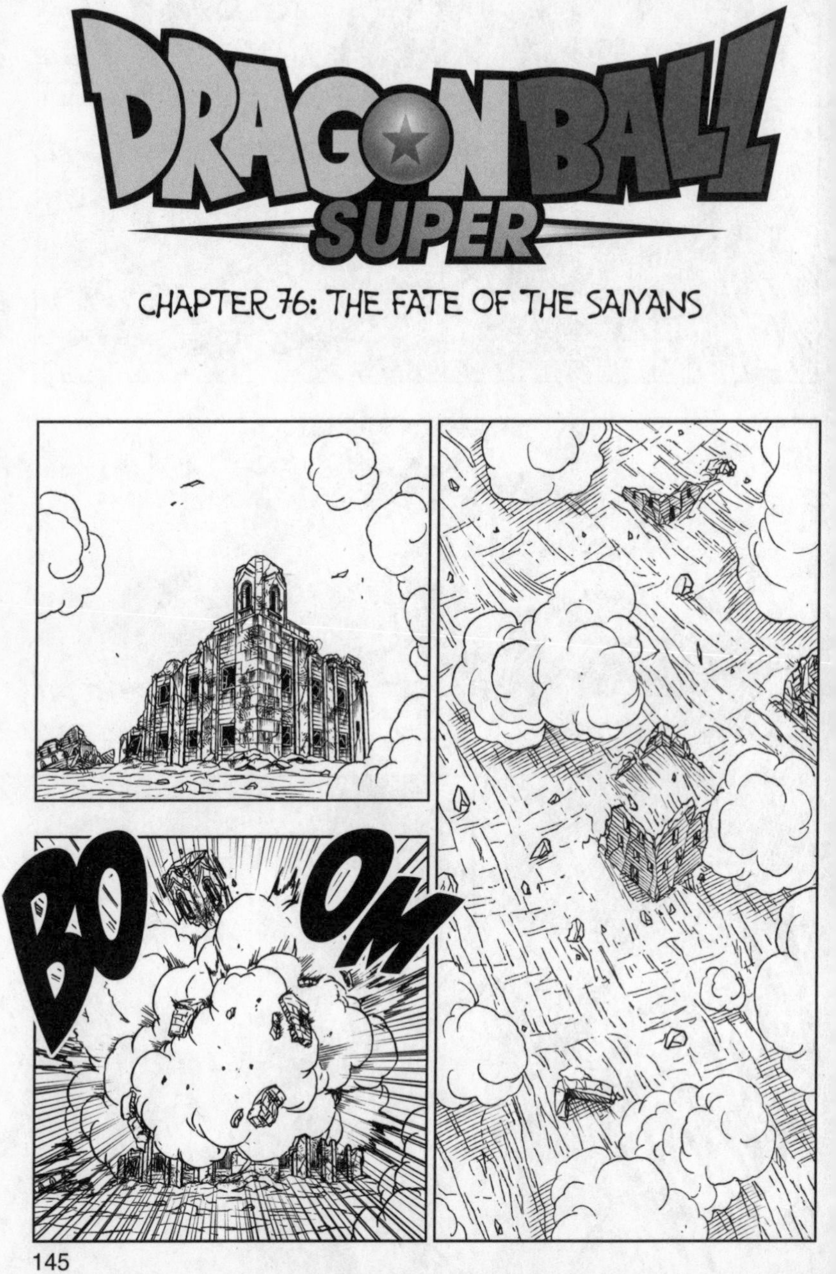
BOOM

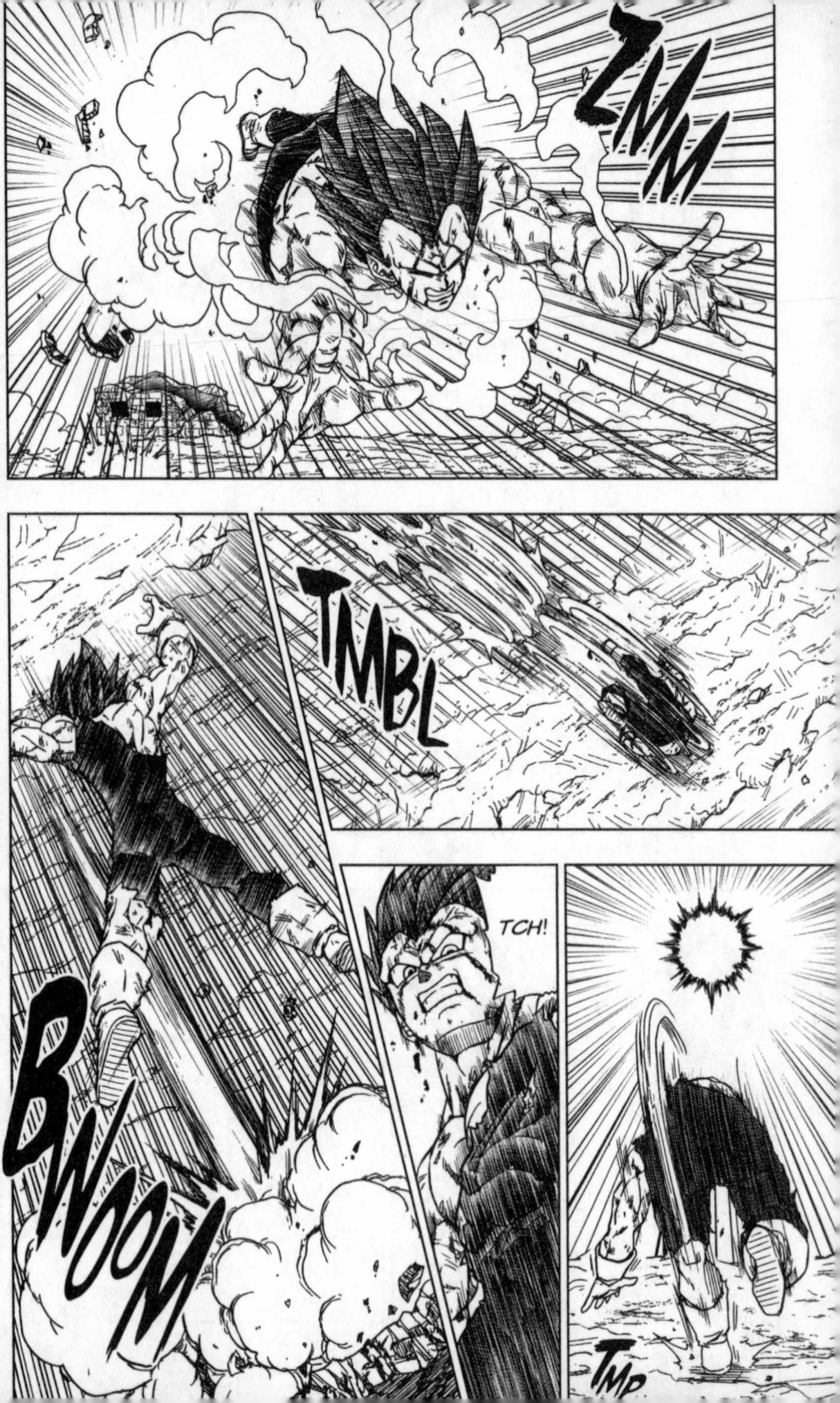
ZMM
TMBL
TMP
TCH!
BWOOM

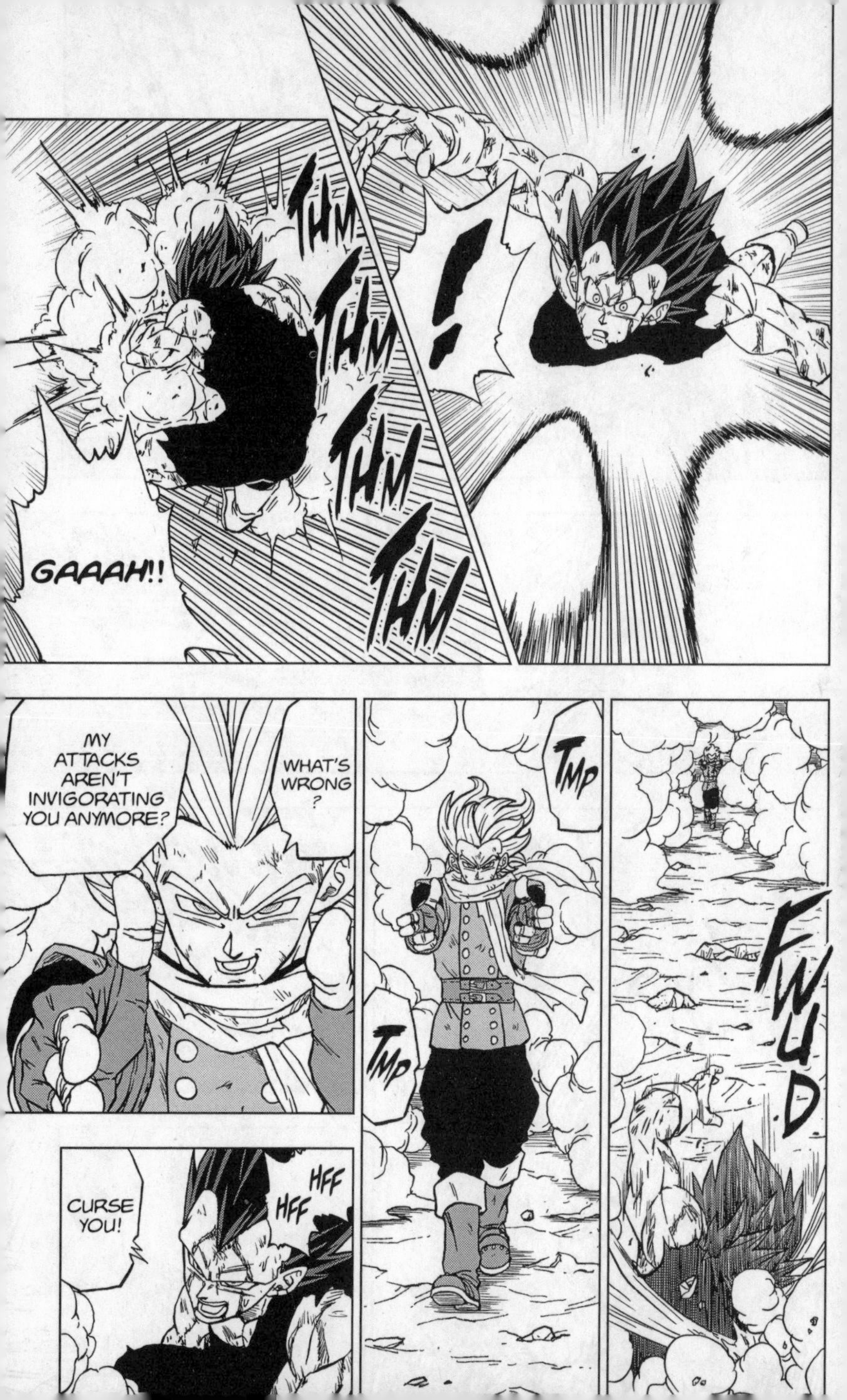

!
THM THM THM THM
GAAAH!!
FWUD
TMP
TMP
WHAT'S WRONG?
MY ATTACKS AREN'T INVIGORATING YOU ANYMORE?
HFF HFF
CURSE YOU!

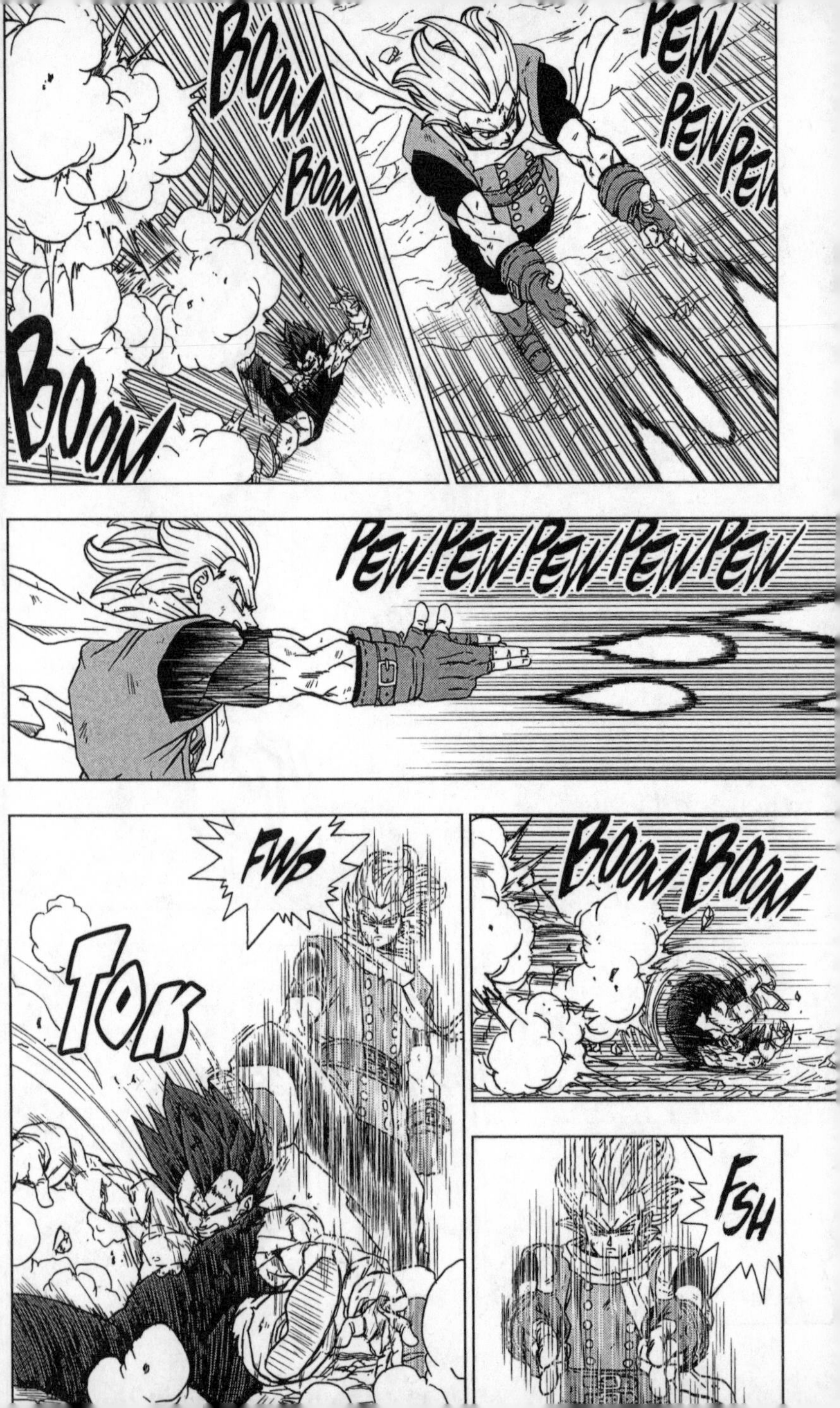
PEW PEW PEW PEW
BOOM
BOOM
BOOM
PEW PEW PEW PEW PEW
BOOM BOOM
FSH
FWP
TOK

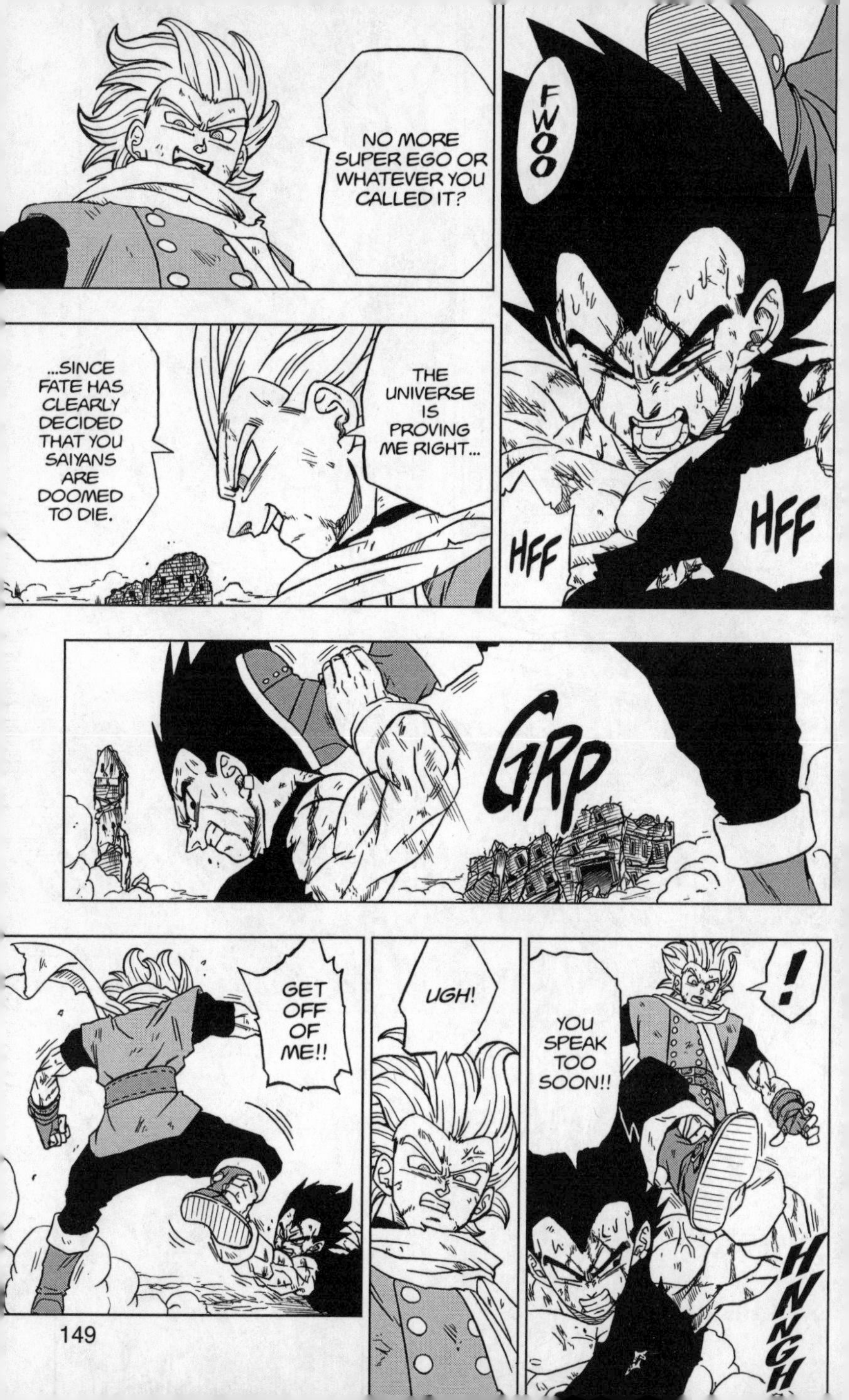

FWOO
HFF
HFF
NO MORE SUPER EGO OR WHATEVER YOU CALLED IT?
THE UNIVERSE IS PROVING ME RIGHT...
...SINCE FATE HAS CLEARLY DECIDED THAT YOU SAIYANS ARE DOOMED TO DIE.
GRP
!
YOU SPEAK TOO SOON!!
HNNGH
UGH!
GET OFF OF ME!!

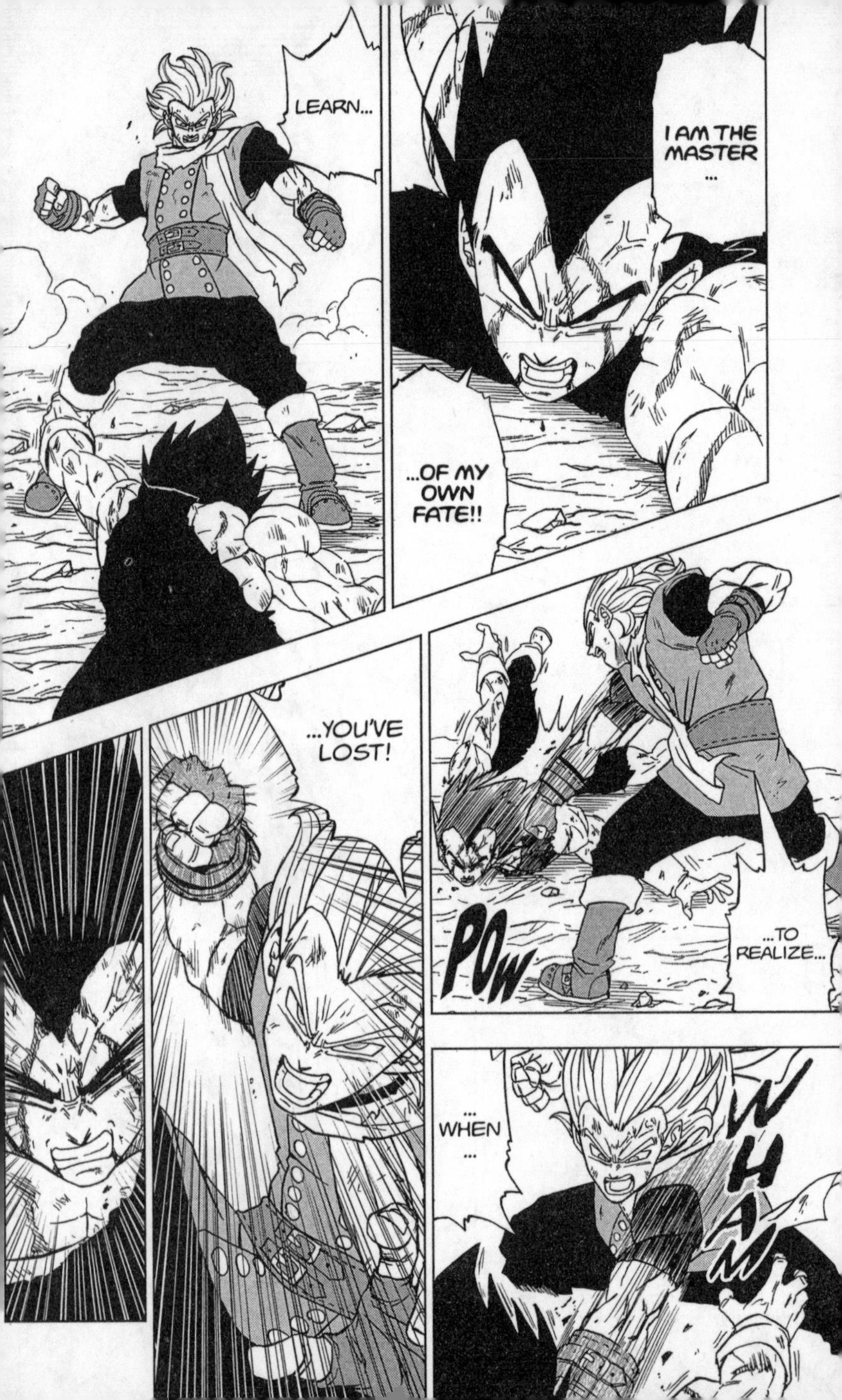
I AM THE MASTER ...
...OF MY OWN FATE!!
LEARN...
...TO REALIZE...
POW
... WHEN ...
WHAM
...YOU'VE LOST!

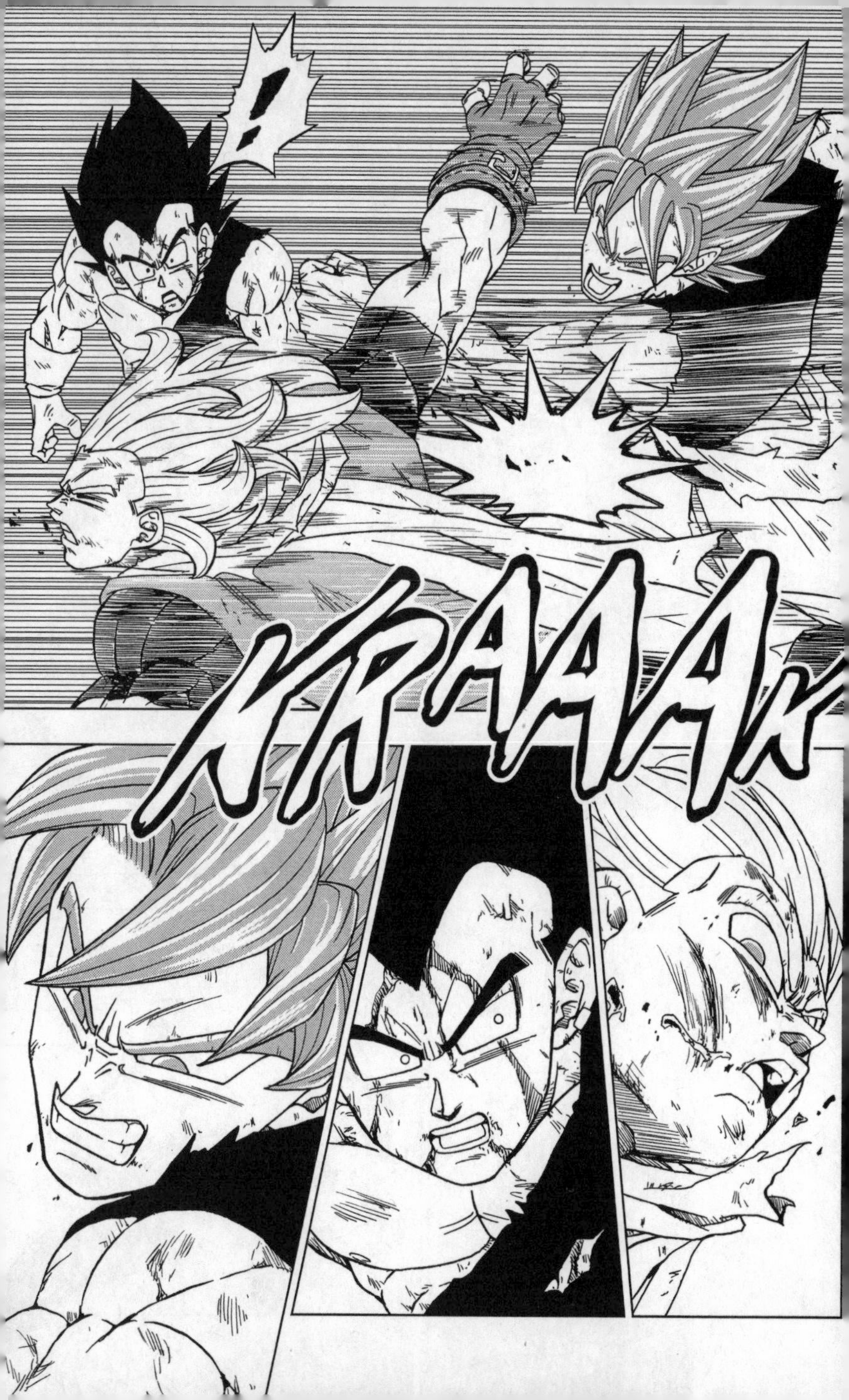
!
KRAAAK

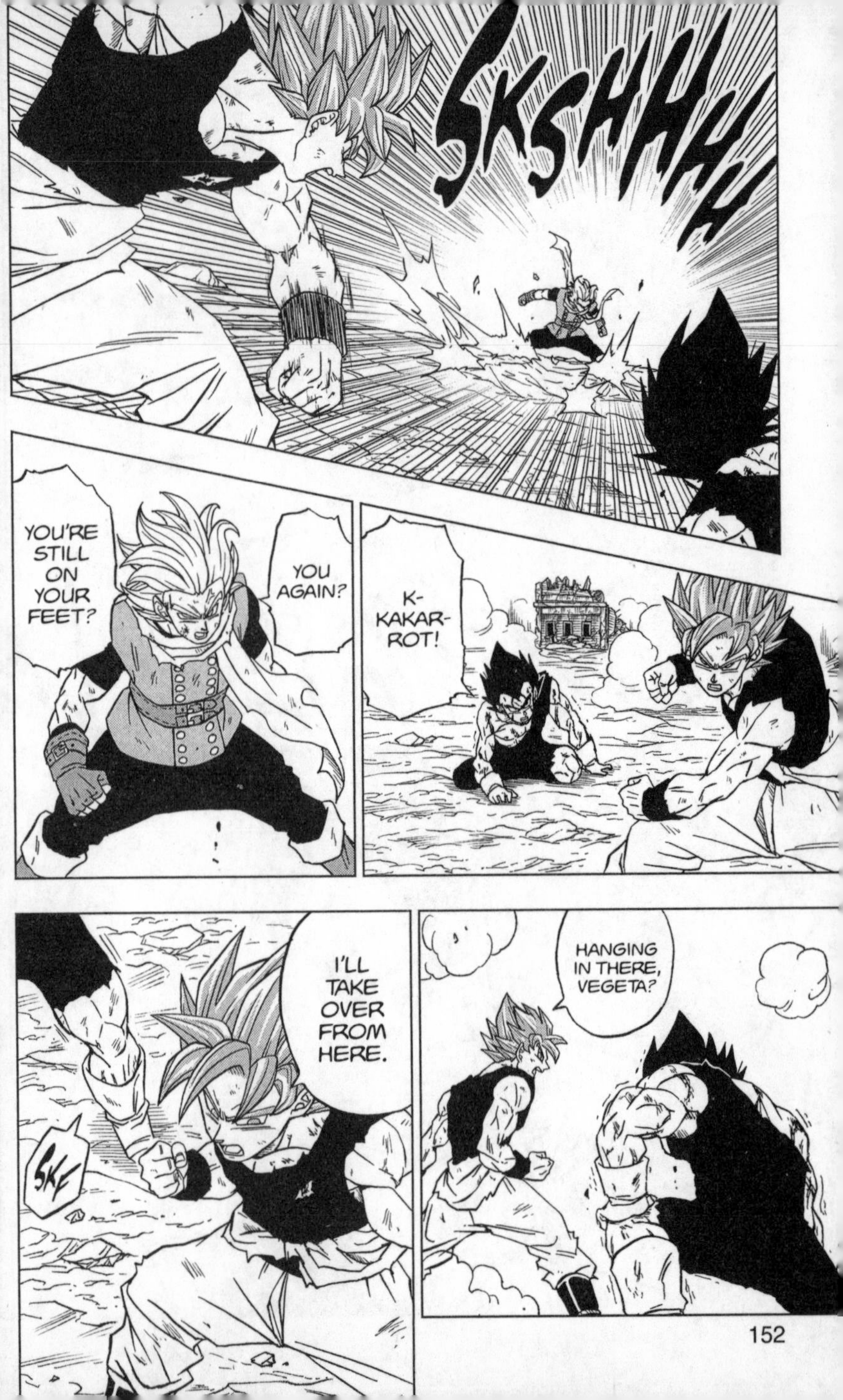
SKSHHHH
K-KAKARROT!
YOU AGAIN?
YOU'RE STILL ON YOUR FEET?
!
HANGING IN THERE, VEGETA?
I'LL TAKE OVER FROM HERE.
SKF

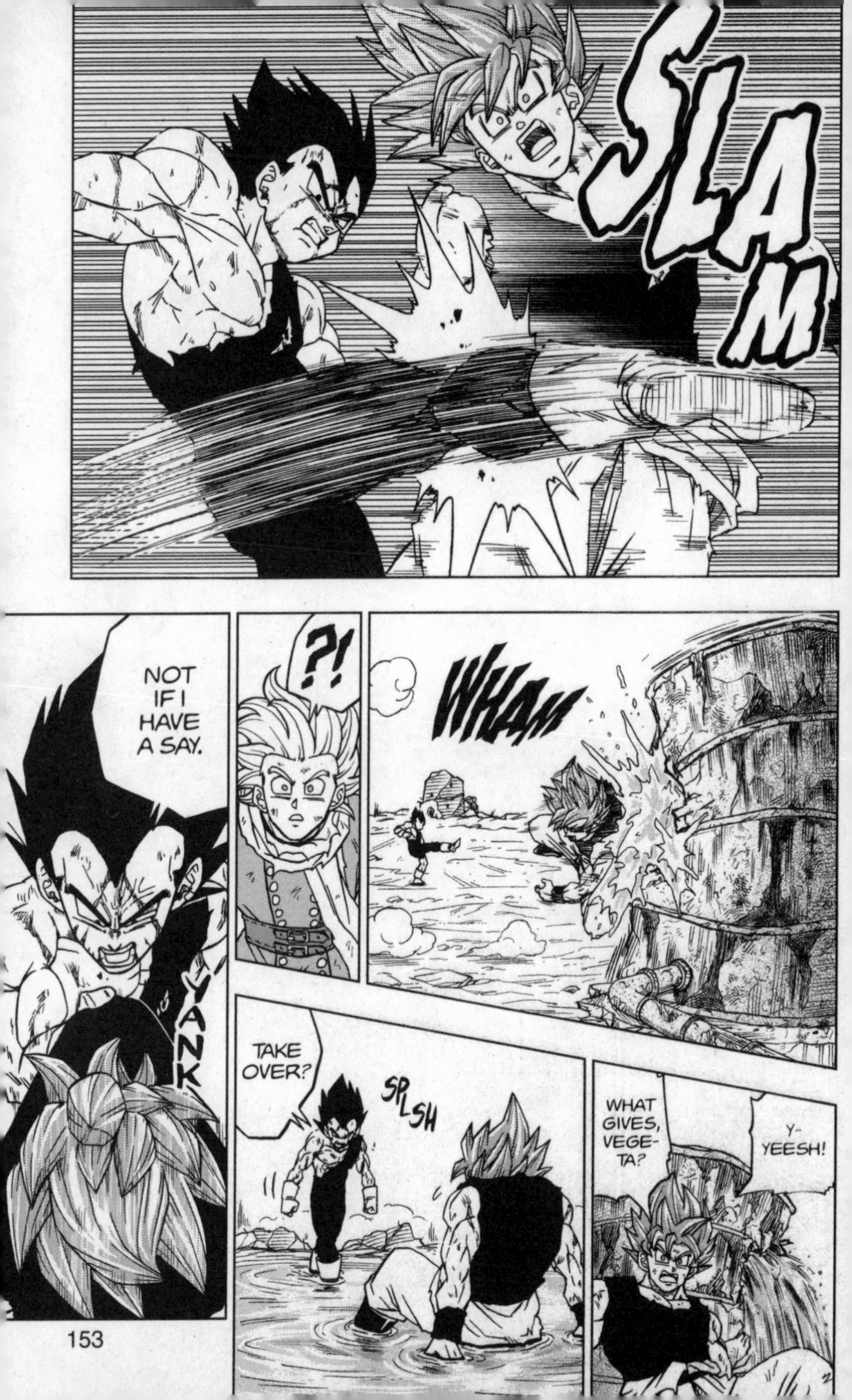
SLAM
WHAM
?!
Y-YEESH!
WHAT GIVES, VEGE-TA?
TAKE OVER?
SPLSH
NOT IF I HAVE A SAY.
YANK

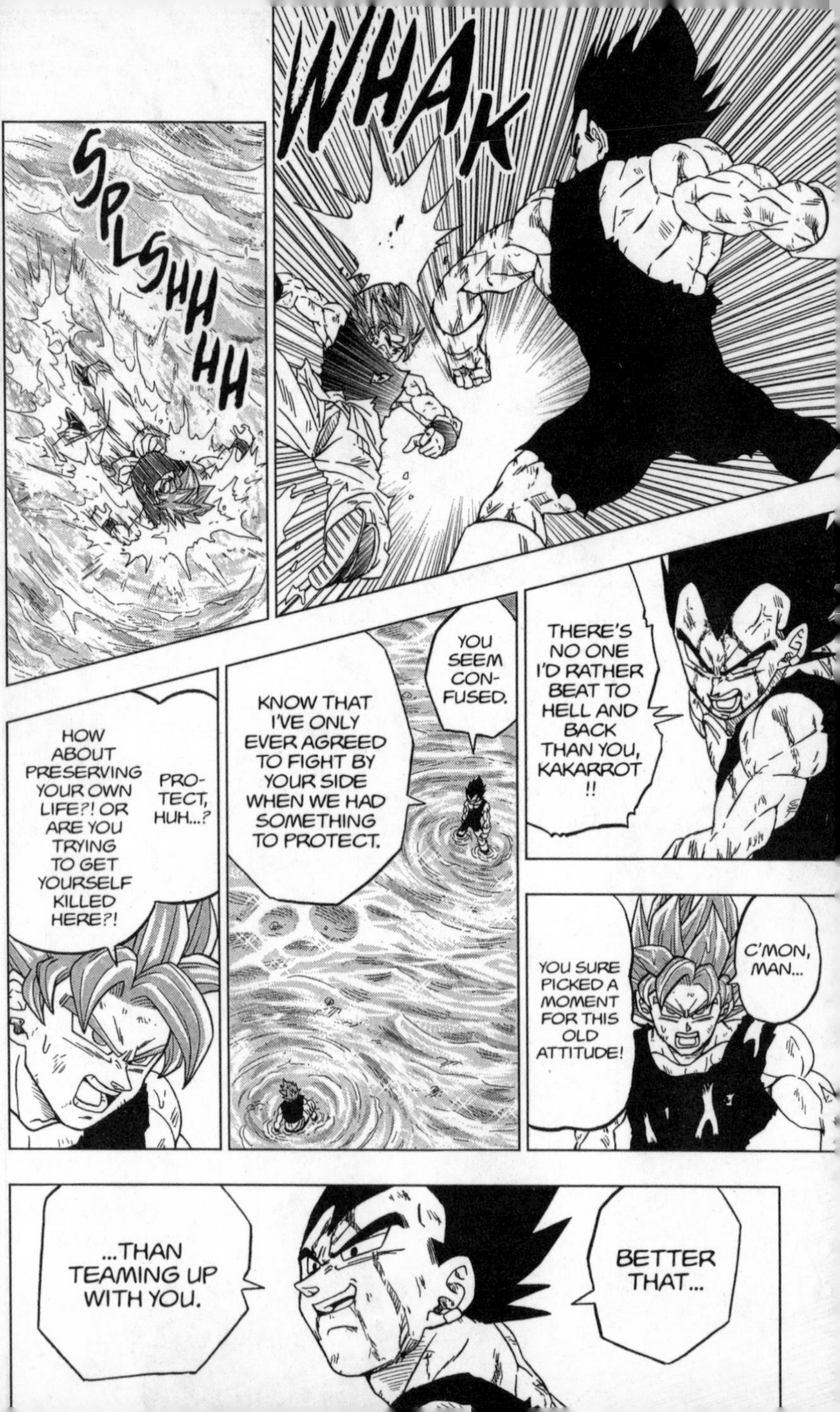
WHAK
SPLSHHHH
THERE'S NO ONE I'D RATHER BEAT TO HELL AND BACK THAN YOU, KAKARROT!!
C'MON, MAN...
YOU SURE PICKED A MOMENT FOR THIS OLD ATTITUDE!
YOU SEEM CONFUSED.
KNOW THAT I'VE ONLY EVER AGREED TO FIGHT BY YOUR SIDE WHEN WE HAD SOMETHING TO PROTECT.
PROTECT, HUH...?
HOW ABOUT PRESERVING YOUR OWN LIFE?! OR ARE YOU TRYING TO GET YOURSELF KILLED HERE?!
BETTER THAT...
...THAN TEAMING UP WITH YOU.

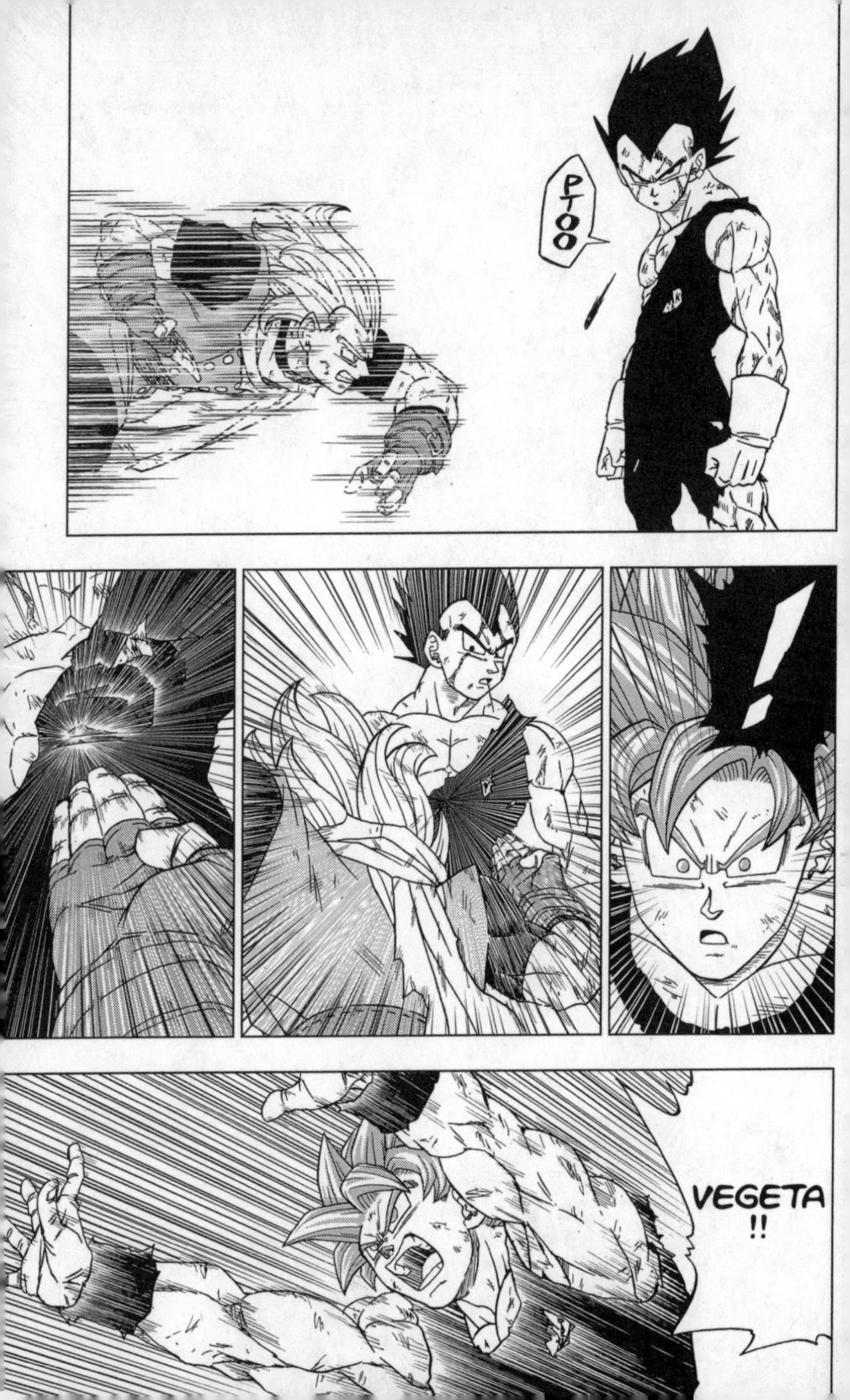
PTOO
VEGETA
!!

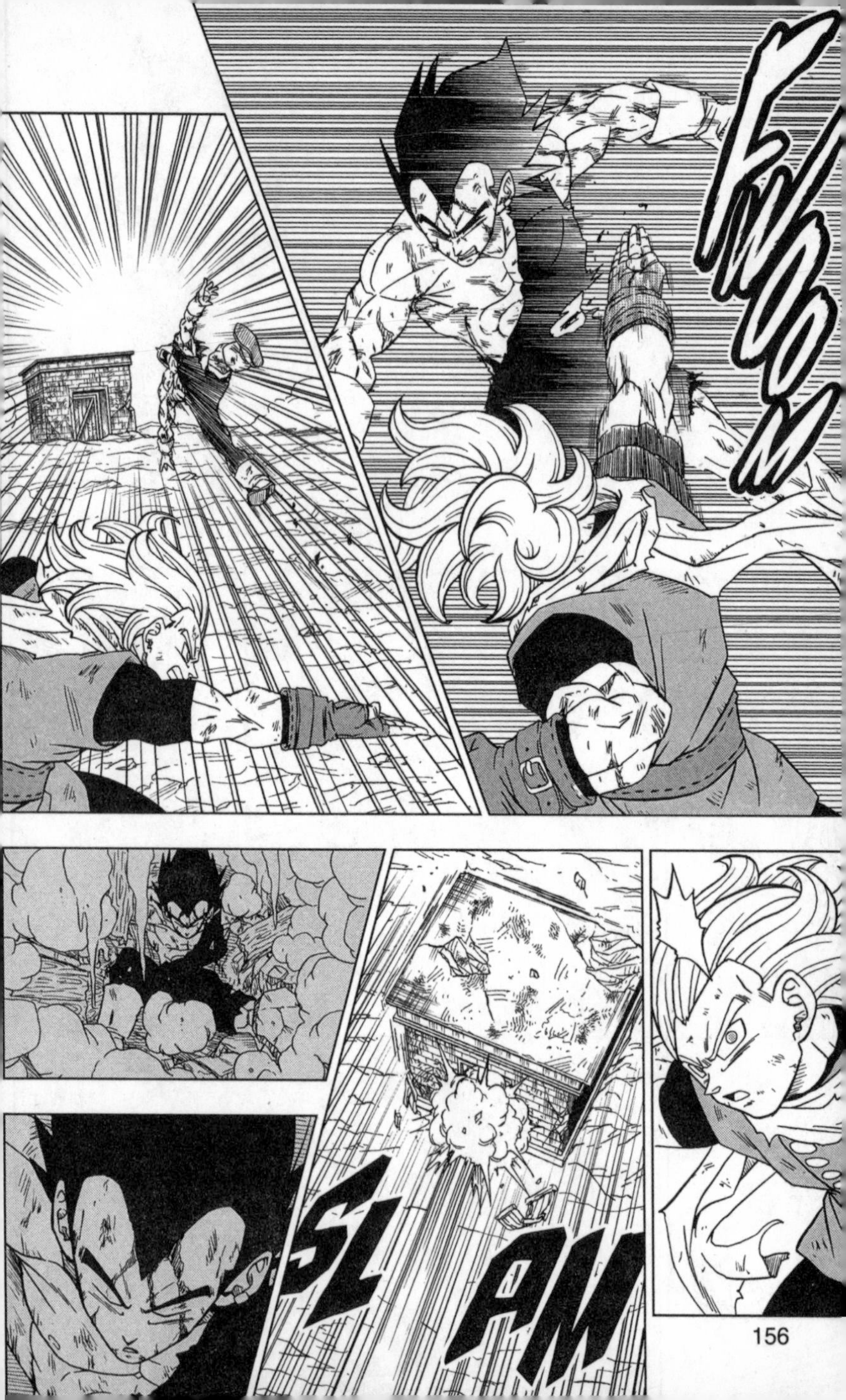
FWOOM
SLAM

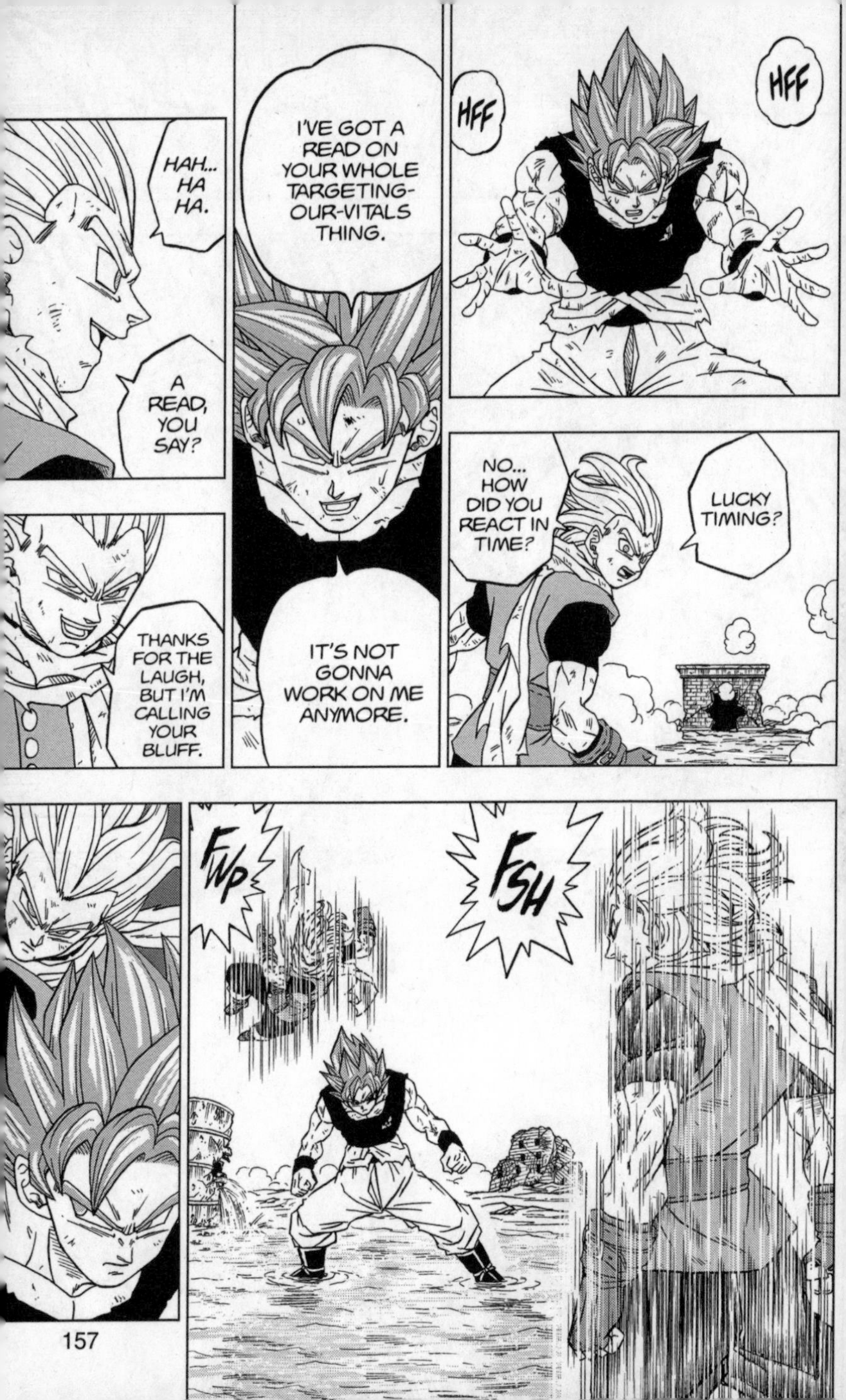
HFF
HFF
NO... HOW DID YOU REACT IN TIME?
LUCKY TIMING?
I'VE GOT A READ ON YOUR WHOLE TARGETING-OUR-VITALS THING.
IT'S NOT GONNA WORK ON ME ANYMORE.
HAH... HA HA.
A READ, YOU SAY?
THANKS FOR THE LAUGH, BUT I'M CALLING YOUR BLUFF.
FSH
FWP

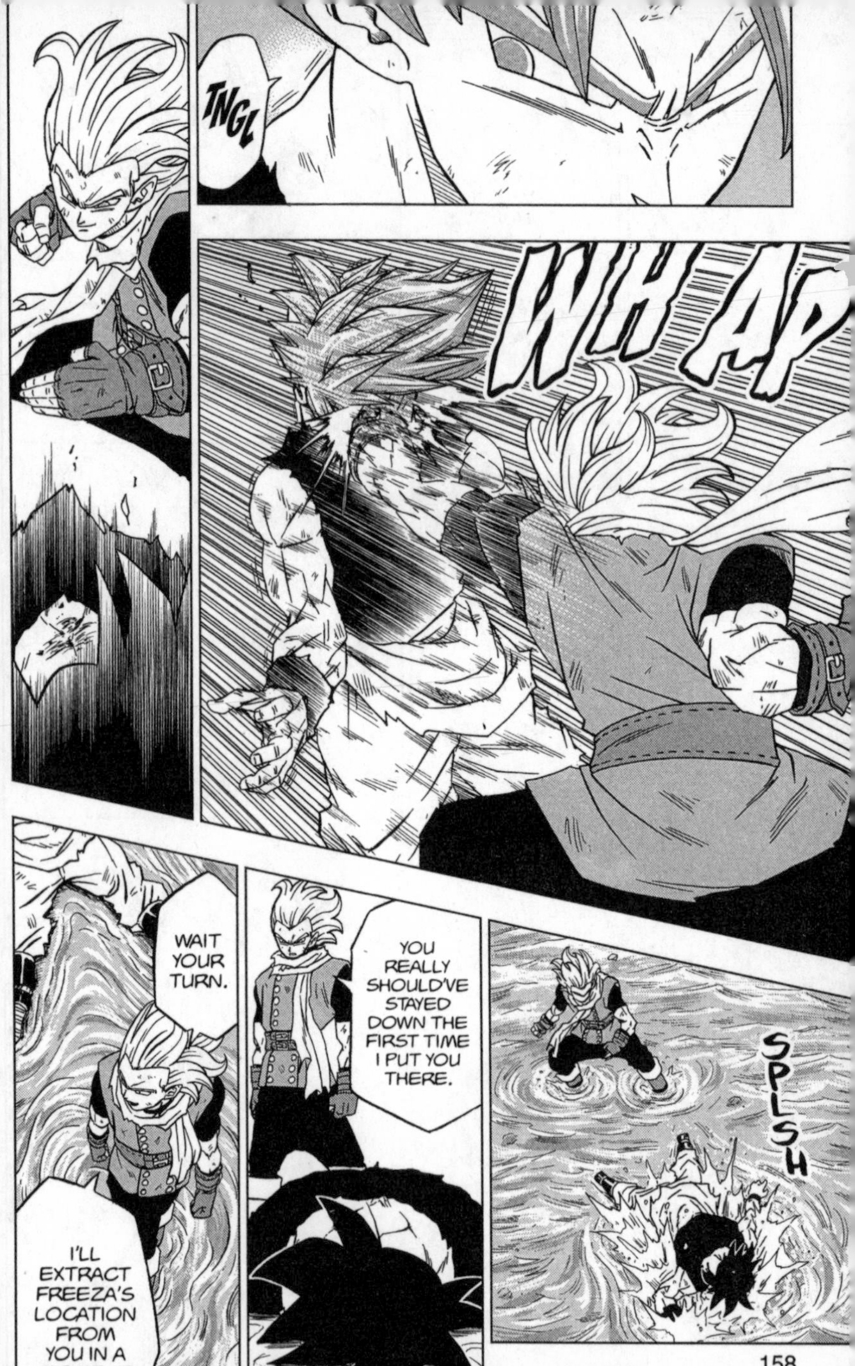

TNGL
WHAP
SPLSH
YOU REALLY SHOULD'VE STAYED DOWN THE FIRST TIME I PUT YOU THERE.
WAIT YOUR TURN.
I'LL EXTRACT FREEZA'S LOCATION FROM YOU IN A MOMENT.

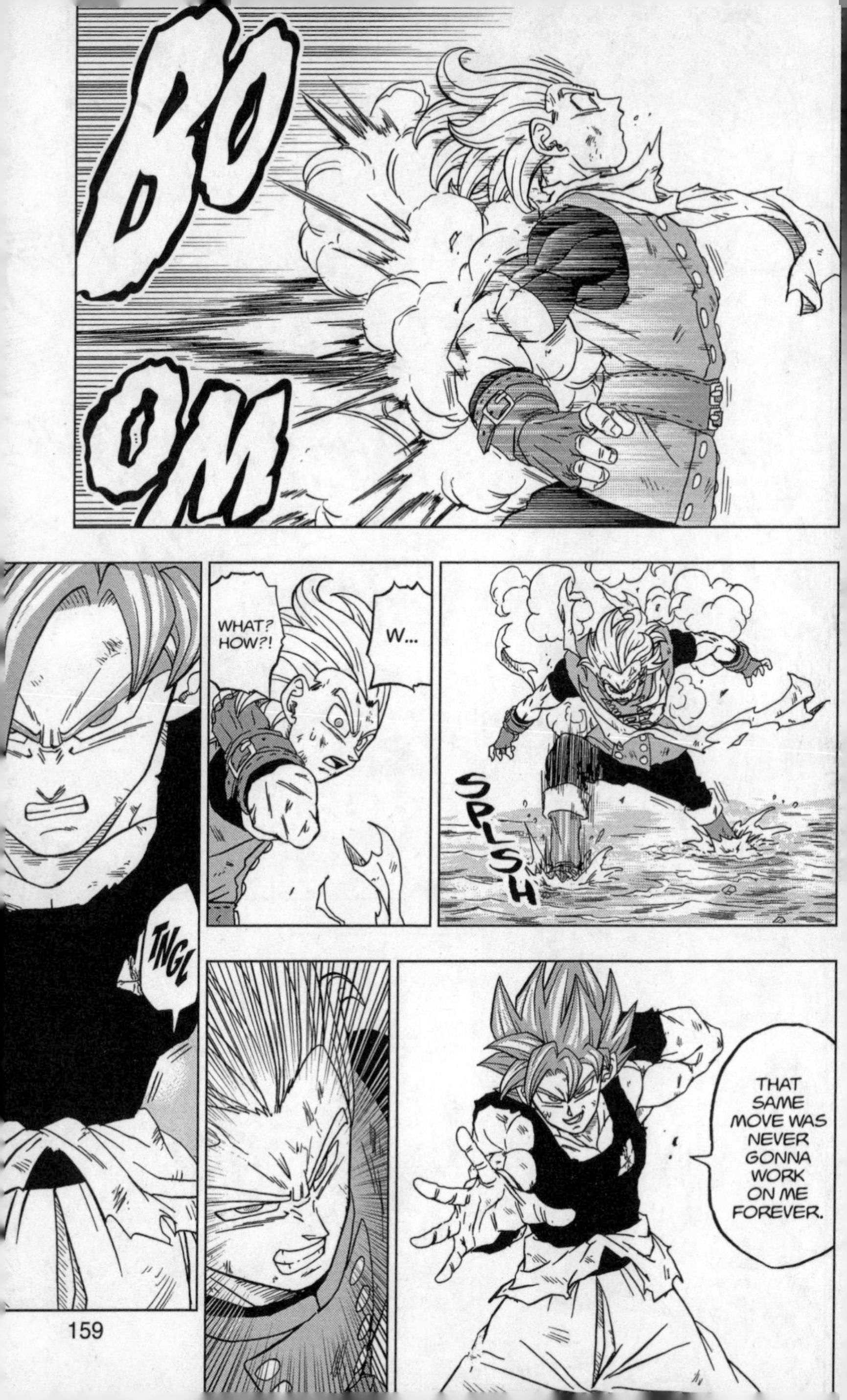
BOOM
SPLSH
W...
WHAT? HOW?!
THAT SAME MOVE WAS NEVER GONNA WORK ON ME FOREVER.
TNGL

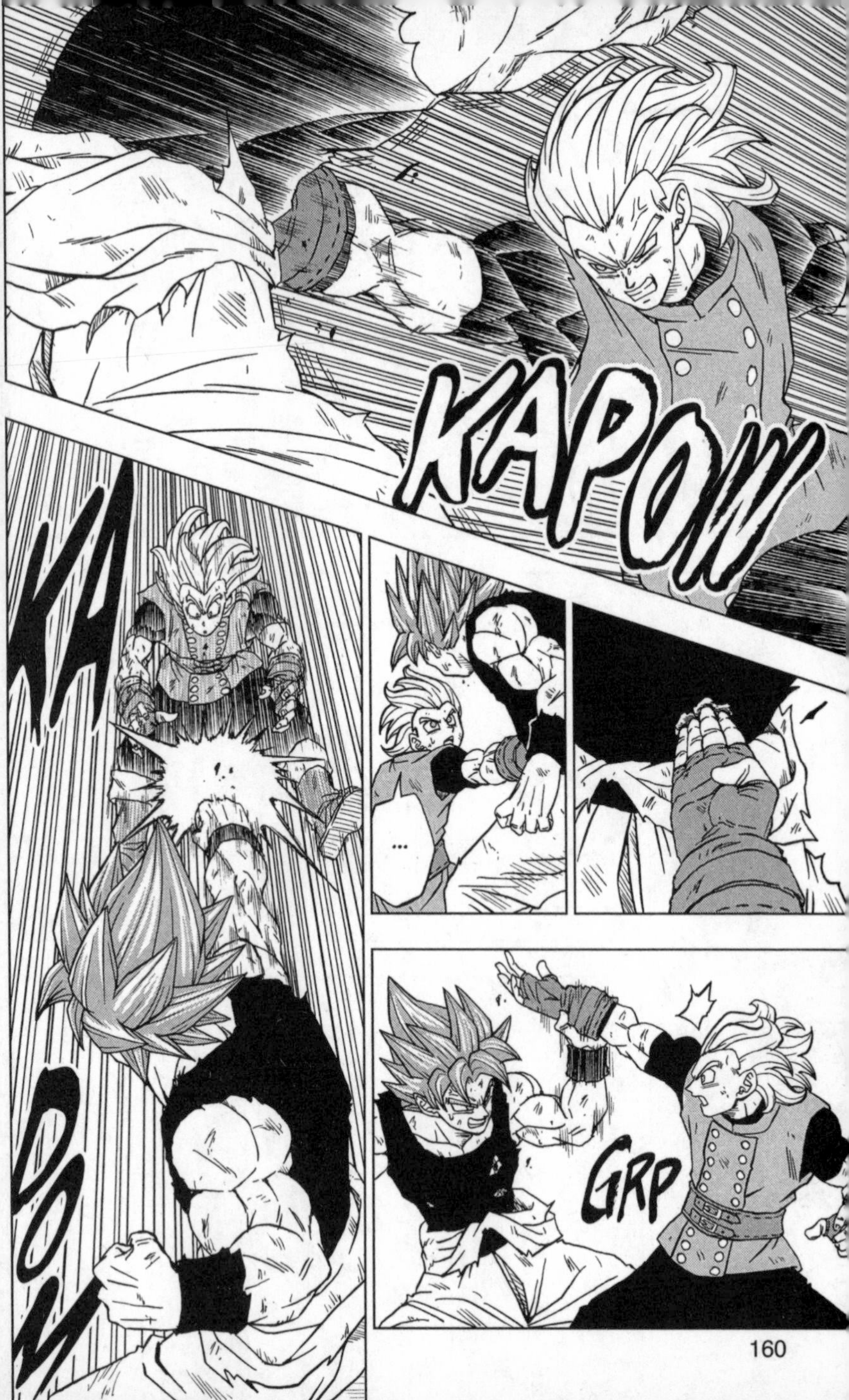
KAPOW
...
GRP

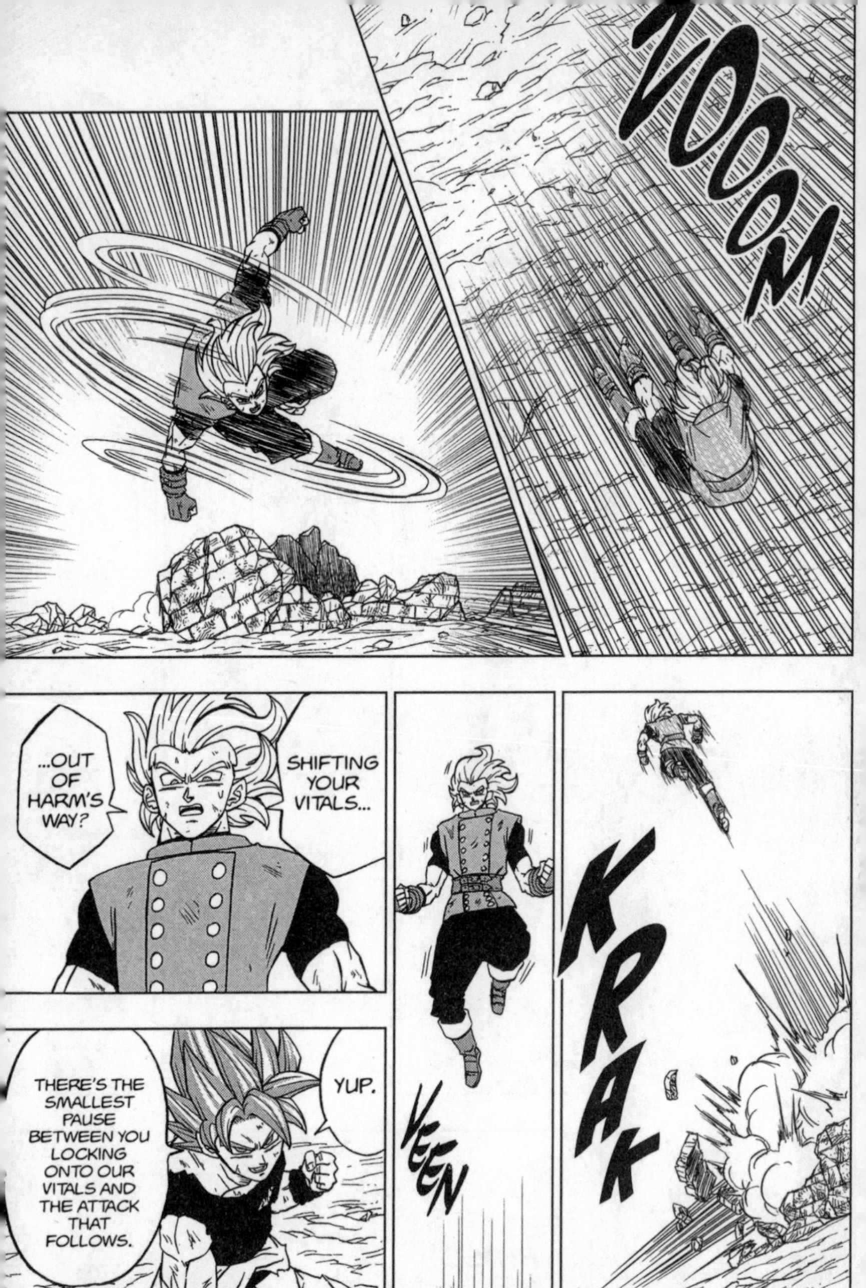
VOOOM
KRAK
VEEN
SHIFTING YOUR VITALS...
...OUT OF HARM'S WAY?
YUP.
THERE'S THE SMALLEST PAUSE BETWEEN YOU LOCKING ONTO OUR VITALS AND THE ATTACK THAT FOLLOWS.

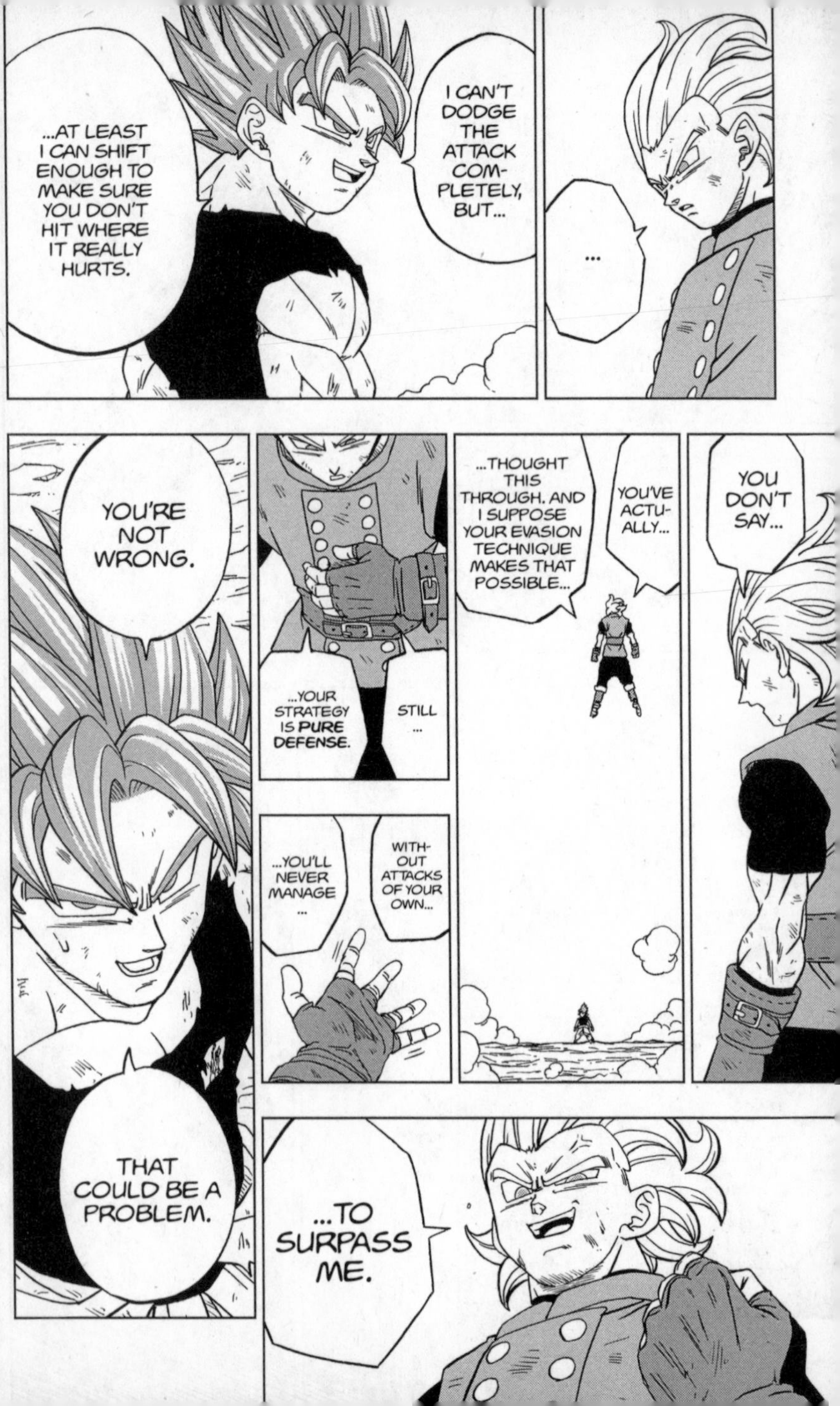
...
I CAN'T DODGE THE ATTACK COMPLETELY, BUT...
...AT LEAST I CAN SHIFT ENOUGH TO MAKE SURE YOU DON'T HIT WHERE IT REALLY HURTS.
YOU DON'T SAY...
YOU'VE ACTUALLY...
...THOUGHT THIS THROUGH. AND I SUPPOSE YOUR EVASION TECHNIQUE MAKES THAT POSSIBLE...
STILL...
...YOUR STRATEGY IS PURE DEFENSE.
WITHOUT ATTACKS OF YOUR OWN...
...YOU'LL NEVER MANAGE...
...TO SURPASS ME.
YOU'RE NOT WRONG.
THAT COULD BE A PROBLEM.

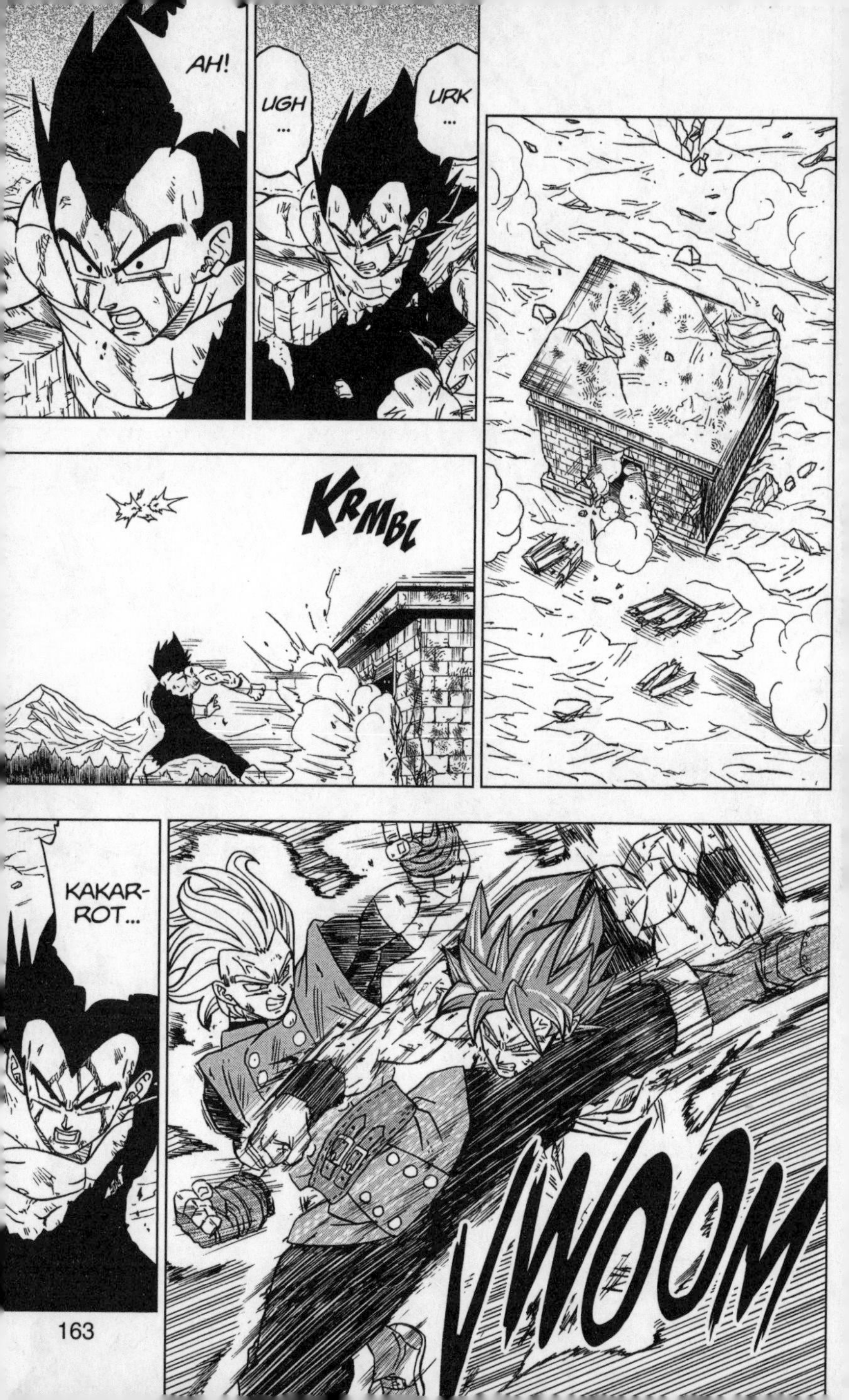
URK ...
UGH ...
AH!
KRMBL
VWOOM
KAKAR-
ROT...

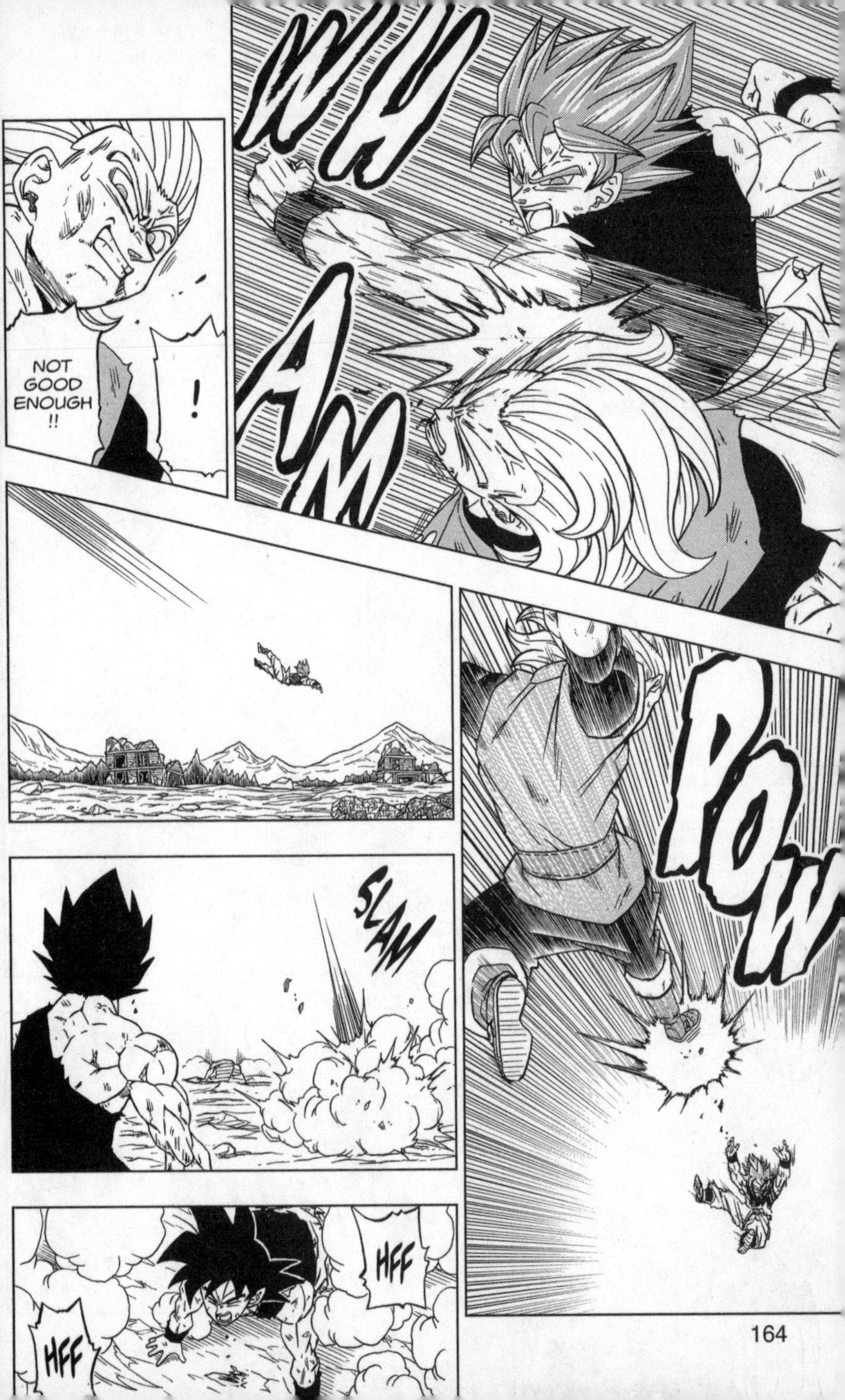
WHAM
!
NOT GOOD ENOUGH !!
POW
SLAM
HFF
HFF

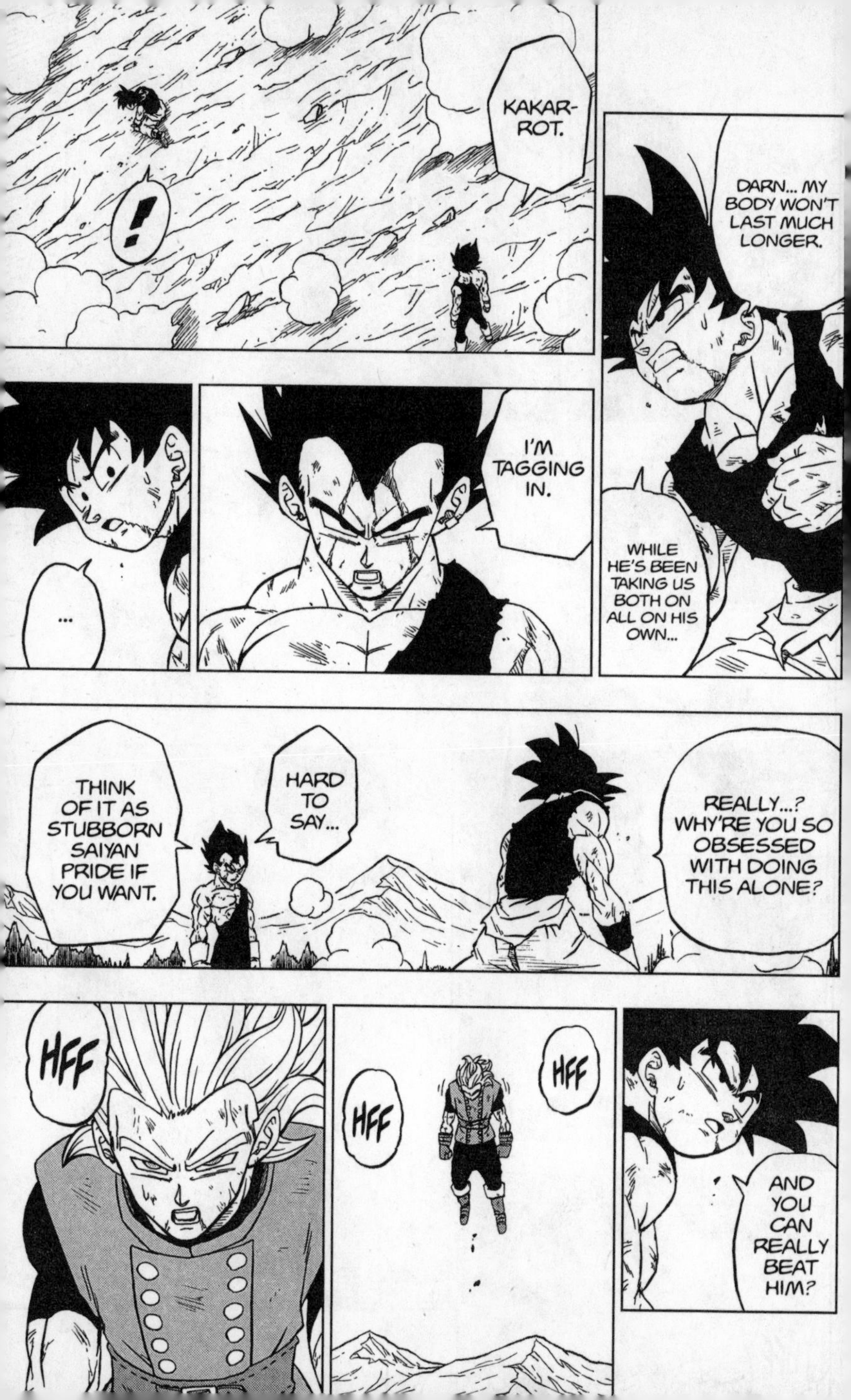

DARN... MY BODY WON'T LAST MUCH LONGER.
WHILE HE'S BEEN TAKING US BOTH ON ALL ON HIS OWN...
KAKAR-ROT.
!
I'M TAGGING IN.
...
REALLY...? WHY'RE YOU SO OBSESSED WITH DOING THIS ALONE?
HARD TO SAY...
THINK OF IT AS STUBBORN SAIYAN PRIDE IF YOU WANT.
AND YOU CAN REALLY BEAT HIM?
HFF
HFF
HFF

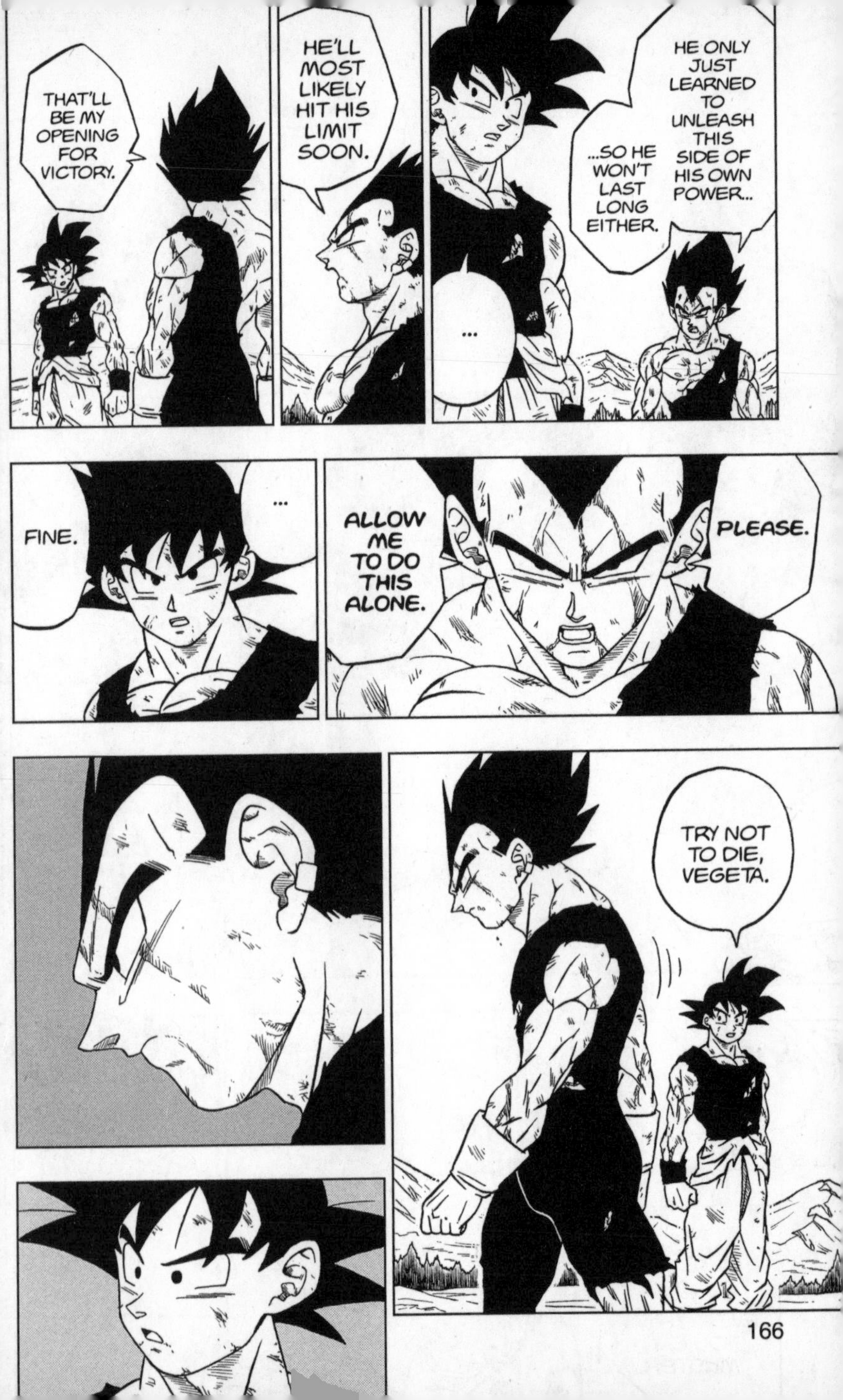
HE ONLY JUST LEARNED TO UNLEASH THIS SIDE OF HIS OWN POWER...
...SO HE WON'T LAST LONG EITHER.
...
HE'LL MOST LIKELY HIT HIS LIMIT SOON.
THAT'LL BE MY OPENING FOR VICTORY.
PLEASE.
ALLOW ME TO DO THIS ALONE.
...
FINE.
TRY NOT TO DIE, VEGETA.

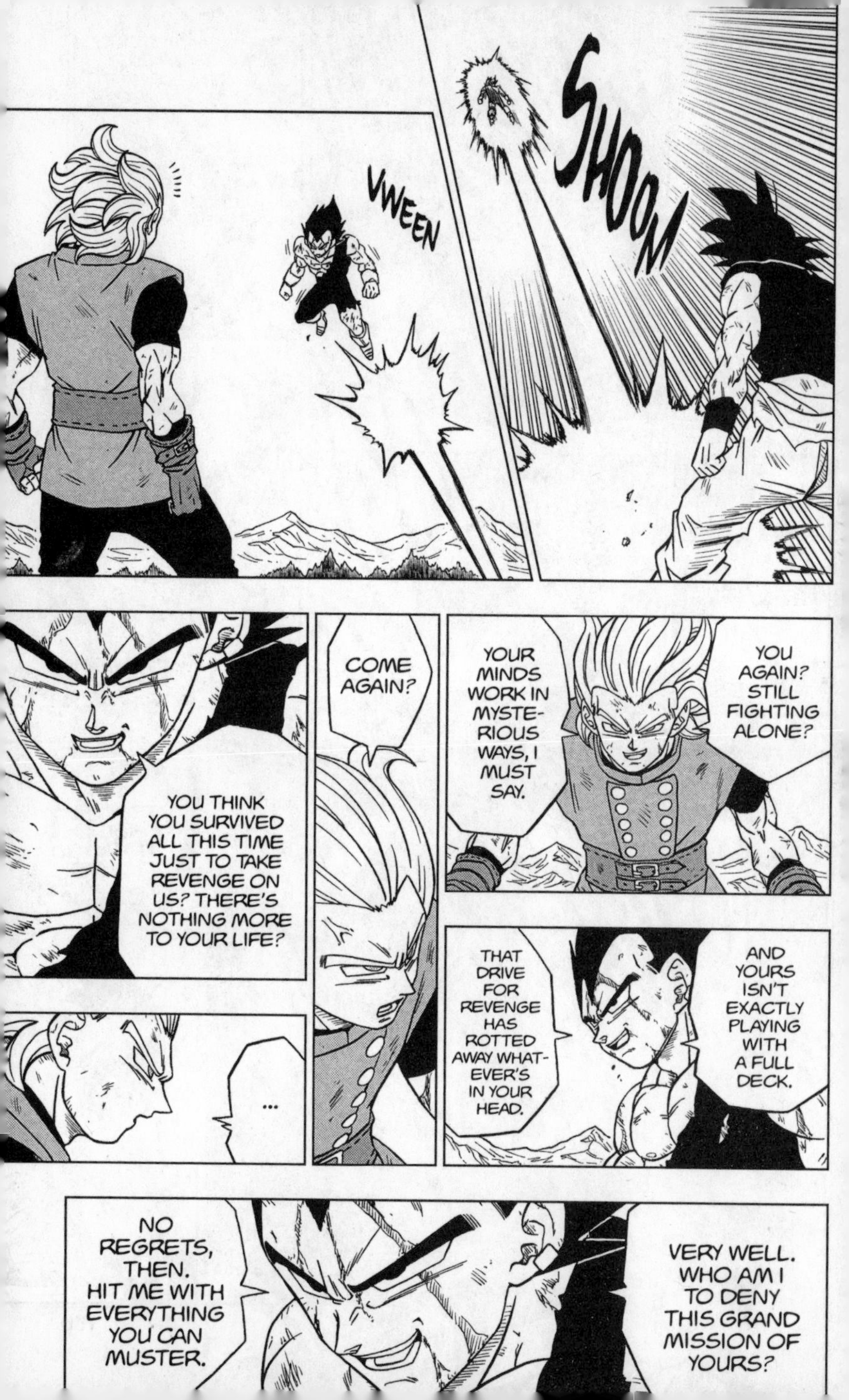
SHOOM
VWEEN
YOU AGAIN? STILL FIGHTING ALONE?
YOUR MINDS WORK IN MYSTE-RIOUS WAYS, I MUST SAY.
AND YOURS ISN'T EXACTLY PLAYING WITH A FULL DECK.
THAT DRIVE FOR REVENGE HAS ROTTED AWAY WHAT-EVER'S IN YOUR HEAD.
COME AGAIN?
YOU THINK YOU SURVIVED ALL THIS TIME JUST TO TAKE REVENGE ON US? THERE'S NOTHING MORE TO YOUR LIFE?
...
VERY WELL. WHO AM I TO DENY THIS GRAND MISSION OF YOURS?
NO REGRETS, THEN. HIT ME WITH EVERYTHING YOU CAN MUSTER.

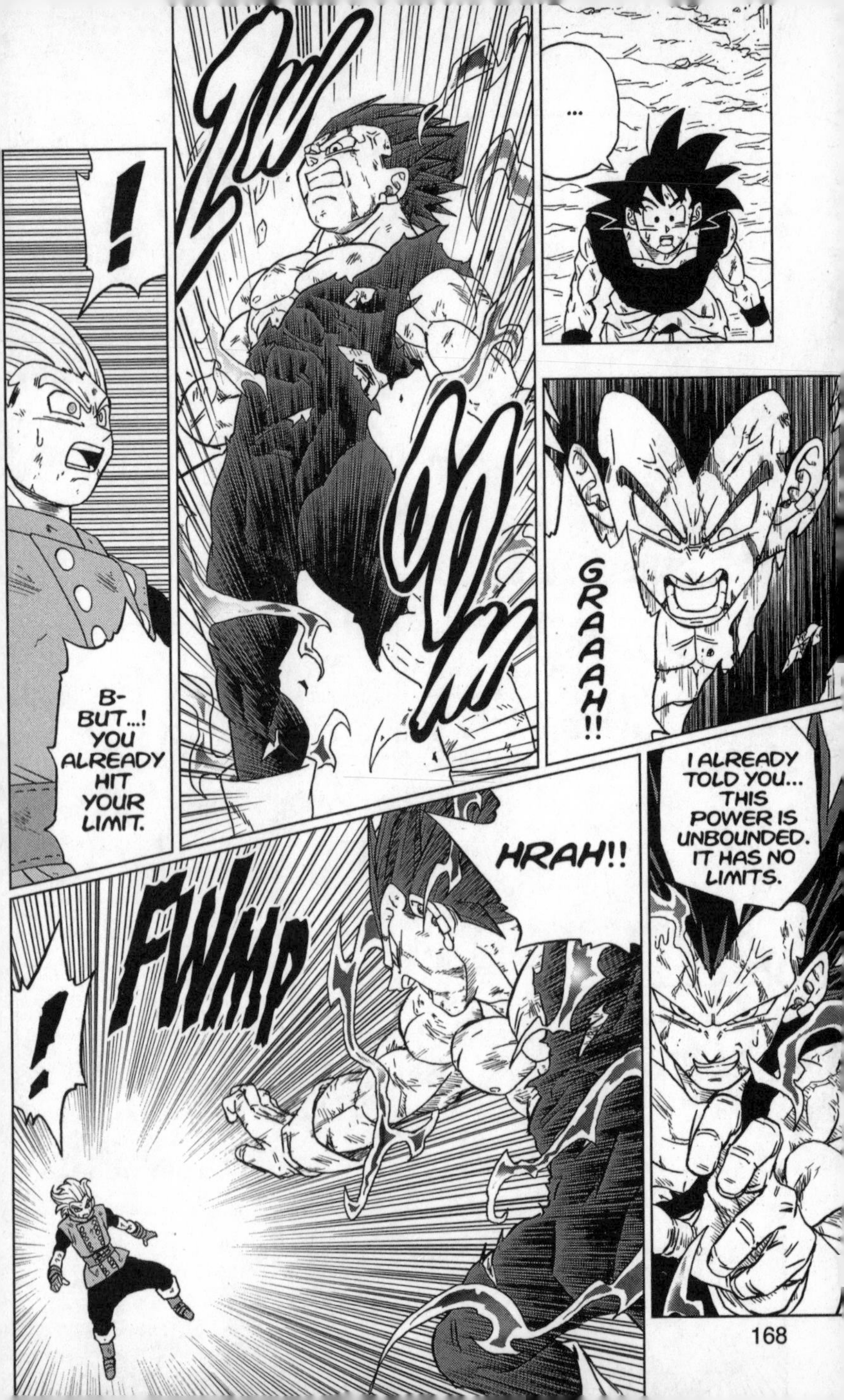
...
GRAAAAH!!
!
B-BUT...! YOU ALREADY HIT YOUR LIMIT.
I ALREADY TOLD YOU... THIS POWER IS UNBOUNDED. IT HAS NO LIMITS.
HRAH!!
FWMP
!!

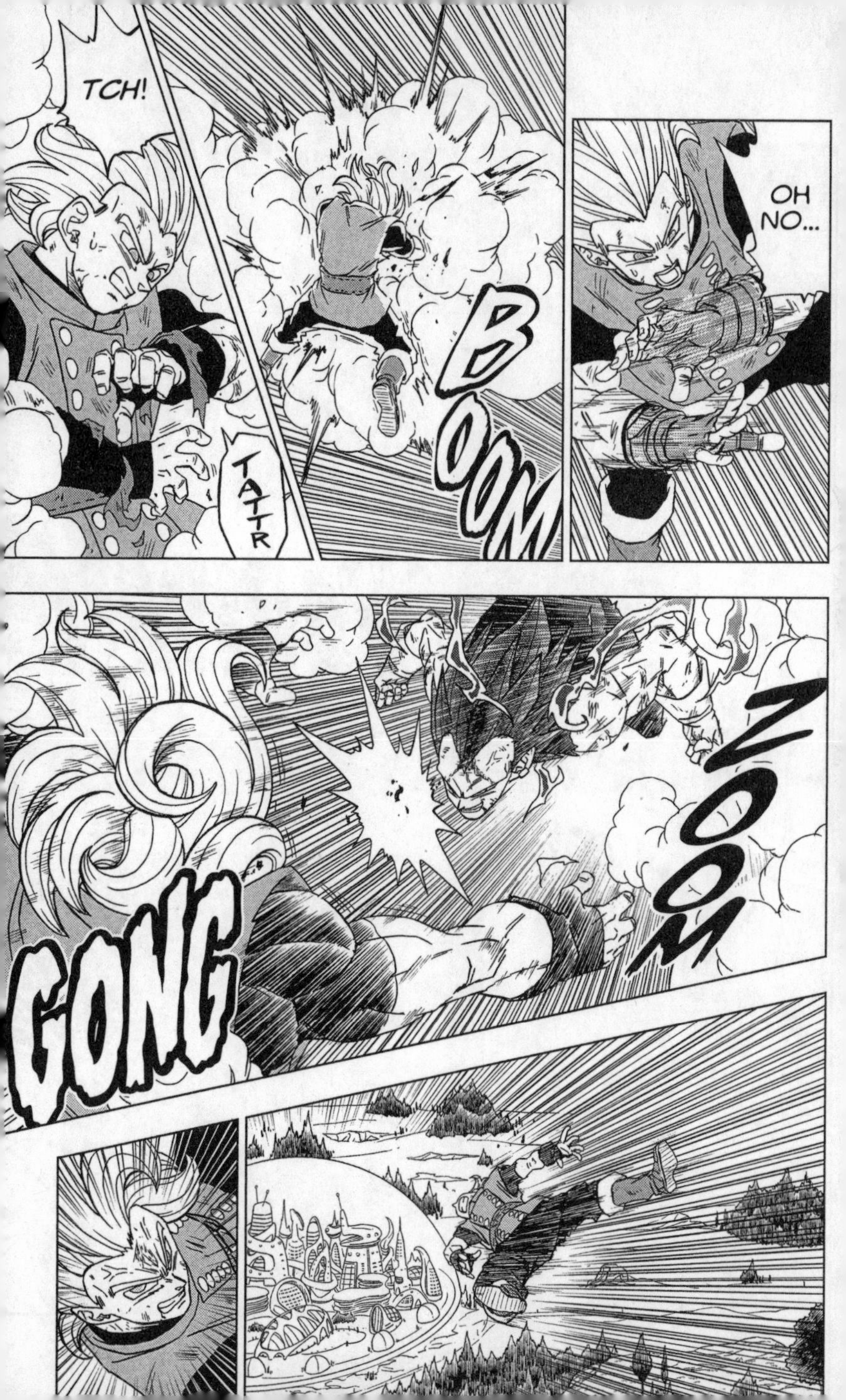
OH NO...
BOOM
TCH!
TATTR
ZOOM
GONG

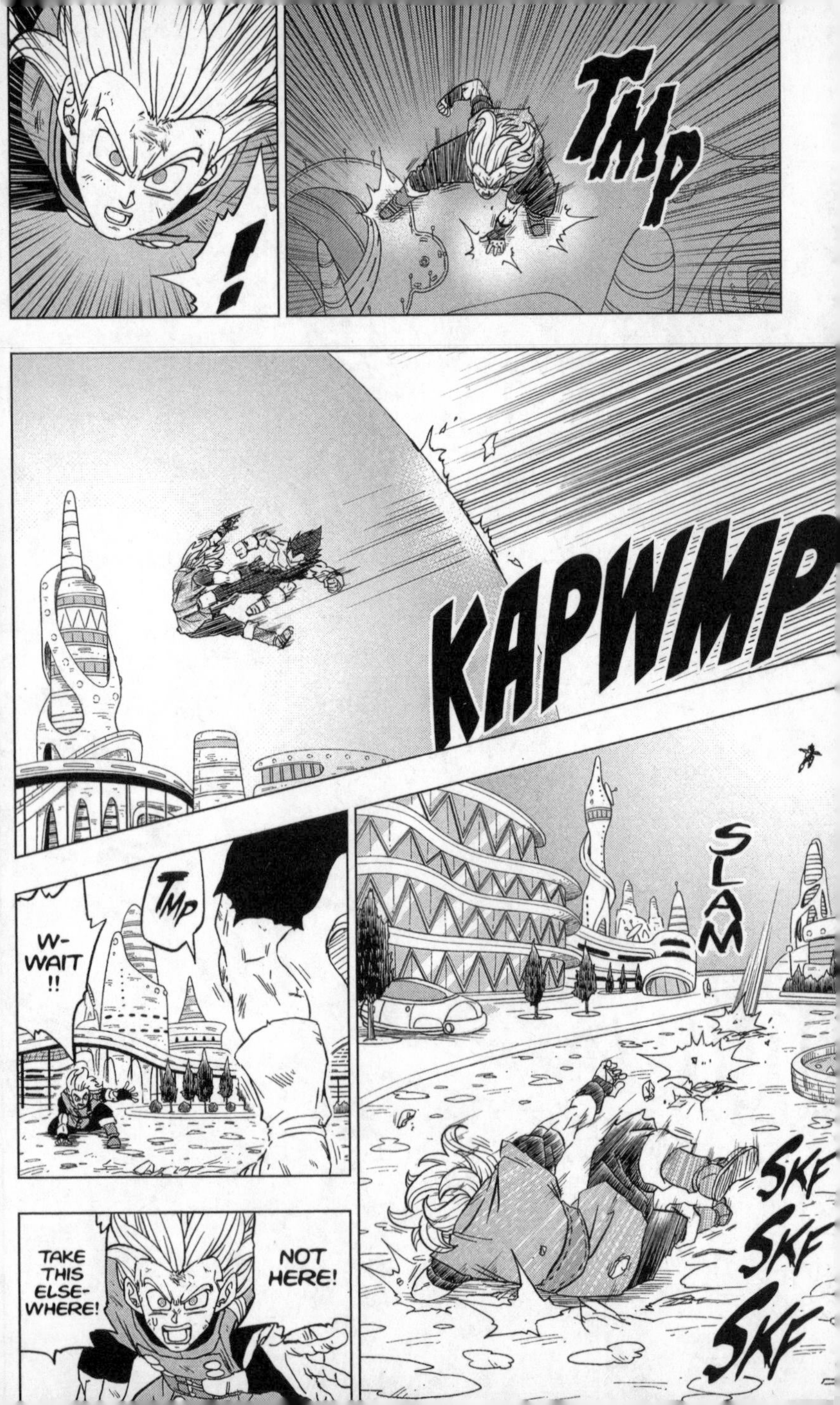
TMP
!
KAPWMP
SLAM
SKF SKF SKF
TMP
W-WAIT!!
NOT HERE!
TAKE THIS ELSE-WHERE!

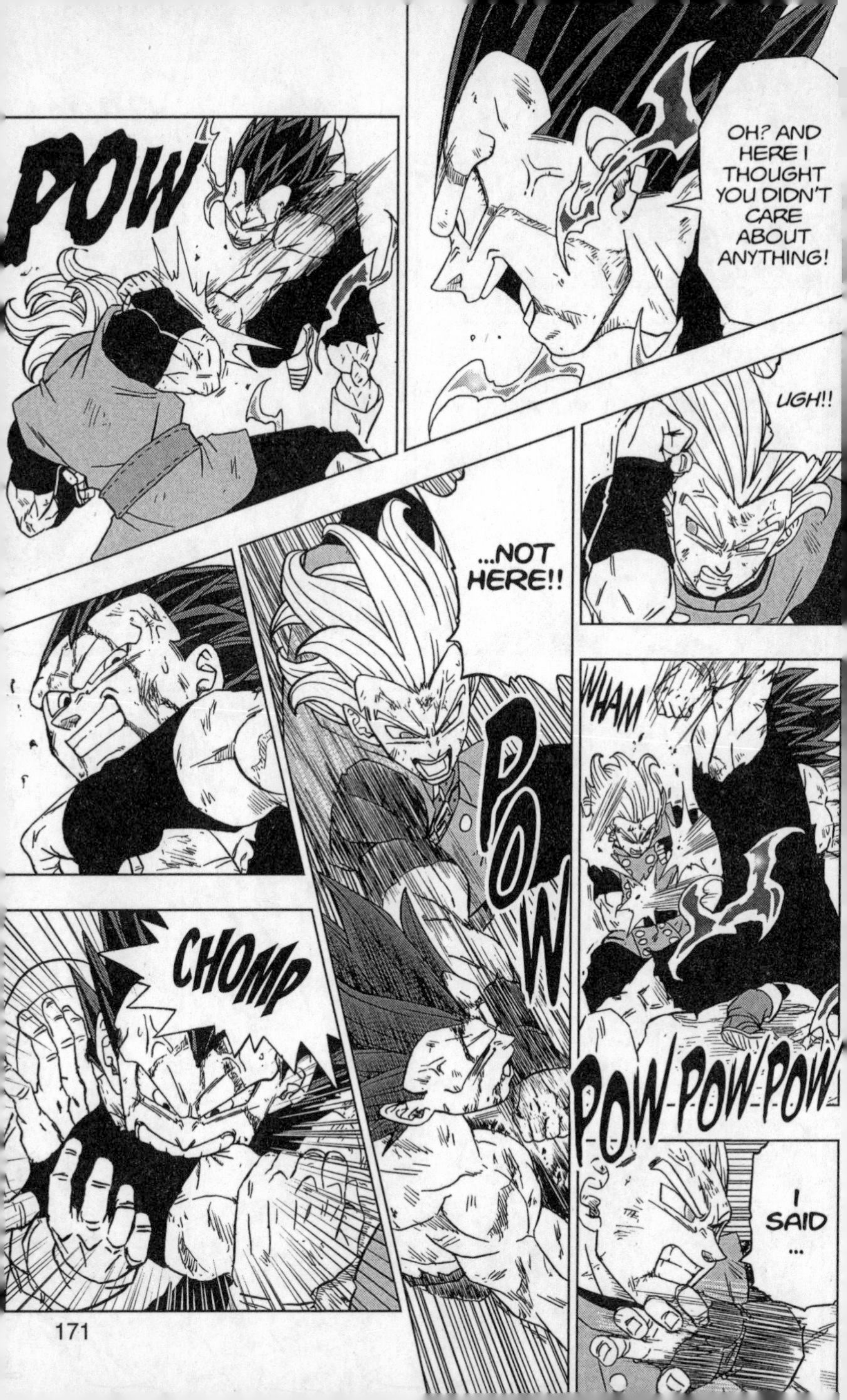
OH? AND HERE I THOUGHT YOU DIDN'T CARE ABOUT ANYTHING!
POW
UGH!!
...NOT HERE!!
POW
WHAM
POW-POW-POW
I SAID ...
CHOMP

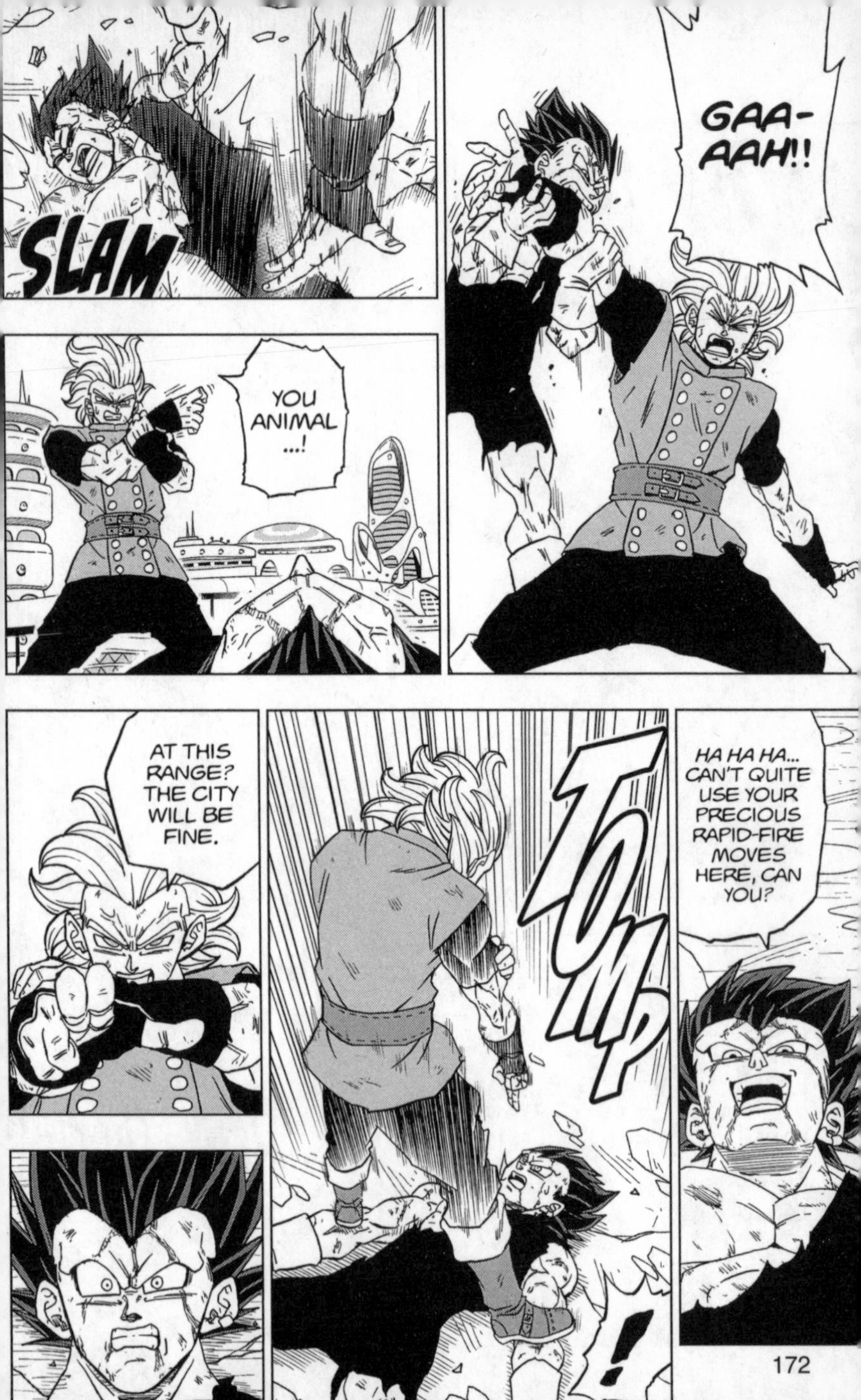
GAA-AAH!!
SLAM
YOU ANIMAL ...!
HA HA HA... CAN'T QUITE USE YOUR PRECIOUS RAPID-FIRE MOVES HERE, CAN YOU?
TOMP
!
AT THIS RANGE? THE CITY WILL BE FINE.

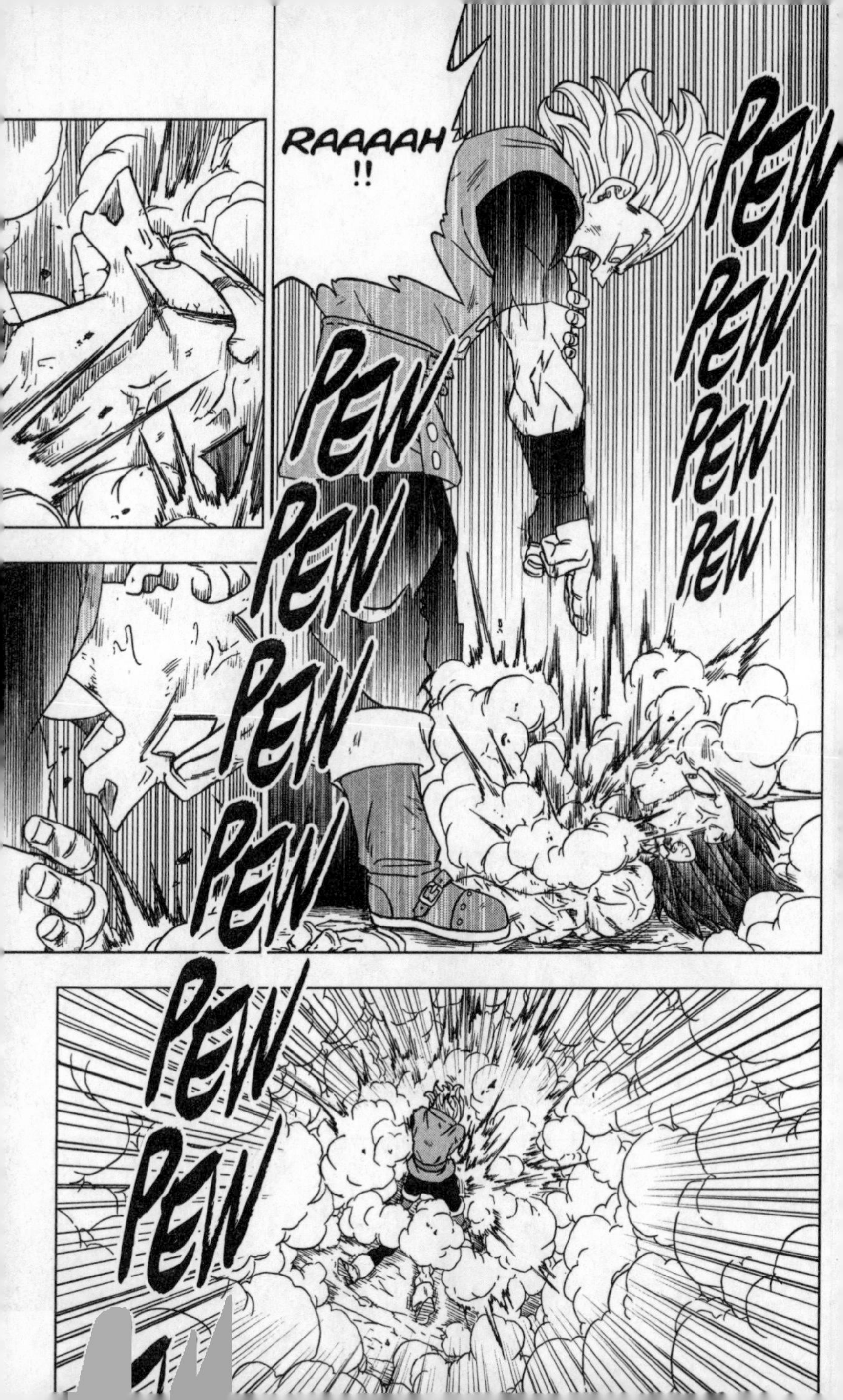
RAAAAH !!
PEW PEW PEW PEW
PEW PEW PEW PEW PEW
PEW PEW

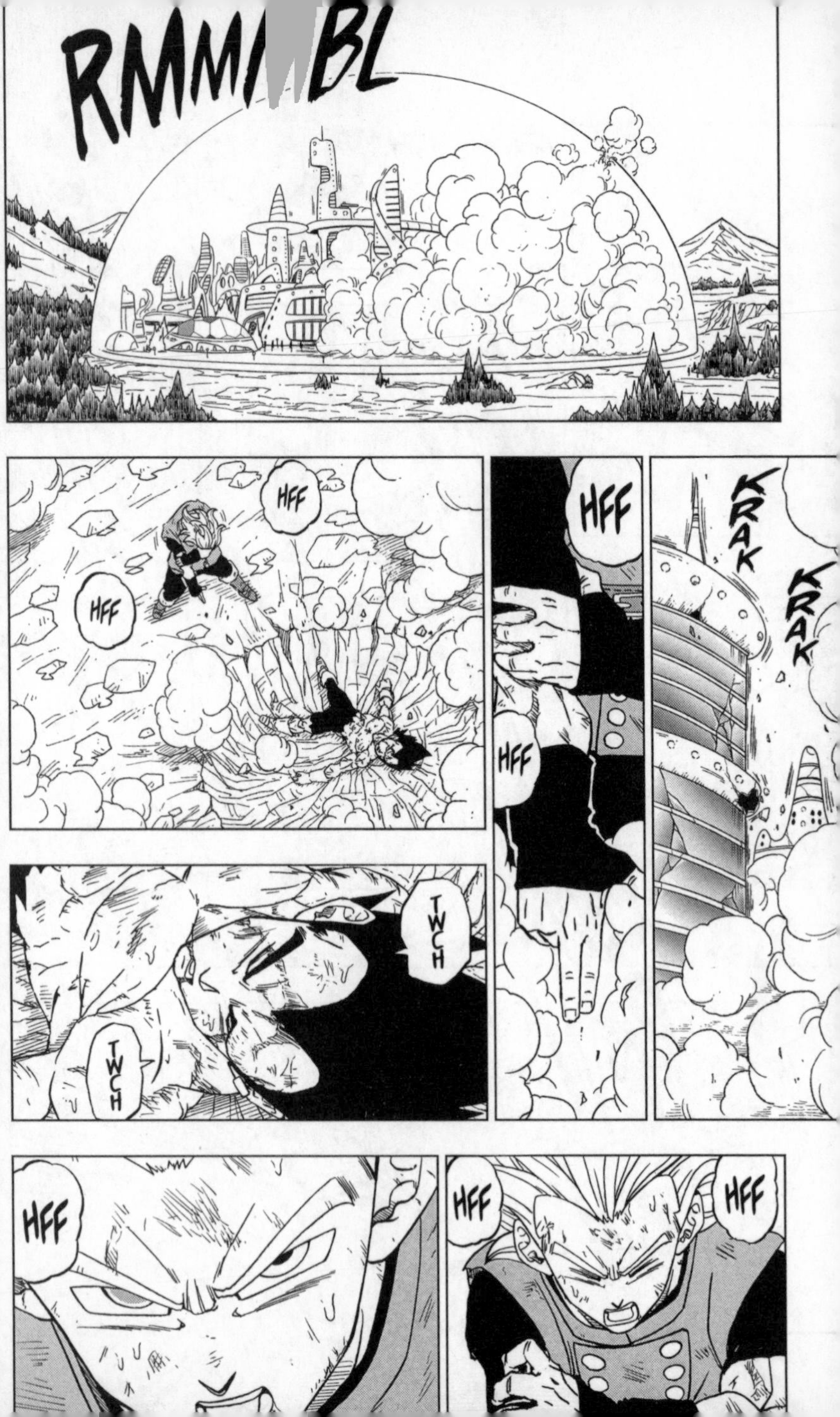
RMM BL
KRAK
KRAK
HFF
HFF
HFF
HFF
TWCH
TWCH
HFF
HFF
HFF

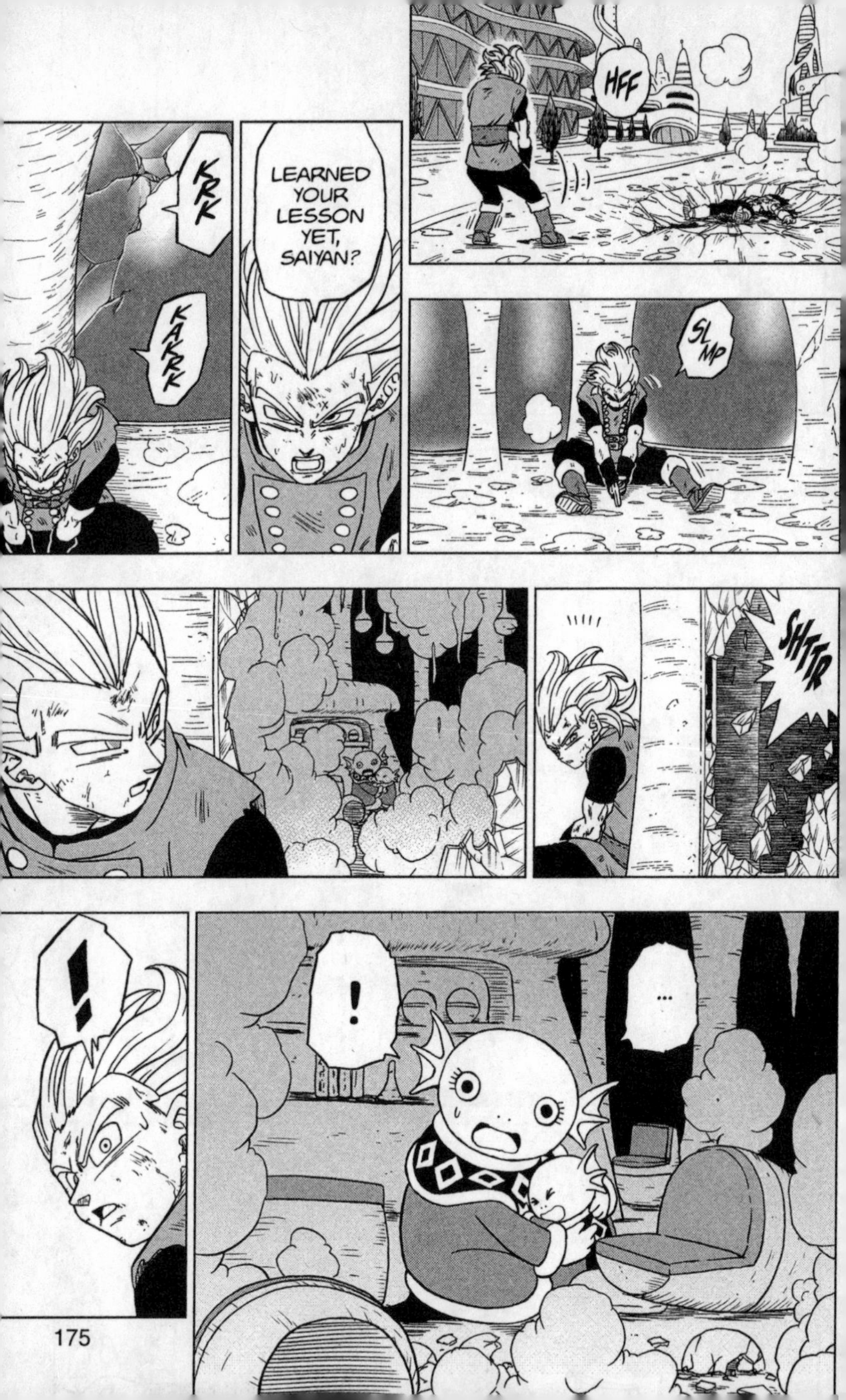
HFF
SLMP
LEARNED YOUR LESSON YET, SAIYAN?
KRK
KAKRK
SHTTR
...
!
!

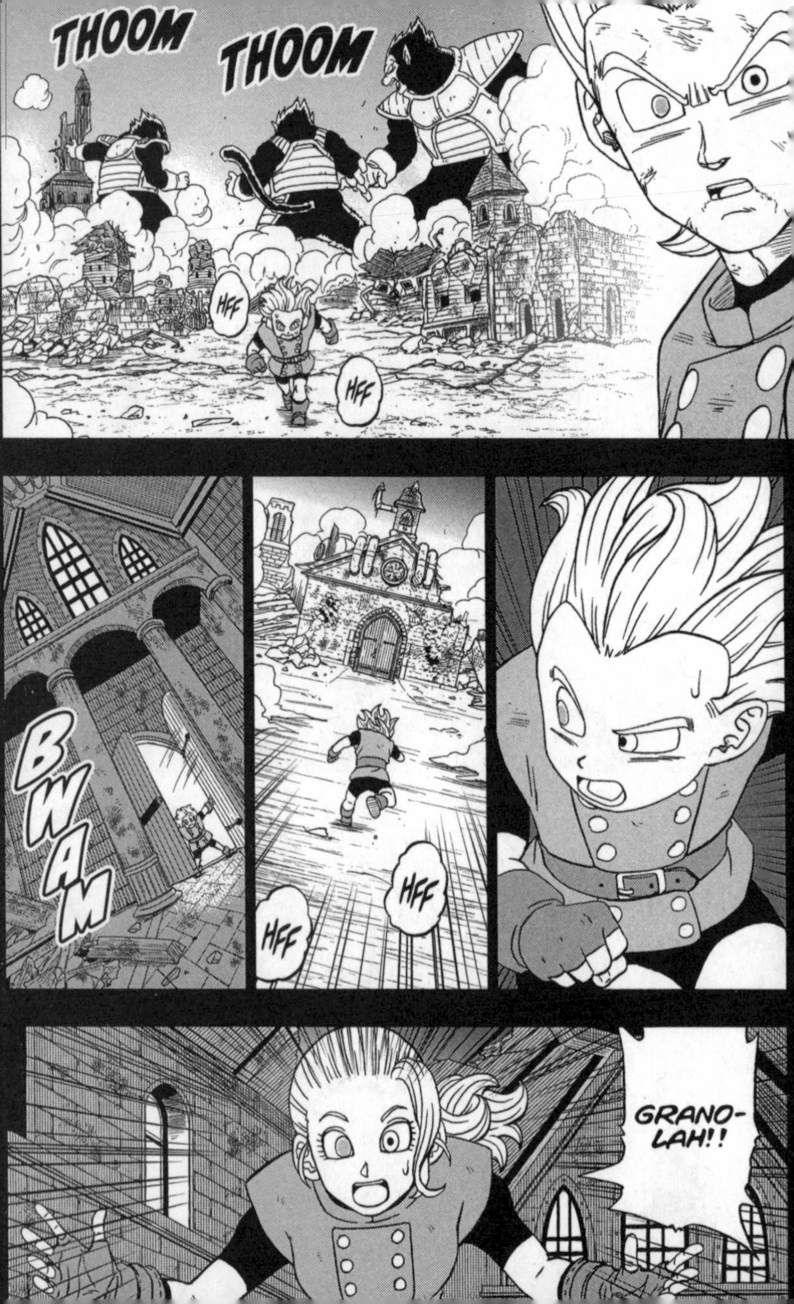
THOOM
THOOM
HFF
HFF
HFF
HFF
BWAM
GRANO-LAH!!

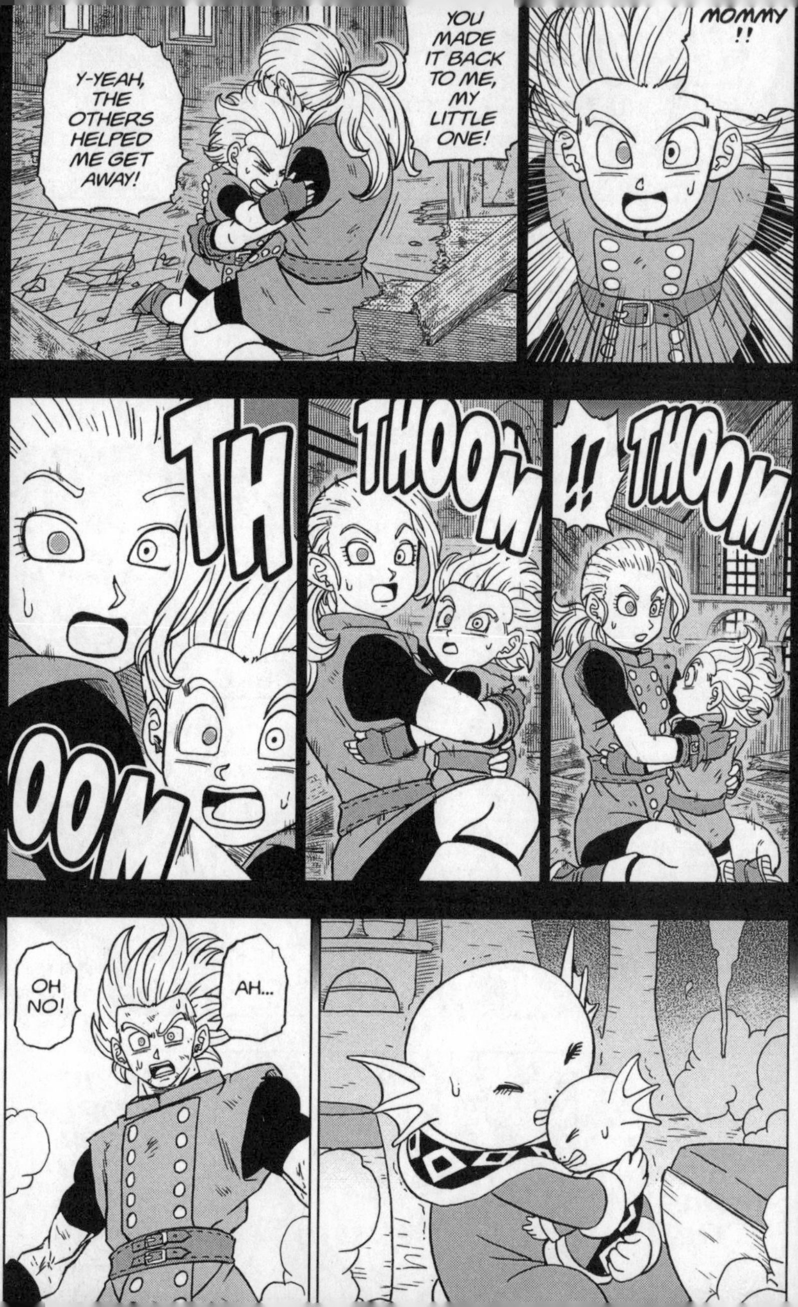
MOMMY !!
YOU MADE IT BACK TO ME, MY LITTLE ONE!
Y-YEAH, THE OTHERS HELPED ME GET AWAY!
THOOM
!!
THOOM
THOOM
AH...
OH NO!

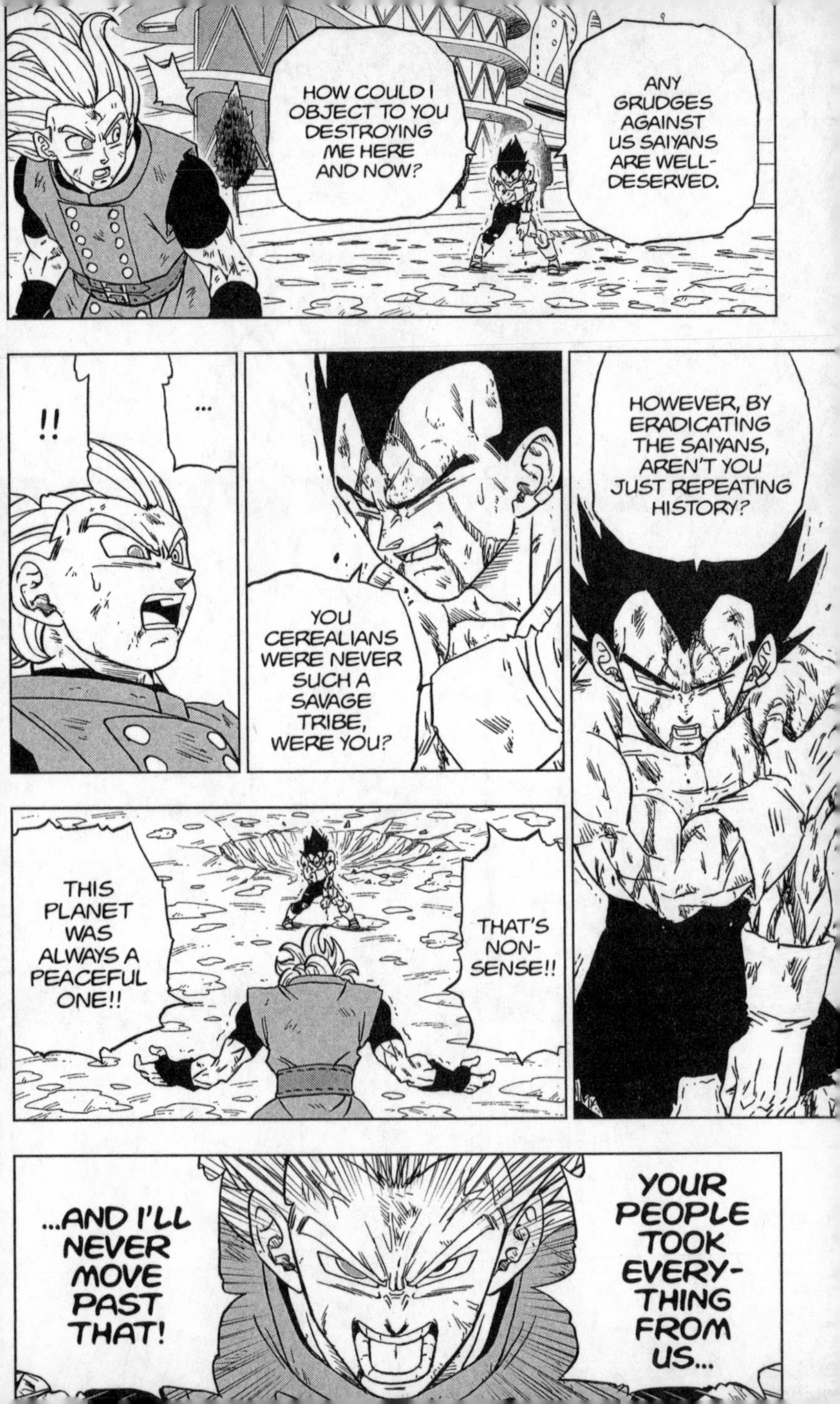
ANY GRUDGES AGAINST US SAIYANS ARE WELL-DESERVED.
HOW COULD I OBJECT TO YOU DESTROYING ME HERE AND NOW?
HOWEVER, BY ERADICATING THE SAIYANS, AREN'T YOU JUST REPEATING HISTORY?
YOU CEREALIANS WERE NEVER SUCH A SAVAGE TRIBE, WERE YOU?
...
!!
THAT'S NON-SENSE!!
THIS PLANET WAS ALWAYS A PEACEFUL ONE!!
YOUR PEOPLE TOOK EVERY-THING FROM US...
...AND I'LL NEVER MOVE PAST THAT!

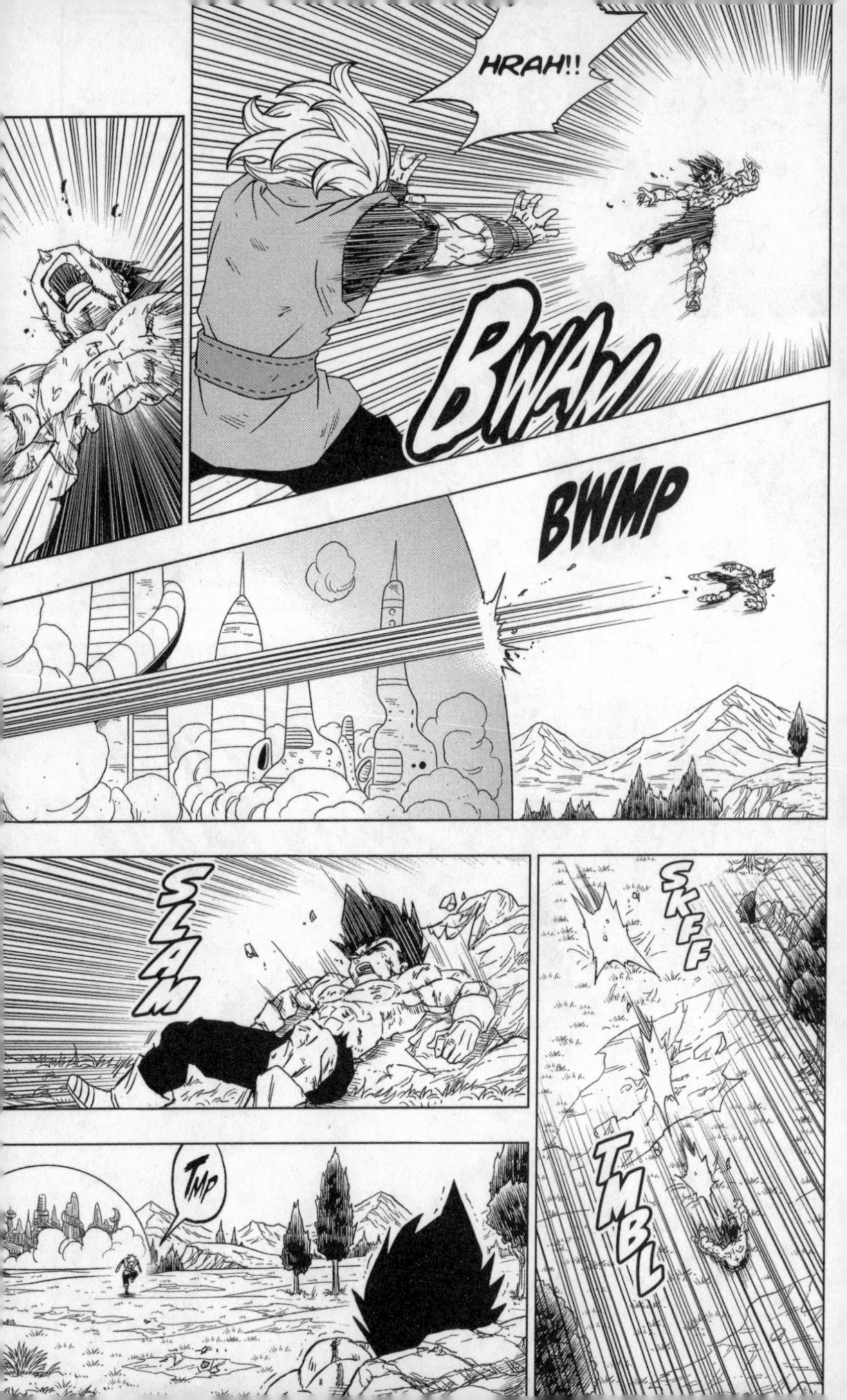
HRAH!!
BWAM
BWMP
SKFF
SLAM
TMBL
TMP

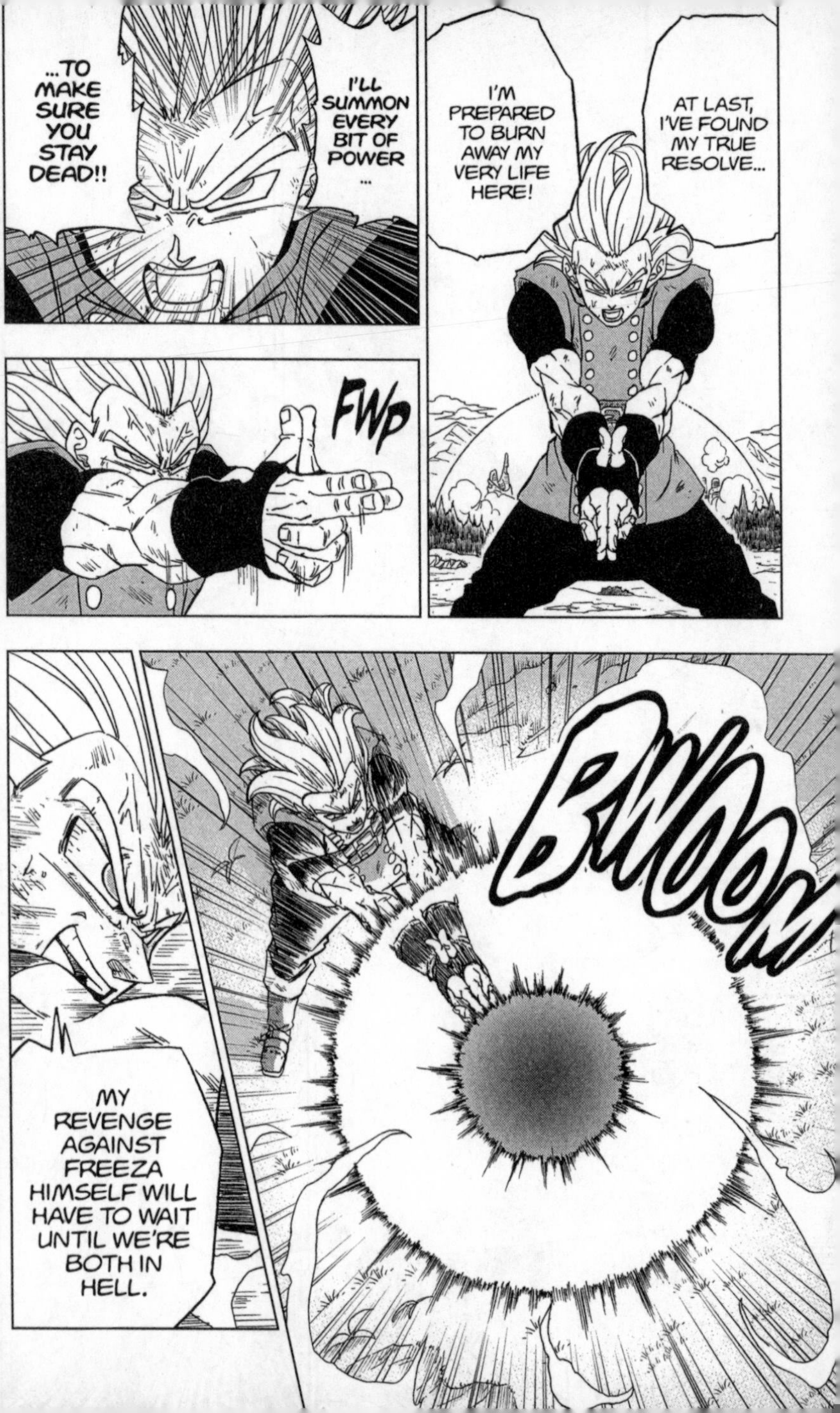
AT LAST, I'VE FOUND MY TRUE RESOLVE...
I'M PREPARED TO BURN AWAY MY VERY LIFE HERE!
I'LL SUMMON EVERY BIT OF POWER ...
...TO MAKE SURE YOU STAY DEAD!!
FWP
BWOOM
MY REVENGE AGAINST FREEZA HIMSELF WILL HAVE TO WAIT UNTIL WE'RE BOTH IN HELL.

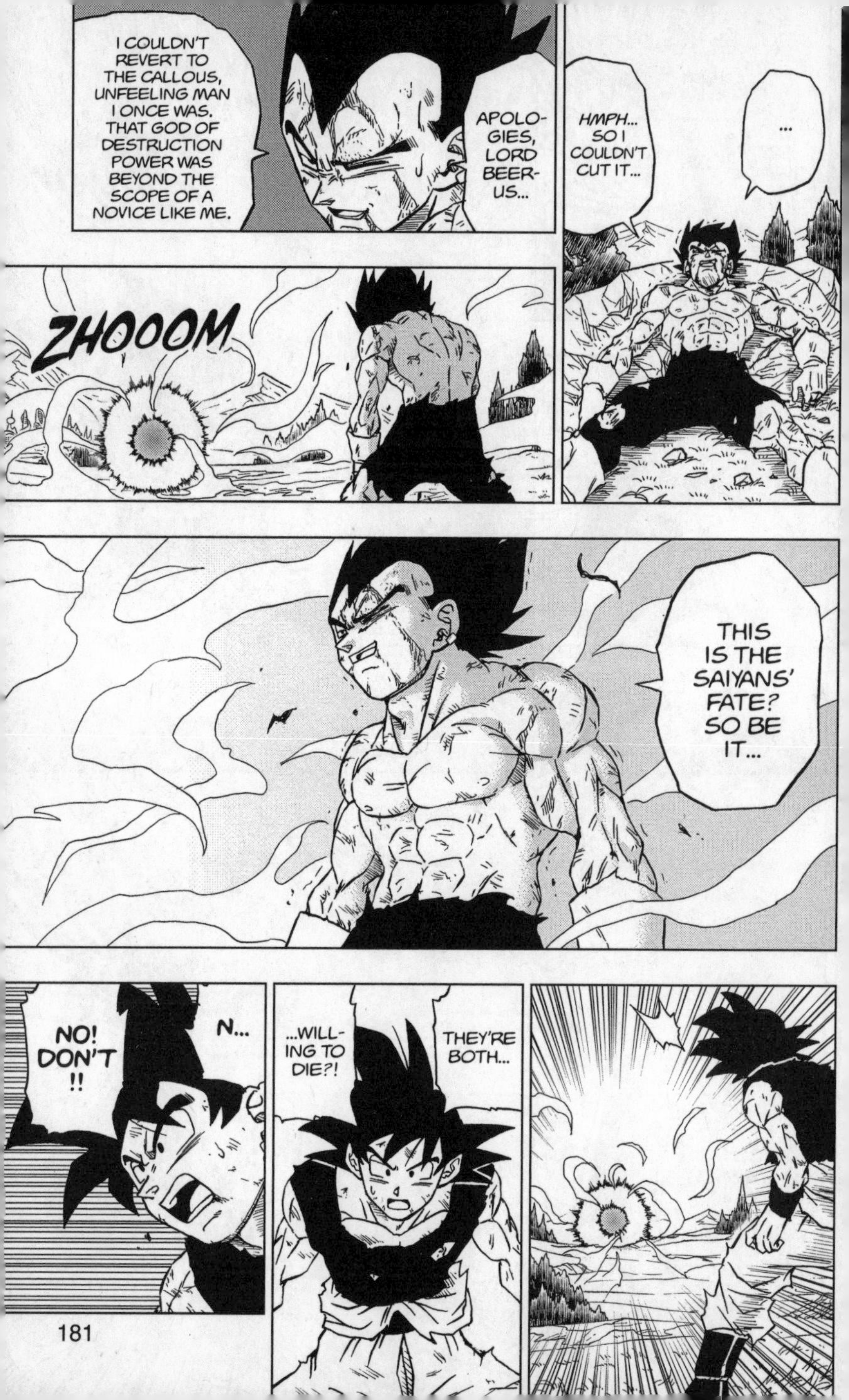
...
HMPH... SO I COULDN'T CUT IT...
APOLOGIES, LORD BEERUS...
I COULDN'T REVERT TO THE CALLOUS, UNFEELING MAN I ONCE WAS. THAT GOD OF DESTRUCTION POWER WAS BEYOND THE SCOPE OF A NOVICE LIKE ME.
ZHOOOM
THIS IS THE SAIYANS' FATE? SO BE IT...
THEY'RE BOTH...
...WILLING TO DIE?!
N...
NO! DON'T!!

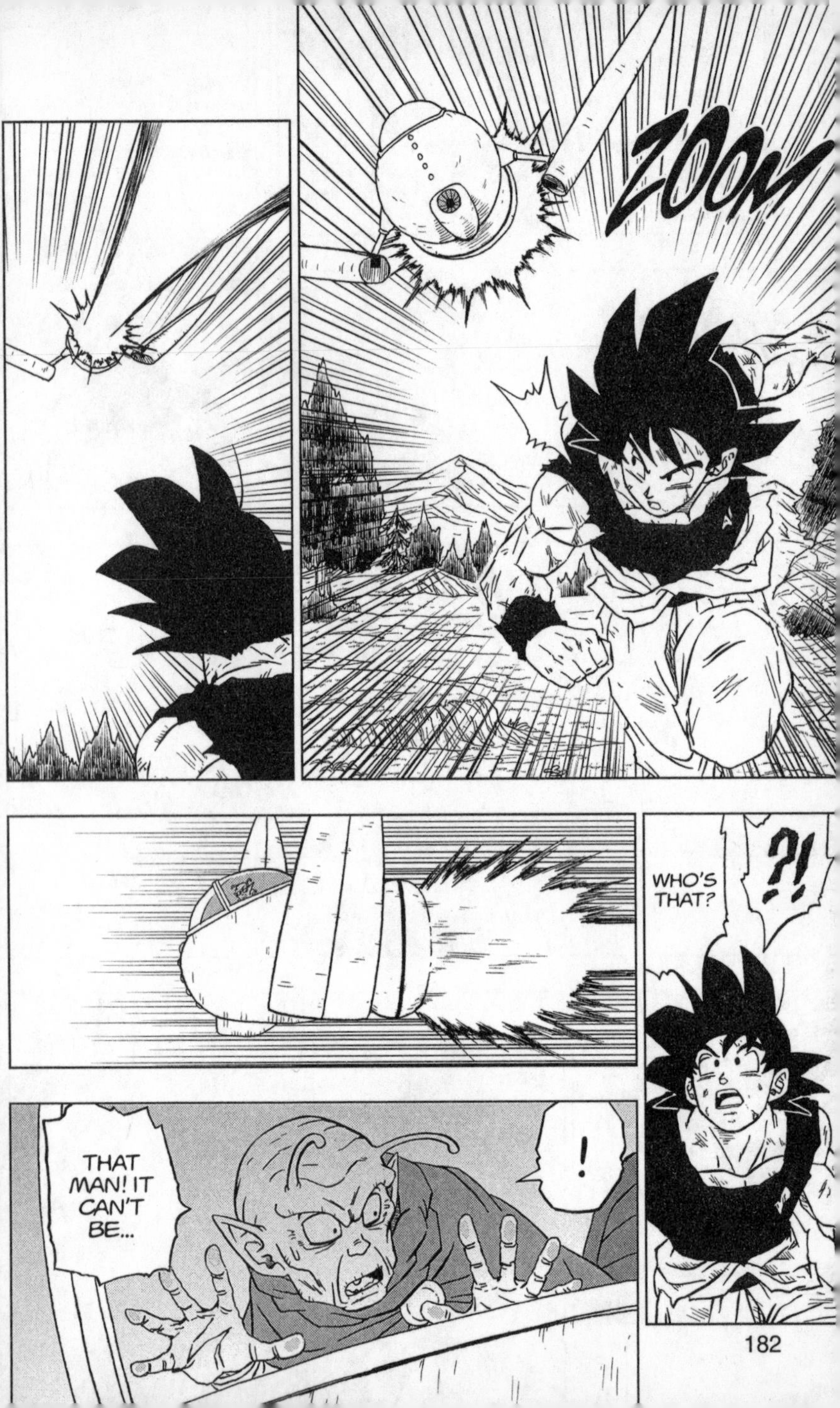
ZOOM
?!
WHO'S THAT?
!
THAT MAN! IT CAN'T BE...

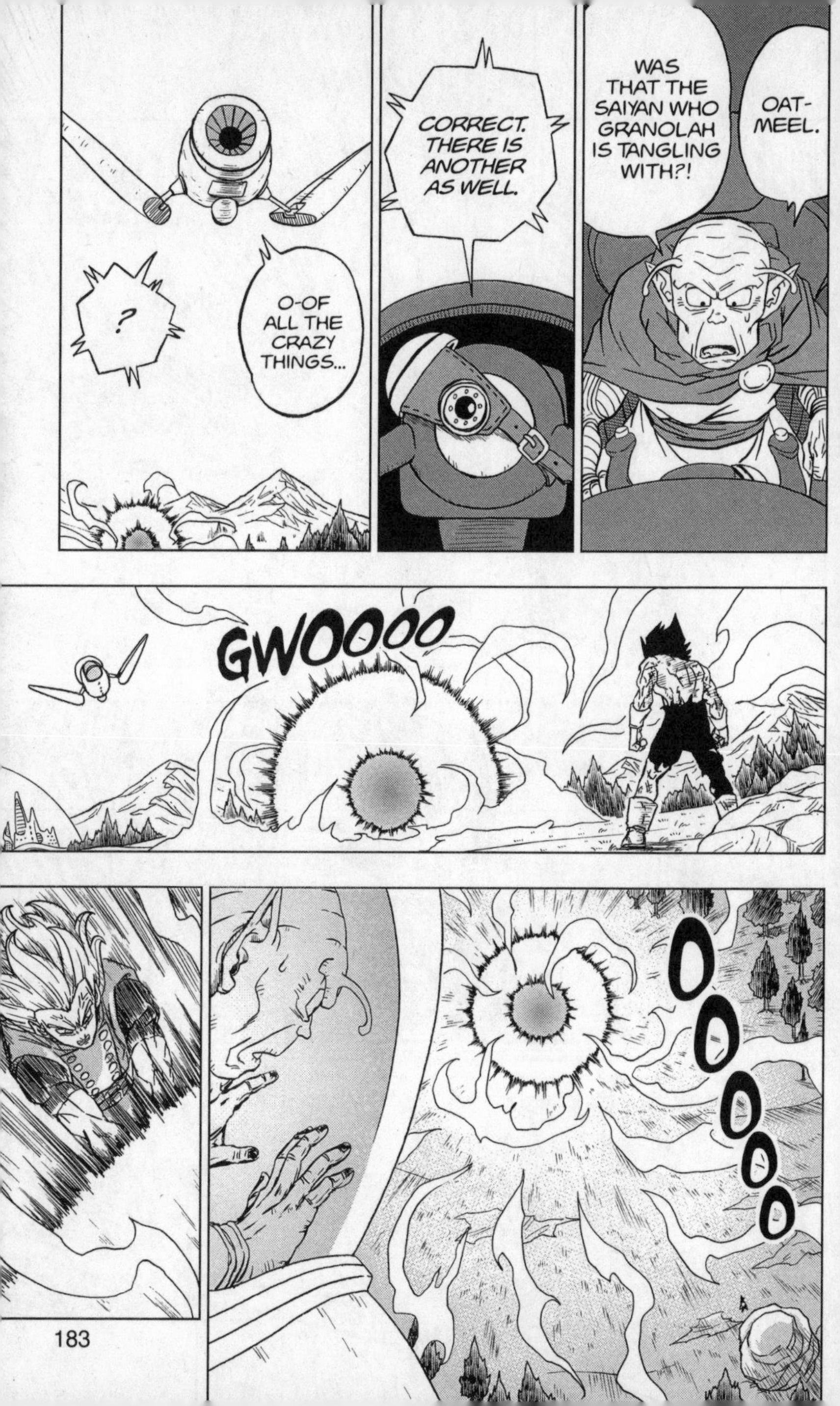
OAT-MEEL.
WAS THAT THE SAIYAN WHO GRANOLAH IS TANGLING WITH?!
CORRECT. THERE IS ANOTHER AS WELL.
O-OF ALL THE CRAZY THINGS...
?
GWOOOO
OOOOOO

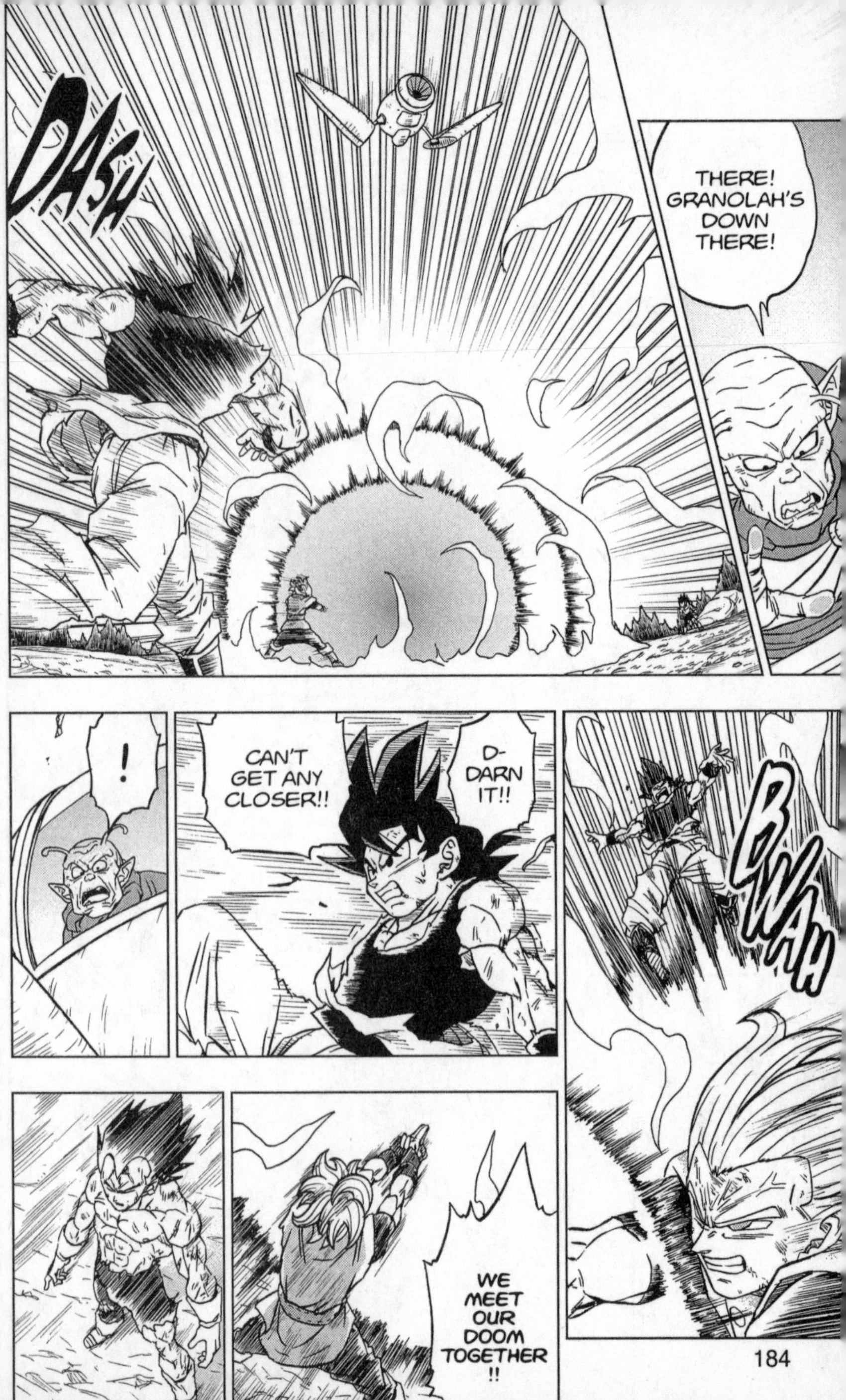
THERE! GRANOLAH'S DOWN THERE!
DASH
BWAH
D- DARN IT!!
CAN'T GET ANY CLOSER!!
!
WE MEET OUR DOOM TOGETHER !!

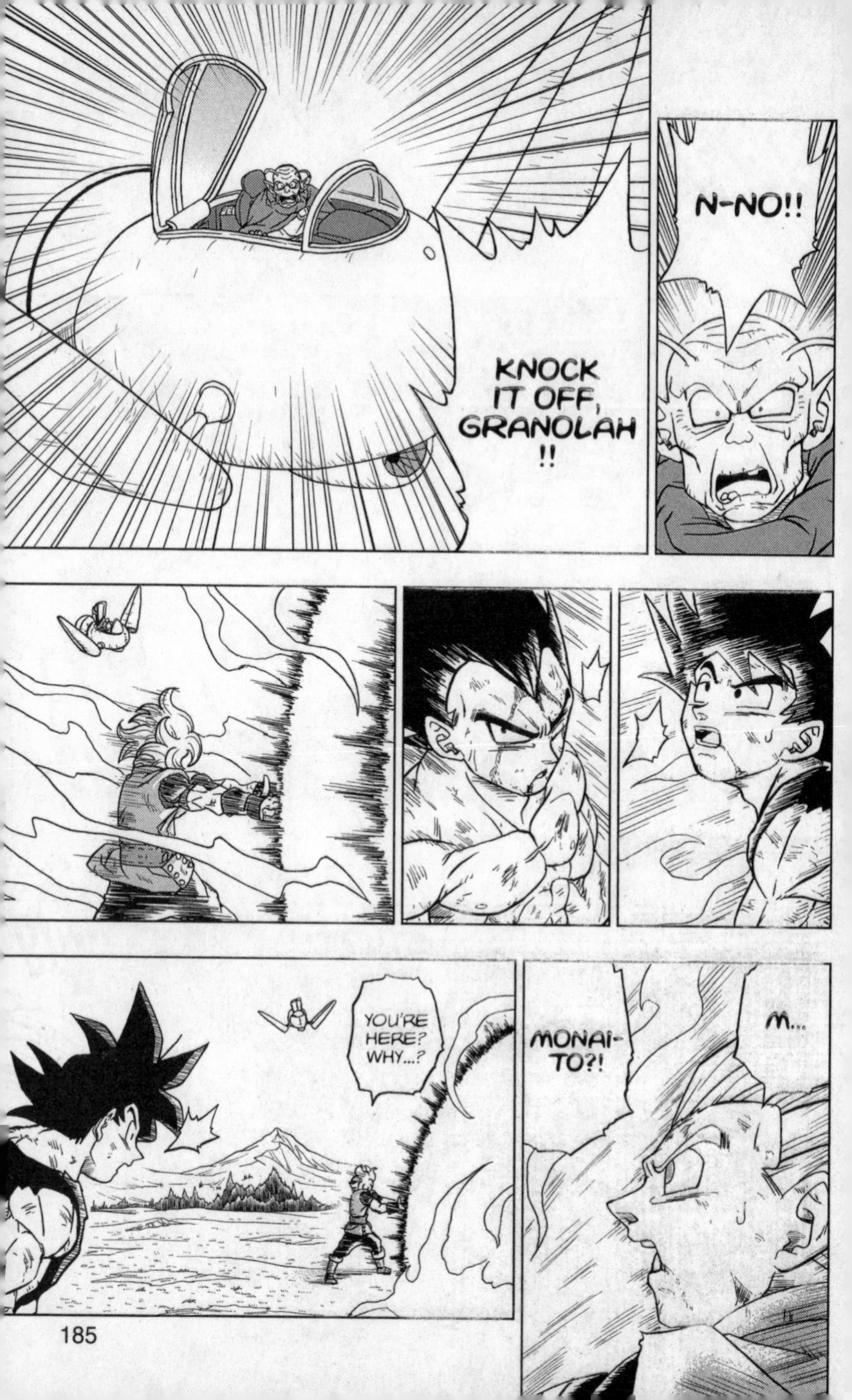
N-NO!!
KNOCK IT OFF, GRANOLAH!!
M...
MONAI-TO?!
YOU'RE HERE? WHY...?

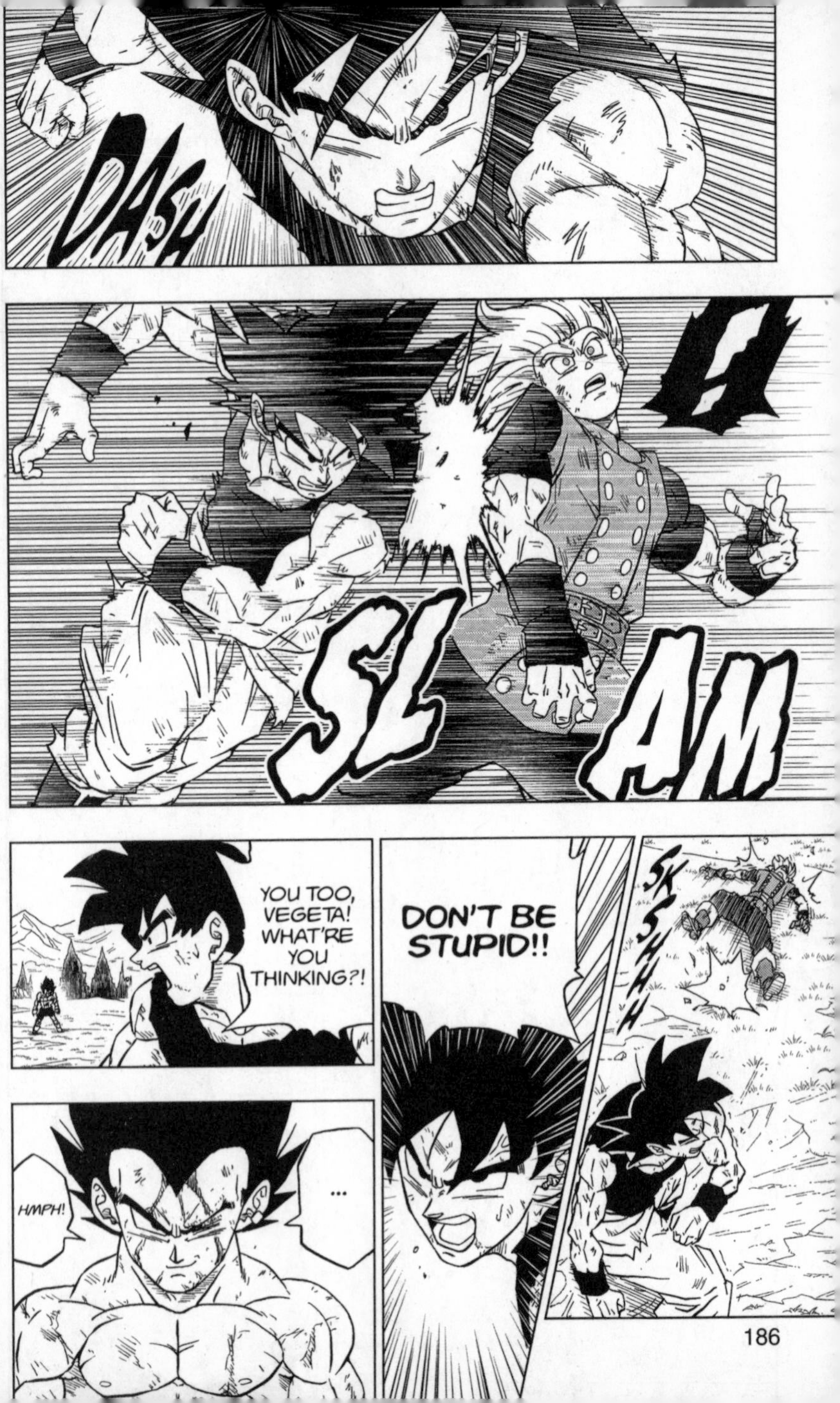
DASH
!
SLAM
SKSHHH
DON'T BE STUPID!!
YOU TOO, VEGETA! WHAT'RE YOU THINKING?!
...
HMPH!

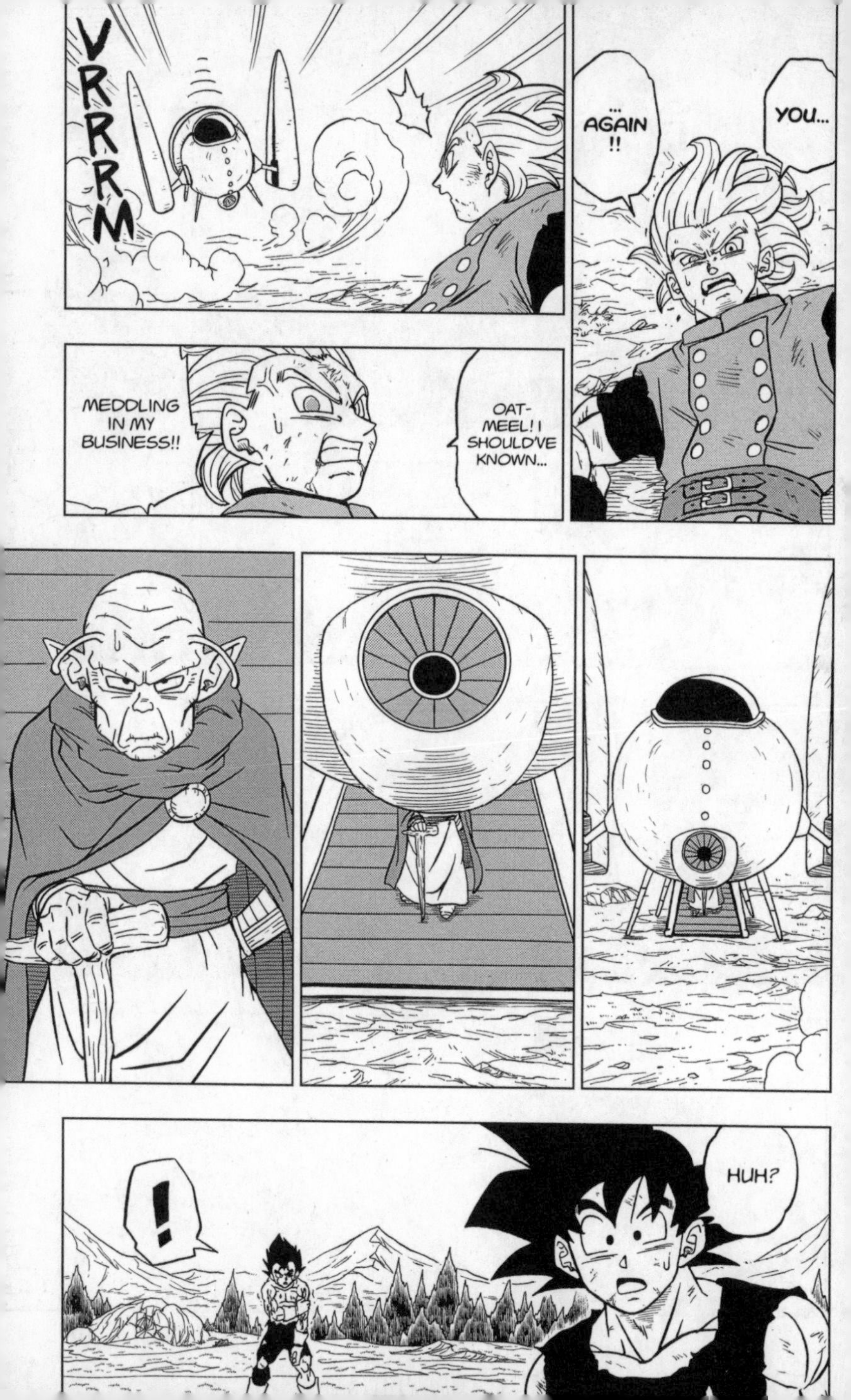
YOU...
... AGAIN !!
VRRRM
OAT-MEEL! I SHOULD'VE KNOWN...
MEDDLING IN MY BUSINESS!!
HUH?
!

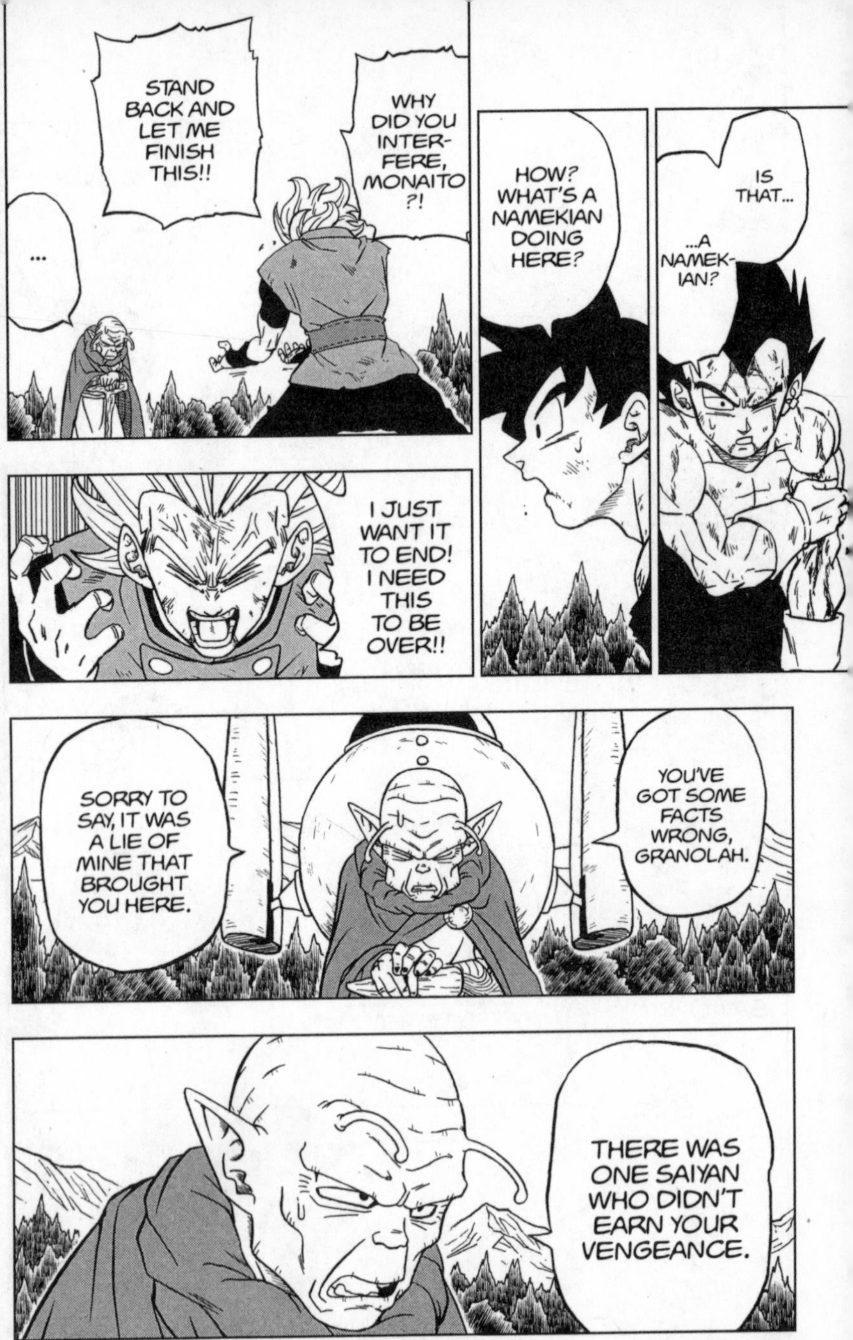
IS THAT...
...A NAMEK-IAN?
HOW? WHAT'S A NAMEKIAN DOING HERE?
WHY DID YOU INTER-FERE, MONAITO?!
STAND BACK AND LET ME FINISH THIS!!
...
I JUST WANT IT TO END! I NEED THIS TO BE OVER!!
YOU'VE GOT SOME FACTS WRONG, GRANOLAH.
SORRY TO SAY, IT WAS A LIE OF MINE THAT BROUGHT YOU HERE.
THERE WAS ONE SAIYAN WHO DIDN'T EARN YOUR VENGEANCE.

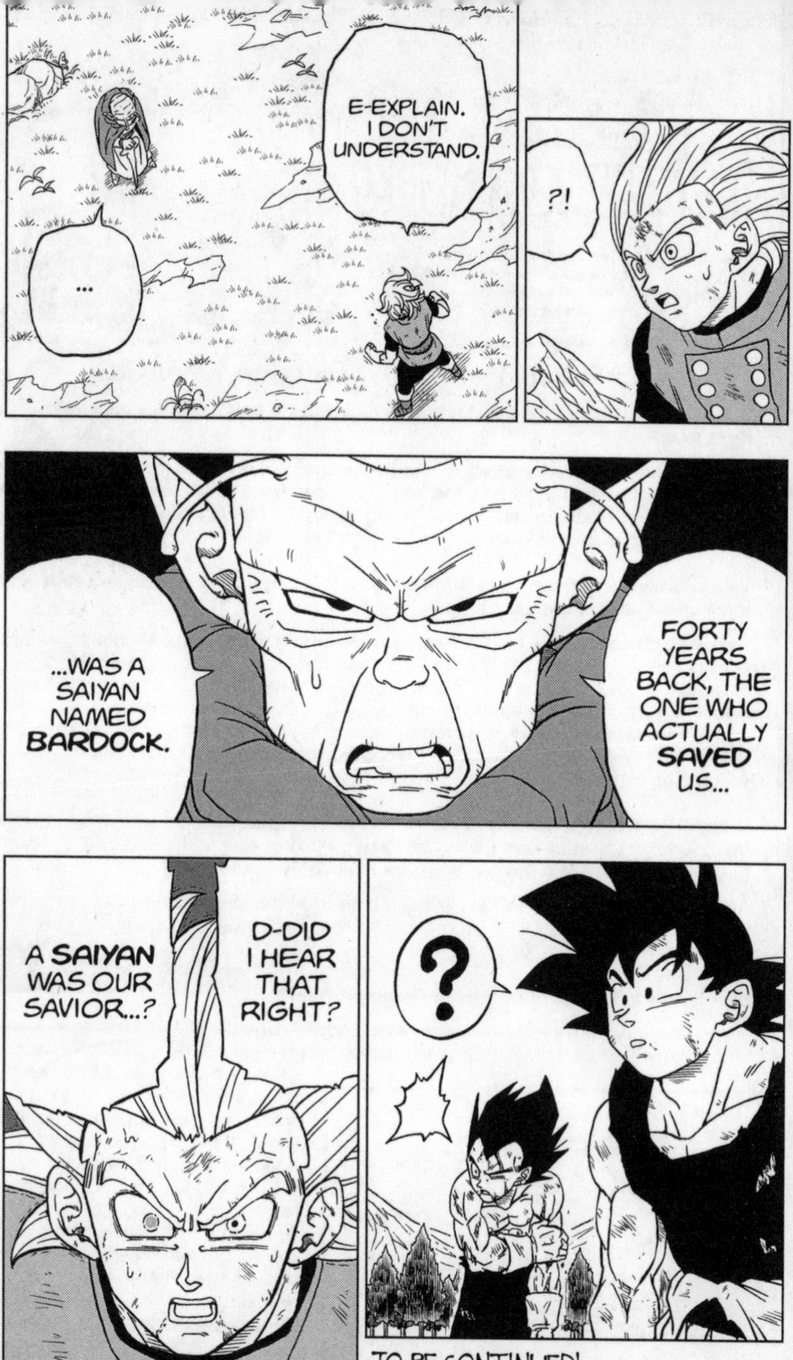
?!
E-EXPLAIN. I DON'T UNDERSTAND.
...
FORTY YEARS BACK, THE ONE WHO ACTUALLY **SAVED** US...
...WAS A SAIYAN NAMED **BARDOCK**.
?
D-DID I HEAR THAT RIGHT?
A **SAIYAN** WAS OUR SAVIOR...?

TO BE CONTINUED!

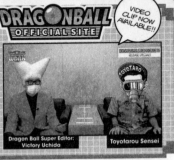

QUESTIONS FOR TOYOTAROU SENSEI!!

DRAGON BALL OFFICIAL SITE

VIDEO CLIP NOW AVAILABLE!!

We've got some highlights from the interview with Toyotarou Sensei, included as a special feature on the Dragon Ball official website! He spoke about the Granolah the Survivor arc!!

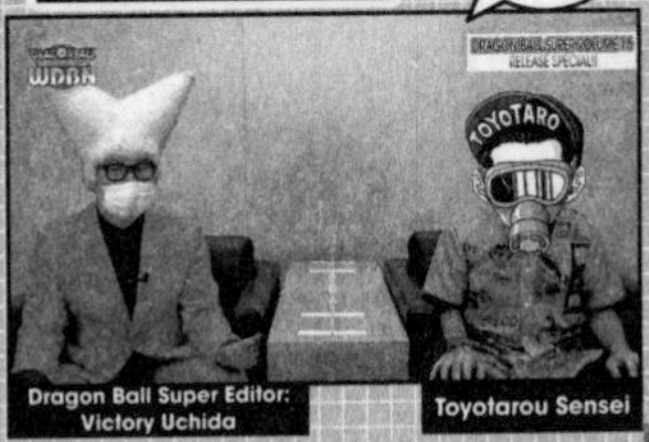
TOYOTARO

Dragon Ball Super Editor: Victory Uchida

Toyotarou Sensei

There's some territory where I dare not tread.

Victory Uchida (V for short): **Granolah, as a character, was originally your idea, right, Toyo?**

Toyotarou Sensei (Toyo for short): Compared to many of my ideas for characters, Granolah came about because the concept of someone with a fateful connection to the Saiyans was really appealing. As for expanding on his story, that was something you and I came up with together and then pitched to Toriyama Sensei.

V: **How does it feel when you submit an idea to Toriyama Sensei and he sends back a full-on original character design?**

Toyo: With characters like the Heeters, Toriyama Sensei would make tweaks and additions of his own. I never expect anything more than a "yes" or "no" in response to my character ideas, but he goes above and beyond by making an effort to understand what I'm trying to convey. It's always a moving experience when he says, "Here's how to make these designs more fun," and hands back the material with those modifications. It ends up being 100–200 times more awesome than whatever I had come up with, which is pretty amazing.

V: **Right. He added a number of elements, like the Namekian, the new Dragon Balls, the new dragon, and so on. He has this way of taking your ideas and adding touches to give them more of a Dragon Ball Super feel. Truly moving.**

Toyo: There's some territory where I dare not tread. Introducing a new set of Dragon Balls is a good example of that, so I'm grateful to Toriyama Sensei for stepping in and bringing those into the story.

V: **You were in charge of designing Granolah, right?**

Toyo: I came up with the "last survivor of his people" aspect, but it was Toriyama Sensei who suggested that while the Cerealians shouldn't necessarily be a tribe of hardcore warriors, they should still be somewhat militant. That led me to the finish line—the conclusion that they should be snipers. The concept of a tribe of snipers then led me to the goggles idea for locking on to targets. Cool, right? As for the rest of Granolah's outfit, we're talking about a tribe that was wiped out forty years ago, so even though he's an alien, I wanted an old-fashioned look, with steampunk-ish elements to it.

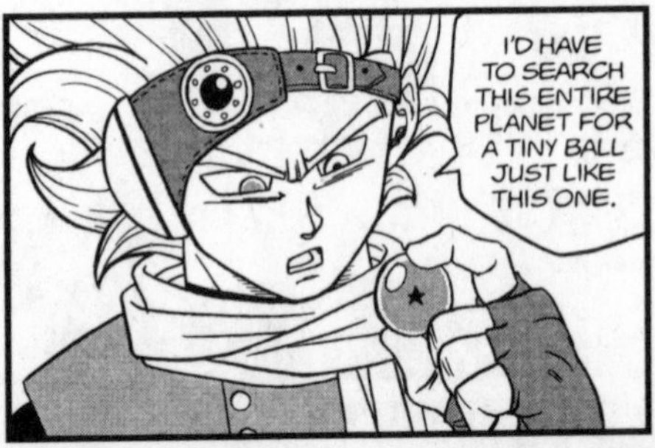
I'D HAVE TO SEARCH THIS ENTIRE PLANET FOR A TINY BALL JUST LIKE THIS ONE.

V: **Who's your favorite new character from this story arc?**

Toyo: It's gotta be Granolah himself, since he's the main character of the Granolah the Survivor arc. I also like Elec from the Heeters. His whole vibe makes it really clear he's a villain.

V: **A villain for the modern ages, yes. Not one who exerts control via terror, but a clever, scheming man who uses money and influence instead. But you struggled with the designs for the Heeters quartet, right?**

Toyo: Toriyama Sensei rejected my designs for them three or four times, and I was almost ready to give up when we finally arrived at the current designs.

V: **Toriyama Sensei puts genuine thought into his critiques. That must feel wonderful.**

V: **One of Toriyama Sensei's designs was the Sugarians, as explained at the end of volume 16. His tweaks ended up making them absolutely adorable.**

Toyo: I submitted two different designs for those guys, and he said, "Their eyes are too creepy." Ha ha!

V: **Their cute designs have that distinct Toriyama Sensei feel to them, especially since the individuals aren't given their own names.**

Toyo: His cute characters are always so iconic. It's amazing how you can immediately recognize the characters designed by Toriyama Sensei.

For the full interview, use the QR code to the left to access the *Dragon Ball* official site!

Search " ドラゴンボールオフィシャルサイト" on the App Store or Google Play!

Japanese ドラゴンボールオフィシャル
@DB_official_jp

English DRAGON BALL OFFICIAL
@DB_official_en

V: **Finally, any hints about upcoming story developments?**

Toyo: There's a lot I can't reveal at this stage, but **rest assured that we've got big surprises in store, so stay tuned!**

YOU'RE READING
THE WRONG WAY!

Dragon Ball Super reads from right to left, starting in the
upper-right corner. Japanese is read from right to left,
meaning that action, sound effects, and word-balloon
order are completely reversed from English order.